Interpreting Company Reports and Accounts

INTERPRETING COMPANY REPORTS AND ACCOUNTS

Geoffrey Holmes and Alan Sugden

FOURTH EDITION

WOODHEAD-FAULKNER
New York   London   Toronto   Sydney   Tokyo   Singapore

Published by Woodhead-Faulkner Limited,
Simon & Schuster International Group,
Fitzwilliam House, 32 Trumpington Street,
Cambridge CB2 1QY, England

First published 1979
Second impression 1980
Third impression 1981
Second edition 1982
Second impression 1983
Third impression 1983
Fourth impression 1984
Third edition 1986
Second impression 1986
Third impression 1986
Fourth impression 1987
Fifth impression 1988
Sixth impression 1988
Seventh impression 1989
Fourth edition 1990
Second impression 1991

© Geoffrey Holmes and Alan Sugden 1979, 1982, 1986, 1990

British Library Cataloguing in Publication Data

Holmes, Geoffrey, *1926–*
    Intepreting company reports and accounts.–4th ed
    1. Companies. Published accounts. Presentation
    I. Title   II. Sugden, Alan
    657.3

    ISBN 0–85941–649–6
    ISBN 0–85941–650–X pbk

Typeset by Vision Typesetting, Manchester
Printed and bound in Great Britain by
Alden Press Ltd, Oxford

CONTENTS

		Page
Preface		ix

1 Introduction to accounting practice

1

Information which reports and accounts must contain. Accounting standards. The Dearing Report. Fundamental accounting concepts. Accounting policies. The balance sheet and profit and loss account.

2 Forming a company

6

Incorporation of a company. Memorandum of Association. Articles of Association. Members' (shareholders') liability. Chartered company. Public company. Private company. Close company. Small and medium-sized companies.

3 Admission to listing

8

Stock Exchange listing – 'quoted companies'. Requirements for listing. Continuing Obligations. Methods of obtaining a listing. The Unlisted Securities Market.

4 Share capital and reserves

11

Share capital. Authorised and issued share capital. Types of share capital. Preference shares. Golden shares. Ordinary shares. Ordinary stock. Non-voting shares. Deferred shares. Partly paid shares. Warrants. ADRs. Share schemes for directors and employees. Limitations on the issue of further equity. Rights issues. Scrip issues. Share splits. Scrip (stock) dividends. Vendor consideration. Supplementary information on shares. Company purchasing its own shares. Reduction of share capital. Arrangements and reconstructions. *Reserves*. Capital and revenue reserves. Share premium account. Revaluation reserve. Foreign currency equalisation. Reserve funds. Capital redemption reserve. Movements to and from reserves.

5 Loan capital

21

The advantages of borrowing. The risk of borrowing. Types of borrowing. Security given to the lender – debentures and unsecured loan stock. Typical characteristics of debentures and ULS. Specific characteristics – the trust deed. Treatment of expenses on issue and of profit or loss on redemption. Deep discount issues. Sinking funds. Yields. Bonds. Notes and Loan notes. Commercial paper. The amount a company can borrow. Convertible loan capital. Terms of a convertible loan. Convertibles with 'put' options. Warrants. Mezzanine finance. Complex capital issues.

6 Fixed assets

33

Definitions. Companies Act requirements on fixed assets. Disclosure requirements on depreciation. Rates of depreciation. Where depreciation is shown in the accounts. Methods of depreciation. The straight line or fixed instalment method. The declining balance or reducing balance method. The sum of the years' digits method. The annuity method. Further points on depreciation. Excess depreciation. The revaluation of assets. Investment properties. Sales and other disposals of fixed assets. Government grants.

7 Investments   43

Types of investment. Balance sheet presentation. Fixed assets – other investments. Investments held as current assets. Points to watch on substantial holdings. Interlocking holdings.

8 Stocks and work in progress   46

Different classes of stock. Subclassification required by SSAP 9. Subclassification required by CA 1985. The matching principle. Consistency. The importance of stock valuation. Problems in valuing stock. Stocks in a large retail business. Stocks in the manufacturing business. Taxation of stock profits. Requirements of the Companies Act 1985 and of SSAP 9 on stocks and WIP. The danger of rising stocks. Long-term contracts. Requirements of SSAP 9 on long-term contracts.

9 Debtors   54

Trade debtors and other debtors. Bad debts and doubtful debtors. The importance of debtors. Debt collection period. Factors affecting the debt collection period. Why it is important to keep a watch upon collection period. *Hire-purchase and credit sale transactions.* Definitions. Timing of profit taking. The rule of 78. Information given in accounts. *Factoring.* Invoice discounting. Factoring in the accounts.

10 Bank loans, overdrafts and other financial instruments   60

Bank facilities. Overdrafts. Bank loans. Loan facilities. *Swaps.* Currency swaps. Interest rate swaps. *Bills of exchange.* Definition. Purpose. Presentation in the balance sheet. Discounting. Acceptance credits. Points for analysts to watch on bills.

11 Creditors, provisions and contingent liabilities   66

Creditors. Provisions. Contingent liabilities. Capital commitments. Other financial commitments. Leases.

12 Turnover, trading profit and pre-tax profit   72

Introduction. How the profit was earned. Effect of accounting policies on profitability. Consequences of abnormal accounting policies. *Sales (Turnover).* Statutory requirements. Stock Exchange requirements. Proposed accounting standard. Analysis of profitability. *Trading profit.* Disclosure of supplementary information – statutory requirements. *Pension costs.* Types of pension scheme. Defined contribution schemes. Defined benefit schemes. *Other pre-tax items.* Investment income. Interest paid. Profit before taxation.

13 Taxation   82

Introduction. Corporation Tax – the imputation system. Tax years and rates of tax. *Corporation Tax with no distribution of dividends.* Inland Revenue's assessment of Corporation Tax. Depreciation and capital allowances. Example of a timing difference. Deferred taxation. Accounting for deferred taxation. Methods of accounting for deferred taxation. Other uses of the deferred taxation account. Asset sales. Further reasons for 'abnormal' tax charges – permanent differences. Effect of previous years. *Corporation Tax with dividend distribution.* Advance Corporation Tax (ACT). Limitations on the use of ACT. Irrecoverable ACT. ACT and relief for foreign tax. Timing of payments of Corporation Tax. *Earnings and dividend cover.* Nil earnings. Net earnings. 'Full distribution' earnings. Dividend cover. Dividend cover with mainly UK operations. Dividend cover with overseas earnings and foreign tax.

14 Profits after tax, exceptional and extraordinary items, dividends and earnings per share   94

Profits after tax. Minorities. Preference dividends. Profit attributable to shareholders. *Exceptional and extraordinary items.* Conflicting concepts of profit. SSAP 6 definition of exceptional and extraordinary items. Presentation of extraordinary items. Importance of extraordinary items. Exceptional items. Prior year items. Examples of items needing special treatment (if material). *Dividends.* Distribution of dividends. Legal restrictions on dividend distribution. Company articles on dividend distribution. Declaration of dividends. *Earnings per share.* The effect of acquisitions on earnings per share. Earnings growth by acquisition. Market rating – the PER. 'Wonder growth' by acquisition. Adjustments to earnings per share – SSAP 3. Net and nil basis. Earnings on more than one class of share. *Movements in reserves.*

15 Acquisitions and mergers   107
Preface. Acquisition accounting. Interests in another company. Acquisition of a subsidiary: revaluation of assets. Capital reserve on consolidation. Subsidiary's profits in year of acquisition or disposal. Acquisition accounting: scope for enhancing profits. *Merger accounting.* Pre-acquisition profits. Criticisms of merger accounting. Avoidance of share premium in acquisition accounting.

16 Subsidiaries and group accounts   114
Holding companies, subsidiaries and groups. Definitions. Statutory requirements for group accounts. *Consolidated accounts.* The consolidated balance sheet. Goodwill on consolidation (purchased goodwill). The consolidated profit and loss account. Unrealised profits on stocks. Exceptions to consolidation of subsidiaries. The parent company's own balance sheet. The parent company's own profit and loss account. The company's financial (accounting) year end. Further statutory requirements in consolidated accounts. Subsidiary's holding of holding company's shares. *The interpretation of consolidated accounts.* Profitability of subsidiaries.

17 Associated undertakings and participating interests   123
New terminology. Equity method of accounting. Example of equity method. Information on associated undertakings. Misuse of SSAP 1.

18 Foreign exchange   127
The problem of variable exchange rates. The UK accounting standard. Individual companies. Group accounts. Current UK practice. Taxation. Mitigating the effect of foreign currency fluctuations. What the analyst should study.

19 Source and application of funds statements   135
Purpose. The requirements of SSAP 10. The interpretation of source and application statements. Interpreting an imaginary funds statement. Limitations of funds statements. Cash flow statements.

20 Historical summaries
Variations in form and content. Difficulties of interpretation. Use of ratios. The key ratios.   142

21 Directors' report, chairman's statement and auditors' report
The directors' report. Contents. Statutory requirements. Listing requirements. Control of the   147
company. The board of directors. *The chairman's statement.* Sequence of study. Contents. Estimating current year profits. Longer-term prospects. Information on the quality of management. *Post balance sheet events.* Types of post balance sheet event. Window dressing. *The auditors' report.* Appointment of auditors. Auditors' access to information. Scope of the report. Qualified auditors' reports. Examples of qualified reports. Fundamental qualifications. Materiality. Emphasis of matter. Delay in publication.

22 Other sources of information   156
Information provided by the company. Interim reports. Prospectuses and listing particulars. Circulars on acquisitions and disposals. Documents issued in a contested bid. Form 20–F. Company newsletters and magazines. Catalogues and sales information literature. Annual General Meeting. Company visits. *External information.* The Registrar of Companies. Extel Cards. ICC Datacards. The Hambro Company Guide. Macmillan's. McCarthy Information Services. Datastream. Other on-line services. Key Notes. The Economist Intelligence Unit (EIU). Government statistical publications. Other government publications – NEDO. Specialist and trade publications.

23 Inflation accounting   164
Introduction. The shortcomings of historical cost accounting. Historical cost (HC) accounting. HC accounting with inflation. The staggering impact of inflation. *The development of inflation accounting systems.* Current purchasing power accounting (CPP). Current cost accounting (CCA). Replacement cost accounting. *Where do we go from here?* Measuring inflation. What inflation accounts should achieve. The future.

24 Trends and ratios   170

How to tackle the analysis. The use of percentages and ratios. Methods of relating items of information. *Trends*. Horizontal analysis – comparison with the previous year. Horizontal analysis – half-yearly comparison. Trend analysis – comparison over several years. The use of published historical summaries. Trends in rates of growth. Vertical analysis. *The use of ratios*. Choice of ratios. Logical grouping. Typical ratio values. Ratios and inflation. *Operating ratios*. Main operating ratios. Further operating ratios. *Financial ratios*. Gearing. Leverage effect. Interest rate sensitivity. Operational gearing. Liquidity ratios. Current ratio. Quick ratio or acid test. Cash flow. Contingent liabilities: Ordinary shareholders' funds. *Investment ratios*. Price earnings ratio (PER). What the PER represents. Dividend policy and the PER. Dividend yield. Dividend cover. Payout ratio. Net asset value (n.a.v.). Market capitalisation.

25 Pro-forma guide to analysis   192

Analysis Sheet 1 – Profit and loss account. Calculation of normalised trading profit. Calculation of normalised pre-tax profit. Calculation of normalised earnings per share. Profitability ratios. *Analysis Sheet 2 – Assets employed. Analysis Sheet 3 – Financing. Summary Sheet 1 – Summary of profit and loss accounts. Summary Sheet 2 – Summary of assets employed. Summary Sheet 3 – Summary of financing. Summary Sheets 4 and 5 – Summary of sources and applications.*

26 Revelation   207

Depreciation. Capitalising expenses. Writing off direct to reserves. Acquisitions and disposals. Extraordinary and exceptional items. Consolidation. Income recognition. Deferred taxation. Fraud.

Appendices   212

Appendix 1 Current SSAPs and EDs. Appendix 2 – Present value. Appendix 3 – Retail Price Indexes since 1950

Index   215

PREFACE

'Published accounts are utterly and absolutely useless.'
Clive Jenkins

Many non-trade-unionists might agree with Clive Jenkins on this point, but we believe they are wrong. Given a sound knowledge of the basic components of a balance sheet and profit and loss account, *anybody with a reasonably enquiring mind* can learn a great deal about a company by studying its report and accounts and by comparing it with other companies, and we have written this book to provide the basic knowledge required and to give the reader (be he student, investor, company director or trade-unionist) a line-by-line guide on how to take a set of reports and accounts to pieces.

A careful, systematic examination of accounts can also provide warning of when a company is taking undue risks, when it is 'window dressing' to cover up a poor performance, or when it is 'netting off' figures to hide embarrassing items.

In addition, an examination of accounts over several years can give a very good picture of the long-term trends of a company's fortunes, distinguishing between a company that is growing at an incredible speed (in which case don't believe it), is growing at a prudent speed (in which case consider investing), or is static or on the decline (in which case avoid or sell).

Analysing accounts, sorting out the good, well-run companies from the less reliable ones, all the time asking further questions and keeping an eye out for warning signals is, in our view, fun. We hope that once you have mastered the nuts and bolts of the process you will find it fun, too.

Note to the fourth edition

Company accounting is currently in a state of some confusion and controversy. Although the 1989 Companies Act has tightened the rules on *off-balance sheet financing*, two serious shortcomings have become apparent in accounting standards since the third edition was published:

(a) On *acquisitions*, companies have the choice between merger accounting and acquisition accounting, although the two methods can produce wildly different results.
(b) On *goodwill*, the writing off of purchased goodwill direct to reserves can grossly distort a company's balance sheet, and make a nonsense of associated ratios.

There is considerable controversy over *intangible assets*, in particular the treatment of *brand names*.

We are glad to say that the machinery for producing accounting standards has recently been changed, with the introduction of a much more powerful Accounting Standards Board; revision is already in hand and we expect standards to improve a great deal in the next few years.

Meanwhile in this edition we have done our best to describe both the problems and the changes in the rules that we think are likely, and we have added a new final chapter to show the many ways in which companies can and do exploit the present rules to enhance their reported profits.

We have called this final chapter 'Revelation', because a number of analysts have been kind enough to refer to this book as their 'Bible' on the subject.

G.H.
A.S.

Acknowledgements

We would like to thank the people who have helped us with
their ideas and comments, and have suggested examples for the
fourth edition, including:

Ray Bowden	Robert Fleming Securities
Chris Bowmer	Bowater Industries
Michael Cairns Janet White	J. Henry Schroder Wagg
Colin Callegari Richard Mountford	Schroder Investment Management
Simon Dawes	Laing & Cruickshank
David Dean	Department of Trade & Industry
Paul Hamilton	Rowe & Pitman
John Jeffrey-Cook	Moores & Rowland
Ruth Keattch	Schroder Securities
John McGee	Warburg Securities
Martin Purvis	The International Stock Exchange
Adam Quinton	Phillips & Drew

and in particular Linette Woods, Schroder Investment
Management's librarian, who has helped us track down the
reports and accounts and other information on well over a
hundred companies.

Chapter 1

INTRODUCTION TO ACCOUNTING PRACTICE

This book is intended as a practical guide to the interpretation of reports and accounts. In it frequent reference is made to the legal, accounting and Stock Exchange requirements that accounts have to meet, but this is done in the context of what interesting information to look out for, rather than to show how a set of accounts should be prepared.

Useful guides to *compiling* accounts include:

The Companies Acts 1985 and 1989 – Accounting and financial requirements, published by the Institute of Chartered Accountants in England and Wales.

Companies Act 1985 – Model reports and accounts, published for the Institute of Chartered Accountants of Scotland by Gee & Co.

Financial Reporting – A Survey of UK Published Accounts, published annually by the Institute of Chartered Accountants in England and Wales.

Information which reports and accounts must contain

The annual report and accounts is usually the principal way in which shareholders and others can keep themselves informed on the activities, progress and future plans of a company.

Although the style and content vary with the directors' views on the use of the report and accounts as a public relations vehicle – an increasing number of companies distribute a summary of their report and accounts to all employees or include one in their house newspaper, and some even produce a separate 'company profile', while others argue the risks of disclosing anything in case it may be of use to competitors – there is a minimum amount of information that *must* be disclosed to comply with the law. Amongst these requirements, the annual report and accounts has to contain four basic components: a directors' report, a profit and loss account, a balance sheet and an auditors' report.

In addition, when the company's shares are listed on The Stock Exchange, London, the report and accounts have to contain more information (see Section 5 of The Stock Exchange's *Admission of Securities to Listing*, known as 'The Yellow Book'). Companies listed on The Stock Exchange also have to produce a half-yearly or interim report.

Accounting standards

Since the 1970s, the Accounting Standards Committee (ASC), a committee representing the Institute of Chartered Accountants in England and Wales, the Scottish and Irish Institutes, the Chartered Association of Certified Accountants, the Institute of Cost and Management Accountants and the Chartered Institute of Public Finance and Accountancy, has been producing papers giving guidance on the treatment and presentation of various aspects of a company's accounts. These papers have been published in two series:

1. *Exposure Drafts* (EDs), which propose methods to be used, and form the basis for discussion and comment in the development of official standards. Once these standards are agreed they are published as:
2. *Statements of Standard Accounting Practice* (SSAPs). These place, on members who are directors or officers of companies, the onus of ensuring that the standards are fully understood by other directors and within the company, and that significant departures are disclosed and explained in the accounts, while members acting as auditors are also required to justify any significant departures if they concur with them.

A number of the accounting requirements contained in SSAPs have subsequently been incorporated in Companies Acts. Companies are required to state whether their accounts have been prepared in accordance with applicable accounting standards, and to give particulars of, and reasons for, any material departures (CA 1989 Sch 1 para. 7).

A list of EDs and SSAPs currently extant is contained in Appendix 1. One of them, SSAP 10, requires the annual report and accounts to contain a fifth basic component, a Source and Application of Funds Statement.

There are also *Statements of Recommended Practice* (SORPs). These are produced by non-accounting bodies in conjunction with the ASC, e.g. the British Bankers' Association's SORP on the treatment of securities.

The Dearing Report

In practice, the ASC standard setting procedure proved too slow and too prone to compromise solutions, particularly in allowing alternative treatments in the SSAPs it produced in order to get the required unanimous approval of all six accounting bodies. A committee was therefore appointed in November 1987, under the chairmanship of Sir Ron Dearing, to review the standard setting procedures.

The Dearing Report recommended the setting up of an Accounting Standards Board (ASB) to replace the ASC. The ASB would issue accounting standards on its own authority, and would be responsible to another new body, the Financial Reporting Council (FRC). The report received widespread support and, after some delay over the question of how the new structure should be paid for, David Tweedie, technical partner at KPMG Peat Marwick, was appointed as the chairman of the new ASB.

Fundamental accounting concepts

Four fundamental concepts are laid down in SSAP 2 *(Disclosure of Accounting Policies)*:

1. *The going concern* concept: the accounts are compiled on the assumption that there is no intention or need to go into liquidation or to curtail the current level of operations significantly.
2. The *accruals* (or matching) concept: revenue and costs are accrued (accounted for) as they are earned or incurred, not as the money is received or paid, and revenue and profits are matched with associated costs and expenses by including them in the same accounting period.
3. The *consistency* concept: accounting treatment of like items is consistent from one period to the next.
4. The concept of *prudence*, which is the overriding concept, demands that:
   (a) Revenue and profits are not anticipated;
   (b) Provision is made for all known liabilities (expenses and losses), whether the amount is known with certainty or has to be estimated.

Accounting policies

SSAP 2 requires the accounting policies (the

Example 1.1   The new company's balance sheet

Liabilities		Assets	
Ordinary share capital	£300,000	Cash	£300,000

Example 1.2   The balance sheet after acquisition of fixed and current assets

Liabilities		Assets	
	£		£
Ordinary share capital	300,000	*Fixed assets*	
		Freehold land and buildings	200,000[1]
		Fixtures and fittings	75,000[2]
		Motor vehicles	10,000[4]
Current liabilities		*Current assets*	
Creditors: due within 1 year	100,000[5]	Stock (of goods)	200,000[3]
Overdraft	90,000[6]	Cash	5,000[6]
	490,000		490,000

various bases on which the accounts have been prepared) to be disclosed. They are usually shown at the beginning of the notes to the accounts and, typically, include the basis of accounting for:

(*a*) sales (treatment of VAT and duties);
(*b*) deferred taxation;
(*c*) depreciation of fixed assets;
(*d*) investment grants;
(*e*) research and development;
(*f*) stocks and work in progress;
(*g*) extraordinary items;
(*h*) translation of currencies;

plus any items specially related to the company's business, such as the treatment of long-term contracts, hire-purchase transactions or growing timber.

The balance sheet and profit and loss account

(The remainder of this chapter provides an introduction to the balance sheet and profit and loss account for those who are not already familiar with them. Experienced readers may like to turn straight to Chapter 2.)

The *balance sheet* is a statement of the assets and liabilities of a company at the close of business on a given day, i.e. on the balance sheet date. The *profit and loss account* is a record of the activities of a company for a given period of time; this period, which is called the accounting period, is normally a year, and the balance sheet always has to be drawn up on the last day of the company's accounting period.

When a company is formed the *members* (shareholders) subscribe for shares. For example, let us suppose that a company is formed with a share capital of 300,000 ordinary shares with a nominal value of £1 each, and that all the shares are issued at *par* (are issued to members at their nominal value of £1 each). At the same time the directors of the company negotiate with their bank manager to allow the company to overdraw by up to £150,000, i.e. they obtain an overdraft facility of £150,000, although this figure does *not* appear in the accounts. The balance sheet will then look like Example 1.1.

Supposing the company then:

1. buys a freehold shop for £200,000
2. fits it out for £75,000, and
3. stocks it with £200,000 worth of goods.

It also:

4. buys a van for £10,000

The shop, the fittings and the van are all paid for with cash, and so are half the goods, but:

5. the other half of the goods are supplied on credit; i.e. the suppliers do not require immediate payment, so they become creditors of the company (*creditors* are people to whom the company owes money);
6. by this time most of the £300,000 capital has been spent, and there is an overdraft: £300,000 − 200,000 − 75,000 − 100,000 − 10,000 = −£85,000. Companies normally have a small amount of cash in hand, even if they have an overdraft. Here it is £5,000, making an overdraft of £90,000.

The balance sheet would then look like Example 1.2 (superior figures refer to items in the above list).

Fixed assets are assets not held for resale but for use by the business. *Current assets* are cash and other assets that the company expects to turn into cash (e.g. stock), and *current liabilities*, usually described as *Creditors: due within 1 year*, are all the liabilities that the company expects to have to meet within twelve months. In modern accounting practice the current liabilities are normally shown below the current assets on the assets side of the balance sheet, and the total of the current liabilities is deducted from the total of the current assets to give what is called *net current assets*.

Let us suppose that the company then trades for a year, during which time it:

7. sells goods for £1,200,000 – their cost plus a profit margin, and
8. buys goods for £850,000 in addition to the initial purchase of £200,000 which is called the *opening stock* (except for the first year this is the stock on hand at the end of the previous year).
9. At the end of the year, on the last day of the company's accounting year, there is £250,000 of stock, valued at cost price, on hand. This is called the *closing stock*.
10. Wages and other expenses for the year amount to £280,000.
11. In addition, a provision is made for the wear and tear on fixed assets during the year. This is calculated so that the cost of each fixed asset is written off over its expected life. The provision is called *depreciation* and, using the most common method of depreciation, the 'straight line' method:

$$\text{Depreciation for the year} = \frac{\text{Cost of asset}}{\text{Expected useful life}}$$

For our company the depreciation charge for the year would be worked out as follows:

Fixed asset	Cost	Life	Annual depreciation £
Building	125,000	50 years	2,500
Fittings	75,000	10 years	7,500
Motor van	10,000	5 years	2,000
Depreciation charge for the year[11]			12,000

Notice that depreciation is charged only on the cost of the building (here assumed to be £125,000 not on the value of the land (assumed to be £75,000), because depreciation is provided only on assets with a finite useful life.

Example 1.3 shows how the profit and loss account for the first year's trading would be calculated, assuming Corporation Tax at 25%.

During the year, in addition to the overdraft facility, the company arranged:

12. a 20-year loan of £100,000 secured on the freehold land and buildings – this is called a mortgage debenture because the lender of the money (the debenture holder) has first claim on the property if the company goes into liquidation.

In Example 1.3 the interest on both types of borrowings has, for simplicity, been included in 'Wages and other expenses'. It would normally be shown separately.

At the end of the year:

13. debtors (customers owing money to the company) owed a total of £80,000;

Example 1.4   The balance sheet after the first year's trading

	£	£
Fixed assets[15]		
Freehold land and buildings		197,500[11]
Fixtures and fittings		67,500[11]
Motor vehicles		8,000[11]
		273,000
Current assets		
Stock	250,000[9]	
Debtors	80,000[13]	
Cash	25,000	
	355,000	
Current liabilities (or Creditors: due within 1 year)		
Trade creditors	120,000[14]	
Taxation payable	27,000	
Dividend payable	30,000	
	177,000	
Net current assets		178,000
Total assets less current liabilities		451,000
Creditors: due after more than 1 year		
Mortgage debenture		100,000[12]
		351,000
Capital and reserves		
Ordinary share capital		300,000
Reserves (retained profits)		51,000
Ordinary shareholders' funds		351,000[18]

Example 1.3   The first year's profit and loss account

	£	£	£
Sales (or Turnover)			1,200,000[7]
less Cost of goods sold:			
Opening stocks	200,000[8]		
Purchases	+850,000[8]		
	1,050,000		
Closing stock	250,000[9]		
Cost of goods sold		800,000	
Wages and other expenses		280,000[10]	
Depreciation		12,000[11]	
			1,092,000
Profit before tax			108,000
Corporation Tax			27,000
Profit after tax			81,000
Dividends (the directors recommend a 10% dividend on the nominal value of the issued share capital)			30,000
Retained profits (to be ploughed back into the company)			51,000

14. trade creditors were £120,000 – so a little less than half the stock was being financed by suppliers.

Our final illustration (Example 1.4) shows the balance sheet at the end of the year drawn up in the modern way, with the assets less creditors above the capital and reserves, rather than assets on one side and liabilities on the other. Notice that:

15. fixed assets are shown at cost *less* depreciation to date;

16. the 10% dividend has not yet been paid;

17. net current assets = current assets – current liabilities, i.e. £355,000 – 177,000 = £178,000;

18. *ordinary shareholders' funds* = ordinary share capital issued plus reserves.

Chapter 2

FORMING A COMPANY

Incorporation of a company

(References: Companies Act 1948, Sch. 1, Tables A and B, which are now incorporated in a statutory instrument.)

When a company is formed by incorporation under the Companies Acts a Certificate of Incorporation is issued and the company assumes a legal identity separate from its shareholders.

Before incorporation can take place, a Memorandum of Association and Articles of Association have to be drawn up and filed with the Registrar of Companies in England and Wales or with the Registrar of Companies in Scotland.

Memorandum of Association

The Memorandum lays down the rules which govern the company in its relations with the ouside world. It states the name of the company; the country in which the Registered Office will be situated; the objects of the company (i.e. activities the company may pursue); the authorised share capital; the nominal value of the shares; a list of initial subscribers and whether the liability of members (shareholders) is limited. An example is given in Table B of the First Schedule to the Companies Act 1948.

Articles of Association

The Articles lay down the internal rules within which the directors run the company. The main items covered are:

(a) the issue of shares, the rights attaching to each class of share, the consent required for the alteration of the rights of any class of shareholders, and any restrictions on the transfer of shares;

(b) the procedure for general meetings and for altering the authorised share capital;

(c) the election and retirement of directors, their duties and their powers, including borrowing powers;

(d) the declaration of dividends;

(e) the procedure for winding up the company.

A model set of Articles is given in Table A of the First Schedule to the Companies Act 1948.

Members' (shareholders') liability

The liability of members (shareholders) of a company can either be limited by shares or by guarantee, or the liability can be unlimited.

Limited by shares

This is the method normally used for a company engaged in business activities. If the shares are *fully paid*, the members' liability is limited to the money they have put up: the maximum risk a shareholder runs is to lose all the money he has paid for his shares, and no further claim can be made on him for liabilities incurred by the company. If the shares are only *partly paid*, shareholders (and to a limited extent former shareholders) can be called upon to subscribe some or all of the unpaid part, but no more than that.

Limited by guarantee

This method is used for charitable and similar organisations, where funds are raised by donations and no shares are issued. The liability is limited to the amount each member personally guarantees, which is the maximum each member may be called upon to pay in the event of liquidation. This form of incorporation is not normally used for a business.

6

Unlimited

This method is used by professional firms that want the tax advantages of being a company; the members have joint and several liability in the same way as a partnership (each member can individually be held entirely responsible).

Chartered company

Companies may also be established by Royal Charter, the method used before any Companies Acts existed; for example, the PENINSULAR & ORIENTAL STEAM NAVIGATION COMPANY was incorporated by Royal Charter in 1840. The legal position of a chartered company is similar to an incorporated company, except that any change to the Articles involves a petition to the Privy Council.

Public company

(Reference: Companies Act 1985, Sections 1(3), 11 and 25.)

A public company is defined as one:

(*a*) which is limited by shares or guarantee, with a minimum issued share capital of £50,000, or such other sum specified by statutory instrument (the shares must be at least 25% paid up, with any share premium fully paid up); and

(*b*) whose Memorandum states that it is a public company; and

(*c*) which has been correctly registered as a public company.

All other companies are private companies.

The name of a public company must in all cases end either with the words 'Public Limited Company' or with the abbreviation 'PLC', neither of which may be preceded by the word 'Limited'.

A public company does not automatically have its shares listed on The Stock Exchange, but the process of obtaining a listing (see Chapter 3) is often referred to as 'going public', as a private company cannot obtain a listing on The Stock Exchange, and the processes of obtaining a listing and of becoming a public company are often carried out together.

Private company

A 'private company' is a company that is not a public company (CA 1985, S.1(3)).

A company limited by shares or by guarantee (not being a public company) must have 'limited' as the last word in its name (CA 1985, S.25). Thus all companies whose names end with 'limited' are private companies.

Close company

(Reference: Income and Corporation Taxes Act 1988, Section 414.)

Broadly speaking, a close company is one which is under the control of five or fewer persons together with their associates *or* is under the control of its directors.

The original rules on close companies, introduced in 1922, were designed to prevent individuals avoiding high rates of personal tax by not making distributions from companies they controlled. With the highest rate of personal tax now only marginally higher than Corporation Tax, these rules, the 'apportionment' provisions, were abolished in the Finance Act 1989. However, a number of fairly obscure tax provisions are still in force for close companies, including special rules on loans to controlling shareholders/directors.

A listed company is not a close company if shares carrying not less than 35% of the voting power are unconditionally and beneficially held by the public.

The Stock Exchange requires a listed company to include, in its annual report, a statement showing whether or not, as far as the directors are aware, the company is a close company.

Small and medium-sized companies

Small and medium-sized companies are defined by Section 13(1) of the Companies Act 1989 as companies meeting two or more of the following criteria:

	Small company	Medium-sized company
Turnover not exceeding	£2m.	£8m.
Balance sheet total not exceeding	£0.975m.	£3.9m.
Number of employees not exceeding	50	250

Small and medium-sized private companies are exempted from some of the requirements of the Companies Acts (CA 1989, Sch. 6).

Chapter 3

ADMISSION TO LISTING

Stock Exchange listing – 'quoted companies'

(Reference: The International Stock Exchange, London's book *Admission of Securities to Listing –* known as 'The Yellow Book'.)

Provided that it meets certain criteria, a public company may have its shares and/or debentures, unsecured loan stocks and warrants 'listed', i.e. included in The Stock Exchange Official List, so that a market is 'made' in the securities. Although it is usual for all the securities of a company to be listed, it is possible for this not to be the case. For example, SAINSBURY's preference shares were listed for many years before its ordinary shares were offered to the public.

Companies which have securities that are listed are often referred to as 'quoted companies', 'having a quotation' or 'being listed', although it is the company's securities that are listed, not the company itself. 'Having a quotation' is simply the old term for being 'listed', and the department which deals with applications for listing, now part of The Stock Exchange's Primary Markets Division, is still often referred to as the Quotations Department.

Requirements for listing

The minimum legal requirements that a company has to meet before any of its securities can be listed are contained in Part 4 of the Financial Services Act 1986, which implements in the United Kingdom four EEC directives, known as the Admission directive, the Listing Particulars directive, the Interim Reports directive, and the Mutual Recognition directive on the UK listing of EEC companies already listed elsewhere in the EEC.

These requirements are incorporated in The Stock Exchange's *Admission of Securities to Listing* (The Yellow Book), together with The Stock Exchange Council's own requirements.

Listing Particulars (prospectus)
Section 3 of The Yellow Book contains details of the contents of Listing Particulars, which have to be supplied to The Stock Exchange for approval prior to listing, and which have to be included in any prospectus inviting initial public subscription for the company's shares.

The Listing Particulars are designed to ensure that the company makes available sufficient information on its history, current position and future prospects to enable the general public to assess the value of the company's shares as an investment, and they are very comprehensive. The prospectus issued by a company when it goes public is therefore a most valuable source of information for the analyst.

Minimum size of issue
The Stock Exchange has to satisfy itself that sufficient dealings are likely to take place in the class of security for which application is being made to make a realistic market, and thus justify a listing. The Yellow Book lays down two minimum criteria for listing – the expected market value of the securities for which listing is sought (the expected market price multiplied by the number of shares issued and to be issued: currently a minimum of £700,000 for shares and £200,000 for debt securities), and the proportion of shares to be held by the public (currently 25% of any class of share).

Keeping the public informed
The Stock Exchange also has to ensure that the general public will be kept satisfactorily informed of the company's activities and progress in the

future, and that the shareholders' interests will be adequately protected: this is done by requiring an applicant for listing to accept 'Continuing Obligations' as a condition of admission to and subsequent maintenance of listing.

Continuing Obligations

Section 5 of The Yellow Book contains details of the *Continuing Obligations* of listed companies, designed to protect shareholders and to keep them properly informed. It requires the company to submit to The Stock Exchange through the company's brokers drafts *for approval* of all circulars to holders of securities, notices of meetings, forms of proxy and notices by advertisement to holders of bearer securities. It also requires the company to notify The Stock Exchange of profit announcements; dividend declarations; material acquisitions; changes of directors; proposed changes in the nature of the business and any other 'information necessary to enable holders of the company's listed securities and the public to appraise the position of the company and to avoid the establishment of a false market in its listed securities'. This information is then immediately transmitted to the market by The Stock Exchange's Company Announcements office.

In addition, amongst various requirements on interim reports, proxy voting, registration of securities and several other topics, the *Continuing Obligations* require companies to include in the annual report and accounts:

(a) the directors' reasons for any significant departure from standard accounting practices;

(b) an explanation if the results differ materially from any forecast published by the company;

(c) a geographical analysis of both turnover and contribution to trading results of operations outside the United Kingdom and Ireland;

(d) the name of the principal country in which each subsidiary operates;

(e) certain particulars of each company in which the group holds 20% or more of the equity capital;

(f) details of bank loans, overdrafts and other borrowings;

(g) the amount of interest capitalised by the company (or group) during the year;

(h) details of each director's beneficial and non-beneficial interests in the company's shares and options;

(i) information on holdings, other than by directors, of 5% or more of any class of voting capital;

(j) a statement of whether the company is or is not a close company;

(k) particulars of significant contracts during the year in which any director is or was materially interested;

(l) particulars of significant contracts with, or for the provision of services by a corporate substantial shareholder (substantial = 30% or more of the voting power);

(m) particulars of the waiving of emoluments by any director, and of the waiving of dividends by any shareholder;

(n) particulars of any authority for the company to purchase its own shares;

(o) details of shares issued for cash other than pro rata to existing shareholders;

(p) short biographical note on each non-executive director.

Companies are also expected to issue their report and accounts within six months of their year end, but may apply for the six-month period to be extended if they have significant overseas interests.

Methods of obtaining a listing

Chapter 3 of Section 1 of The Yellow Book describes the five ways in which a company can obtain a listing. Briefly, they are as follows:

1. *Offer for sale*, the most common method; both new and/or existing shares can be offered to the public. The issuing house or the sponsoring broker purchases the shares from existing shareholders and/or from the company, and offers them on to the general public at a slightly higher price.

2. *Offer for sale by tender*, a variation on method 1 which allows applicants to bid for securities at or above a minimum issue price. The shares are then all sold at one price, the 'striking price', which may be the highest price at which all the shares can be sold, or a little lower if this is necessary to ensure a good spread of shareholders.

3. *Public issue by prospectus*, a rare method; shares are offered direct to the public by the company. Only new shares can be offered.

4. *Selective marketing*, also known as *placing*, used for small issues (under £15 million); the shares are sold mainly to institutional investors. Where the issue exceeds £2 million, not less than 25% must either be made available to the general public or be distributed by another, independent, Stock Exchange member firm.

5. *Introduction*, used where the company's shares are already widely held and/or are already listed outside the United Kingdom, or where a new holding company issues its shares in exchange for those of one or more listed companies; there is no formal offer of shares, but a listing is obtained for existing shares.

Methods 1 to 4 are referred to broadly as 'new issues', because the company's shares are new to the stock market, although methods 1, 2 and 4 do not necessarily involve the issue of any new shares.

The Unlisted Securities Market

(Reference: The Stock Exchange, London's booklet *Unlisted Securities Market* – known as 'The Green Book'.)

The Unlisted Securities Market (USM) was launched by The Stock Exchange in November 1980 to provide a recognised market for the securities of smaller, less mature companies. Although companies on the USM do not have the same status as Listed companies, and their shares are in law 'unlisted', the shares are dealt in on The Stock Exchange just like any listed shares. Entry to the USM has been made easier than obtaining a full listing:

1. Only 10% of the equity need be made available to the general public rather than the 25% normally required for the full listing.
2. The company is required to have been trading for only two years (full listing three years).
3. Both the cost of entry and the annual charge are considerably less than for a full listing.

Chapter 4

SHARE CAPITAL AND RESERVES

SHARE CAPITAL

Authorised and issued share capital

When a company is formed the authorised share capital and the nominal value of the shares are established and written into the company's Memorandum of Association, and the procedure for increasing the authorised share capital is included in the company's Articles of Association. This procedure usually requires the passing by simple majority of an ordinary resolution at a general meeting of shareholders. Thereafter the directors of the company cannot issue new shares in excess of the authorised limits, nor can they issue any form of securities which have rights to subscribe for shares (e.g. convertibles and warrants: see below) if the full exercising of these rights would involve the issue of shares in excess of the authorised share capital.

Both the authorised share capital and the issued share capital are shown in the company's balance sheet.

Types of share capital

Although all shares are referred to generally as 'risk capital', as the shareholders are the first investors to lose if the company fails, the degree of risk can vary within the same company from hardly any more than that of an unsecured lender to highly speculative, with prospects of reward usually varying accordingly. The main types of shares, in increasing order of risk, the order in which they would rank for distribution in the event of liquidation, are:

(a) preference shares;
(b) ordinary shares;
(c) deferred shares;
(d) warrants to subscribe for shares.

Unlike interest paid on loan capital, distributions of profits to shareholders are not an 'allowable expense' for company taxation purposes; i.e. dividends have to be paid out of profits *after* Corporation Tax has been deducted, although the present imputation tax system does concede to shareholders an associated tax credit on dividends, as explained in Chapter 13.

Preference shares

Preference shares carry a fixed rate of dividend, normally payable half-yearly, but unlike the holders of loan capital, who can take action against a company in default of interest payments, preference shareholders have no legal redress if the board of directors decides to recommend that no preference dividends should be paid. However, if no preference dividend is declared for an accounting period, no dividend can be declared on any other type of share for the period concerned, and the preference shareholders usually become entitled to vote at shareholders' general meetings. (Provided their dividends are paid, preference shares do not normally carry a vote.)

Varieties of preference shares (see Example 4.1) can include one or a combination of the following features:

1. *Cumulative.* If the dividend on a cumulative preference share is not paid on time, payment is postponed rather than omitted. When this happens, the preference dividend is said to be 'in arrears', and these arrears have to be paid by the company before any other dividend can be declared. Arrears of cumulative preference dividends must be shown in a note to the accounts.

2. *Redeemable.* The shares are repayable, normally at their nominal (par) value, in a given year, e.g. 1995, or when the company chooses within a given period, e.g. 1993/98.
3. *Participating.* In addition to receiving a fixed dividend, shareholders participate in an additional dividend, usually a proportion of any ordinary dividend declared.
4. *Convertible.* Shareholders have the option of converting their preference shares into ordinary shares, usually on an unchanged nominal value basis within a given period of time, the conversion period.

Example 4.1 Varieties of preference share

A company has four types of share, listed below. In 1986 it pays no dividends; in 1987 it pays preference dividends only, including arrears of cumulative preference dividends, and in 1988 and 1989 it also pays ordinary dividends of 4p and 12p respectively. The participating preference shareholders are entitled to half the ordinary dividend in addition to their fixed 3.5% per annum, but neither they nor the redeemable preference shares are cumulative.

The net dividend payable on each type of share, all of £1 nominal value, would be

	1986	1987	1988	1989
5.6% Cumulative preference	Nil	11.2p	5.6p	5.6p
7% Redeemable preference 1987	Nil	7p	Nil (redeemed)	Nil
3.5% Participating preference	Nil	3½p	5½p	9½p
Ordinary £1 share	Nil	Nil	4p	12p

(The rate of dividend on a preference share is normally quoted not of associated credit (see page 95).)

Golden shares

Where nationalised industries have been privatised, the Government has, in some cases, retained a 'golden share' to prevent takeover and/or has placed limits on the maximum size of any one holding or on the percentage that can be held by foreigners, e.g. the Secretary of State for Transport holds a Special Rights redeemable preference share of £1 in BAA, and BAA's articles of association limit the holding of any one shareholder to 15% of the ordinary shares.

Ordinary shares

Ordinary shares usually form the bulk of the share capital of a company. Ordinary shareholders are normally entitled to all the profits remaining after tax and preference dividends have been deducted although, as explained later, not all these attributable profits are likely to be distributed. Ordinary shareholders are entitled to vote at general meetings, giving them control over the election of directors.

However some companies, e.g. STOREHOUSE, put a clause in their articles of association to allow them to disenfranchise a shareholder where the shares are held in a nominee name and the nominee holder fails to respond to a request for information on the underlying holder (CA 1985, S.216). This protects the company against the building up of anonymous holdings prior to a possible bid.

Until recently companies were not allowed to issue redeemable ordinary shares. Under Section 159 of the Companies Act 1985 they are now allowed to do so, provided they also have shares in issue which are not redeemable; i.e. the share capital of a company cannot consist solely of redeemable shares. A company may now also purchase its own shares, subject to a large number of conditions, including the prior approval of its shareholders (see page 17).

Ordinary stock

Ordinary stock is a historical legacy from the days when every share in issue had to be numbered; some companies used to convert their shares into stock when they became fully paid (as this avoided the bother of numbers), and a few companies continue to use the term.

Ordinary stock is equity capital. It can, in theory, be transferred in any monetary amount, while shares can only be bought and sold individually; in practice ordinary stock is normally traded in multiples of £1, so the terms 'ordinary share' and 'ordinary stock' are effectively synonymous.

Non-voting shares

A number of companies have more than one class of share (other than preference shares), with differing rights on voting and/or dividends and/or on liquidation. The most common variation is in voting rights, where a second class of share, identical in all other respects to the ordinary class, carries either no voting rights (usually called N/V or 'A' shares), or carries restricted voting rights (R/V shares).

The trend over the last few years has, however, been towards the abolition of non-voting shares, and it is becoming increasingly difficult (if not actually impossible) to raise new money by the issue of non-voting shares. Several companies, led by MARKS & SPENCER in 1966, and including SEARS and RANK, have enfranchised their non-voting shares, giving modest scrip (free) issues to voting shareholders by way of compensation, but there are still some notable exceptions, including GREAT UNIVERSAL STORES (£1.3m ordinary shares, £61.3m 'A' non-voting) and WHITBREAD (£4.1m 'B' ordinary shares, £104.8m 'A' limited voting). The ordinary shares stand at a substantial premium over the other shares, and WHITBREAD's share structure (where the 'B' shares each carry 20 votes to the 'A' share's one vote, and are virtually all held by the Whitbread family) has undoubtedly helped to keep unwelcome predators away from the company.

Investing in shares that do not have full voting power is very much a case of *caveat emptor* (buyer beware). You may find yourself invested in a company like C. H. BAILEY, where the 'B' ordinary shares, largely family-held, carry 100 times the voting rights of the more widely held ordinary shares and where the chairman, Mr C. H. Bailey, pays himself more than £120,000 per annum although the shareholders have not had a dividend for years. The company discourages them from complaining by holding the AGM inconveniently close to Christmas at a dry dock in South Wales. Or you may find yourself invested in a company like ACROW, where the founder, Bill de Vigier, and his son-in-law between them held over 50% of the voting shares; de Vigier ran ACROW extremely successfully for many years but, in making acquisitions, built up a mountain of debt because he steadfastly refused to enfranchise the N/V shareholders and have a rights issue to broaden his equity base. When, in the early 1980s, the bottom fell out of the crane market and the strength of sterling hit exports (a very large part of ACROW's turnover), the bankers finally withdrew their support. When we asked de Vigier, two years earlier, why he didn't enfranchise and have a rights issue, he replied 'Not while I'm alive. The banks have never refused to lend me money in the past, why should they do so in the future?'

The same warning applies to companies where all shares (other than preference shares) carry equal voting rights, and one person effectively controls more than 50% of the votes; other shareholders are relying very heavily on that one person, but at least the controlling shareholder doesn't enjoy power that is disproportionate to his stake in the company.

Deferred shares

Another, but now quite rare, class is the deferred share, where no dividend is payable either:

(*a*) until ordinary shareholders' dividends have reached a certain level,
   or
(*b*) until several years after issue: e.g. CRODA in 1978 made a scrip issue of deferred ordinary shares which did not rank for dividends until 1988, when they became ordinary shares.

Partly paid shares

When a company does not need all the proceeds of an equity issue immediately (e.g. an oil exploration company with a lengthy drilling programme) or wishes to have guaranteed recourse to further equity finance in certain circumstances (e.g. a merchant bank wanting ample cover for liabilities), it may issue partly paid shares, i.e. shares for which subscribers pay for only part of the nominal price at the time of issue. Partly paid shares, once issued, place an obligation on the holder to subscribe the unpaid-up portion at the company's call, and there are legal safeguards to prevent the device of holders transferring their shares to a non-creditworthy person in order to avoid paying the call.

Details of partly paid shares issued by a company are shown in the balance sheet. Where a company holds partly paid shares, details should be shown under 'contingent liabilities' (CA 1985, Sch. 4, para. 50 (2)).

Shares can be issued with part of the issue price payable on application and the remainder payable shortly afterwards, before registration (i.e. before the company registers the shares in the holder's name). However, if shares are to remain partly paid after registration, The Stock Exchange will not normally allow them to be admitted to listing.

Warrants

Warrants are transferable options granted by the company to purchase new shares from the company at a given price, called the 'exercise price'. The warrant is normally exercisable only during a given time period, the exercise period, although one or two perpetual warrants have been issued.

Warrants can be issued on their own, but are usually issued attached to new issues of unsecured loan stock to give the stockholder an opportunity of subsequently participating in the equity of the company; the warrant element makes the issue more attractive and is sometimes referred to as the 'sweetener' (see Chapter 5).

Once the loan stock plus warrants 'package' is issued the warrants can be detached ('stripped') and sold separately, providing a high risk/high reward form of equity investment. For example, if the ordinary shares of a company stood at 100p, warrants with an exercise price of 75p would then be worth a minimum of 25p. If the ordinary shares doubled to 200p then the warrants would be worth a minimum of 125p, a fivefold increase. In practice warrants command a premium over the ordinary price minus exercise price, although this premium tends to fall over the life of the warrant, reaching zero at the end of the exercise period. Warrants are comparatively rare in the United Kingdom, where the majority have been issued in bid situations.

A very clear explanation of the behaviour of warrant prices in practice is given in R. A. Brearley's book *Security Prices in a Competitive Market*.

ADRs

ADRs (American Depositary Receipts) are used in America to simplify the holding of securities in non-United States companies. The securities purchased on behalf of the American investor are deposited abroad in a custodian bank, and the corresponding ADR certificates are issued by a US depository bank. The ADR bank then acts both as depositary and stock transfer agent, dealing with the payment of dividends and the handling of proxies and rights issues for the American investor.

ADRs can be unsponsored, normally traded on the Over-The-Counter (OTC) market, or sponsored by the non-US company. Sponsored ADRs can be traded on the New York and American stock exchanges, but the non-US company must register with the Securities and Exchange Commission (SEC) and meet the specific requirements of the exchange, including the filing of an annual report (usually Form 20–F).

Share schemes for directors and employees

A number of companies have encouraged share ownership amongst their staff for many years (ICI, for example, introduced a profit-sharing scheme as long ago as 1954, under which employees received a salary-related allocation of shares each year, according to the profitability of the company), but it is only in the last few years that governments have actively encouraged wider share participation by the introduction of substantial tax concessions. These concessions now apply to three types of scheme: savings related share option schemes (SAYE schemes), profit-sharing schemes and, most recently, share option schemes. They have all proved very popular, particularly the share option scheme; by the end of 1989, 869 SAYE, 879 profit-sharing, and 4,199 share option schemes had been approved by the Inland Revenue.

Savings related share option schemes (SAYE schemes)
In this type of scheme, if 'approved' under the Finance Act 1980, an employee enters into a 'save as you earn' contract for a maximum of £150 per month for a minimum of five years and at the same time is given an option to subscribe for shares with the sum saved at a given price, which must be not less than 80% of their market value on the date the option is granted.

At the end of the SAYE contract period the employee can either use the lump sum from the SAYE contract to exercise the option, if the shares have done well in the mean time, or he can keep the cash. In either case he will not be charged income tax, but any profit on disposal is subject to assessment for capital gains tax. Details of options outstanding under the scheme will be shown in the annual report and accounts (e.g. LEADING LEISURE, illustrated here).

LEADING LEISURE *Note to the 1988 accounts*

Called up share capital
. . .

Options were outstanding under the 1988 savings related share option scheme to subscribe for shares as follows:

Shares	Option Price	Exercise Date
533,975	80p	1 July 1993
90,825	80p	1 July 1995

The options are normally exercisable during a period of 6 months following the exercise date.

Profit-sharing schemes
In this type of scheme, introduced by Labour under pressure from the Liberals, companies have, since 1978, been allowed to allocate up to a maximum sum per employee (currently £2,000 p.a. or 10% of earnings if more) to be used to purchase shares at full market value through specially created trusts.

The shares have to be held in trust for at least two years; income tax has to be paid only if the shares are sold within five years, and then only on a reducing scale according to how long they have been held, but normal capital gains tax rules apply.

Executive share option schemes
Executive share option schemes are like warrants, except that they are not normally transferable, and may lapse on termination of the holder's directorship of or employment by the company. Options may be granted to full-time directors and employees, at not less than the average market price at the time. There is an annual limit per person of £100,000 (number of shares × exercise price) or four times relevant emoluments, if more, (ICTA 1988).

Under the Finance Act 1984 there is no tax liability when the options are exercised between 3 and 10 years after being granted, but when the shares are sold there is an assessment for capital gains tax on the amount by which the selling price exceeds the exercise price.

Details of the number of options granted, the period during which they may be exercised and the subscription price payable should be shown in the accounts. For example:

LEADING LEISURE *Note to the 1988 accounts*

Called up share capital
. . .

Options were outstanding under the 1984 and 1988 share option schemes to subscribe for shares as follows:

Shares	Option Price	Date of Grant
385,889	39.5p	30 November 1984
133,529	56p	25 May 1986
198,037	69p	2 April 1987
1,263,005	91p	1 June 1988

The options are normally exercisable during the period between 3 and 10 years following the date of grant.

Partly paid shares
As the amount paid up is usually very small, and the call is normally payable at the holder's request, partly paid shares issued under executive incentive schemes are very similar to options from the company's point of view. From the holder's point of view the tax advantages of share options under the Finance Act 1984 are so great that partly paid shares are unlikely to be used as executive incentives in the future.

Details of all types of partly paid shares are shown in the balance sheet under 'Share capital' (e.g. BRITISH LAND, shown here).

BRITISH LAND *Balance sheet*

Note 8 Shareholders' Funds

	1989
Shares of 25p each issued:	
Fully paid	224,894,238
Share incentive scheme – 2.5/3.5p	44,000

Strictly speaking, options granted and partly paid shares issued to directors and employees under incentive schemes produce potential dilution of equity earnings in the same way as warrants, but in practice they are usually sufficiently small in relation to a company's issued equity to be ignored.

Shares purchased with loans
Section 153 (4) (c) of the Companies Act 1985 allows loans to employees, but not to directors, for the purpose of purchasing fully paid shares in the company; the aggregate amount of any outstand-ing loans must be shown in the company's balance sheet. Because of the tax advantages of other schemes, loans for the purchase of shares are likely to become increasingly rare.

The investors' viewpoint
Companies that encourage employee share participation on favourable terms are generally regarded as more likely to prosper than those which do not. In particular, companies that grant options to executive directors and key senior staff, on whose efforts the success of a company largely depends, can expect better than average performance. In short, giving the directors and employees a 'slice of the action' should be regarded as a plus point for investing in a company.

Limitations on the issue of further equity

There are three limitations to the issue of further equity.

First, as already mentioned, there must be sufficient share capital authorised.

Secondly, The Stock Exchange's *Continuing Obligations* for listed companies forbids the issue of equity, convertibles, warrants or options for cash, other than to the equity shareholders of the company, except with the prior approval of ordinary shareholders in general meeting, and the approval of The Stock Exchange. The Stock Exchange normally restricts issues of equity capital by way of placings to protect the interests of existing shareholders (see The Yellow Book, Section 1, Chapter 2, para. 14), but these restrictions can be relaxed when market conditions or the individual circumstances of a company justify doing so.

Thirdly, Section 100 of the Companies Act 1985 prohibits the issue of shares at a discount, i.e. for less than their nominal value.

Rights issues

A rights issue is an issue of new shares offered to shareholders in proportion to their existing holdings at a discount to the current market price. The discount varies according to the 'weight' of the rights issue; 1 new share offered for every 8 or 10 shares already held would be regarded as a 'light' issue, probably requiring a discount of around 15%, while more than 1-for-4 would be 'heavy' and likely to need about 20% discount, or more if the company is in poor health. At these discounts underwriting would be arranged to ensure buyers for any shares not taken up by shareholders, but companies occasionally choose to make a rights issue at very much below the market price, the lowest price normally permitted being the par value of the shares.

The effect on the balance sheet of an issue at par is to add the total nominal value of the shares being issued to the issued share capital, and to show the cash received on the assets side. The expenses of the issue would normally be written off either to profit and loss account or against share premium account.

If the new shares are issued above par, the nominal value of the shares issued is added to the issued share capital and the difference between the issue price and the nominal price of each new share, i.e. the premium at which the shares were issued, is added to the share premium account. For example, in June 1989 RTZ made a 1-for-7 rights issue of 113,052,000 ordinary 25p shares at 435p per share. The issue added £28.3m to the ordinary share capital (113.05m × 25p) and £450.3m (113.05m × 410p premium), less expenses, to the share premium account, as illustrated here.

RTZ *Rights issue*

	Pre-rights £m	Post-rights £m
Issued share capital		
Ordinary shares of 25p each	200.4	228.7
Share premium		
Pre-rights	330.0	330.0
Premium on shares issued		463.5
Expenses of rights issue		(13.2)
	330.0	780.3

There are two methods of dealing with convertible stock in a rights issue. Either the holders are offered new shares on the basis of the number of ordinary shares they would hold on full conversion, or the stock has its conversion terms adjusted to allow for the rights issue, whichever method is laid down in the convertible's trust deed (see Chapter 5). Similarly, either warrant holders are offered new shares or the warrant's exercise price is adjusted.

Scrip issues

A scrip issue, also known as a bonus or capitalisation issue, is a free issue of additional new shares to existing shareholders, made by capitalising reserves. For example, ALBERT FISHER made a 1-for-2-scrip issue in December 1987, with the following effect on the balance sheet:

	Pre scrip £000	Post scrip £000
Ordinary share capital	11,260	16,890
Share premium account	23,725	18,095
Shareholders' funds	34,985	34,985

As a scrip issue is basically a bookkeeping transaction, the share price would normally be expected to adjust accordingly (e.g. would fall from 150p to 100p with a 1-for-2), and it is open to debate as to whether scrip issues serve any useful purpose. The main arguments in favour are the following:

(a) Scrip issues are popular with the investing public, and therefore enhance share prices. Research shows that shares tend to outperform the market after the announcement of a scrip issue, but that companies make scrip issues only when they are doing well, i.e. when their share price would be expected to outperform just as much without the scrip issue.

(b) A 'heavy' share price in the market, say over £2, tends to make the shares harder to trade and artificially depresses the price. Scrip issues can be used to scale the price down.

(c) A scrip issue, being 'paid for' out of reserves, enables retained profits and/or the increased value of assets to be reflected by an increased share capital.

(d) The rate of dividends, expressed as a percentage of an unrealistically small share capital, can look excessive.

(e) An issued share capital of at least £1 million is needed for Trustee status.

The last argument appears to be the only factual one in favour of scrip issues; the remainder are psychological, although only a sound and flourishing company is likely to be able to make substantial scrip issues every few years. ALBERT FISHER's record illustrates this well: the company also made a 1-for-3 scrip issue in 1983, a 1-for-2 in 1984, a 1-for-3 in 1986 and a 1-for-2 in 1987.

The arguments against scrip issues are firstly the administrative costs incurred and secondly the increased risk of the share price subsequently falling very close to or below par, thus precluding a rights issue. The cost is relatively small, but reducing the market price can cause serious embarrassment if the company wants, at a later date, to make a rights issue only to find that its share price is too low to do so.

Share splits

Where a company feels its share price is 'heavy' but does not want to capitalise reserves – i.e. it does not want to make a scrip issue – it can split its shares into shares with a smaller par value. For example, in 1982 GEC split its 25p shares, which were standing at around £12 at the time, into 5p shares, and the share price moved to around 240p.

Scrip (stock) dividends

There are two types of scrip or stock dividends:

(*a*) where the company issues shares instead of paying cash dividends – shareholders have no choice (as ULTRAMAR did in the 1970s);

(*b*) where each shareholder can choose whether he or she wishes to receive a cash dividend or a stock dividend.

Stock or scrip dividends can only avoid tax if they are *not* an alternative to cash dividends, i.e. type (*a*) above, which is in effect a scrip issue with no dividends!

In type (*b*) shareholders are sent a form of election in advance of each dividend payment, giving them the opportunity to opt for a scrip dividend, although a nominal cash dividend also has to be paid at least once each year in order to preserve 'wider range' investment status under the Trustee Investment Act 1961 (i.e. to allow trustees to invest in the shares). The number of shares is calculated to give the same value as the *net* dividend payable, and counts as income, so there is no tax advantage, and a positive disadvantage for 'gross' funds (pension funds and charities, which pay no tax).

Scrip dividends are popular with private shareholders, because they can add to their holding at middle market price without paying stockbrokers' commission. For example RTZ get about 20% of their shareholders opting for scrip dividends, representing about 4 or 5% of the ordinary share capital.

From the company's point of view, it is able to raise additional equity capital from its existing shareholders without the expense of a rights issue. Providing the response from shareholders is sufficient to justify the administrative costs, scrip dividends provide a useful addition to the cash flow.

Vendor consideration

This is the use of new shares to pay for an acquisition. In the balance sheet the value of the shares issued is shown as an increase in liabilities under share capital and share premium account, balanced on the other side by the assets acquired. If the value of the tangible assets falls short of the market value of the shares issued, the difference (i.e. the premium the acquirer has paid) can either be written off straight away against reserves, or taken into the balance sheet as 'goodwill' – an intangible asset.

For example, in 1988/89 HENRY BARRETT made four acquisitions and gave details of assets acquired and how their purchase was funded at the bottom of its source and application of funds statement (see illustration opposite). The sum of £20,892,000 was provided by the issue of shares, and the overall cost exceeded the value of the tangible assets acquired by £16,250,000.

HENRY BARRETT *Extract from group source and application of funds statement 1988/89*

The figures in the Consolidated Statement of Source and Application of Funds include the following amounts that relate to the acquisition of subsidiaries.

	£000	£000
Assets acquired:		
Tangible fixed assets		4,249
Goodwill		16,250
Stocks		2,607
Debtors		2,958
Cash and bank balances		2,255
		28,319
Less: Bank overdraft	383	
Creditors	6,602	
Deferred taxation	62	(7,047)
		21,272
Discharged by:		
Cash		80
Deferred cash payment		300
Shares		20,892
		21,272

Supplementary information on shares

Details of shares and debentures issued during the year should be given in a note to the balance sheet (CA 1985, Sch. 4, paras 39 and 41). The terms for redemption of all redeemable shares and the details of all outstanding rights to acquire shares either by subscription or conversion should also be given (CA 1985, Sch. 4, paras 38 (2) and 40).

Company purchasing its own shares

Under Sections 162 to 169 of the Companies Act 1985, a company may purchase its own shares, providing it doesn't buy in all its non-redeemable shares. Each contract for purchases outside the normal market must be authorised in advance by a special resolution. General authority may be given for market purchases up to a maximum number of shares, within a given price range and within a maximum of 18 months from the date the resolution is passed but, to protect investors, The Stock Exchange does not allow companies to purchase their own shares within two months before the announcement of half-yearly or full-year results or when price-sensitive information has become known to the company but has not been released to the public.

Several property companies were quick to take advantage of this concession to purchase their ordinary shares at a price below asset value, thus increasing the asset value of the remaining shares. For example the chairman of CLAYFORM

PROPERTIES, in his statement for 1988, reported that:

'In January 1988, the Company made market purchases of 692,500 of its own 5p ordinary shares for an aggregate consideration of £1,431,000. In December 1988 a further 200,000 shares were purchased for an aggregate consideration of £471,000. In total these purchases represent 2.6% of the issued share capital at the beginning of the year ... As a result of the cancellations both earnings and net assets per share will be enhanced.'

The authority to continue purchasing shares (at a maximum price of 105% of the average middle market quotation on the previous ten business days) was renewed at CLAYFORM's subsequent AGM.

A few companies outside the property sector, most notably GEC, have purchased their own shares, but the general reaction from investors has been that if a company can't find a better use for its cash it needs to find better management!

Reduction of share capital

Under Section 135 of the Companies Act 1985 a company may, with court approval, reduce its share capital in any way and, in particular, may:

(a) reduce or extinguish liability on share capital not fully paid up;

(b) cancel any paid-up share capital which is lost or unrepresented by available assets; and

(c) repay any paid-up share capital in excess of its requirements.

Where the net assets no longer exceed the paid-up value of the issued share capital, the reserves will appear negative in the balance sheet. Take, for example, the balance sheet of a company which has 1 million £1 ordinary shares in issue and reduces this to 1½ million 25p shares to remove a substantial accumulation of losses (Example 4.2):

Example 4.2   Effect of share capital reduction on the balance sheet

	Before reduction £000	After reduction £000
Issued share capital	1,000	375
Share premium account	206	—
Other reserves	(831)	—
Shareholders' funds	375	375

The amount of £625,000 nominal of capital and the share premium account of £206,000 have been cancelled.

Arrangements and reconstructions

If a company wishes to make an arrangement with its creditors or shareholders, including a reorganisation of the company's share capital by consolidation of different classes and/or division into different classes, it can do so under Section 425 of the Companies Act 1985. A meeting has to be called for each class of creditor or shareholder concerned, at which a resolution to make the arrangement requires at least three-fourths by value of those present and voting to vote in favour; after subsequent sanction by the court, the arrangement is then registered with the Registrar of Companies and becomes binding on all creditors and shareholders concerned.

RESERVES

Reserves can arise in several ways:

(a) by the accumulation of profits, either by retained profits from the profit and loss account or from the sale of assets;

(b) by the issue of shares or loan capital at a premium, i.e. at more than their nominal value: the issue can be either for cash or as consideration (payment) in an acquisition;

(c) by the purchase or repayment of loan capital below its nominal value;

(d) by upward revaluation of assets (see page 39);

(e) by the acquisition of assets at below their balance sheet value.

They can be reduced by losses, issue and redemption expenses, revaluation deficits and the writing-off of goodwill. In addition, foreign currency translation differences are taken direct to reserves (see Chapter 18).

The balance sheet formats in Schedule 4 of the Companies Act 1985 require reserves to be shown in three main subdivisions: Share premium account, Revaluation reserve, and Other reserves. Reserves should not include provision for deferred taxation, or any other provision.

Capital and revenue reserves

By law certain reserves are non-distributable (cannot be paid out as dividends) and the Articles of a company may further restrict distribution.

Prior to the Companies Act 1967 a company was required to distinguish between reserves available for dividend (revenue reserves) and non-distributable reserves (capital reserves), and although in law this distinction is no longer compulsory some companies still make the division between capital reserves and revenue reserves in their accounts, e.g. BASS:

BASS *Note on reserves*

	Share premium account £m	Revaluation reserve £m
a) **Undistributable reserves**		
At 30 September 1988	155	1,051
Premium on allotment of ordinary shares (net)	22	—
Revaluation surplus on intangible fixed assets (note 11)	—	2
Realised revaluation surpluses transferred to profit	—	(24)
Revaluation element in depreciation charge (note 21b)	—	(3)
Net debenture issue costs	(2)	—
At 30 September 1989	175	1,026

b) **Profit and loss account** . . .

Share premium account

(Reference: Companies Act 1985, Section 130.)

When shares are issued at a premium over their nominal value, the premium element must, by law, be credited to the share premium account, unless the rules of merger accounting apply (see page 111).

The share premium account has to be shown separately on the balance sheet and no part may be paid out to shareholders except on liquidation or under a capital reduction scheme authorised by the court. It is permissible, however:

(*a*) to capitalise the share premium account to pay up unissued shares for distribution to shareholders as a *bonus* issue (otherwise known as a scrip or capitalisation issue), for instance:

Ordinary share capital	£100,000
Share premium account	£85,000

Company makes 1-for-2 scrip issue:

Ordinary share capital	£150,000
Share premium account	£35,000

(*b*) to charge to the share premium account:

(i)   the preliminary expenses of forming a company;

(ii) the expenses and commissions incurred in any issue of shares or debentures;

(iii) any discount on the issue of loan capital;

(iv) any premium paid on the redemption of debentures.

Revaluation reserve

The surplus (or shortfall) on the revaluation of assets should be credited (or debited) to a separate reserve, the revaluation reserve. The amount of the revaluation reserve shall be shown 'under a separate sub-heading in the position given for the item "revaluation reserve" in the balance sheet formats, *but need not be shown under that name*'. (*Our italics!* CA 1985, Sch. 4 para. 34.)

Foreign currency equalisation

Some companies with overseas borrowings and overseas assets keep a running total of the effect of currency exchange rates in a separate reserve.

Reserve funds

Where a reserve is represented by earmarked assets (e.g. quoted securities, an endowment policy and/or cash specifically set aside), it is called a reserve *fund*.

For example, if a company issues a £250,000 debenture repayable in 20 years and decides to set aside £8,000 each year towards the cost of eventual redemption (the old-fashioned type of sinking fund as described in Chapter 5), it will treat it as a separate fund, investing the money in earmarked assets, usually risk-free gilt-edged securities, to earn interest between now and the redemption date.

Debenture redemption reserve funds are comparatively rare these days as almost all debenture issues now either have no sinking fund at all or provide for a small proportion of the debenture to be redeemed by drawings or repurchase each year, rather than setting the money aside in a fund.

Capital redemption reserve

Shares may only be redeemed or purchased by the company out of distributable profits or out of the proceeds of a new issue of shares. Where redemption or purchase is out of distributable profits, an amount equal to the amount by which the company's issued share capital is diminished must, by law, be transferred to a reserve, called the *capital redemption reserve* (CA 1985, S. 170). This reserve is shown separately under Other reserves.

The idea behind the law is to prevent a company's overall share capital plus nondistributable reserves from being reduced when share capital is repaid: the reserve can never be distributed except upon liquidation or in a capital reduction scheme, but it can be capitalised by a bonus issue, as in Example 4.3.

Example 4.3   Capital redemption reserve

1. Initial position:

Issued share capital	£
30,000 £1 Redeemable preference shares	30,000
100,000 £1 Ordinary shares	100,000
	130,000

Reserves

Revenue reserve (retained profits)	75,000

2. Company then uses retained profits to redeem all the preference shares:

Issued share capital	£
100,000 £1 Ordinary shares	100,000
	100,000

Reserves

Capital redemption reserve	30,000
Revenue reserve (retained profits)	45,000

3. Company then decides to make a 3-for-10 scrip issue, which brings the issued share capital back to £130,000.

Issued share capital	£
130,000 £1 Ordinary shares	130,000
	130,000

Reserves

Revenue reserve (retained profits)	45,000

Movements to and from reserves

The Companies Act 1985 requires the source of any increase and the application of any decrease in reserves to be disclosed (Sch. 4, para. 46 – see example on page 106).

Chapter 5

LOAN CAPITAL

The advantages of borrowing

If a company confidently expects that its return on capital (i.e. the trading profit expressed as a percentage of the capital the company employs) will exceed the cost of borrowing, then borrowing will increase the profit attributable to the ordinary shareholders.

There are, however, various limitations on the amount a company can·borrow, which we will discuss later in this chapter, and borrowing also increases risk.

The risk of borrowing

The risk of borrowing is twofold: firstly the interest on most borrowings has to be paid promptly when due (unlike dividends on shares, which can be deferred or omitted altogether) and secondly most borrowings have to be repaid by a certain date (unlike most share capital, which is only repayable on liquidation).

In a poor year, interest charges can drastically reduce the pre-tax profits of a heavily borrowed company. Take, for example, two companies that are identical except that one, Company A, is financed entirely by shareholders while the other, Company B, is financed half by shareholders and half by borrowing, which bears a rate of interest of 10% per annum.

The table in Example 5.1 shows the profitability of the two companies with varying rates of return on capital employed: in an average year Company B earns 15% on money borrowed at 10%, and so gains 5% on 2,000,000, adding £100,000 to pre-tax profits. This extra profit, after tax, adds 3p to the earnings attributable to each of the 2,000,000 shares that Company B has issued, making the earnings per share 12p compared with 9p for Company A.

In a good year the advantage of borrowing will enhance Company B's earnings per share even more (24p compared with 15p for Company A) but in a poor year, as our table shows, all the trading profit is used servicing the borrowings of Company B, while Company A still manages to earn £120,000 after tax for its shareholders.

The point at which the two companies do equally well as far as their shareholders are concerned is shown on the graph in Example 5.1. Their earnings per share are both 6p when the return on capital employed is 10% per annum; as one would expect, borrowing at 10% to earn 10% neither adds to nor detracts from Company B's profits. As the graph also shows, borrowing makes a company's profits more volatile, and the risk of borrowing is further increased when money is borrowed at a variable rate of interest (e.g. on overdraft). If interest rates had risen above 10% in our example's 'poor year', Company B would have actually made a loss.

We will come back to the effects of borrowing in Chapter 24, but let us now look in detail at various types of borrowing.

Types of borrowing

There are many ways in which a company can borrow money, the main characteristics of different types of debt being:

(a) the length of time for which the money is borrowed;
(b) the rate of interest paid;
(c) the security offered to the lender by way of charges on the assets of the company;
(d) the negotiability of the debt instrument (i.e. does the lender receive a piece of paper which he can sell if he wishes to disinvest before the date of repayment?);

Example 5.1   Financing by share capital and by borrowing

	Company A			**Company B**		
Issued equity (£1 shares)	£4,000,000			£2,000,000		
Borrowings (10% interest)	Nil			£2,000,000		
	Good year	Average year	Poor Year	Good year	Average year	Poor year
Rate of return	25%	15%	5%	25%	15%	5%
	£000	£000	£000	£000	£000	£000
Trading profit	1,000	600	200	1,000	600	200
Interest	—	—	—	200	200	200
Pre-tax profit	1,000	600	200	800	400	0
Taxation (40%)	400	240	80	320	160	0
Profit after tax	600	360	120	480	240	0
Earnings per share	15p	9p	3p	24p	12p	0p

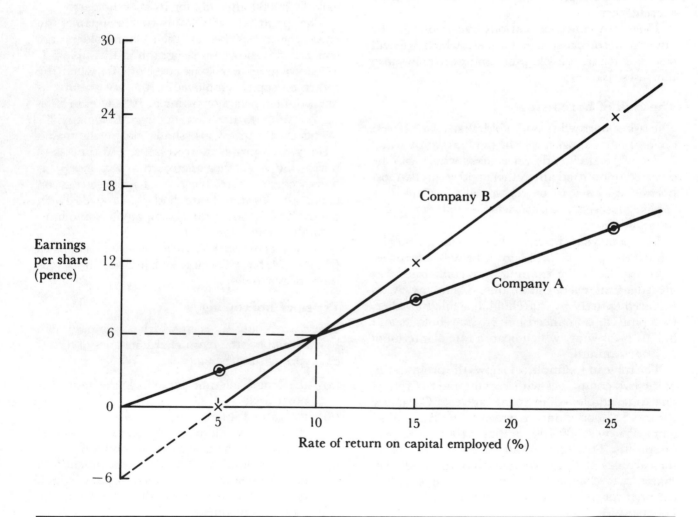

(*e*) the flexibility to the company and to the lender in the timing of borrowing and repayment;

(*f*) any deferred equity option given to the lender.

A company's borrowings fall broadly into three categories:

1. Issues of debentures and unsecured loan stock, which can be held by the general public, and can be bought and sold in the same way as shares.
2. Loans from banks and other financial institutions.
3. Bank overdrafts (described in Chapter 10).

Categories 1 and 2 are shown separately in the balance sheet, with a note describing the terms on which each loan is repayable and the rate of interest, dividing them into secured and unsecured loans, and giving the aggregate amount of:

(*a*) bank loans;
(*b*) other loans wholly repayable within five years;
(*c*) other loans, wholly or partly repayable more than five years after the balance sheet date.

Loans that are wholly repayable within one year should appear under 'Creditors: amounts falling due within one year' where Format 1 in the Companies Act 1985 is used, but in Format 2 all creditors come under a single heading. This is an important point to watch, because a loan coming up for repayment may significantly weaken the company's liquidity position, and can be a very serious threat to a company that is already short of funds if it is likely to have any difficulty refinancing the loan.

Security given to the lender – debentures and unsecured loan stock

When a company wishes to issue loan capital it can offer the lender some specific security on the loan. If it does so, the loan is called a debenture (£100 units) or debenture stock (usually units of £1); if not it is an unsecured loan stock (ULS), and these are the two main types of loan capital raised from the general public.

Debentures

Debentures can be secured by fixed and/or floating charges described below, the most common type of debenture being one that is secured on specific land or buildings, sometimes called a mortgage debenture.

Fixed charge

A fixed charge is similar to a mortgage on a house.

The company enters into a debenture deed which places a charge on specific identifiable assets. This gives the debenture holder a legal interest in the assets concerned as security for the loan, and the company cannot then dispose of them unless the debenture holder releases the charge (which he is unlikely to do unless he is offered some equally good alternative security). If the company defaults or falls into arrears on interest payments or capital repayments, the debenture holder can either:

(*a*) appoint a Receiver to receive any income from the assets (e.g. rents) *or*
(*b*) foreclose, i.e. take possession and sell the assets, using the proceeds of the sale to repay the debenture holders in full; any surplus remaining is then paid to the company, but if the proceeds of selling the assets charged are insufficient to repay the debenture holders in full, the debenture holders then rank equally with unsecured creditors for the shortfall.

Floating charge

This is a general charge on the assets of a company. But the debenture holder has no legal interest in the assets unless and until an event specified in the debenture deed occurs; for example, if the company goes into liquidation or ceases trading, or falls behind with interest payments or capital repayments, or exceeds specified borrowing limits. In the event of default the debenture holder can then appoint a Receiver, who takes physical possession of the assets of the company. The Receiver can also be appointed as the Manager or a separate Manager can be appointed to continue running the company, or the Receiver can sell off the assets; the former course is adopted if possible, because a company can normally be sold as a going concern for more than the breakup value.

The ranking of ULS

In a liquidation the holders of unsecured loan stock rank equally with other unsecured creditors, that is after debenture holders and preferential creditors (tax, rates and certain obligations to employees). In practice trade creditors often restrict a company to 'cash with order' terms if they see it running into difficulties, and to that extent a ULS tends to rank behind suppliers.

Typical characteristics of debentures and ULS

Interest

Most debentures and ULS carry a fixed annual rate of interest (known loosely as the 'coupon') which is payable (normally half-yearly) regardless of the company's profitability. Interest is deductible before the company is assessed for tax, i.e. it is an allowable expense for tax purposes, and therefore costs the company less than the same amount paid out in dividends on shares.

Redemption

Each issue is normally for a given term, and is repayable at the end of the term (at the redemption date) or, where there is a redemption period (e.g. 1993/97), it is repayable when the company chooses within that period. A few irredeemable stocks do exist, e.g. BET 5% Perpetual Debenture, redeemable (at 130%) only in the event of voluntary liquidation, but they are rare.

Liquidation

In the event of liquidation, debenture holders are entitled to repayment in full from the proceeds of disposal of the charged assets. Then the ULS holders and other unsecured creditors, and the fixed charge debenture holders if not already fully satisfied, rank equally after preferential creditors, and have to be repaid before the shareholders are entitled to anything.

Specific characteristics – the trust deed

Where a debenture or loan stock is to be issued to more than a very small number of holders, and particularly when it is going to be listed on The Stock Exchange, a trustee or trustees are appointed to represent the holders collectively, and the company enters into a trust deed rather than a debenture deed.

For listing, The Stock Exchange also requires that at least one trustee must be a trust corporation which has no interest in or relation to the company which might conflict with the position of the trustee. A large insurance company or the specialist LAW DEBENTURE CORPORATION is often appointed as trustee.

The deed contains all the details of the issue, except the issue price, including:

(a) details of fixed and floating charges, together with provision for *substitution* (securing further assets to replace secured assets which the company may subsequently wish to dispose of during the term of the loan). Provision may also be made for *topping up* (securing further assets if the value of secured assets falls below a given limit);

(b) redemption price and redemption date or period, together with any sinking fund arrangements;

(c) conditions under which the company may repurchase in the market, by tender and from individual holders;

(d) redemption price in the event of liquidation;

(e) conditions for further *pari passu* (equal rank-

ing) issues, restrictions on prior borrowings and, for ULS, overall borrowing limits;

(f) minimum transferable unit;

(g) powers to approve modifications to the terms and conditions.

The trust deed may also include restrictive clauses, for example:

(h) to prevent the nature of the company's business being changed; this is known as a 'Tickler' clause, after the celebrated case of the jam manufacturer who was taken to court by the holders of an unsecured loan stock;

(i) to prevent major disposals of the company's assets – a 'disposals' clause;

(j) to restrict the transfer of assets between charging subsidiaries (those within the charging group, i.e. included in the charge on assets) and other subsidiaries – sometimes known as a 'ring fence' clause.

Treatment of expenses on issue and of profit or loss on redemption

The expenses of issuing debentures and ULS, and any profit or loss on issues not made at par, are normally taken direct to reserves. For example, in September 1988 LAND SECURITIES made a £200 million issue of 10% First Mortgage Debenture Stock 2030 at £97.336%, and charged the expenses of the issue, including the discount, direct to reserves:

LAND SECURITIES *Note on reserves*

Other reserves:	£m
At 1 April 1988	201.8
Realised on sale of properties	30.8
Costs of raising loan capital	(6.4)
At 31 March 1989	226.8

Any profit or loss on redemption is usually taken direct to reserves, but may be shown as an extraordinary item. For example HAMMERSON in 1987 included 'Surplus on repayment of borrowings £417,000' in its extraordinary items. Profit on redemption should not be taken 'above the line', i.e. should not be included in the calculation of earnings per share.

Deep discount issues

Some companies issue loan capital at a substantial discount to par value in order to reduce the coupon, i.e. to reduce the amount of interest they have to pay during the life of the security concerned. The investor is compensated for receiving less interest by getting back appreciably more than he paid when the security is redeemed.

For tax purposes, a *deep discount* security is one:

(a) where the discount on issue represents more than 15% of the capital amount payable on redemption, *or*

(b) where the discount is 15% or less but exceeds half the number of complete years between issue and redemption.

The *income element* is calculated as the percentage rate at which the issue price would have to grow on a compound basis over each income period to equal the redemption price at the date of redemption. The income element is treated as income of the holder and as a deductible expense of the issuer, as COMMERCIAL UNION shows in its accounting policies:

COMMERCIAL UNION *Extract from accounting policies*

Loan capital and other loans

Borrowings issued at a discount are included in the balance sheet at their issue price together with the amortised discount to the balance sheet date. The amortised interest has been charged to loan interest in the profit and loss account.

An extreme example of a deep discount issue is GREYCOAT's £50 million Zero coupon bond 1995, issued in April 1987 at £43.6496% to finance property development. The accounts to 31 March 1989 showed an increase in the bond's book cost of £2.557 million, and explained the accounting policy being adopted:

GREYCOAT *Note to the 1989 accounts*

Creditors – amounts falling due after one year

	1989 £000	1988 £000
Unsecured loan stocks:		
£50,000,000 zero coupon bonds 1995	26,557	24,000

The discount implicit on the issue of the bond is being capitalised as part of the development cost until the properties are completed. On completion, the discount will be covered by part of the anticipated growth in the value of the related properties and written off to the share premium account. By this treatment, the discount

will be matched with the underlying capital growth. The amount capitalised for the year to 31 March 1989 was £2,532,000 and the amount charged to share premium account was £25,000 in respect of a completed property.

For tax purposes the discount will continue to be amortised and be treated as a deductible expense until redemption, but the expense will not be shown in the accounts; i.e., the pre-tax profits will be inflated by the amortised amount each year. In our view, the accounting treatment should be the same as the tax treatment.

Sinking funds

Some debenture and loan stock issues make provision for part or all of the stock to be redeemed gradually over a period of time by means of a sinking fund, e.g., SAINSBURY's mortgage debentures.

The normal method for a sinking fund to redeem stock is by annual or six-monthly drawings (lotteries of stock certificate numbers), with the company in some cases having the option of purchasing stock in the market if it can do so at or below the drawing price. The company may also be allowed to invite holders to tender stock for redemption.

There are three types of sinking fund, described below.

Original concept – no early redemptions
The sinking fund or redemption reserve fund, as originally conceived, was a fund into which a company put a given sum each year, the money being invested in government or other safe fixed-interest securities rather than being used to make early redemptions. The sums, together with interest earned, went on accumulating in the balance sheet year by year until the redemption date. This method is now rarely used.

Non-cumulative
Each year in which the sinking fund is in operation the company normally sets aside enough cash to redeem a fixed amount of stock, expressed as a given percentage of the total issue, and uses it to redeem stock on or by the date of the second interest payment (Example 5.2).

Example 5.2 Non-cumulative sinking fund

A 25-year stock with a 2% sinking fund starting at the end of the 5th year would be redeemed at the rate of 2% per annum at the end of years 5 to 24, leaving 60% of the stock to be redeemed at redemption date.

Provided redemptions each year are by drawings at par, the *average life* of a stock can be calculated by working out the average life of the stock redeemed by the sinking fund, in this case 14½ years, and then weighting it by the percentage redeemed by the sinking fund, in this case 40%:

$$\text{Average life} = \frac{(14\frac{1}{2} \times 40\%) + (25 \times 60\%)}{100\%}$$

$$= 20.8 \text{ years}$$

Cumulative

In a cumulative sinking fund the cash used for redemption each year is variable and normally consists of a fixed amount of cash plus the amount of interest saved by prior redemption (Example 5.3).

Yields

The yield on an irredeemable security is the gross amount of income received per annum divided by the market price of the security. Redeemable securities have two yields, their running yield and their gross redemption yield.

Running yield

The running yield is the same as the yield on an irredeemable security: it measures *income* and is concerned purely with the annual gross interest and the price of the stock; for instance, an 8% unsecured loan stock issued at £98% will yield 8% ÷ 0.98 = 8.16% at the issue price, or a 4½% debenture purchased at £50% will give the purchaser a yield of 9%, ignoring purchase expenses.

Redemption yield

The *gross* redemption yield is rather more complicated, as it measures 'total return'; i.e. it takes into account both the stream of income and any capital gain (or loss) on redemption. It is *not* just the sum of the running yield and the capital gain per annum, but is obtained by discounting the future interest payments and the redemption value at a rate that makes their combined *present value* equal to the current price of the stock. (The concept of discounting to obtain *present value* is explained in Appendix 2.) The rate required to do this is the gross redemption yield (Example 5.4).

Typical gross redemption yields for a well secured debenture are ¾% to 1½% above the yield on the equivalent gilt-edged security (i.e. a UK government stock of similar life and coupon), and 1% up to 5% or more for ULS, depending very much on the quality of the company and the amount of prior borrowings (borrowings that would rank ahead in a liquidation). *Net* redemption yields (i.e. the yields after tax) vary with the individual holder's rate of income tax payable on the stream of interest payments and the rate of tax payable on any capital gain on redemption.

Redemption date

When a stock has a final redemption period, e.g. 1999/2004, it is assumed in computing redemption yields that the company will choose the earliest date for redemption, 1999, if the stock is currently standing above par, otherwise the latest date, 2004.

When there is a sinking fund which allows redemptions only by drawings, the average life can be calculated accurately and should therefore be used as the number of years to redemption in calculating redemption yields. However, if the company is allowed to redeem by purchase in the market or by inviting tenders, the stockholder can no longer be sure that early drawings at par will

---

Example 5.3   Cumulative sinking fund

If our previous example had been a £10m. issue of a 25-year stock with a 10% coupon and a cumulative sinking fund starting at the end of year 5, and if all redemptions were made by drawings at par, then the annual redemptions would be:

End of year	Fixed amount of cash £	Variable amount (interest saved) £	Stock redeemed in year £	Total stock redeemed £	Stock remaining £
4	Nil	Nil	Nil	Nil	10,000,000
5	200,000	Nil	200,000	200,000	9,800,000
6	200,000	20,000	220,000	420,000	9,580,000
7	200,000	42,000	242,000	662,000	9,338,000
8	200,000	66,200	266,200	928,200	9,071,800

and so on. The average life can be calculated by time-weighting each year's redemption, e.g. 200,000 × 5 years plus 220,000 × 6 years, etc. ÷ 10,000,000. However, if redemptions are made by purchases in the market or by tender at below the redemption price, the amount redeemed will be greater, the amount of interest subsequently saved will be larger and the whole process of redemption will accelerate.

---

take place, and the average life is therefore ignored.

Example 5.4   Gross redemption yield

A 6% debenture due for redemption at £105% in four years' time is standing in the market at £90. Interest is payable in the normal manner, half-yearly in arrears (at the end of each six months). The present value of the stock is the sum of the present values of the eight future six-monthly interest payments discounted at $\sqrt{(1+i)}$ per half-year (where i expressed as a decimal = gross redemption yield).

$$\frac{3}{(\sqrt{1+i})} + \frac{3}{(\sqrt{1+i})^2} + \ldots + \frac{3}{(\sqrt{1+i})^8}$$

plus the present value of the sum received on redemption in eight half-years' time:

$$\frac{105}{(\sqrt{1+i})^8}$$

Solving for i by trial and error:

Value of i		Present value of income		Present value of redemption		Total
10%	=	19.48	+	71.72	=	£91.20
11%	=	19.09	+	69.15	=	£88.24

Inspection suggests that the gross redemption yield on a market price of £90 is about 10½%, and a more accurate figure can be obtained by further manual calculation or by computer. Alternatively, the yield can be obtained from Bond Tables.

Bonds

A bond is the generic name given to loan capital raised in the Eurobond market and in the US and other domestic markets. Issues in the Eurobond market may be denominated in sterling or in a foreign currency, and are normally of between 7 and 10 years' duration.

The Eurobond market began with the issue of Eurodollar bonds: US$ denominated securities issued *outside* the United States, but it now encompasses offshore issues in a variety of currencies, and an increasing number of UK companies make use of this market, e.g. GRAND METROPOLITAN:

GRAND METROPOLITAN *Extract from note on Group Borrowings*

Other loans

		Year-end interest rates %	1989 £m
Guaranteed notes 1990	Sterling	10.875	50
Deutschemark bonds 1992	Deutschemark	6.625	45
Euro bonds 1993	US dollar	10.25	62
Notes payable 1995	US dollar	11.5	62
Redeemable loan notes 1998	Sterling	11.3125	55
Extendible notes 1999	US dollar	12.0	62
Subordinated convertible bonds 2002	Sterling	6.25	100
. . .			
Commercial paper	Sterling/US dollar	8.36–14.03	270

Notes and Loan notes

These are promissory notes issued to one or a small number of other companies or individuals, and are normally of between 1 and 10 years' maturity on issue. They are often issued to individuals in an acquisition in lieu of cash to defer the individuals' liability to Capital Gains Tax.

Commercial paper (CP)

This is a short-term loan vehicle between the borrower (the issuer) and the purchaser (the investor); the issuer can sell direct to the investor or use banks as intermediaries.

Commercial paper takes the form of negotiable unsecured promissory notes. In the Sterling CP market notes have a maximum maturity on issue of 1 year and a minimum of 7 days; they are usually for £½m. or £1 m., with a minimum of £100,000. They are bearer securities which are issued at a discount to allow for interest, i.e., there is no separate payment of interest.

In the UK commercial paper with an original maturity of between 1 and 5 years is referred to as medium-term notes. By far the largest CP market is in the United States, where over $400 billion is outstanding; elsewhere CP is becoming increasingly popular both in the EuroCP market and in over a dozen other domestic markets: rates are very competitive, it is easy to administer and costs are low.

The amount a company can borrow

The amount a company can borrow may be limited by the following:

(a) Its borrowing powers. The directors' borrowing powers are normally limited by a company's Articles of Association, and cannot be altered except with the approval of shareholders at a general meeting. Borrowing powers are usually expressed as a multiple of shareholders' funds (issued share capital plus reserves, excluding intangible assets such as goodwill, although some companies, e.g., CADBURY SCHWEPPES, now include purchased goodwill in defining the directors' borrowing powers).

(b) Restrictions imposed by existing borrowings. The terms of the trust deeds of existing loan capital may restrict or preclude the company from further borrowing. In particular the terms of an unsecured loan stock may include a clause preventing the company from issuing any loans that rank ahead of the stock concerned, and unduly restrictive clauses are often the reasons for companies redeeming loan capital in advance of the normal redemption date.

(c) The lender's requirement for capital and income cover.

(d) The lender's general opinion of the company and its overall borrowing position.

Capital and income covers

These are two standard measures the intending purchaser of a debenture or loan stock may use to assess the security of his investment.

The *capital* or asset cover can be calculated in two ways, on a simple basis or on a 'rolled-up' basis.

Using the simple basis, the cover is the total capital less all prior-ranking stocks, divided by the issued amount of the stock in question.

Using the 'rolled-up' basis, the cover is the total capital divided by the stock in question plus all prior-ranking stocks.

As Example 5.5 shows, the two equal-ranking ULS issues are three times covered on a simple basis (£60 million total capital less £15 million prior-ranking debenture, divided by the total of £15 million ULS), but only twice covered on a rolled-up basis. The more conservative rolled-up basis is normally used for assessing capital covers.

For a floating charge debenture a rolled-up capital cover of at least 3 or 4 is expected by the lender, and 2½ times is the normal minimum for an unsecured loan stock, but both depend on the quality of the assets, i.e. the likely realisable value of the assets on the open market in the event of a liquidation.

The *income* cover is normally worked out on a rolled-up rather than a simple basis: i.e. it is the number of times the interest on a stock plus the interest on any prior-ranking stocks could be paid out of profits before interest and tax. This cover can also be expressed as a *priority percentage*, showing the percentile ranking of a stock's interest, with earnings before interest and tax representing 100% (Example 5.6).

Interest should normally be several times covered, although a lower income cover may be acceptable in some highly geared situations, e.g. in some property companies, where assured rental income provides safe cover.

A company's overall borrowing position

There are a variety of methods of measuring a company's overall borrowing position: the two main ones are *gearing* and *debt/equity ratio* (which is known as 'leverage' in the United States).

Gearing is most commonly defined as loan capital plus bank and other borrowings expressed as a percentage of capital employed (Example 5.7).

Example 5.5   Capital cover

Capital	Amount	Cumulative total	Simple cover	Rolled-up cover
	£000	£000		
6% Debenture	15,000	15,000	4.0	4.0
8% ULS	10,000	30,000	3.0	2.0
10%	5,000			
Ordinary shares	12,000	60,000		
Reserves (less goodwill)	18,000			
Total capital	60,000			

Example 5.6   Income cover

A company has £5.76 million of earnings before interest and tax, and the following loan capital, with the ULS and the CULS ranking equally:

Nominal value of issue	Annual interest	Cumulative interest	Times covered	Priority percentage
£12m. of 6% Debenture	£0.72m.	£0.72m.	8.0	0–12½%
£10m. of 8% ULS	£0.80m. }	£1.92m.	3.0	12½–33⅓%
£8m. of 5% CULS	£0.40m. }			

Example 5.7   Gearing and debt/equity ratio

Loan capital	£24,000 }	£34,000
Bank overdrafts	£10,000 }	
Ordinary shares	£14,500 }	£36,000
Reserves (*less* goodwill)	£21,500 }	
Capital employed		£70,000

$$\text{Gearing} = \frac{34,000}{70,000} = 49.1\%$$

Debt/equity ratio = 34,000 : 36,000 = 0.94 or 94%

Gearing of 33.3% (debt/equity ratio of 50%) would be a reasonable level for an average company, although companies with steady profits can borrow more highly, while those in cyclical industries would be wise to have little or no gearing.

Convertible loan capital

Convertible loan capital, which is usually convertible unsecured loan stock (CULS) rather than convertible debentures, entitles the holder to convert into ordinary shares of the company if he so wishes (see also convertible preference shares, Chapter 4).

The coupon on a convertible is usually much lower than the coupon needed for the issue of a straight unsecured loan stock with no conversion rights. This is because a convertible is normally regarded by the market as deferred equity, valued on the basis of the market value of the shares received on conversion plus the additional income enjoyed before conversion (the coupon on issue being higher than the yield on the ordinary shares).

Because convertibles are a form of deferred equity, listed companies can issue them without shareholders' prior approval only as a rights issue or as part or all of the consideration in an acquisition. In a takeover situation the bidder can use a suitably pitched convertible to provide the shareholders of the company being acquired with a higher initial income than they would receive from an equivalent offer of the bidder's ordinary shares. This is particularly useful when a bidder with low-yielding shares wants to avoid the shareholders of the company he wishes to acquire suffering a fall in income if they accept his offer.

CULS is attractive to investors seeking higher income, for example to an Income unit trust, and it also provides greater security than ordinary shares for both income and capital. From a company's point of view, CULS is cheaper to service than convertible preference shares, as the interest on the former is deducted in the assessment of Corporation Tax, but this advantage has been considerably eroded by the reduction in the rate of Corporation Tax. Most companies now prefer to issue convertible preference shares rather than CULS in order to reduce rather than increase their gearing.

Terms of a convertible loan

The holder has the option of converting into ordinary shares during a given period in the life of the debenture or ULS (the conversion period), at a given conversion price per share, expressed as so many shares per £100 of stock, or as so much nominal stock per ordinary share (Example 5.8).

Example 5.8   Convertible loan: GREAT PORTLAND ESTATES

In January 1988 GREAT PORTLAND ESTATES made a rights issue of a 9½% convertible loan stock 2002 at par, on the basis of £1 nominal of CULS for every 4 ordinary 50p shares held. The stock, when issued, was convertible into 30.303 ordinary shares per £100 stock (equivalent to a price of 330p per share when issued at par) in the August of any year between 1992 and 2002 inclusive; these conversion terms will be adjusted for any *scrip issues* to the ordinary shareholders in the meantime, and were in fact adjusted for a 1 for 5 scrip issue made in 1989.

Any *rights issues* to ordinary shareholders will *either* be made to the holders of the convertible as if they had been converted, *or* an adjustment will be made to the conversion terms (most CULS specifies only one method).

In the event of a *bid*, the company will endeavour to ensure that a like offer is made to the CULS holders as if they had converted; they would, however, lose any income advantage they enjoyed over the ordinary shareholders. This is a risk you have to take if you buy the CULS rather than the ordinary shares.

If more than 75% of the stock is converted, GREAT PORTLAND has the right to force remaining stockholders to convert or redeem straight away; this is a fairly standard condition in a convertible stock, enabling the company to clear a convertible off its balance sheet once most of it has been converted. Stock that remains unconverted at the end of the conversion period will be redeemed by GREAT PORTLAND at par on 1 December 2002.

The period between issue and the first date for conversion is sometimes called the 'rest period', and the period from the last date for conversion and the final redemption date the 'stub'. Diagrammatically the GREAT PORTLAND convertible can be shown as:

Stub

Rest period	Conversion period	

1988   1992   2002

A rest period of two or three years is normal, and most conversion periods run for at least four or five years. Some convertibles have a stub of several years, which is more prudent because if convertible holders decide not to exercise their conversion rights the company concerned is probably not doing very well and would not want to be faced with having to redeem the stock almost as soon as the conversion rights lapsed.

Another piece of convertible jargon is the *conversion premium*. This is the premium one pays by buying the ordinary shares via the convertible rather than buying them direct. For example, if the GREAT PORTLAND convertible in Example 5.8 was standing at £120% (per £100 nominal) and the ordinary shares were standing at 300p, the cost of getting into the ordinary shares through the convertible would be £120 ÷ 36.3636 (30.303 adjusted for the 1-for-5 scrip issue in 1989) = 330p, a conversion premium of 10%.

A good indication of the likely market price of a convertible can be obtained by discounting the future income advantage to present value and adding it to the market value of the underlying equity. Where conversion terms vary during the conversion period, sometimes called *stepped conversion* (e.g. DRAYTON CONSOLIDATED TRUST's 7½% CULS 1993), the calculation has to be done for each set of terms and the highest result taken. One caveat to this method is that if the price of the ordinary shares is very depressed, the price of the CULS in the market can become mainly dependent on its value as a fixed-interest security, particularly if the conversion period has not long to run.

Convertibles with 'put' options

In the euphoria before the market fall in October 1987, several companies were so confident that their share price was going on up for ever that they agreed to the innovation suggested by fee-hungry US Investment banks to include a 'put' option in the terms of their convertibles. This 'put' option gave the convertible bond holders the option to redeem after four or five years at a substantial premium, which was calculated to give a specified gross redemption yield. For example NEXT gave this option to two issues:

NEXT *Note to the 1989 accounts*

Creditors due after one year	£m
. . .	
6.75% Convertible bonds due 2002	47.9
5.75% Convertible bonds due 2003	100.0
. . .	

The convertible bonds are unsecured. Further details of these bonds are:

	6.75% Convertible Bonds due 2002	*5.75% Convertible Bonds due 2003*
Bondholders may convert into ordinary shares at a price per share of	286p	430p
Bondholders may redeem on	15.1.92	14.10.92
at an interest yield to redemption of	11.55%	10.46%
The company may redeem subject to a minimum share price of	372p	559p

Giving this option was asking for trouble, and trouble it got. Shortly after the second issue the stockmarket fell, the consumer boom faltered and NEXT's share price started to tumble. From a peak of 378p it plunged to less than 100p and unless it stages an extraordinary recovery it is highly likely that the bondholders will opt for early redemption at a time when the company may still be struggling. An early 'put' option in a convertible puts the investor in a 'heads I win, tails you lose' situation. From a company's point of view it is sheer folly.

To allow for the possibility of early redemption, the potential increased interest charge should be accrued and charged to the profit and loss account, as NEXT's directors decided to do:

NEXT *Extract from the directors' 1989 report*

Convertible Bonds

The Directors have decided that the true effective rate of interest on the convertible bonds should be charged against the profits irrespective of whether the supplemental interest will actually be paid. Consequently, net interest payable includes £8.1m. supplemental interest which represents the difference between the interest yield to redemption and the coupon rate payable on the convertible bonds.

Warrants

Where a company is reluctant to raise loan capital when very high long-term interest rates prevail, or investors are reluctant to commit themselves to purely fixed-interest securities, loan capital can be raised with a lower coupon by attaching warrants to issues of stock. For example, TRUSTHOUSE FORTE attached warrants to their issue of £85 million 10¼% Eurobond issue in 1987.

Warrants, already described in Chapter 4, are long-term options granted by the company, entitling holders to subscribe for ordinary shares during some specified period in the future at some specified price, called the exercise price. They are normally detachable and exercisable as soon as the stock to which they are attached is fully paid, and in some issues stock can be surrendered at its nominal value as an alternative to cash payment when the warrants are exercised.

In a takeover situation, warrants can provide a more flexible way for the bidder to give loan stock an equity interest than convertibles, because the number of warrants, sometimes called the 'equity kicker', can be varied as the company wishes, while the quantity of ordinary shares to which convertible holders are entitled is defined within a narrow range by the limit the market will accept on the conversion premium.

On the other hand, a drawback to warrants is that they will seldom be exercised until close to the final exercise date, because they are bought by investors who want the gearing they provide, so the future flow of money into the company's equity is more chancy than with a convertible.

Details of a warrant's exercise rights are normally shown in the company's annual report and accounts; for example TRUSTHOUSE FORTE:

TRUSTHOUSE FORTE *Note to the 1988 accounts*

Share capital

. . .

On 10 March 1987, 41,225,000 option warrants were issued in conjunction with the 10.25% Eurobond 1992, each of which entitles the holder to subscribe for one ordinary 25p share at a price of 226p until 10 March 1992 (market value at 10 March 1987 – 208p).

Mezzanine finance

Mezzanine finance is a term used to describe finance that lies between straight debt and share capital. It is used in situations, e.g. Management Buy-Outs (MBOs), where the amount of debt that can be raised is limited, and the amount of cash available to subscribe for shares is insufficient to make up the total required.

It is usually in the form of a loan that ranks after the normal debt (the 'senior' debt) and, because of the higher risk, bears a higher rate of interest and carries *either* an option to convert part of the loan into equity *or* has a warrant to subscribe for equity.

For example, the £165 million MBO of GRAND METROPOLITAN's contract services division in the summer of 1987, when it became the COMPASS GROUP, was financed as follows:

COMPASS GROUP *Financing of management buy-out*

	£m	
Senior medium-term loan @ 1.5% over LIBOR	70	(Note 1)
Mezzanine loan @ 3.5% over LIBOR	30	(Note 2)
30m. Cumulative redeemable preference shares (CRP)	30	(Note 3)
Ordinary shares	30	(Note 4)
Overdraft	5	
	165	

Notes:
1. Repayable in equal instalments over 5 years, commencing 31 July 1990.

2. Reducing to 1.25% over LIBOR on flotation; repayable in equal instalments over 5 years commencing 31 July 1992; included a warrant to subscribe for up to 375,824 ordinary 1p shares at par.
3. CRP 1p shares, allotted for cash at a premium of 99p; dividend of 7p net per share per annum.
4. 3,500,000 Cumulative convertible participating preferred ordinary shares of 1p (CCPPO), allotted for cash at a premium of £8.57. Dividend of 30p net per share per annum, plus 5% of pre-tax profit divided pro rata to the CCPPO holders. 250,000 ordinary 1p shares allotted to the management at 99p premium. 50,000 ordinary 1p shares allotted at 99p premium included in the CRP and CCPPO package, which was subscribed by institutional investors.

Compass subsequently reduced its exposure to variable interest rates by an agreement with the lending bank which limited the maximum interest payable on £50 million of the senior loan to 12.375% until 31 July 1989 (known as an 'interest rate cap'), and by an interest rate swap exchanging the LIBOR element of the mezzanine loan for a fixed rate of 9.4% until 31 January 1990.

Compass's contract services business had a strong cash flow, sufficient to service the £100 million of debt and pay the preference dividends,

and it obtained a listing on The Stock Exchange in December 1988, but highly geared (leveraged) deals are high risk: hence the need for the mezzanine debt to have an equity 'sweetener'.

Complex capital issues

There is almost no limit to the ingenuity of companies and their financial advisers in devising innovative terms for the issue of loan capital. In addition to the deep discount bonds and convertibles with 'put' options that we have described, complex capital issues include:

(a) *Stepped bonds*, where the interest payable increases by fixed steps over its life, e.g. 5% for the first two years, 7% in the next two and so on until redemption. In these cases the profit and loss account should normally be charged at the effective rate computed over the anticipated life of the bond, irrespective of the amount of interest paid each year.

(b) *Bonds with variable redemption payments*, where the loan is repayable at a value adjusted by the Retail Price Index or some other index. An annual charge should be made against profits to reflect the increased burden of repayment caused by the movement in the relevant index during the year.

Chapter 6

FIXED ASSETS

(References: SSAP 12 *Accounting for Depreciation*; SSAP 19 *Accounting for Investment Properties*; SSAP 22 *Accounting for Goodwill*.)

Schedule 4 to the Companies Act 1985 requires fixed assets to be presented in the balance sheet under three headings: *Intangible assets*, *Tangible assets* and *Investments*; we deal with the first two in this chapter, and with Investments in Chapter 7.

Definitions

Intangible (fixed) assets

These include capitalised development costs (see page 74); concessions, patents and trademarks; and goodwill. Goodwill is the amount by which the value of a business as a whole exceeds the value of its individual assets less liabilities; it is normally only recognised in the accounts of a company when it acquires another business as a going concern, i.e. when purchased.

SSAP 22, published in December 1984, stated that purchased goodwill (sometimes called goodwill cost of control) should normally be written off immediately against reserves. Alternatively it may be carried in the balance sheet, in which case it should be amortised (written off) through the profit and loss account over its estimated useful life. Few companies adopt this alternative method, because amortisation reduces reported profits in future years. (See Chapter 16 for goodwill on consolidation.)

The treatment of purchased goodwill has given rise to considerable controversy: some companies, unwilling to write off purchased goodwill immediately because doing so would erode their reserves, and equally unwilling to reduce their profits by amortising it, have resorted to placing a value on acquired brands and trade names to reduce the goodwill element in an acquisition. They then put the brand values on the balance sheet but do not amortise them, claiming that their brands do not suffer any diminution in value.

For example, when LADBROKE acquired the HILTON hotel chain in 1987, the premium of £276.7 million was originally deducted from reserves; but the directors subsequently decided to attribute this premium to the Hilton International brand name and, in the 1988 accounts, showed it as an intangible asset of £276.7 million, having added that amount back into the reserves.

Proposals have now been made to amend SSAP 22 to require purchased goodwill to be carried in the balance sheet and to be amortised, which will bring it into line with US practice. Meanwhile, where companies are amortising purchased goodwill, the amount amortised each year should be added back to pre-tax profits to make them comparable with companies which write off purchased goodwill immediately against reserves.

Tangible (fixed) assets

Those long-lived assets not held for resale in the ordinary course of business but for the purpose, directly or indirectly, of earning revenue. Thus they include not only things like plant and machinery which are actually used to provide the product, but assets used to house or support its operations, such as land, buildings, furniture, vehicles, ships and aircraft. They may also contain leased assets (see pages 70–1).

Depreciation

A measure of the loss of value of an asset due to use, the passage of time and obsolescence, including the amortisation of fixed assets whose useful life is predetermined (e.g. leases) and the depletion of wasting assets (e.g. mines).

Book value

Traditionally fixed assets are shown in the balance sheet at cost less aggregate depreciation to date (i.e. at net book value). This book value is not, and does not purport to be in any sense, a valuation, though fixed assets, particularly land and buildings, are quite frequently revalued. Sometimes, but by no means always, the valuation is taken into the books.

Companies Act requirements on fixed assets

The requirements of the Companies Act 1985 with regard to fixed assets are complex. In summary they are as follows:

(a) Fixed assets may be shown on a historical cost basis, or at valuation, or at current cost (see Chapter 23), and should be classified under headings appropriate to the business.
(b) Land must be analysed into freehold, long leaseholds (over 50 years unexpired) and short leaseholds.
(c) Where fixed assets are included on a historical cost basis, the aggregate figure for the following amounts must be shown under each heading:
    (i) cost;
    (ii) provision for depreciation since acquisition;
    (iii) the book value (i minus ii).
(d) Where fixed assets are included at a valuation, the amount so included must be shown, together with the years and amounts of the valuations and, for assets valued during the year, the names of the valuers and the basis of valuation (see page 40, Example 6.8).
(e) Where fixed assets are included at valuation or at current cost, historical cost details must also be disclosed.
(f) Particulars must be given of additions and disposals during the period.

Disclosure requirements on depreciation

Schedule 9 of the Companies Act 1985 requires companies to disclose:

(a) the amount of depreciation charged to revenue;
(b) if depreciation has been calculated on other than book value;
(c) any amounts, additional to depreciation, charged by way of provision for renewal of fixed assets;
(d) if no provision has been made for depreciation or replacement; or the method used if other than by depreciation charge or provision for renewals.

SSAP 12 requires companies to disclose the method of depreciation used for each category of asset, together with the effective useful lives assumed.

Rates of depreciation

The following are typical rates (using the straight line method of depreciation, described below):

Freehold land	Nil
Freehold buildings	2% = 50 year life
Leasehold property:	
Long leases (over 50 years)	2% = 50 years
Short leases	Over life of the lease
Plant and machinery	10% = 10 years
Vehicles	20% = 5 years
Ships, according to type	4–10% = 10–25 years
Furniture and equipment	10% = 10 years

Subnormal depreciation charges

Where a company is charging a subnormal rate of depreciation, or is omitting to charge depreciation on assets (other than freehold land), it will report higher than normal pre-tax profits, and the figures should be adjusted accordingly in any analysis. For example, an increasing number of companies in the retail sector, including KINGFISHER, MARKS & SPENCER, SAINSBURY and TESCO, no longer provide depreciation on their freehold and long leasehold properties, and explain why in their accounts, e.g., KINGFISHER:

KINGFISHER *Note on accounting policies*

Depreciation

Depreciation of fixed assets is provided where it is necessary to reflect a reduction from book value to estimated residual value over the useful life of the asset to the group. It is the group's policy to maintain its properties in a state of good repair to prolong their useful lives, and in the case of freehold and long leasehold properties the directors consider that the lives of these properties and their residual values are such that their depreciation is not significant. Accordingly, no depreciation is provided on freehold and long leasehold properties.

Depreciation of other fixed assets . . .

Analysts need to check and make allowances for differing depreciation policies when making comparisons with other companies, for instance with ASDA which, in 1989, was depreciating freehold buildings and long leasehold property over 67 years, showing a charge for the year of £9.4 million.

Where depreciation is shown in the accounts

Depreciation appears in several places; EDBRO (HOLDINGS) provides an example of what a good set of accounts shows:

1. In the profit and loss account, as a note to the item 'Operating profits' (below): the charge for the year.
2. In the balance sheet, as a note to the item 'Fixed assets' (below): the charge for the year and the cumulative amount to date.
3. In the statement of accounting policies:

EDBRO (HOLDINGS) *Note on accounting policies*

Depreciation

The charge for depreciation is calculated to write off the cost of tangible fixed assets less government grants over the shorter of their expected useful lives or the lease terms. Depreciation rates are: freehold land, nil; freehold and long leasehold buildings, 4% (reducing balance); plant and machinery, 10% to 14% (straight line); office equipment and motor vehicles, 20% (straight line).

Methods of depreciation

The most common method or basis of depreciation, used by over 80% of major companies, is the straight line (or fixed instalment) method. Other methods include:

(a) the declining balance (or reducing balance) method;
(b) the sum of the years' digits method;
(c) the production unit method;
(d) the annuity method;
(e) the sinking fund method.

The straight line or fixed instalment method

Depreciation under the fixed instalment method is computed as follows (see also Example 6.1):

$$\text{Annual depreciation} = \frac{\text{Cost} - \text{Residual value}}{\text{Expected useful life}}$$

The straight line method is ideal where the service provided by the asset continues unabated throughout its useful life, as might be the case with a 21-year lease of a building; and it is *generally used wherever the equal allocation of cost provides a reasonably fair measure of the asset's service*, for example, for buildings, plant, machinery, equipment, vehicles and patents. It is easy to calculate, and conceptually simple to understand.

The declining balance or reducing balance method

The declining balance method used to be the most popular method of depreciation; but it has largely been supplanted in recent years by the straight line method.

Under the declining balance method, the annual depreciation charge represents a fixed percentage of the net book value brought forward (i.e. cost less aggregate depreciation). The calculation of the annual charge is simple enough once the appropriate percentage has been determined, but this requires the use of tables, a slide rule or a calculator.

EDBRO (HOLDINGS) *Profit and loss account, note on operating profits*

	£000
Operating profits are shown after charging:	
depreciation of owned fixed assets	999
depreciation of assets held under finance leases	181
auditors' remuneration . . .	

EDBRO (HOLDINGS) *Balance sheet, note on tangible fixed assets*

	Land and buildings Freehold	Long leasehold	Plant and equipment	Total
	£000	£000	£000	£000
Depreciation at start of year	197	1,185	5,829	7,211
Exchange differences	(2)	(2)	(37)	(41)
Charge for the year	19	127	1,034	1,180
Eliminated on disposals	—	(1)	(237)	(238)
Depreciation at end of year	214	1,309	6,589	8,112

Example 6.1   Straight line depreciation

If a machine having an estimated useful life of five years is purchased for £10,000, and is expected to have a residual value of £1,000 at the end of that life, depreciation will be:

$$\frac{£10,000-£1,000}{5}=\frac{£9,000}{5}=£1,800 \text{ per annum}$$

and the accounts will show:

End of year	Depreciation for the year (shown in the P & L account)	Cost	Provision for depreciation to date	Net book value
	£	£	£	£
1	1,800	10,000	1,800	8,200
2	1,800	10,000	3,600	6,400
3	1,800	10,000	5,400	4,600
4	1,800	10,000	7,200	2,800
5	1,800	10,000	9,000	1,000

For the middle columns: ← shown in the balance sheet →

Example 6.2   Declining balance depreciation

The rate for the machine in Example 6.1 would be computed as follows:

$$\text{Depreciation rate}=1-\sqrt[5]{\left(\frac{£1,000}{£10,000}\right)}=1-0.631=0.369=36.9\%$$

Thus the rate to apply is 36.9%.

End of year	Depreciation for the year (shown in the P & L account)	Cost	Provision for depreciation to date	Net book value
	£	£	£	£
1	3,690	10,000	3,690	6,310
2	2,328	10,000	6,018	3,982
3	1,470	10,000	7,488	2,512
4	927	10,000	8,415	1,585
5	585	10,000	9,000	1,000

For the middle columns: ← shown in the balance sheet →

$$\text{Depreciation rate (as a decimal)} = 1 - \sqrt[n]{\frac{\text{Residual value}}{\text{Cost}}}$$

where n = useful life in years.

Example 6.2 illustrates the calculation.

Among the disadvantages of the declining balance method are these:

(a) Most users do not calculate the rate appropriate to each particular item of plant, but use standard percentages, which tend to be too low rather than too high.

(b) Unless notional adjustments are made to cost and residual value, it is impossible to calculate satisfactorily a declining balance rate if the residual value is nil – the net book value can never get to nil, as it can only be reduced by a proportion each year.

(c) Even if the asset is assigned a nominal scrap value (say £1 so that it is not overlooked in the books) or if there is some residual value but it is small in relation to cost, the method is unlikely to be satisfactory without notional adjustments, because it leads to such high charges in the early years, as Example 6.3 shows.

The sum of the years' digits method

The sum of the (years') digits method is not commonly found in the United Kingdom, though it is used a good deal as a method of allowing accelerated depreciation in the United States (where accounting depreciation, provided it is computed by an acceptable method, is used for tax purposes too). It is occasionally found in the United Kingdom in connection with activities like leasing which involve heavy outlays in early years.

Example 6.3   Declining balance depreciation, small residual value

Taking our previous example of plant costing £10,000, but with a residual value of £200 instead of £1,000, we get:

Year	Year's depreciation £	Compared with £
1	5,425	3,690
2	2,482	2,328
3	1,135	1,470
4	520	927
5	238	585
Accumulated depreciation at the end of year 5	9,800	9,000
Residual value	200	1,000

In this method, the cost less any residual value is divided by the sum of the years' digits to give what, for the purpose of this explanation, may be termed a unit of depreciation. In the last year of expected life, one unit of depreciation is provided; in the next to last, two; in the one before that, three; and so on.

The sum of the years' digits is simply the sum of the series: $(1 + 2 + 3 + 4 + \ldots\ldots + n)$, where n represents the expected life of the asset.

The formula for computing the sum of the digits is $n(n + 1) \div 2$, where n is the number of years. Thus, to apply the sum of the digits to an asset having a life of 5 years, the divisor (i.e. the sum of the years' digits) is $5(5 + 1) \div 2 = 15$, and the first year's depreciation is 5/15ths of (cost minus residual value), the second year's 4/15ths, and so on (see Example 6.4).

It is interesting to compare the balance sheet value of this asset year by year with the value under the straight line and the declining balance methods, as shown in Example 6.5.

It can be seen that if the annual book value

Example 6.5   Comparison of depreciation methods (for an asset costing £10,000, residual value £1,000, useful life 5 years)

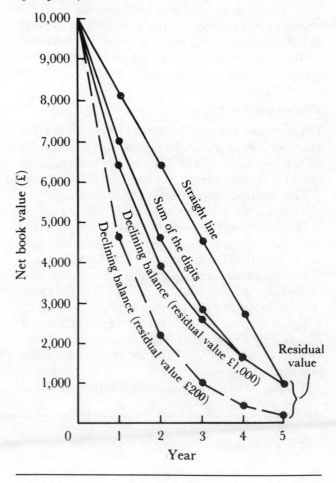

Example 6.4   Sum of the years' digits method of depreciation

Taking our example of a machine costing £10,000, with an estimated life of five years and a residual value estimated at £1,000: the sum of the year's digits is 15, and a unit of depreciation is thus $(£10,000 - £1,000) \div 15 = £600$, so:

End of year	Depreciation for the year (shown in the P & L account) £	Cost £	Provisions for depreciation to date £	Net book value £
1	3,000	10,000	3,000	7,000
2	2,400	10,000	5,400	4,600
3	1,800	10,000	7,200	2,800
4	1,200	10,000	8,400	1,600
5	600	10,000	9,000	1,000

(the columns Cost, Provisions for depreciation to date, and Net book value are shown in the balance sheet)

under the declining balance method is plotted, it follows a curve which in mathematical terms is asymptotic, that is, it gets nearer and nearer to the horizontal axis (i.e. to 0), but if the residual value is zero it would never quite get there (i.e. a charge for depreciation is made however long the asset lasts, be that charge ever so small), whereas the value under the sum of the digits method is reduced in decreasing steps, year by year, reaching residual value at the end of the asset's expected life, regardless of the size of the residual value, if any. Thus, although there is a similarity in the charges produced by the two methods, the sum of the digits method does not need the notional adjustments of the declining balance method to cope with small or nil residual values.

The annuity method

The annuity method is sometimes used for the amortisation of leasehold properties, i.e. to write off the premium (the initial cost of the lease) over the term of the lease.

The annual depreciation charge under the annuity method is calculated by dividing the cost of the asset (less the present value of any expected residual value) by the present value of an annuity of 1 per annum for the estimated life of the asset.

An *annuity* is simply an annual payment, normally for a defined number of years (or for someone's lifetime), so the present value of an annuity of 1 for n years is the present value of 1 receivable in one year's time, plus that of a further 1 receivable in two years' time and so on, up to the last payment of 1 in n years' time.

A more detailed explanation of the concept of present value is given in Appendix 2, together with examples of a present value table and an annuity table.

Example 6.6 gives a simple illustration of the calculation:

Example 6.6 Calculating present value of an annuity

If $n = 3$ and the interest rate is 15%, then the present value of an annuity of 1 is

$$\frac{1}{(1.15)} + \frac{1}{(1.15)^2} + \frac{1}{(1.15)^3} = 2.283$$

Returning to the calculation of depreciation – as we said, the cost of the asset less the present value of any expected residual value is divided by the present value of an annuity of 1 per annum for the estimated life of the asset to produce the annual depreciation charge. At the same time notional interest on the net book value (cost less accumulated depreciation) is taken on the credit side of the profit and loss account (Example 6.7).

Alternative annuity method
An alternative way of using the method, at one time used by public utilities, and used by property companies in Canada, shows the net amount (i.e. depreciation less notional interest) as 'depreciation', and not a depreciation charge and a separate credit for interest. This has the effect of producing a rising charge: a low charge in the early years and a high one in the later years.

Example 6.7 Annuity method of depreciation

Take the case of a five-year lease costing £9,000,000, with no residual value; if interest is taken to be 15% the present value of an annuity of 1 for 5 years is 3.352 (see table in Appendix 2) and the depreciation charge is thus:

$$\frac{£9,000,000}{3.352} = £2,685,000$$

The computation then proceeds as follows:

Year	1	2	3	4	5
	£000	£000	£000	£000	£000
Cost	9,000				
Balance b/f	—	7,665	6,130	4,364	2,334
Notional interest at 15% p.a.	1,350	1,150	919	655	351
	10,350	8,815	7,049	5,019	2,685
Depreciation charge	2,685	2,685	2,685	2,685	2,685
Balance c/f	7,665	6,130	4,364	2,334	—

This method puts the company in a position similar to investing the £9,000,000 rather than purchasing the lease, and renting the asset for £2,685,000 per annum.

Further points on depreciation

Change in expected useful life

Where, through experience or changed circumstances, it is considered that the original estimate of useful life of an asset needs to be revised, the unamortised cost of the asset (net book value less residual value) should be charged over the revised remaining useful life. Changes in useful life can have a significant effect on profits. For example CITYVISION, the video hire company, reported an increase in pre-tax profits from £1.06 million in 1987 to £5.43 million in 1988, but a note on tangible assets showed that nearly half the increase was due to doubling the estimated useful life of the tape libraries (although this was not mentioned in the chairman's statement):

CITYVISION *Extract from note on tangible assets*

During the year the directors reconsidered the estimated useful life of the tape libraries. These are now depreciated over a 30-month period. They were previously depreciated over a 15-month period. The effect has been to reduce the depreciation charge for the year by £2 million. The growth of the business, along with the opportunity for the Group to circulate its tapes through a wider range of outlets, means that the average video tape now has a longer life.

The writing down of asset values

SSAP 12 requires that, if there is a permanent diminution in the value of an asset, it should be written down immediately to the estimated recoverable amount, which should then be written off over the remaining useful life of the asset. For example, in August 1986 the chairman of BOC wrote to shareholders to tell them about the Group's problem with the Graphite Electrodes business in the US and the decision to recognise the diminished value of the assets employed in the light of the contraction of the steel industry:

BOC *Extract from chairman's letter to shareholders*

We will write-down the assets of this business at 30 September 1986 by £128 million and will reflect this loss in our results for the final quarter of the current financial year. This write-down will reduce the estimated assets employed in this business at the year end to approximately £125 million.

We will write-down substantially all of our older and less efficient graphite electrode manufacturing assets at St. Mary's and Niagara Falls. We have also recognised that part of our facilities at Seadrift represents excess capacity for the long term, and that some of the facilities at Ridgeville, which were over-sized for future expansion, will no longer be needed.

The write-down will have the effect of reducing depreciation charged in this business and correspondingly increasing profits. The effect in 1987 will be approximately £11 million.

Changing method

Under SSAP 12 a change from one method of providing for depreciation to another is permissible only on the grounds that the new method will give a fairer presentation of the results and of the financial position. Where such a change is made, the unamortised cost should be written off over the remaining useful life commencing with the period in which the change is made, and the effect of the change should be disclosed in the year of change, if material.

Freehold land and buildings

Traditionally, freehold land and buildings used not to be depreciated, though the majority of companies have been depreciating freehold buildings in recent years, and SSAP 12 makes this obligatory, except for investment properties. In addition, freehold land should be written down if its value is adversely affected for any reason.

Excess depreciation

A few companies make an additional charge for depreciation to allow for the cost of replacing fixed assets, rather than just writing off the original cost of an asset over its useful life. The amounts involved should be added back for the purposes of inter-company comparison.

The revaluation of assets

Traditionally, under historical cost accounting, assets appear at cost less depreciation, and they are not revalued to show their current worth to the company. But because of the effects of inflation, the practice has grown up in the United Kingdom of revaluing assets, particularly freehold land and buildings, from time to time.

Indeed, Schedule 7 para. 1 of the Companies Act 1985 requires the difference between the market value of property assets and the balance sheet amount to be disclosed in the directors' report if, in the opinion of the directors, it is significant. UK companies thus face the choice; they must either:

(a)   incorporate any revaluation in the accounts,
      or
(b)   disclose it in the directors' report.

Where assets are revalued and the revaluation is incorporated in the accounts, both sides of the balance sheet are affected, and depreciation from then on is based on the revalued amounts, as Example 6.8 illustrates.

Example 6.8   Effects of revaluation

A company has freehold land which cost £100,000 and buildings which cost £420,000, have a useful life of 50 years and were 10 years old on 31 December 1989. Depreciation to that date would therefore be 2% p.a. for 10 years on £420,000 = £84,000, so the balance sheet would show:

Freehold land and buildings at cost	£520,000
less depreciation to date	84,000
Book value at 31 December 1989.	436,000

On 1 January 1990 the land was revalued at £380,000 and the buildings at £810,000. After the revaluation the accounts would show freehold land and buildings at the valuation figure of £1,190,000, an increase of £754,000. On the other side of the balance sheet the reserves would normally be increased by £754,000. (If, however, the company has decided in principle to dispose of the buildings, SSAP 15, para. 12 requires a provision to be made out of the revaluation surplus for the tax which would be payable on disposal, and this would be credited to deferred tax, the remainder of the surplus being credited to reserves.)

The 1990 accounts would be required to disclose:

(a)   the basis of valuation used and the name or qualification of the valuer (CA 1985, Sch. 4, para. 43(b));

(b)   the effect of the revaluation on the depreciation charge, if material (SSAP 12, para. 20).

The revaluation will affect the company in several ways:

1.   The annual depreciation charge on the buildings, based on the new value and the current estimate of the remaining useful life (40 years), will increase from £8,400 to £20,250 (2½% p.a. on £810,000), thus directly reducing the pre-tax profits by £11,850 in each future year.

2.   The overall profitability of the company, as measured by the ratio Return on Capital Employed (ROCE, described in Chapter 24), will also appear to deteriorate because the capital employed will have increased by £754,000. For instance, if the company in our example went on to make £300,000 before interest and tax in 1990, and had £2 million capital employed before the revaluation, the 1990 return on capital employed would be:

No revaluation	*Revaluation*
$\dfrac{311,850}{2,000,000} = 15.59\%$	$\dfrac{300,000}{2,754,000} = 10.89\%$

3.   The borrowing powers of most companies are expressed as a multiple of share capital and reserves, so the increase in reserves will raise the borrowing limits, and improve the capital cover of existing lenders.

4.   The higher property value may give more scope for borrowing on mortgage.

5.   The increase in reserves will also increase the n.a.v., the net asset value per share, described in Chapter 24.

Revaluation deficits

Although unrealised surpluses on the revaluation of fixed assets should be credited direct to reserves, revaluation deficits should be charged to the profit and loss account to the extent that they exceed any surplus held in reserves identified as relating to previous revaluations of the same assets (SSAP 6).

Investment properties

SSAP 12 requires annual depreciation charges to be made on fixed assets, and makes it clear that an increase in the value of a fixed asset does not remove the necessity to charge depreciation. It is, however, accepted that a different treatment should be applied to fixed assets held as disposable investments.

Under SSAP 19, 'investment properties' (properties held as disposable investments rather than for use in a manufacturing or commercial process) are not depreciated, but are revalued each year at their open market value, and the valuation is reflected in the balance sheet.

Changes in the value of investment properties should be treated as a movement on an 'investment property revaluation reserve'. If, however, there is a fall in value that exceeds the balance in the investment property revaluation reserve, the excess should be charged to the profit and loss account; i.e. the reserve cannot 'go negative'.

Sales and other disposals of fixed assets

Where fixed assets are disposed of for an amount which is greater (or less) than their book value, the surplus (or deficiency) should be reflected in the results of the year, and should be disclosed separately if material (SSAP 12).

Some companies, for instance MARKS & SPENCER, habitually include an item 'profit (loss) on sales of tangible fixed assets' in a note to their profit and loss account, and show the *net book cost* of the disposals (book cost less accumulated depreciation) as a source in their funds statement. Others, like AARONSON overleaf, deduct the profit on the sale of fixed assets in their funds statement and then show the *proceeds* of the sale (i.e. net book cost plus profit on disposals).

If the profit/loss on disposals is not shown, it can be calculated; it is the difference between the proceeds of disposal and the net book value of disposals: in AARONSON's case £1,656,000 minus £1,227,000 = £429,000.

There is nothing particularly significant in a company making small gains or losses on disposals, but it may give some indication of whether fixed assets tend to be worth more or less than their net book value.

When disposals arise because of the discontinuation of a significant part of the business, they should be dealt with as extraordinary items (see Chapter 14); in these cases the release of capital and the profit or loss previously being made by the discontinued part are probably more important than the amount by which the proceeds of the sale varies from the book value of the assets sold.

AARONSON BROS *Disposal of fixed assets in 1988 accounts*

(a) In the note on tangible fixed assets

	£000
Cost or valuation	
At 1 October 1987	47,888
Additions at cost	10,789
Eliminated on disposals	(2,079)
. . .	
Depreciation	
At 1 October 1987	20,501
Charge for the year	3,560
Eliminated on disposals	(852)
. . .	

The net book value of disposals is thus £2,079,000 − 852,000 = £1,227,000.

(b) In the Source and Application of Funds

Profit before taxation	5,823
Adjustments for items not involving the movement of funds:	
(Profit)/loss on sale of fixed assets	(429)
. . .	
Funds from other sources:	
Proceeds on sale of fixed assets	1,656

This produces the same result as showing the net book value of disposals (£1,656,000 − £429,000 = £1,227, 000).

Government grants

(Reference: SSAP 4 and ED 43 *The Accounting Treatment of Government Grants.*)

Capital-based grants, such as regional development grants, introduced by the Industry Act 1972, and similar grants found in other countries, are grants which provide a refund of part of the purchase price of fixed assets. SSAP 4 requires capital-based grants to be credited to revenue (i.e. to profit) over the expected useful life of the asset concerned. There are two ways of achieving this:

1. By deducting the grant from the cost of the fixed assets (and thus reducing the subsequent annual depreciation charges). In the accounts the fixed assets simply appear net of grants, although some companies mention this in their note on accounting policies and a few describe 'additions at cost' in their note on fixed assets as '(less grants receivable)'.

2. By treating the grant as a deferred credit, and transferring it to revenue by annual instalments over the life of the asset concerned. Under this method government grants normally appear in several places in the accounts; for example, ENGLISH CHINA CLAYS' 1989 consolidated balance sheet included a figure of £5.7 million for capital grants, showed movements on the capital grants account in the Source and Application of Funds statement and explained its accounting policy in a note to the accounts, as illustrated.

However, some companies using this method deduct the balance in their government grants account from the net book value of their tangible assets in a note, rather than showing it in the balance sheet.

ENGLISH CHINA CLAYS *1989 accounts – government grants*

Source and Application of Funds

	1989 £m	1988 £m
Adjustments for items not involving the movement of funds:		
Capital grants	(1.2)	(1.1)
. . .		
Other sources:		
Capital grants received	1.7	1.2

Note on Accounting Policies

Capital grants
Capital grants shown in the balance sheet represent total grants received or receivable to date less amounts transferred to the profit and loss account.

This transfer is made over a period of ten years.

The arguments in favour of method 1 are, first, that commercial decisions on capital investment are (or should be) made on a 'net of grants' basis, i.e. the return on capital employed to consider is the return on the capital the company would have to put up, not the 'gross' cost, and, second, that method 1 makes accounting so much simpler. Method 2 has the advantage of showing the extent to which government grants are contributing to and may be influencing the company's investment programme.

Less than half of UK listed companies mention government grants in their accounts, presumably because they are not material. Of those that do, about twice as many use method 1 as use method 2. From the analyst's point of view, the only disadvantage to method 1 is that companies using it seldom if ever report the amount of government grants received, although they could easily do so.

Revenue-based grants are simply credited straight to revenue in the same period as the related expenditure and are seldom shown in the accounts.

Chapter 7

INVESTMENTS

Types of investment

Investments fall into three categories:

(*a*) Investment in subsidiaries.
(*b*) Investment in associated undertakings.
(*c*) Other participating interests.
(*d*) Other investments, which may appear in the balance sheet as fixed assets, or as current assets.

Investment in subsidiaries

In simple terms, a subsidiary undertaking is a company, partnership, or unincorporated association, where the company owning the investment (the holding company) is able to control the board of directors, either by virtue of its voting power or in some other way. The holding company is required by law to produce group accounts, in which the profits, assets and liabilities of the subsidiary are combined with those of the holding company, as described in detail in Chapter 16.

Investment in associated undertakings

For accounting purposes, an associated undertaking is a non-subsidiary undertaking in which the investing group or company's position in it is:

(*a*) effectively that of a partner in a joint venture or consortium; *or*
(*b*) long-term and substantial (i.e. not less than 20% of the equity voting rights) and can include partnerships and unincorporated associations as well as companies.

In each case the investing group must be in a position to exercise a significant influence over the operating and financial policy of the undertaking; this is usually by representation on the board of directors.

The investing group's share of the associated company's turnover, profits before tax, taxation, extraordinary items and net profit retained are shown separately in the group's consolidated accounts, as described more fully in Chapter 17.

Participating interests

A participating interest is an interest held by the investing group or company on a long-term basis to secure a contribution to its activities by the exercise of control or influence. A holding of 20% or more of the shares of an undertaking is presumed to be a participating interest unless the contrary is shown. An *interest* includes convertible securities and options as well as shares (CA 1989 S.22). A participating interest is only an interest in an associated undertaking where a significant influence is exercised over its operating and financial policy.

Other investments

Where at first sight it may seem that these will consist entirely of investments of less than 20% this is not always the case, but where a company has a holding of 20% or more in another undertaking but does not treat it as an associated undertaking or as a participating interest, its accounts should explain why, e.g., HIGHLAND DISTILLERIES:

HIGHLAND DISTILLERIES *Note on accounting policies*

Group accounts

The HIGHLAND DISTILLERIES COMPANY PLC owns 35.4 per cent of the issued ordinary share capital of ROBERTSON & BAXTER LIMITED and 34.0 per cent of the issued share capital of its subsidiary, DUNARD INSURANCE GROUP LIMITED. These companies . . . are not, in the opinion of the Directors, associate companies within the definitions laid down in SSAP 1, because both are the subsidiaries of another company. THE HIGHLAND DISTILLERIES COMPANY PLC is not in a position to exercise significant influence over their policies. Dividends received are included in Group profits.

Companies sometimes use surplus cash to make short-term investments in various securities, and show these under current assets.

Balance sheet presentation

Schedule 4 of the Companies Act 1985 (amended by CA 1989) requires other investments to be shown in the balance sheet either under fixed assets and/or under current assets. Where shown as fixed assets a further breakdown should be given, if individual amounts are material, either in the balance sheet itself or in notes:

(a) shares in group undertakings;
(b) loans to group undertakings;
(c) interests in associated undertakings;
(d) other participating interests;
(e) loans to undertakings at (c) and (d);
(f) other investments other than loans;
(g) other loans;
(h) own shares.

Fixed assets – other investments

Listed investments should be shown at cost, divided into those listed on a recognised stock exchange in the United Kingdom and those listed overseas. The aggregate market value should also be shown where it differs from cost (CA 1985, Sch. 4, para. 45). *Unlisted investments*, which include securities on the USM, should be shown at cost or valuation. See example from HARRISONS & CROSFIELD's accounts:

HARRISONS & CROSFIELD *Note to the balance sheet*

Other investments held as fixed assets

	1988	
	Book value £m	Valuation £m
Shares		
Quoted in the United Kingdom	0.1	0.1
Quoted elsewhere	0.8	2.3
Unquoted	0.3	0.3
	1.2	2.7

Quoted share valuations are at market value; unquoted share valuations are at directors' valuation.

Significant holdings

Schedule 3 of the Companies Act 1989, para. 24, requires that where a company:

(a) holds 10% or more of the nominal value of any class of shares in an undertaking, *or*
(b) the holding exceeds one-tenth of the company's assets the accounts must state:

    (i) the name of the undertaking;
    (ii) the country in which it is incorporated (if other than Great Britain); *or* (if incorporated in Great Britain) whether it is registered in England & Wales or in Scotland; *or*, if unincorporated, its address;
    (iii) the identity of each class held, and the proportion held.

This information need not be disclosed in respect of undertakings established or carrying on business outside the United Kingdom if the directors of the investing company consider disclosure would be harmful and the Department of Trade and Industry agrees (CA 1989, S.6).

Holdings of 20% or more in another undertaking

Where a company has a significant holding of 20% or more, the aggregate amount of the capital and reserves and the profit or loss for the most recent year must also be given (CA 1989, Sch. 3, para. 25).

In addition The Stock Exchange listing agreement, section 5 (continuing obligations) para. 20 (e), requires disclosure of:

(i) the principal country of operation;
(ii) its issued capital and debt securities; and
(iii) the percentage of each class of debt securities held.

For example, ECC gave the following information on its interest in BRYANT HOLDINGS:

ECC *Extract from note on investments*

Bryant Group plc's business is housebuilding and property development, principally in England. At 30 September 1989, Bryant Group plc had in issue 204,986,501 ordinary shares of 25p each and 250,000 5.6% cumulative preference shares of £1 each in which the Group's interest amounted to 29.1% and nil respectively. The market value at 30 September 1989 of the Group's holding of 59,748,234 ordinary shares *(1988 59,748,234 ordinary shares)* was £59.2m. *(1988 £82.5m.)*. Bryant Group plc is registered in England and Wales and is listed on The International Stock Exchange.

Investments held as current assets

Other investments shown as current assets also need describing in detail (CA 1985, Sch. 4, para. 45). For example:

HARRISONS & CROSFIELD *Note to the balance sheet*

Investments held as current assets

	1988 £m	1987 £m
Shares quoted in the United Kingdom at cost less provisions	0.6	0.4
Shares unquoted at directors' valuation	—	0.3
Short term deposits	32.3	21.7
	32.9	22.4

The market value of investments quoted in the UK at 31 December 1988 was £0.7m (1987 – £0.4m).

Most companies are not in business to deal in shares, nor are equities really suitable as a holding medium for liquidity (notice HARRISONS & CROSFIELD's holdings of quoted investment represented only 2% of liquid resources), and the investor should be wary of any substantial amount of short-term investments (other than short-dated government stock): they may indicate a wheeler-dealer style of management.

Points to watch on significant holdings

A holding may indicate:

(*a*) the possibility of an eventual bid, particularly if the holder is predatory by nature;
(*b*) a blocking position taken by the holder to protect his trade interests from the risk of the company concerned being taken over by some (larger) competitor.

There is no hard and fast rule about which is which, and a holding could indicate a blocking position pending a possible bid in the distant future. In this context it is worth checking whether directors have substantial holdings and, if so, whether any are nearing retirement age.

If the holding is of *20% or more* and the company is *not* treated as an associate, the chances are probably more in favour of a bid than a blocking position – the unwelcome holder of a substantial stake being unlikely to be given a seat on the board. If the holding is of *25% or more* the holder is in the strong position of being able to block any arrangements and reconstructions that the company might wish to make with creditors and members under Section 425 of the Companies Act 1985, which require three-fourths to vote in favour.

A substantial holding may also be the legacy of a thwarted bid, as it was with the 29.3% holding of BRYANT GROUP shown in the note to ECC's 1988 accounts.

Interlocking holdings

Where a number of companies under the same management have substantial holdings in each other or in another company, the holdings may be entirely innocent; but interlocking holdings can give scope for manipulation to the detriment of outside shareholders and should be viewed with caution.

A classic illustration of the dangers of inter-locking holdings was provided by the affairs of several companies in the LOWSON GROUP, which came under investigation by the Department of Trade in 1973. The appointed inspectors found that a number of defaults in the management 'were knowingly committed by Sir Denys [Lowson] and constituted grave mismanagement of the affairs of the companies concerned' and that in some trans-actions 'his motive was to obtain a very substantial gain for himself and his family'.

Chapter 8

STOCKS AND WORK IN PROGRESS

(Reference: SSAP 9 *Stocks and Work in Progress*.)

Different classes of stock

Most manufacturing companies have traditionally shown stocks as a single figure under current assets, described either as 'stocks', as 'inventories' or as 'stocks and work in progress', but these terms cover three very different classes of asset:

(a) items in the state in which they were purchased; these include raw materials to be used in manufacture, components to be incorporated in the product and consumable stores (like paint and oil) which will be used in making it;

(b) items in an intermediate stage of completion ('work in progress', or in the United States 'work in process');

(c) finished goods.

For wholesalers and retailers, stocks are almost entirely goods purchased for resale.

Subclassification required by SSAP 9

SSAP 9 calls for the accounts to show the subclassification of stocks and work in progress 'in a manner which is appropriate to the business and so as to indicate the amounts held in each of the main categories'; for example, BASS's accounts give a subclassification of stocks in a note which is illustrated at the top of the next column.

Subclassification required by CA 1985

The Companies Act 1985 is more stringent than SSAP 9, requiring stocks to be analysed under the following subheadings:

(a) raw materials and consumables;

(b) work in progress;

BASS *Note to the 1988 accounts*

Stocks

	£m
Raw materials	52.6
Consumable stores	25.3
Work in progress	59.0
Finished stocks	154.0
Bottles, cases and pallets	14.6
	305.5

(c) finished goods and goods for resale;

(d) payments on account (for items of stock not yet received).

The matching principle

Where a business incurs in one accounting period expenditure on stocks which remain unsold or unconsumed at the balance sheet date, or upon work in progress which is incomplete at that date, these costs are carried forward into the following period so that they may be set against the revenue when it arises. This is an application of what accountants term the matching principle: that of matching cost and revenue in the year in which the revenue arises rather than charging the cost in the year in which the cost is incurred.

If, however, there is no reasonable expectation of sufficient future revenue to cover costs already incurred (for instance because of deterioration, obsolescence or a change in demand pattern), any irrecoverable cost should be charged to revenue in the year under review, and not carried forward. For this reason the value of stock and work in progress in the balance sheet at the end of the year (i.e. the book value) should be the lower of cost and net realisable value.

Consistency

The method of valuing stock should be consistent, and most sets of accounts include a brief statement in the notes on how stocks have been valued, e.g.:

AARONSON BROS. 'Stocks are valued at the lower of purchase price or production cost and net realisable value. In the case of work in progress and finished goods, production cost comprises the purchase price of raw materials and attributable costs of production.'

RTZ. 'Stocks are valued at the lower of cost and net realisable value. Cost for raw materials and stores is purchase price and for partly processed and saleable products is generally the cost of production including the appropriate proportion of depreciation and overheads.'

A particular point to look for is any statement of a *change* in the basis between year ends and, when one is made, whether any indication is given of how much difference the change has made to the year-end stock figure and to profits.

The importance of stock valuation

The accurate valuation of stock on a consistent basis is important, because quite small percentage variations can very significantly affect the profits reported in any period (Example 8.1):

Example 8.1 Stock valuation

	£000	£000
Sales		2,000
less Cost of goods sold:		
Opening stock	600	
add Purchases in period	1,500	
	2,100	
less Closing stock	400	
		1,700
		300
less Wages, overheads, etc.		200
Trading profit		100

If the closing stock had been valued 10% lower at £360,000 and the opening stock 10% higher at £660,000, the cost of goods sold would have increased by £100,000 and the trading profit would have been wiped out.

Problems in valuing stock

Three main problems arise in valuing stock:

(a) the price to be used if an item has been supplied at varying prices;

(b) the value added in manufacture both to incomplete items (work in progress) and to completed items (finished goods);

(c) the assessment of net realisable value.

Stocks in a large retail business

Having defined the main principles and problems, let us now look at stocks in practice, beginning with the control of stocks in a large retail business, where virtually all stocks are goods purchased for resale and the complications of WIP (work in progress) and finished goods do not arise.

The central management of most supermarkets controls the efficiency and honesty of local stores by charging goods out to those stores at *selling* price, and by maintaining overall stock control accounts in terms of selling price by broad product groups. By suitably analysing takings it will then be possible, for each of these product groups, to compare theoretical stock with actual stock:

Opening stock at selling price	Deliveries at + selling price	− Takings	Theoretical closing = stock at selling price

With this sort of operation, it is usual for the purpose of monthly, quarterly, half-yearly and annual accounts to deduct from the value of stock at selling price the normal gross profit margin, as MARKS & SPENCER's accounting policy on retail stocks illustrates:

MARKS & SPENCER *Accounting policies*

Stocks

Retail stocks consist of goods for resale and cost is computed by deducting the gross profit margin from the selling value of stock. When computing net realisable value an allowance is made for future markdowns.

But SSAP 9 requires that before such a figure is used for the purposes of the annual accounts, it be tested to ensure that it gives a 'reasonable approximation of the actual cost'.

Stocks in the manufacturing business

Most manufacturing businesses employ a system of cost accounting. They do so:

(a) as an aid to price fixing (so that they can

charge the customer with the materials used and the time actually taken to complete his job – as is the case with a motor repair garage, or jobbing builder); *or*

(*b*) in order to provide the estimating department with information on which to base future estimates or tenders; *and/or*

(*c*) as a means of controlling operating efficiency.

The type of record employed varies widely, from a few scribblings on the back of an envelope, to a cost system parallel to the normal financial system, reconciled with it but not part of it, right up to a completely integral cost and financial accounting system. In all but the first of these there would normally be some form of stock record.

A problem often arises in the case of the manufacturing business over the pricing of issues from stock. When there are relatively few items, and where they are easily identifiable and can each be kept separate, each stock issue can be priced at its *specific price*, and no problem arises. But in many cases it is not possible, or not convenient, to keep identical items from different purchase consignments separate.

Several different methods of pricing issues from stock are commonly employed, and the value of the stock remaining depends on the pricing method used, of which there are several:

First-in-first-out (FIFO)

Good storekeeping demands that goods should, so far as is possible, be used in the order in which they are received; that is to say, that those which came in first should be the first to go out, otherwise the danger of being left with stock which has deteriorated through lapse of time is greatly increased. The first-in first-out method of stock pricing merely assumes for accounting purposes that the normal rules of good storekeeping have been followed.

Average or weighted average price

When an organisation receives a number of deliveries during an accounting period at a series of different prices, it is reasonable to take the average price or, for more accuracy, the weighted average price.

Standard price

Many businesses employ a standard cost system; that is to say, they predetermine for each type of unit manufactured the price which ought to be paid for material, the material usage, the wage rate of the personnel employed to produce it, the time they should take, and so on. In such a system materials issued from store are priced at standard cost, as are work in progress at all stages and any finished goods in stock. Any variances from standard are written off as operating losses (or profits) at the time they occur. Provided the standard price represents fairly the average cost of the material in stock, it may be employed for financial accounting purposes.

These different methods of pricing issues each give rise to a slightly different closing stock value and thus to a slightly different profit for the year. But this is not important *provided* that a company adopts the same method consistently in each accounting period. It is not permissible to chop and change.

Replacement cost and NIFO

In the past, items in stock were occasionally stated in the accounts at replacement cost when this was lower than both cost and net realisable value. The effect of this was to increase the cost of goods sold for the period, and thus reduce reported profits. The statement of stocks at the lowest of cost, net realisable value and replacement cost is no longer (under SSAP 9) an acceptable basis of stock valuation.

LIFO

Another method of valuation, unacceptable under SSAP 9, but commonplace in the United States, is the last-in first-out (LIFO) basis in which issues are charged at the latest price at which they could conceivably have come. This has the advantage of charging the customer with the most recent price; but in the balance sheet stocks appear at the price of the earliest delivery from which they could have arisen, on the basis that the rule of good storekeeping is (in theory only) reversed, and goods received latest are used first, and those in stock remain in stock.

Thus, in a time of rising prices LIFO has the effect of:

(*a*) showing stocks in the balance sheet at a cost appropriate not to recent purchases but to those many months or even years earlier; and, consequently,

(*b*) reducing profit made on holding stock.

Taxation of stock profits

Suppose that a company has an opening stock of raw materials of £10 million at the beginning of the year. At the end of the year the closing stock comprises exactly the same material quantities as the opening stock but, because of inflation, the value has risen to £11 million:

Opening stock of raw materials	£10,000,000
Closing stock of raw materials	11,000,000
Increase in value of stock	1,000,000

This increase in value of £1 million reduces the cost

of goods sold by £1 million, which adds £1 million to pre-tax profit. This stock profit, although unrealised, bears Corporation Tax at 35% = £350,000 tax, which has to be paid even though the physical amount of stock is unchanged.

In the early 1970s, when almost all prices were rising rapidly with inflation, companies that needed to carry large stocks were very hard hit: they were taxed on their stock profits and had to find more working capital each year just to maintain the same *volume* of stock. Their plight was eventually recognised by the government, which introduced stock relief in the Finance Act 1975, but discontinued it in 1984 after inflation had eased (see Chapter 13).

The problems of stocks in an inflationary situation will be discussed further in Chapter 23.

Requirements of the Companies Act 1985 and of SSAP 9 on stocks and WIP

SSAP 9 requires that the amount at which stock and work in progress, other than long-term contracts, are stated in periodic financial statements should be 'the total of the *lower of cost and net realisable value* of the separate items of stock and work in progress or groups of similar items', i.e. each item or each group of similar items should be assessed separately.

The Companies Act 1985 allows the use of FIFO, LIFO, weighted average price or any other similar method to be used for *fungible assets* (assets substantially indistinguishable from one another) but, where the amount shown differs materially from the replacement cost (or the most recent purchase price or production cost), the amount of that difference must be disclosed (Sch. 4, para. 27).

The inclusion of overheads in cost
It was at one time accepted that companies should be free to choose whether to value work in progress and finished goods:

(*a*) at prime cost: that is to say, to exclude all overheads, *or*

(*b*) at variable (or marginal) cost: that is to say to exclude all *fixed* overheads, but include prime cost plus variable overheads, *or*

(*c*) at the full cost of purchase plus the cost of conversion (including fixed overheads too).

The Companies Act 1985 and SSAP 9 both regard (*c*) as the only proper method. The classification of overheads between fixed and variable is regarded as an unsuitable one for determining whether or not they should be included in the cost of conversion: the dividing line is considered too imprecise.

Costs of general management, as distinct from functional management, are excluded unless directly related to current production (as they may be to some extent in smaller companies), but the Companies Act 1985 does allow a reasonable proportion of interest on capital borrowed to finance production costs to be included in the value of stock; however, if this is done the amount must be disclosed (Sch. 4, para. 26).

Net realisable value
Net realisable value is 'the actual or estimated selling price (net of trade but before settlement discounts) less:

(*a*) all further costs to completion; and

(*b*) all costs to be incurred in marketing, selling and distributing'.

When stocks are held which are unlikely to be sold within the turnover period normal to the company (i.e. where there are excess stocks), the impending delay in realisation will increase the risk of deterioration and/or obsolescence, and this needs to be taken into account in assessing net realisable value.

The danger of rising stocks

Although SSAP 9's requirement to include production overheads in costing finished goods gives a fair picture when stocks are being maintained at prudent levels in relation to demand, their inclusion can produce unduly optimistic profits when a manufacturer leaves production unchanged in periods of lower demand. This is illustrated by Example 8.2.

In practice, the profit from full production would be likely to be reduced by interest charges to finance carrying increased stock, but even so management can bolster profits a great deal in the short term by continuing high production in the face of falling demand. Rising stocks unmatched by rising turnover may give some warning here, and this can be monitored by the ratio Stocks/Turnover. For example in 1988 the chairman of CRAY ELECTRONICS began his annual statement:

'On behalf of the Board of Directors, I am pleased to report a further year of successful achievement by your Group.

Profits before tax advanced to £13.1m. (1987 £10.6m, adjusted), an increase of 24%, with the fourteenth successive increase in earnings per share from 8.7p to 10.3p. The Group's operating margin on sales continued to improve. Your Directors are recommending once again an improved final dividend . . .'

Example 8.2   Rising stocks

Let us look at a single-product factory facing a year in which demand is forecast to fall by 30% due to an economic recession:

Production overheads (rent of factory, etc.) = £1 million.
Production capacity 100,000 units per annum.
Variable costs = £10 per unit. Selling price = £25 per unit.
Sales last year 100,000 units.

The management is faced with the decision of whether:

(a)   to continue at full production, hoping that demand will pick up sharply the following year if not sooner, and that it possibly won't fall quite as sharply as forecast; *or*
(b)   to cut production by up to 30%.

Under SSAP 9, assuming demand does fall by 30%, the figures that will be reported at the end of the year under these two choices will be:

	(a) Full production Units	(b) Production cut by 30% Units
Opening stock	20,000	20,000
Units manufactured	100,000	70,000
	120,000	90,000
Units sold	70,000	70,000
Closing stock	50,000	20,000
	£	£
Fixed costs	1,000,000	1,000,000
Variable costs (£10 per unit)	1,000,000	700,000
Total costs (costs per unit made)	2,000,000 (£20)	1,700,000 (£24.285)
Sales (£25 per unit)	1,750,000	1,750,000
Cost of goods sold:		
Opening stock (£20 per unit)	400,000	400,000
add Cost of units manufactured	2,000,000	1,700,000
less Closing stock by FIFO method	− 1,000,000 (£20)	− 485,700 (£24.285)
Cost of goods sold	1,400,000	1,614,300
Profit (Sales *less* Cost of goods sold)	350,000	135,700

and he continued in the same vein. But the figures for stocks and overdrafts in the accounts suggested that all was not well; the Stock/Turnover ratio had deteriorated from 27.1% to 33.6% (a change of more than 1 or 2% is significant) and the bank overdraft had almost quadrupled:

CRAY ELECTRONICS *Extracts from 1988 accounts*

Year ended 30 April	1987 £000	1988 £000	*Change*
Turnover	64,244	75,500	+17.5%
Stocks:			
Raw materials and consumables	2,011	4,070	+102.4%
Work-in-progress	8,657	10,510	+21.4%
Finished goods	3,671	5,498	+49.8%
Long-term contract work-in-progress	12,875	17,169	+33.3%
	27,214	37,247	+36.9%
Less payments received on account on long-term work-in-progress	(9,772)	(11,879)	+21.6%
	17,442	25,368	+45.4%
Bank overdrafts	3,259	12,701	+289.4%
Trade creditors	5,987	10,538	+76.0%
Interest payable (net)	322	857	+166.1%
Stocks/Turnover ratio (our calculation)	27.1	33.6%	

The £4.5 million increase in trade creditors was an indication that the company might be strapped for cash, while interest payable rising more slowly than bank overdrafts suggested that things might be getting worse. This proved to be the case, and within 18 months new management had to be brought in.

Long-term contracts

A *long-term contract* is defined by SSAP 9 as 'a contract entered into for manufacture or building of a single substantial entity or the provision of a service where the time taken to manufacture, build or provide is such that a substantial proportion of all such contract work will extend for a period exceeding one year'.

Shipbuilders, constructional engineers and the like frequently engage in long-term contracts. Because of the length of time such contracts take to complete, to defer taking profit into account until completion would result in the profit and loss account reflecting not a true and fair view of the activity of the company during the year, but rather the results of those contracts which, by the accident of time, were completed by the year end.

It is normal with long-term contracts to have an arrangement under which the contractor receives payment on account on the basis of the 'work certified' by an architect or surveyor. Traditionally, there are two ways of computing the profit to be taken. The 'work certified' is an essential piece of information whichever of the two ways of arriving at the profit to date is adopted.

Under the first method, profit to date is computed as follows:

$$\begin{matrix} \text{Work certified at balance sheet date} \end{matrix} - \begin{matrix} \text{Costs incurred on contract to date} \end{matrix} = \begin{matrix} \text{Profit to date} \end{matrix}$$

The second method takes a proportion of the overall profit expected:

$$\left\{ \begin{matrix} \text{Total contract price} \end{matrix} - \begin{matrix} \text{Total costs incurred on contract to date} \end{matrix} - \begin{matrix} \text{Total estimated further costs to completion} \end{matrix} \right\}$$

$$\times \quad \frac{\text{Work certified to date}}{\text{Total contract price}} = \begin{matrix} \text{Profit to date} \end{matrix}$$

If the first formula is used it is still necessary to have regard to the costs likely to be incurred in completing the job, for it is clearly wrong to take a profit on the first stage of a contract if the profit is likely to be lost at a later stage. In either case, in considering future costs, it is necessary to allow for likely increases in wages and salaries, likely increases in the price of raw materials and rises in general overheads in so far as these items are not recoverable from the customer under the terms of the contract: inflation can play havoc with the profitability of fixed-price or inadequately

51

protected contracts, as many companies have learned to their cost.

In neither case is it usual to take up the entire profit to date. Some companies take only two-thirds, others only three-quarters. Many multiply by a further fraction:

$$\frac{\text{Amount received to date}}{\text{Work certified to date}}$$

Where the customer is entitled (as is usually the case) to retain, say, 10% of the amount certified as 'retention monies', so as to ensure satisfactory rectification of any defects, the use of this further fraction of, in this case, 9/10ths, has the effect of

disregarding that part of the profit appropriate to the amount retained.

The amount reflected in the year's profit and loss account will be the appropriate proportion of the total profit by reference to the work done to date, less any profit already taken up in prior years on the contracts still on hand. The aim of using a multiplying factor of two-thirds or three-quarters is to ensure that unless the remaining work on a contract is disastrous, some profit remains to be taken when the contract is finally completed. Example 8.3 illustrates the treatment of long-term contracts in the accounts of an imaginary company, 'COMMERCIAL CONTRACTS LTD'.

Example 8.3 Long-term contracts: 'COMMERCIAL CONTRACTS LTD'

'COMMERCIAL CONTRACTS LTD' is engaged in a long-term bridge-building contract.

	£
Work certified to 31 December 1990	1,250,000
Total contract price	2,000,000
Costs incurred on contract to 31 December 1990	1,025,000
Estimated further costs to completion	575,000
Amount received from customer by 31 December 1990	1,125,000
Profit taken on the contract in 1989	45,000

The company takes up three-quarters of the profit earned to date, reduced by the fraction: amount received to date ÷ work certified to date. What profit will be taken up on the contract in 1990?

Using the first formula:

$$\text{Work certified at balance sheet date} - \text{Costs incurred on contract to date} = \text{Profit to date}$$

Profit to date = £1,250,000 − £1,025,000 = £225,000

Of which: $\frac{3}{4} \times \frac{1,125,000}{1,250,000} = 67\frac{1}{2}\%$ will be taken up = £151,875

but £45,000 of this was taken up in 1989, so only £106,875 remains to be taken up in 1990

Using the second formula:

$$\left\{ \begin{array}{c} \text{Total contract price} \end{array} - \begin{array}{c} \text{Total costs incurred on contract to date} \end{array} - \begin{array}{c} \text{Total estimated further costs to completion} \end{array} \right\} \times \frac{\text{Work certified to date}}{\text{Total contract price}} = \text{Profit to date}$$

$$\text{Profit to date} = (£2,000,000 - £1,025,000 - £575,000) \times \frac{1,250,000}{2,000,000} = £250,000$$

Of this £250,000 profit, 67½% will be taken up (as before) i.e. £168,750, less the £45,000 already taken up in 1989 = £123,750.

The difference between the two figures for profit to date is due to the difference between the profit margin on that part of the contract completed to date (£225,000 on £1,250,000 in the first formula = 18%) and that estimated on the contract as a whole (£400,000 on £2 million in the second formula = 20%).

The second formula requires an estimate to be made of future costs and is therefore open to subjective judgement. Results should be viewed with caution if the overall profitability margin is estimated to be higher than the margin to date; i.e. if the second formula allows a higher profit to be taken now than the first formula would allow.

Requirements of SSAP 9 on long-term contracts

In the past, accounting treatment of long-term contracts has varied enormously from company to company. BOVIS, for example, in its 1972 accounts noted that 'no provision is made for anticipated future losses' and a year later had to be rescued by P. & O. At the other end of the scale companies like JOHN LAING pursued policies of extreme prudence: all losses were taken when they were foreseen, but no account was taken of profits on contracts unfinished at the end of the year.

SSAP 9 requires that 'The amount at which long-term contract work in progress is stated in periodic financial statements should be cost plus any *attributable profit*, less any foreseeable losses and progress payments received and receivable', and the amount of attributable profit included should be disclosed. Attributable profits on contracts are, however, only required to be taken up when 'it is considered that their outcome can be assessed with reasonable certainty before their conclusion'; if the outcome cannot be reasonably assessed, 'it is prudent not to take up any profit', so management is still left with a certain amount of latitude, and the key point to watch for is undue anticipation of profits.

SSAP 9 also requires balance sheets to show how the amount included for long-term contracts is reached by stating:

(a) the amount of work in progress at cost plus attributable profit (i.e. profit or loss taken to date), less foreseeable losses;

(b) cash received and receivable at the accounting date as progress payments on account of contracts in progress.

Thus, if the bridge contract we discussed in Example 8.3 was the only contract of Commercial Contracts Ltd to appear in the balance sheet at 31 December 1990, and if the first formula is used, it would appear as follows:

	£	£
Work in progress, at cost *plus* Profit taken to date	1,176,875	
less Cash received from customer	1,125,000	
		51,875

Chapter 9

DEBTORS

TRADE DEBTORS AND OTHER DEBTORS

Debtors (also known as 'receivables') are a current asset, representing amounts owing to the business.

The balance sheet formats in Schedule 4 of the Companies Act 1985 require debtors to be subdivided into:

(a) *trade debtors* – those arising from the sale of goods on credit,

(b) *amounts owed by group undertakings* – see Chapter 16,

(c) *amounts owed by undertakings in which the company has a participating interest* – see Chapter 17,

(d) *other debtors* – for example debts due form the sale of fixed assets or investments, and

(e) *prepayments and accrued income* – for example rent or rates paid in advance.

The amount falling due after more than one year should be shown separately for each item included under debtors (CA 1985, Sch. 4, note (5) to the balance sheet formats). Most companies show a single figure for debtors in their balance sheet, and give details in a note, as illustrated here:

ULTRAMAR *Details of debtors*

Balance sheet

	Note	1988 £ million	1987 £ million
Current assets			
Stocks		125.4	128.6
Debtors	20	277.0	283.3
. . .			

20. Debtors	1988 £ million	1987 £ million
Amounts falling due within one year:		
Trade debtors	144.7	165.1
Other debtors	25.1	18.9
Prepayments and accrued income	17.0	23.7
	186.8	207.7
Amounts falling due after one year:		
Indonesian debt service equalisation	78.6	69.4
Other debtors	11.6	6.2
	277.0	283.3

(A paragraph under 'Accounting Policies' described how the amount for Indonesian debt service equalisation arose in connection with long-term liquified natural gas (LNG) contracts.)

Bad debts and doubtful debtors

The granting of credit inevitably involves some risk that the debtor will fail to pay, that is, will become a bad debt. When a business recognises that a debt is bad, the debt is written off to profit and loss account. That is to say, the balance appearing as 'debtors' falls by the amount of the debt, and 'bad debts' appears as an expense. This expense is shown separately in the published accounts only if the amount is material.

In addition, it is normal to set up a 'provision for doubtful debtors'. To do so a charge is made to profit and loss account and, in the balance sheet, the cumulative provision for doubtful debtors is deducted from the total debtors. Once again, the provision for doubtful debtors is disclosed separately in the published accounts only if it is material.

A provision for doubtful debtors may be *specific*, that is to say based upon the businessman's estimate of the probable loss, studying each debt in turn; for instance, there is a 10% probability that Smith will fail to pay his debt of £12,100, therefore we must provide £1,210; or it may be *general*, e.g. 2½% of total debtors; or a combination of the two.

The importance of debtors

Companies such as supermarket chains, whose turnover is almost entirely for cash, will have very few debtors; the figure appearing in the balance sheet is likely to be largely prepayments and non-trade debtors, and usually has no particular significance. SAINSBURY, for example, with sales of £4,791 million p.a., showed trade debtors of a mere 6.2 million in its 1988 accounts. At the other extreme are companies whose entire turnover is on credit terms, in which case very large amounts of working capital may be tied up in debtors. Here the efficiency with which credit accounts are handled, and the timing of the taking of profit where payments are by instalment, are of considerable interest to the analyst.

Debt collection period

The ratio Trade Debtors/Turnover can be used to monitor a company's credit control, as we describe in Chapter 24, and this is possibly a more meaningful measure if expressed in terms of time, as the *debt collection period*:

Debt collection period (in days) =

$$\frac{\text{Trade Debtors}}{\text{Sales (Turnover)}} \times 365$$

It is interesting to compare this ratio in similar companies:

BASS *Debt collection period*

	1988 £m	1989 £m
Turnover	3,734	4,036
Trade debtors	281	256
Debt collection period	27.5 days	23.2 days

WHITBREAD *Debt collection period*

	1988 £m	1989 £m
Turnover	2,059.9	2,259.8
Trade debtors	131.3	119.5
Debt collection period	23.3 days	19.3 days

Both companies have improved their debt collection periods significantly. Had the periods been the same in 1989 as they were in 1988, BASS would have had a further £48 million tied up in trade debtors in 1989 (£304m. ÷ £4,036m. × 365 = 27.5 days), and WHITBREAD would have had £25 million more.

Some companies and analysts take 360 days to the year, or compute in terms of, say, 260 *working* days.

In a seasonal business it is more accurate to compute the collection period on a month-by-month basis, but this is not possible without inside knowledge. Indeed, the analyst can tell comparatively little about debtors unless a significant proportion of debtors are due after more than one year or unless the company discloses more than the minimum information required by law. Among the things which one would like to find out are the following:

1. What is the customer concentration? Is an undue proportion due from one major customer, or from customers in one industry? Would failure of one or two customers have a material effect upon the company's financial future?

2. What is the age pattern of debtors? Are some unduly old? Is there adequate provision for bad and doubtful debts?

3. Are any of the debts falling due after more than one year very long-term in nature? In the United Kingdom debtors appear at their face value regardless of when they are due. In the United States, if a debt is not due within one year, it may be necessary to discount it, i.e. to take account of imputed interest. Thus, a debt of $1 million due three years hence might appear, taking interest into account at 10%, as $751,300.

Factors affecting the debt collection period

A short debt collection period is, other things being equal, preferable to a longer one; but as with many ratios one has to qualify this general principle. For by restricting credit, and selling entirely for cash, a business can have a zero debt collection period; but if this drives its customers into the arms of competitors it is scarcely an improvement so far as the business as a whole is concerned. Subject to that qualification, any improvement in collection period, since it represents a reduction in overall debtors, means that more capital is available for other purposes, or that there is less need to borrow money from the bank.

At first sight it may seem that an increase in collection period represents a fall in the efficiency of the debt collection section. This is likely to be the case, but it is not necessarily so. The debt collection period may increase (decrease) between one period and another for a number of reasons:

1. If there is a *policy change* with regard to:
    (a) credit terms to existing customers; if, for example, the board of directors, to obtain a valuable order from a major customer, offers two months' credit instead of one;
    (b) the granting of credit; for instance, if potential customers whose credit rating was formerly insufficient for them to be granted credit, are granted credit – for such customers are unlikely to be among the fastest payers.
2. If there is *poor credit management*:
    (a) if credit is given to unsatisfactory customers;
    (b) if the invoicing section falls behind; customers will not pay until they receive an invoice and, in general, pay at a fixed

time determined by the date on which they receive an invoice, e.g. at the end of the month in which they receive an invoice;
    (c) if statements are late – some businesses wait until they receive a statement;
    (d) if there is no consistent follow-up of overdue debts, by letter and/or telephone, or even in person.
3. If a subsidiary with an atypical debt collection period is disposed of or acquired, e.g., MARLEY's sale of its DIY cash-and-carry chain 'Payless' increased the group's debt collection period by several days.
4. If factoring or invoice discounting is introduced or discontinued (see page 59).

Why it is important to keep a watch upon collection period

Although it is necessary for most businesses to offer some credit, any unnecessary credit is bad management because it ties up money which (normally) earns no return, and which is subject to increased risk. The customer who is short of money, and who finds he can order things from a company without having to pay for them at the end of the month, tends to place more and more of his orders with that company; if he subsequently goes into liquidation, he is likely to do so owing a hefty amount.

HIRE-PURCHASE AND CREDIT SALE TRANSACTIONS

(Reference: SSAP 21 *Accounting for leases and hire purchase contracts*.)

Definitions

A *hire-purchase transaction* is a transaction in which the *hirer* agrees to hire goods from their *owner* in return for which he pays (usually) a deposit and a series of weekly, monthly, quarterly or yearly payments. The intention is that when the hiring period comes to an end, the ownership of the goods will pass to the hirer, sometimes on the payment of a nominal sum, sometimes with the final instalment; ownership, therefore, does not pass to the hirer until all payments have been made.

A *credit sale* is an outright sale (usually by a retailer) where payment by instalments is agreed in writing as a condition of the sale. Under a credit sale arrangement the property in the goods passes immediately to the purchaser, who becomes the owner of the goods, but payment is required to be made over a period.

Interest is normally charged by the seller both in

credit sale and hire-purchase arrangements; the great difference between them is that in a credit sale the 'purchaser' owns the goods from the outset, whereas in the case of a hire-purchase sale, they do not become his until the final payment is made. Thus the seller cannot reclaim the goods in the case of a credit sale if the purchaser defaults, whereas, subject to the terms of the agreement and the law on hire-purchase, he can in the case of a hire-purchase transaction.

Amounts due under credit sale transactions are debtors, and normally appear with other trade debtors, though they may be shown separately. In the case of a hire-purchase transaction, there has, strictly speaking, been no sale, and the goods involved are still an asset of the seller; but, adopting the principle of 'substance over form', most companies refer to the item as 'hire-purchase debtors' or 'instalments due under hire-purchase agreements'.

Timing of profit taking

Whether the sale is a credit sale or on hire-purchase, there are two elements of profit: the profit on the sale of the goods themselves and interest upon the amounts outstanding. There are a number of ways in which these two forms of profit can be spread over the accounting periods involved; but essentially these break down into two:

1. Take all the profit on the sale immediately, and spread only the interest element.
2. Spread both the profit on the sale and the interest over the life of the agreement.

Although method 1 is permissible for credit sales, method 2 is the more prudent. Method 1 is not recommended for hire-purchase, as the goods have not actually been sold.

Where a credit sale is made on truly 'interest-free' terms, there is no interest to spread, though logically there is an interest cost so far as the selling company is concerned. This is not normally taken into account, though it could be, by taking into account imputed interest. But it is always necessary to make provision for collection costs. Such a provision might, for instance, be 10% of the credit sale account debtors outstanding on balance sheet date.

The rule of 78

Finance companies frequently apply the 'rule of 78' in spreading either the interest alone, or the whole profit and interest, over the life of the agreement. This is simply a form of the 'sum of the years' digits method' already discussed in connection with depreciation in Chapter 6. What happens is this: the period of the agreement is set down in months (or it could be weeks in the case of a weekly agreement, or years where payments were on an annual basis), and the sum of the digits represents the sum of $1 + 2 + 3 + 4 \ldots$ to n, where n is that number of months (or weeks or years). It is called the rule of 78 because for a year's agreement, the sum of $1 + 2 + 3 + \ldots + 12$ is 78. Any interest charge is then spread as follows (in this case a year's agreement):

First month 12/78ths of total interest
Second month 11/78ths
Third month 10/78ths
. . .
Twelfth month 1/78th

See Example 9.1.

Some companies use this same method for hire-purchase transactions, but it is generally considered more prudent to spread both profit and interest over the life of the transaction (Example 9.2), rather than to take profit at the outset.

The rule of 78 is a simple, though not totally accurate, way of spreading interest or profit over the period of an agreement. Some companies use more sophisticated techniques, spreading interest or profit by what is termed the 'actuarial method', taking into account interest (at the true effective rate payable) on the balance outstanding period by period.

Example 9.1   Credit sale, method 1: 'HIGH FIDELITY LTD'

Hi-fi equipment costing £425 is sold by 'High Fidelity' to a customer for £600, to be spread by means of a credit sale agreement over nine months. Taking into account interest and collection costs of £45, High Fidelity is to be paid a total of £645, i.e. £71.67 per month, commencing with delivery of the goods on 1 November 1990. High Fidelity Ltd prepares accounts to 31 December annually. How much profit will be taken upon the customer's agreement in 1990 (assuming he pays two instalments, one on 1 November and one on 1 December) and how much in 1991, the final payment being made on 1 July 1991?

All the profit on selling goods, purchased for £425, for £600 – i.e. £175 – will fall into 1990, the year in which the sale was made, as will the interest for two months, computed as follows:

November 9/45ths of £45 = £9
December 8/45ths of £45 = £8
(since the sum of the digits 1, 2, 3 . . . 9 is 45).

At 31 December 1990 there would appear among debtors seven instalments of £71.67 (£501.69) less a provision for unearned interest and collection costs (£45 − £9 − £8 = £28) = £473.69.

Example 9.2   Hire-purchase, method 2: 'DEFERRALS LTD'

The hire-purchase trading account of 'DEFERRALS LTD' for 1990 is as follows:

Hire-purchase sales	£120,000
less Cost of goods sold	£80,000
Gross profit on HP sales (33⅓%)	£40,000

Receipts from 1990 HP sales	= £36,000
Profit to be taken in 1990	
£36,000 × 33⅓% profit margin	= £12,000
Provision for unearned profit	
carried forward on 1990 HP sales	
= £40,000 − £12,000 = £28,000	

HP sales in 1990	£120,000
less Cash received	£36,000
	£84,000
less Provision for unearned profit	£28,000
Hire-purchase debtors (from 1990 sales)	£56,000

If, say, £63,000 is received in 1990 in respect of transactions from 1989 and £42,000 from 1988, when the profit margins were 30% and 35% respectively, the total profit from HP sales to be taken in 1990 would be:

From 1990	£12,000
From 1989 (30% of £63,000)	£18,900
From 1988 (35% of £42,000)	£14,700
Total profit	£45,600

Hire-purchase information given in accounts

A good set of accounts will give quite a lot of information on hire-purchase and credit sale business; e.g. GREAT UNIVERSAL STORES states how the profit is taken and how the interest is brought in, and shows the amount of provisions made (see illustration below).

Some companies arrange for their credit sales and hire-purchase transactions to be handled by a separate finance company, so that they receive payment for goods at once and thus reduce their requirements for working capital. In these cases, of course, the amounts outstanding are of no concern to the selling company and do not appear in its accounts.

GREAT UNIVERSAL STORES *Information on hire purchase*

Debtors	1989		1988	
	Due within one year	Due in more than one year	Due within one year	Due in more than one year
The Group	£m	£m	£m	£m
Trade debtors:				
Instalment and hire purchase debtors	903.8	460.5	789.0	414.4
Deduct: Provision for unearned finance charges	70.7	40.9	67.5	30.2
	833.1	419.6	721.5	384.2
Add: Other trade debtors	39.5		39.0	
Total trade debtors	872.6	419.6	760.5	384.2

. . .

Accounting policies

(e) Instalment and hire purchase debtors (SSAP 21)
The gross profit and finance charges on goods sold under hire purchase and certain instalment agreements are brought into profit as and when instalments are received. Interest receivable by finance companies on their hire purchase and personal loan agreements is credited to profit using the sum of the digits method. Interest on other personal loan agreements is brought into profit on an accruals basis in proportion to the reducing balance outstanding.

FACTORING

Factoring involves the sale of a company's trade debtors to a factoring house. Factoring houses offer three facilities:

1. the provision of finance for working capital;
2. a credit management and sales accounting service;
3. bad debt protection.

The provision of finance

This is the main reason why companies use factoring. The factor assesses the client's business and arrives at an agreed debt-collection period. Suppose the client offers 30-day terms but, in fact, is taking 60 days to collect the average debt. A reasonable assessment might be 45 days, and the factor will doubtless aim to get the average collection period down to below that.

The factor then, upon receiving invoices, forwards typically 80% of their value immediately, charging interest of around 2% to 4% over base rate from that date to the normal collection date (in our example 45 days). The remaining 20%, less charges, is paid over at the end of the agreed period.

This form of factoring can be especially useful to the seasonal business and to the small, rapidly expanding company because, unlike a bank overdraft facility, the amount of finance varies automatically with the volume of business.

Alternatively the factor can undertake to make the entire payment on the invoices at the end of the agreed debt-collection period, in our example 45 days; in either method the liquidity of the company would be improved.

Credit management and sales accounting

The factor takes over responsibility for credit control, sales accounting and debt collection. Credit management is of particular advantage to companies with foreign customers. Most factors tend to be either subsidiaries of UK clearing banks or part of an international factoring organisation. In either case, the factor tends to have expert knowledge of the credit standing not only of customers in the United Kingdom, but also of those abroad, whereas the ordinary company has some difficulty running a credit check upon a potential overseas customer.

Bad debt protection

The factor pays whether or not the customer does. Factoring tends to provide greater protection against credit risks than credit insurance, which is normally limited to a proportion of the debt, say, 70%. The factor charges a commission for these services of around 2%, but much depends upon the nature and volume of the business. Clearly, the service costs more where the business has a large number of smaller accounts and/or is in a risky industry, and less where it has few, large, accounts, all of which are companies with household names.

Invoice discounting

As explained earlier, most factoring is upon a non-recourse basis, the factor taking the entire credit risk; but it is possible to make other arrangements, especially where debt collection might prove a problem, and the client wishes to handle this himself. In the case of non-recourse factoring, the existence and identity of the factor are both known to the customer. In what is termed invoice discounting (or confidential factoring), the company maintains its own accounting records, and collects the money from customers in the ordinary way; but each time an invoice is raised, a copy is forwarded to the factor, who advances, say, 80% of the value of the invoice. As cheques are received from customers, they are passed to the factor, who banks them, deducts the amount already advanced, plus his charges, and remits the balance. The customer then does not even know of the existence of the factor.

Factoring in the accounts

In general, it is impossible from an inspection of published accounts to say with certainty whether or not a factor is involved; but a single sharp reduction in collection period and total debtors outstanding might make one suspect that factoring had been introduced.

Chapter 10

BANK LOANS, OVERDRAFTS AND OTHER FINANCIAL INSTRUMENTS

Bank facilities

There are three main methods by which a company can borrow money from a bank: by overdrawing on its current account, by loans and by the use of acceptance credits. The bank normally agrees with a company the maximum amount that can be borrowed under each method, and this is called granting a facility. For example, a company that has the bank's permission to run an overdraft of up to £1 million has overdraft facilities for that amount.

What is shown in the balance sheet is, however, not the limit of each facility but the amount the facility is being used at the year end; only the amounts actually borrowed from the bank on the balance sheet date appear in the balance sheet, although some idea of the average amount overdrawn during the year can be gained from the interest charges reported in the profit and loss account. The bank facilities available to a company are not normally published, although broad statements may be made about the company having 'ample overdraft facilities' or being 'well within its bank facilities', although some companies may be more specific, e.g. BRITISH PETROLEUM:

BRITISH PETROLEUM *Note to the 1988 accounts*

Finance debt

. . .

At 31 December the group had substantial amounts of undrawn borrowing facilities available including approximately £4,993 million (£2,307 million) which was covered by formal commitments.

Schedule 4 of the Companies Act 1985 requires bank loans and overdrafts falling due within one year to be shown separately from those falling due after more than one year. The use being made of acceptance credit facilities is included in 'Bills of exchange payable'.

Overdrafts

The traditional method of clearing bank lending is to allow the customer to overdraw on his current account. It was originally designed to cover fluctuations in the company's cash during the year and gives the company complete flexibility of drawing within a given limit, which is normally reviewed annually.

Bank advances on overdraft are technically repayable on demand and, although this is seldom enforced, the bank when granting overdraft facilities may expect the customer to produce budgets and cash flow forecasts to show the purposes for which the facilities are intended and the plans for eventual repayment. Bank lending on overdraft is traditionally short-term in character, designed to cover fluctuations in working capital requirements rather than to provide permanent capital for the company.

In recent years, however, long-term interest rates have been driven so high by inflation that few finance directors have been willing to commit their companies to long-term debt. Instead they have resorted more and more to borrowing from their banks, where interest on an overdraft is charged at an agreed percentage over the clearing bank's base rate (see below) which they hope will average less than current long-term rates, and where the company is free to reduce its borrowing whenever it wishes. Although it is now quite common for companies to finance a large part of their working capital in this way, clearing banks are usually reluctant to let companies increase their overdraft ad lib, even against a floating charge, preferring their clients to convert any 'hard-core' borrowing that has built up on overdraft into loans (see Bank loans below).

The cost of borrowing on overdraft
The interest a company has to pay on its overdraft is usually set at a given percentage above its bank's base rate, depending on the standing of the customer; a financially stable, medium-sized company might pay a fixed 1½% above base.

The base rate, the datum on which the rates of interest are based, is adjusted up and down to reflect fluctuations in short-term interest rates. Each bank sets its own base rate according to supply and demand and the fluctuations of short-term interest rates, though in practice the clearing banks' base rates keep very much in line with each other.

Fluctuations of the overdraft
As we have said, the overdraft figure given in the balance sheet is the amount the overdraft facility is being used at the year end; as companies normally choose their year end to fall when business is at its slackest, the balance sheet figure is unlikely to be the maximum amount the company has overdrawn during the year.

For example, a company in a seasonal business, with peak sales in the summer, could be expected to build up stocks from early spring and to carry high debtors across the summer. With an annual turnover of say £15 million, an overdraft of £100,000 at its year end (31 December) and £150,000 bank interest paid (reflecting an average overdraft of £1,500,000 during the year, bearing interest on average at 10%), the amount the company was actually overdrawn during the year would be likely to fluctuate with the sales cycle as shown in Example 10.1.

In practice, profit on sales and depreciation on assets would accumulate during the year, steadily improving the overdraft position, but sharp increases would be expected with the payment of dividends and Corporation Tax, and capital expenditure would also have an immediate effect on the overdraft position.

Vulnerability of borrowing on overdraft
Companies which rely heavily on borrowing on overdraft and on floating-rate loans (see below) are vulnerable to rising interest rates, particularly if their profit margins are small, and those which let their overdrafts steadily increase year by year without raising further equity or

Example 10.1 Example of annual fluctuation in overdraft

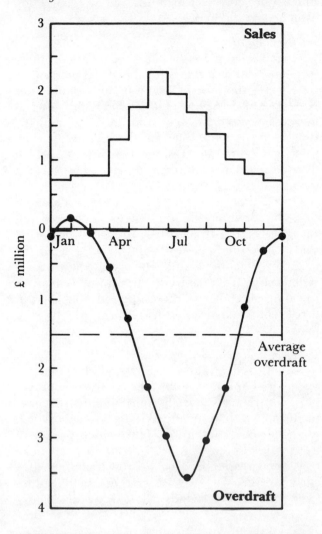

fixed-interest capital are steadily increasing their interest rate risk.

Another hazard of financing on overdraft is that the government has from time to time clamped down on bank lending; in addition, the banks are also liable to restrict credit on their own account when they find themselves up against their own overall lending limits or too heavily lent in the particular sector in which the company operates. As credit controls often come when conditions are unfavourable for capital raising, a company which is financed extensively on overdraft can all too easily find its operations severely constrained by its immediate cash position.

Bank loans

The simplest type of bank loan is one where the full amount is drawn by the borrower at the outset and is repaid in one lump sum at the end of the period.

61

The duration (or 'term') of the loan is seldom more than seven years but, unlike an overdraft, a bank loan cannot be called in before the end of the term unless the borrower defaults on any condition attached to the loan.

Interest charged

Interest is charged either at a fixed rate or, more frequently, at a *floating* rate: an agreed percentage over base rate, or over London Inter-Bank Offer Rate (LIBOR). Where LIBOR is used, an interest period is agreed between the borrower and the bank and the bank then, on the first day of each interest period, determines the rate at which deposits are being offered in the interbank market for the relevant period.

For example, if a rate of ½% over LIBOR and a three-month interest period have been agreed and the three-month LIBOR rate is 10.7% at the start of the period, the borrower will pay 11.2% for the next three months, and the rate will then be redetermined. Banks frequently allow borrowers to vary their choice of interest period – one month, three months or six months – during the life of a loan.

Drawing and repayment by instalments

Where the borrower doesn't need all the money at once, the bank may allow the loan to be drawn down in tranches (specified instalments). Repayments may also be arranged in instalments, which may often be a stipulation of the lender; banks like to see money coming back gradually to make repayment easier for the borrower and to give early warning of a borrower getting into difficulties over repayment. Details of drawing down and repayment are agreed in advance, together with the rate of interest payable and the security to be given, although any of these features can be altered subsequently by mutual agreement.

Security

Bank loans are sometimes secured on assets acquired by the loan or on other assets of the company, but a floating charge is more usual. If the loan is not secured at all, the company may be required to give a *negative pledge*, i.e. to undertake not to give security to any new or existing creditor or to borrow further amounts under existing security without the bank's prior agreement in writing.

Loan facilities

There is an increasing trend, particularly in European banking, to provide companies with more flexible financing by means of loan facilities. Drawing down (usually with a minimum limit on any one drawing) can be allowed at any time given a little notice, repayment is flexible, and subsequent redrawing may possibly be allowed, but the borrower will be charged for this flexibility by a *commitment commission* payable on any unused portion of the facility for as long as the facility is left open. Facilities giving this flexibility are called *revolving*, and can be single or *multi-currency*.

Banks can also provide *multi-option* facilities, where companies have the option of borrowing in a variety of financial instruments; they are usually backed up by a committed standby facility, for which companies pay an underwriting fee.

SWAPS

Companies have traditionally borrowed in foreign currencies to help finance overseas investment and reduce exposure to currency risk.

This still holds true, but the suspension of UK exchange controls in 1979 has led to total mobility of capital. This, and the increasing sophistication of the financial markets, has led to the development of a wide range of financial instruments to hedge against both currency and interest rate risk. It no longer follows that you borrow French francs long term at fixed rates of interest to finance long-term investment in France; it may be advantageous to borrow variable rate in sterling and do a currency swap and an interest rate swap.

Currency swaps

A currency swap is, in effect, the same as a *reciprocating* or *back-to-back* loan: the company borrows foreign currency for a given period and, in the same transaction, lends an equivalent amount of sterling for the same period.

For example, a UK company wants to borrow US dollars, but also wants to avoid the currency risk on the principal amount borrowed, i.e. it wants to hedge the currency risk. So it raises, say, £100 million by a 7-year 10% Eurobond issue and swaps it for 7 years with a bank for say $160 million at 7½%. During the 7 years the company pays interest to the bank in dollars at 7½% per annum on the $160 million and the bank pays interest to the company in sterling at 10% per annum on the £100 million. At the end of the 7 years the swap is reversed, so the company gets its £100 million back regardless of the sterling/US$ exchange rate and in time to redeem the Eurobond issue.

Currency swaps normally appear in a note to the accounts, e.g. BRITISH PETROLEUM:

BRITISH PETROLEUM *Note to the 1988 accounts*

Finance debt

. . .

Borrowings which are swapped into currencies other than the original currencies of denomination are recorded as liabilities in the currencies under the swap agreements.

Interest rate swaps

An interest rate swap can be used by a company to protect itself against the impact of adverse fluctuations in interest rates on the interest charge it has to pay on its floating rate debt. The company agrees a fixed rate with bank on a nominal sum for a given period; the company then pays the bank the fixed rate and the bank pays the company the floating rate. For example ALLIED LYONS report in 1989; see next column.

ALLIED LYONS *Note to the accounts*

Loan capital and other borrowings

. . .

There are interest exchange agreements which fix the rate of interest at between 7% and 8.1% on US$155 million for periods of up to four years, at approximately $8\frac{1}{2}\%$ on C$60 million for three years, at $9\frac{1}{2}\%$ on £50 million for eight years, at between 5.1% and 6.9% on guilders 180m. and at 8.3% on ECU 30m. for periods up to nine years.

When used in conjunction with a currency swap, it enables a company to lock in at a fixed rate of interest in one currency to cover floating rate interest charges in another currency.

Companies may also use interest rate swaps in the reverse direction to reduce the proportion of their fixed-rate interest charges (e.g. if they take the view that interest rates will fall). In neither case is there any transfer of principal (capital).

The swap market has grown in recent years for another reason: to exploit the differences that exist between the fixed rate and the extremely competitive floating rate credit markets in order to reduce the cost of borrowing, as illustrated in Example 10.2:

Example 10.2   Use of swaps to reduce the cost of borrowing

Two companies both want to borrow money for five years. One has a AAA Standard & Poor's credit rating and wants to borrow floating rate, while the other, rated BBB, wants to borrow fixed. Market conditions are:

Company rating	AAA	BBB
Cost of 5-year fixed rate bond	10%	$11\frac{1}{2}\%$
Cost of 5-year bank loan	LIBOR $+\frac{1}{8}\%$	LIBOR $+\frac{5}{8}\%$
Cost of a swap:		
Company pays:	LIBOR	$10\frac{1}{2}\%$
Company receives:	$10\frac{3}{8}\%$	LIBOR

The AAA company, wanting to borrow floating, would issue 5-year bonds at 10% and swap; cost of borrowing floating $= 10\% + \text{LIBOR} - 10\frac{3}{8}\% = \text{LIBOR} - \frac{3}{8}\%$ compared with the 5-year bank loan's cost of LIBOR $+\frac{1}{8}\%$.

Similarly the BBB company, wanting to borrow at a fixed rate, would take out a bank loan at LIBOR $+\frac{5}{8}\%$ and swap; cost of borrowing fixed $= \text{LIBOR} + \frac{5}{8} - \text{LIBOR} + 10\frac{1}{2}\% = 11\frac{1}{8}\%$, which is cheaper than issuing bonds at $11\frac{1}{2}\%$.

BILLS OF EXCHANGE

Definition

A bill of exchange is, briefly, an order in writing from one person (the *drawer*) to another (the *drawee*) requiring the drawee to pay a specified sum of money on a given date. When the drawee signs the bill he becomes the *acceptor* of the bill, and the person to whom the money is to be paid is the *payee*.

The main legislation on bills is contained in the Bills of Exchange Act 1882, and their use in practice is clearly and concisely described in a book, *The Bill on London*, produced by Gillett Brothers, one of the discount houses.

Purpose

The primary purpose of a bill of exchange is to finance the sale of goods when the seller or exporter wishes to obtain payment at the time the goods are despatched and the buyer or importer wants to defer payment until the goods reach him, or later.

In these circumstances A, the supplier of goods to B, would draw a bill of exchange for the goods, which B 'accepts', acknowledging the debt and promising payment at some future date, normally three months ahead. Bills of this type are called *trade bills*.

A can then sell the bill to a third party, C, at a discount to the face value of the bill; and C in turn can endorse it and sell it on to D. In this case if B subsequently defaults, D can claim payment from A, and if A also defaults D can then claim on C.

Alternatively A can retain the bill, which gives a legal right to payment at a given date in the future (the date of maturity), or the bill can be deposited at a bank as a security against borrowings.

Presentation in the balance sheet

If Company A's year ends before the bill has reached maturity, then:

(a) if A still holds the bill, it would be included in debtors; *or*
(b) if A has discounted the bill, it would not appear in the balance sheet, but should be shown as a contingent liability, in case B subsequently defaults on payment.

In Company B's balance sheet the outstanding bill would be shown under creditors as a *bill of exchange payable*.

Discounting

When a bill of exchange is discounted, i.e. sold to a third party at a discount to its face value, this is usually done through one of the discount houses, which will trade it in the money market. The discount on a trade bill depends on prevailing interest rates, on the creditworthiness of the drawer, the acceptor and any subsequent endorsers, and on the nature of the underlying transaction. In the case of a *bank bill*, that is one where a bank is the acceptor of the bill, or has endorsed it, the discount rate will be less than on a trade bill. The finest rates are obtained in discounting bills drawn against exports or imports and accepted by 'eligible banks' (i.e. those banks whose acceptances are eligible for rediscount at the Bank of England.

Acceptance credits

Many eligible banks specialise in accepting bills for customers. They provide this type of short-term finance by granting the client an acceptance credit facility up to a given limit for an agreed period, and the client can then draw bills of exchange on the bank as he wishes, provided the running total of bills outstanding does not exceed the prescribed limit (in other words, it is a revolving credit facility). The bank 'accepts' the bills, which can then be discounted in the money market at the finest rate, and the customer receives the proceeds of the sale, less the acceptance commission he has to pay to the accepting house (normally between $\frac{3}{8}\%$ and $\frac{1}{2}\%$ p.a. for good-quality borrowers). When the bill falls due for payment (usually three months later), the customer pays the bank the full face value of the bill and the bank in turn honours the bill when it is presented by the eventual purchaser. The bank has to honour the bill even if the customer defaults, because it had 'accepted' responsibility for meeting the bill when it fell due.

The acceptance of bills by banks is related to commercial transactions, either specifically matched or linked to the general volume of business, so that the bills are self-liquidating.

Unlike an overdraft, the interest on discounted bills is paid *in advance* by the deduction of discount charges from the face value of the bill and, in addition, if the bills have been accepted by a bank, the company will also have to pay the acceptance commission in advance. In spite of these extra costs, variations of interest rates often make the use of acceptance credit facilities cheaper than an overdraft or a bank loan.

Acceptance credits in the balance sheet
The future obligation of a company to provide cash cover to meet bills that have yet to mature under an acceptance credit facility must, if material, be shown separately in a company's balance sheet under creditors as 'Bills of exchange payable' (CA 1985, Sch. 4 formats), as illustrated here:

LONDON INTERNATIONAL GROUP *Note on other creditors*

	1988 £000	1987 £000
Amounts falling due within one year:		
Trade creditors	45,624	25,802
Bills of exchange payable	156	320
Taxation on profits . . .		

Points for analysts to watch on bills

The discounting of bills is a traditional method of providing finance for many businesses, particularly importers and exporters, and acceptance credits are a standard form of short-term finance available to companies, so there is nothing inherently wrong with finding 'bills payable' or 'bills receivable' in a company's accounts, but a sharp change in the amounts involved can be a symptom of cash shortage:

Bills payable
If bills are not normally used by the company or in the particular trade, or if there is a marked increase in the total involved, the company may be resorting to the use of bills in lieu of cash to satisfy creditors.

Bills receivable
A drop from normal levels in bills receivable is also of interest: the company may be discounting bills (selling them at a discount in advance of their maturity date) to obtain cash in order to ease liquidity problems.

Chapter 11

CREDITORS, PROVISIONS AND CONTINGENT LIABILITIES

(References: SSAP 18 *Accounting for Contingencies*; SSAP 21 *Accounting for Leases and Hire Purchase Contracts*.)

Creditors

The two balance sheet formats in Schedule 4 of the Companies Act 1985 present creditors in different ways:

Format 1 shows them under two headings, *Creditors: amounts falling due within one year* and *Creditors: amounts falling due after more than one year;*

Format 2 shows them under a single heading, *Creditors*, in which case the amounts falling due within one year must be shown separately for each item and in aggregate.

Most companies use Format 1, which nets out *Creditors falling due within one year* (also known as Current liabilities), against *Current assets* to produce Net current assets (liabilities). For example:

Types of creditor

The following items are required to be shown, if material:

(a) debenture loans (see Chapter 5);
(b) bank loans and overdrafts (see Chapter 10);
(c) payments received on account;
(d) trade creditors;
(e) bills of exchange payable (see Chapter 10);
(f) amounts owed to group undertakings;
(g) amounts owed to undertakings in which the company has a participating interest;
(h) other creditors, including taxation and social security;
(i) accruals and deferred income.

Details of types of creditor are usually given in notes to the balance sheet, rather than in the balance sheet itself. For example:

LUCAS *Balance sheet*

	Notes	1989 £m	1988 £m
Fixed assets . . .		677.0	499.1
Current assets . . .		1,115.8	937.2
Creditors falling due within one year	14	(630.7)	(500.1)
Net current assets		485.1	437.1
Total assets less current liabilities		1,162.1	936.2
Creditors falling due beyond one year	15	(246.3)	(162.4)
Provisions for liabilities and charges		(95.4)	(96.2)
		820.4	677.6

LUCAS *Notes to the balance sheet*

Note 14   Creditors: due within one year

	1989 £m	1988 £m
Bank loans and overdrafts	77.7	64.1
Trade creditors	239.1	200.5
Finance lease obligations	8.9	10.4
Bills of exchange payable	31.9	20.3
Corporate taxation	27.9	23.5
Social security and other taxes	53.3	45.7
Accruals and deferred income	161.2	110.4
Proposed final dividends	30.7	25.2
	630.7	500.1

Note 15   Creditors: due beyond one year

Bank loans	38.4	57.8
Loans other than from banks	162.7	61.4
Finance lease obligations	33.0	33.5

Trade creditors	0.2	0.2
Accruals and deferred income	12.0	9.5
	246.3	162.4

Payments received on account
These arise where a customer is asked as a sign of good faith to deposit money in respect of a contemplated purchase. If the purchase goes through, the deposit becomes a part payment and ceases to be a creditor. Should the sale not be consummated, the deposit would normally be returned, though it could conceivably be forfeited in certain circumstances.

Trade creditors
Trade creditors are people who are owed money for *goods* supplied. The size of trade creditors shows the extent to which suppliers are financing a company's business.

Other creditors including taxation and social security
Taxation and social security are each shown separately. Taxation due within 12 months will normally include one year's mainstream Corporation Tax (see Chapter 13), ACT on any dividends recently paid, ACT on any proposed dividends, and any foreign tax due.

Accruals and deferred income
An *accrual* is an apportionment of a known or determinable future liability in respect of a service already partly received. Thus, a business paying rent of £60,000 half-yearly in arrears on 30 June and 31 December would, if it had an accounting year ending 30 November, show an accrual of £50,000 (the five months' rent from 1 July to 30 November unpaid at the end of its accounting year). *Deferred income* is money received by or due to the company but not yet earned.

The following items may also appear under creditors:

Other types of borrowing
These include bonds, loan notes and commercial paper (see Chapter 5).

Dividends proposed
Under Section 8 of the Companies Act 1989, the directors' report must state any amount which the directors recommend be paid by way of dividend. Although the company cannot, in law, pay these proposed dividends until they have been approved at the annual general meeting, companies always show them as a liability.

Deposits
In addition to deposits in respect of a contemplated purchase (included under *payments received on account*), deposits may have been charged where goods have been despatched in containers, drums, barrels or boxes, to ensure their return. The container, etc., remains part of the stock of the despatching company, until it becomes apparent that it will not be returned, e.g. when the return period has elapsed, when it will be treated as having been sold.

In financial companies, where deposits are a major item, representing money deposited to earn interest, deposits are shown as a separate heading.

Provisions

A 'provision' (as defined by CA 1985, Sch. 4, paras 88 and 89) is either:

(a) any amount written off by way of providing for depreciation or diminution in the value of assets (the amount would normally be deducted from the value of the assets, rather than being shown separately); *or*

(b) any amount retained to provide for any liability or loss which is *either* likely to be incurred, *or* certain to be incurred but uncertain as to the amount or as to the date on which it will arise.

Provisions for liabilities and charges
Under this heading are shown provisions for:

(a) pensions and similar obligations, see page 78.
(b) taxation, including deferred taxation; *and*
(c) other provisions.

Pension schemes can be either funded (contributions paid away to separate funds, see page 79), or unfunded.

In an unfunded scheme, which is the norm in some foreign countries, the company makes a provision for future liabilities in its accounts, e.g. GLAXO:

GLAXO *Note on provisions for liabilities and charges*

	Pensions and similar obligations £m	Deferred taxation £m	Other provisions £m	Total £m
At 1 July 1988	22	33	24	79
Exchange adjustments	1	1	1	3
Applied	(2)	—	(4)	(6)
Charge for the year	5	19	1	25
At 30 June 1989	26	53	22	101

Particulars should also be given of any pension commitments for which no provision has been made (CA 1985, Sch. 4, para. 50(4)(b)).

The item taxation will normally only include deferred taxation (see page 86), as other taxation will be shown under creditors, unless the amount is uncertain.

Other provisions may include provisions for deferred repairs or deferred maintenance with a view to equalising the charge against profits from year to year. For example, the balance sheet of claymining company WATTS, BLAKE, BEARNE makes a provision for 'Deferred revenue expenditure' for repairs and over-burden removal.

Contingent liabilities

A contingent liability is a potential liability which had not materialised by the date of the balance sheet. By their nature, contingent liabilities are insufficiently concrete to warrant specific provision being made for them in the accounts, and none is in fact made.

However, under the Fourth Schedule of the Companies Act 1985 a company must show by way of note or otherwise:

(*a*) any arrears of cumulative dividends (para. 49);

(*b*) particulars of any charge on the assets of the company to secure the liabilities of any other person, including, where practicable, the amount secured (para. 50 (1));

(*c*) the legal nature of any other contingent liabilities not provided for, the estimated amount of those liabilities, and any security given (para. 50 (2)).

Examples of contingent liabilities include:

(*a*) bills of exchange discounted with bankers;

(*b*) guarantees given to banks and other parties;

(*c*) potential liabilities on claims (whether by court action or otherwise);

(*d*) goods sold under warranty or guarantee;

(*e*) any uncalled liability on shares held as investments (i.e. the unpaid portion of partly paid shares held).

The extract below from the accounts of PORTALS HOLDINGS will serve to illustrate this. Note that:

(*a*) Contingencies frequently arise in respect of an acquisition as the result of an 'earn-out', where part of the consideration is based on future profits.

(*b*) Parent companies often guarantee the borrowings of their subsidiaries, but these borrowings appear in the group accounts as part of the debt of the group.

PORTALS HOLDINGS *Note to the 1988 accounts*

Contingent Liabilities and Guarantees

There is a contingency in respect of further consideration associated with the acquisition of subsidiaries dependent on the results of the subsidiaries for the 2 years to 31 July 1989. This is estimated to amount to not more than £2,760,000.

The holding company has guaranteed the overdrafts and loans of certain subsidiaries up to a maximum of £21,890,000 (1987 £27,227,000). The holding company has also guaranteed contract bonding on behalf of certain subsidiaries amounting at 31 December 1988, to £23,773,000 (1987 £23,042,000).

The Group has entered into recourse liabilities under export credit arrangements amounting at 31 December 1988 to £36,631,000 (1987 £30,635,000). There are also contingent liabilities in respect of guarantees as to plants installed or under construction and engagements in the ordinary course of business. No security has been given for any contingent liability. No contingent liability is expected to result in any material financial loss.

Court actions

There is some reluctance in the United Kingdom to disclose potential liability in actions before the court, though this is normal practice in the United States and is becoming more common in the United Kingdom. The note from T & N's accounts illustrated here is an example of this.

T & N *Note to the 1988 accounts*

The Company and certain subsidiaries are among many companies named as defendants in a large number of court actions concerned with alleged asbestos-related diseases in the USA and are among a number of defendants to claims in the UK from employees and former employees. Because of the slow onset of these diseases, the directors expect that similar claims will be made in future years but the expenditure which may arise from such claims cannot be determined. Provision will continue to be made in respect of the estimated cost of meeting claims notified and outstanding at each accounting date.

The significance of contingent liabilities
In many cases notes on contingent liabilities are of no real significance, for no liability is expected to arise, and none does. Occasionally, however, they are very important indeed, and points to watch for are a sharp rise in the total sums involved, and liabilities that may arise outside the normal course of business: to guarantee the liabilities of someone, or some company, over which one has no control entails undue risk, and guaranteeing the borrowings of associated undertakings or joint ventures may also be dangerous.

In particular, experience suggests that any contingent liability in respect of a subsidiary that has been disposed of can be extremely dangerous. For example, when COLOROLL took over JOHN CROWTHER it accepted more than £20 million of contingent liabilities in order to help the MBO of Crowther's clothing interests, which it wanted to get rid of quickly:

COLOROLL *Note to the accounts*

Contingent liabilities

At 31 March 1989 the group had contingent liabilities in connection with the following matters:

(a) the sale with recourse of £7,500,000 of redeemable preference shares and £14,250,000 senior and subordinated loan notes in RESPONSE GROUP LIMITED which were received as part consideration for the sale of the clothing interests of JOHN CROWTHER GROUP PLC;
(b) the guarantee of borrowings and other bank facilities of . . .

In February 1990 the RESPONSE GROUP called in the receivers! and COLOROLL followed four months later!

Capital commitments

Schedule 4, para. 50 (3) of the Companies Act 1985 requires that, where practicable, the aggregate amounts or estimated amounts, if they are material, of:

(*a*) contracts for capital expenditure (not already provided for) *and*
(*b*) capital expenditure authorised by the directors, which has not been contracted for,

be shown by way of note, as the extract below from OCEAN TRANSPORT & TRADING shows.

Such a note provides *some* indication of the extent to which the directors plan to expand (or replace) the facilities of the group, and thus of the potential call upon its cash resources. It should be read in conjunction with the directors' report and chairman's statement and any press announcements by the company, but it is not a particularly reliable guide to cash flows unless it gives some information on timing. It is impossible to tell from the note below how long the various ships to which OCEAN is committed will take to build, or when payments will fall due.

Other financial commitments

The Companies Act 1985 requires particulars to be given of any other financial commitments which have not been provided for and which are relevant to assessing the company's state of affairs

OCEAN TRANSPORT & TRADING *Note on capital commitments, 1988 accounts*

Capital commitments

	£m Group	
	1988	1987
Capital expenditure for which contracts have been placed but which is not otherwise provided for in these accounts	4.0	5.4
Capital expenditure authorised by the Directors but for which contracts had not been placed at the balance sheet date	8.4	3.9

(Sch. 4, para. 50 (5)). This requirement covers such things as leasing commitments, where the sums involved can be very large indeed, as illustrated by ROYAL DUTCH/SHELL's note on leasing arrangements, shown here.

ROYAL DUTCH/SHELL *Note to the 1988 accounts*

Leasing arrangements

The future minimum lease payments under operating leases that have initial or remaining terms in excess of one year, and under capital leases, together with the present value of the net minimum lease payments at 31 December 1988, were as follows:

	Operating leases	Capital leases
	£ million	
1989	392	75
1990	256	67
1991	222	60
1992	194	57
1993	170	35
1994 and after	1,257	148
Total minimum lease payments	2,491	442

. . .

The note distinguishes between operating leases and capital (finance) leases, which are explained below.

Leases

SSAP 21, *Accounting for leases and hire purchase contracts*, published in August 1984, divides leases into two types, *finance* leases and *operating* leases, and requires quite different accounting treatment for each type. A *finance* lease is defined as a lease which transfers substantially all the risks and rewards of ownership of an asset to the *lessee*. All other leases are *operating* leases.

Finance leases: the lessee

Prior to SSAP 21 a company could enter into a finance lease instead of borrowing the money to purchase an asset, and neither the asset nor the commitment to pay leasing charges would appear in the balance sheet. This was known as 'off-balance-sheet financing', which produced 'hidden gearing', as the company had effectively geared itself up just as much as if it had borrowed the money to purchase the asset, except that it had to pay leasing charges rather than paying interest and bearing depreciation charges.

SSAP 21 requires a finance lease to be recorded in the balance sheet of the lessee as an asset and as an obligation to pay future rentals. The initial sum

to be recorded both as an asset and as a liability is the present value of the minimum lease payments, which is derived by discounting them at the interest rate implicit in the lease. The method of accounting is illustrated in Example 11.1.

Example 11.1 Accounting for a finance lease

A company acquires a small computer system on a finance lease. Lease payments are £10,000 p.a. for five years, with an option to continue the lease for a further five years at £1,000 p.a. Payments are made annually in advance, i.e. the first payment is made on taking delivery of the computer. The interest rate implicit in the lease is 10%, and the estimated useful life of the system is five years.

The *present value* of the minimum lease payments discounted at 10% p.a. can be calculated using figures from the table *Present value of 1 in* n *years' time* in Appendix 2:

Payment date	Present value of 1 (from table)	Present value of £10,000 payment
On delivery	1.0	£10,000
In 1 year	0.909	9,090
In 2 years	0.826	8,260
In 3 years	0.751	7,510
In 4 years	0.683	6,830
Present value of minimum lease payments		£41,690

The computer system will thus be recorded as an asset of £41,690 and the liability for future rental payments will also be recorded as £41,690. After the first year:

(a) the asset will be depreciated over the shorter of the lease term (the initial period plus any further option period, i.e. a total of ten years in this case), and its expected useful life (five years). Annual depreciation charge on a straight line basis is therefore one-fifth of £41,690 = £8,338, reducing the asset value to £33,352.

(b) the present value of the remaining minimum lease payments is recomputed. There is no longer a payment due in four years' time (£6,830 in our table above), so the present value of future payments is now £41,690 − 6,830 = £34,860. £6,830 is deducted from the future liability and the remaining £3,170 of the £10,000 payment made on delivery is shown as interest paid.

These calculations would then be repeated each subsequent year:

End of year	Balance sheet		P & L account	
	Asset value	Remaining payments	Interest charge	Depreciation charge
1	£33,352	£34,860	£3,170	£8,338
2	25,014	27,350	2,490	8,338
3	16,676	19,090	1,740	8,338
4	8,338	10,000	910	8,338
5	Nil	Nil	Nil	8,338

Finance leases: the lessor

In the past the practice of 'front-ending', taking a high proportion of the profits on a lease in the first year, has got a number of companies into serious difficulties, e.g. SOUND DIFFUSION, which went into liquidation primarily as a result of taking 60% of profits on leasing electrical equipment – telephone switchboards, fire-alarm and public-address systems – in the first year.

Under SSAP 21, front-ending is not allowed. The amount due under a finance lease should be recorded as a debtor at the net investment after provisions for bad and doubtful rentals etc., and the earnings in each period should be allocated to give a constant rate of return on the lessor's net investment (SSAP 21, paras. 38 and 39).

Operating leases

An operating lease is normally for a period substantially shorter than the expected useful life of an asset; i.e. the *lessor* retains most of the risks and rewards of ownership.

Under an operating lease the lease rentals are simply charged in the profit and loss account of the lessee as they arise. Leased assets and the liability for future payments do not appear in the balance sheet, even though companies can enter into operating leases of several years' length, as the extract from ROYAL DUTCH/SHELL's accounts illustrated opposite.

71

Chapter 12

TURNOVER, TRADING PROFIT AND PRE-TAX PROFIT

INTRODUCTION

As described briefly in Chapter 1, the profit and loss account, sometimes referred to as the revenue account, is a score-card of how the company has done over the last year (or whatever period is being reported on). It can conveniently be divided into three parts:

(a) how the profit (or loss) was earned;
(b) how much was taken by taxation;
(c) what happened to the profit (or loss) that was left after taxation.

This chapter covers the first part, and the next two chapters will cover the second and third parts.

How the profit was earned

The Companies Act 1985 offers the company the choice of four profit and loss account formats. Formats 1 and 2, shown in Examples 12.1 and 12.2, start with sales invoiced (turnover) and deduct operating costs to produce trading profit; they then add other income and deduct other charges to reach pre-tax profits. Formats 3 and 4, which are rarely used by listed companies, show charges and income separately, and are effectively two-sided versions of Formats 1 and 2.

The difference between Format 1 and Format 2 is the way they show operating costs. *Format 1* breaks down operating costs by function into:

Cost of sales (which will include all costs of production, such as factory wages, materials and manufacturing overheads, including depreciation of machinery)
Distribution costs (costs incurred in getting the goods to the customer)
Administrative expenses (e.g. office expenses, directors' and auditors' fees).

Format 2, on the other hand, breaks down operating costs by their nature:

Raw materials and consumables
Staff costs
    Wages and salaries
    Social security costs
    Other pension costs
Depreciation and other amounts written off fixed assets
Other external charges
Change in stock of finished goods and work in progress.

Example 12.1   Profit and loss account: Format 1

	£000	£000
Turnover		7,200
Cost of sales		3,600
Gross profit (or loss)		3,600
Distribution costs	1,100	
Administrative expenses	900	
		2,000
		1,600
Other operating income		50
[Trading profit]		1,650
Income from interests in associated undertakings		30
Income from other participating interests		10
Income from other fixed asset investments		5
Other interest receivable		120
		1,815
Amounts written off investments	15	
Interest payable	600	
		615
[Pre-tax profit on ordinary activities]		1,200

In Examples 12.1 and 12.2:

(*a*) the items in square brackets, 'Trading profit' and 'Pre-tax profit', have been included because they are important to the analyst, although they do not appear in the formats in Schedule 4 of the Companies Act 1985;

(*b*) the item 'Income from shares in group companies', which would appear in the profit and loss account of the holding company of a group, has been omitted because the profit and loss account of a holding company is seldom if ever published (see Chapter 16);

(*c*) associated undertakings and participating interests, and their contribution to the profit and loss account, are described in Chapter 17.

Example 12.2   Profit and loss account: Format 2

	£000	£000
Turnover		7,200
Changes in stocks of finished goods and work in progress		160
Other operating income		50
		7,410
Raw materials and consumables	1,700	
Other external charges	1,120	
Staff costs		
Wages and salaries	2,050	
Social security costs	300	
Other pension costs	120	
Depreciation and other amounts written off tangible and intangible fixed assets	400	
Other operating charges	70	
		5,760
[Trading profit]		1,650
Income from interest in associated undertakings		30
Income from other participating interests		10
Income from other fixed asset investments		5
Other interest receivable		120
		1,815
Amounts written off investments	15	
Interest payable	600	
		615
[Pre-tax profit on ordinary activities]		1,200

The formats reflect the increased disclosure requirements of the EEC Fourth Directive, as a result of which the information gap which formerly existed in UK accounts between turnover and profit has disappeared. In the past some companies included value added statements in their accounts to fill the gap, but they are now becoming increasingly rare.

Most retailers follow Format 1; manufacturing companies are divided fairly evenly between Formats 1 and 2, while some use a combination of both. For example, UNILEVER shows cost of sales, distribution and selling costs, and administrative expenses (i.e. Format 1) in the profit and loss account, and then gives a detailed breakdown of staff costs, raw materials and packaging, depreciation, etc. (i.e. Format 2) in a note.

Effect of accounting policies on profitability

Before going on to discuss individual components, it is worth noting three important points of interaction between the profit and loss account and the balance sheet, where abnormal accounting policies can materially alter the reported profits:

1. *Valuation of stock* The higher the value at the end of the period, the lower the cost of goods sold and the higher the profits.

2. *Depreciation* The lower the charge for depreciation in a particular year, the higher the book value of fixed assets carried forward and the higher the profits. For example, in 1988 CHRISTIAN SALVESEN reported a change in its depreciation policy:

CHRISTIAN SALVESEN *Note on trading profit*

Depreciation rates on cold-store buildings and related machinery and equipment have been changed to reflect more accurately their useful economic life. The effect on the year to 31 March 1988 is to increase the profits by £4.3m.. The impact of this change on 1987 would have been £3.9m.

Although the change was mentioned in the Chairman's statement and its effect was given in the note, the profit and loss account, read in isolation, was very misleading, as the 1987 figures had *not* been adjusted. Without the change, the pre-tax profits for 1988 would only have been up a tiny £0.3 million on the previous year's £42.0 million, rather than up a respectable £4.6 million.

3. *Capitalising expenditure* All expenditure incurred by a company must either add to the value of

the assets in the balance sheet or be charged in the profit and loss account. In the sense that it would otherwise be a charge against profits, any amount that can be capitalised will increase profits directly by the amount capitalised at the expense of the profits in future years, when increased capital values will require increased depreciation. Items which are sometimes capitalised include:

(a) research and development;
(b) interest;
(c) starting-up costs.

Research and development

Under SSAP 13, the standard accounting practice on research and development, all expenditure on research and development should normally be written off in the year in which it is incurred. However, where development is for clearly defined projects on which expenditure is separately identifiable and for which commercial success is reasonably certain, companies may if they wish defer charging development expenditure 'to the extent that its recovery can reasonably be regarded as assured'. Capitalised development expenditure should be separately disclosed.

Interest

Capitalising interest on a project during construction is a normal and reasonable practice provided interest is not capitalised outside the planned timescale of the project. It would be reasonable, for example, to capitalise interest on a new refinery while it was being built, but not on the cost of the site before work had begun (it might lie undeveloped for years), nor on the overall cost once the refinery was completed but hadn't been put into production because demand for the product had slumped. For example, LADBROKE GROUP's accounting policies on interest charges are as follows:

(a) Interest accruing on certain hotel and retail development expenditure to the date of commencement of trading is capitalised.
(b) Interest accruing on investment and development properties before full letting is capitalised to the extent that it exceeds income receivable, and provided that the capital value of each individual property does not thereby exceed its market value. Once fully let and income earning, all income and charges are taken through the profit and loss account.

Policy (a) is prudent, but policy (b) could raise difficulties if properties remain unlet, or only partially let with income falling short of interest payments. Interest is then capitalised up to 'market value', but market values are very much a matter of subjective judgement, and can fall disastrously, as many property companies discovered in the big shake-out in 1973/74.

Where capital is borrowed to finance the production of fixed and/or current assets, the Companies Act 1985 allows the interest charge incurred during the period of production to be included in the value of the assets, but if it is included, the amount must be separately disclosed (Sch. 4, para. 26 (3)). The annual accounts must state the amount of interest capitalised during the year (*Admission of Securities to Listing*, Section 5, Chapter 2, para. 21(g)). For example it is SAINSBURY's policy to capitalise interest on borrowings to finance specific property developments, and their 1989 accounts showed:

J SAINSBURY *Note to 1989 accounts*

Tangible fixed assets

. . .

The amount included in additions in respect of interest capitalised during the year amounted to £21.7 million after deducting tax relief of £11.3 million.

Starting-up costs

The starting-up costs of a new factory, including the costs of removal from old premises, the initial losses of a new unit (e.g. a hotel or supermarket), and the advertising, promotional and other expenses of launching a new product, should normally all be charged to revenue as they are incurred.

Where a company capitalises starting-up costs it may be expanding faster than is prudent, and if the new project fails to live up to expectations the company could run into serious trouble. SOCK SHOP provides a good example; the accounts for 17 months to 28 February 1989 showed:

SOCK SHOP *Extracts from the accounts*

Accounting policies

Overseas subsidiary set-up costs

Costs incurred in establishing overseas operations in the first year are capitalised as intangible assets and amortised over 4 years on a straight-line basis commencing at the end of the first year.

Intangible assets

	£000
Overseas subsidiary set-up costs	
At beginning of period	—
Additions	354
At end of period	354

The capitalising of £354,000 was not, in itself, significant; it only represented 8% of reported pre-tax profits of £4.32 million, but the overseas expansion proved disastrous: less than a year later the company reported an interim loss of £3.97 million and heavy write-offs on the closure of 17 loss-making US outlets and went into receivership in 1990.

Consequences of abnormal accounting policies

If a company does overstate its profits in the year being reported on, the assets carried forward in the balance sheet will make future profits harder to earn: the opening stock for next year will be the figure for this year's overvalued closing stock, underdepreciated plant will wear out before it has been written off, and capitalised expenditure will inflate capital values, thus reducing the apparent return on capital employed and increasing the provision for depreciation. (Understating liabilities also has the same effect: profits for the year are inflated, but the liability will catch up with the company later on.)

The company's accounting policies, which appear either as 'Note 1' to the accounts, or as a separate statement, should be read carefully to see if there are any unusual features that might affect the company's reported profits. The statement should also point out any changes to policies, and companies are required to report 'any material respects in which any items shown in the profit and loss account are affected by any change in the basis of accounting' (CA 1985, Sch. 9, para. 18(6)(b). Changes in accounting policies can have a dramatic effect on reported profits, as we showed in Chapter 6: CITYVISION, the video hire group, added almost 60% to its pre-tax profits in 1988 by doubling the estimated useful life of its tapes.

In contrast, in 1989 the property company REGENTCREST prudently changed its policy on capitalising interest on loans to fund developments to *exclude* interest accrued during the period in which a development was being planned. This added £2.969 million to the interest charged in the profit and loss account, reducing pre-tax profits to £1.540 million; without the change in the accounting policy the pre-tax profits would have been over £4 million!

Any changes that are not explained, or that increase profits without reasonable accounting justification, should be viewed with caution, and with downright suspicion when 'new and thrusting, management is involved.

We now turn to the individual items on the profit and loss accounts.

SALES (TURNOVER)

Statutory requirements

Companies are required by the standard formats of the Companies Act 1985 to disclose turnover (i.e. total sales) in their profit and loss account. Turnover is the amount derived from the provision of goods and services falling within the company's ordinary activities (after deduction of trade discounts and before adding VAT and other sales-based taxes). The following information must also be given:

1. If a company carried on *two or more classes of business* during the year which in the directors' opinion differ substantially from each other, it should describe the classes and show each one's turnover and pre-tax profit (Sch. 4, para. 55(1)).
2. If in the year a company supplied *geographical markets* which in the directors' opinion differ substantially, the amount of turnover attributable to each should be stated. (Sch. 4, para. 55(2)).

However this information need not be disclosed if, in the opinion of the directors, it would be seriously prejudicial to the interests of the company to do so, but the fact that it has not been disclosed must be stated (Sch. 4, para. 55(5)).

Stock Exchange requirements

The Stock Exchange's *Continuing Obligations* for listed companies require a listed company to circulate with the annual report of the directors a geographical analysis of turnover *and* of contribution to trading results of those trading operations carried on by the company (or group) outside the United Kingdom and Ireland. However, although companies are required to make shareholders 'aware of significant contributions derived from activities carried out in any one territory', 'No analysis of the contribution to trading results is required unless the contribution to profit and loss from a specific area is "abnormal" in nature'. (*Admission of Securities to Listing*, Section 5, Chapter 2, para. 21.2.)

Proposed accounting standard

ED 45 'Segmental Reporting' published in November 1988 proposes that turnover, pre-tax profits and capital employed should be shown for each class of business and for each geographical area, together with an analysis of inter-segment sales, if material.

Some companies, like REED (illustrated overleaf), already give some details of capital employed by segment.

REED INTERNATIONAL *Note to the 1989 accounts*

Segmentation

The business segment analysis has been revised to reflect the restructuring of the Group following divestment of its manufacturing activities and the additional investment in publishing and information businesses. The analysis has been expanded to include capital employed.

£ million	Turnover		Operating profit		Capital employed	
	1989	1988	1989	1988	1989	1988
Class of business						
Business publishing – Europe	278.0	246.0	56.5	33.4	93.7	62.5
Business publishing – USA	321.4	286.6	45.6	39.7	405.4	303.6
Books	323.7	211.4	47.7	29.9	495.7	354.8
Consumer publishing	327.5	281.3	36.1	26.9	134.2	43.4
Continuing activities	1,250.6	1,025.3	185.9	129.9	1,129.0	764.3
Reed Manufacturing Group	270.1	785.6	19.8	62.5		
North American Paper	78.7	186.9	16.4	39.5		
Others	29.2	134.9	(4.3)	11.7		
Discontinued activities	378.0	1,107.4	31.9	113.7		
Total	1,628.6	2,132.7	217.8	243.6		

Country of origin . . . ⎫
Geographical market . . . ⎬ (only Turnover shown)

Analysis of profitability

The analyst can do a good deal of work on a segmental table such as REED's, calculating various ratios, using them to compare performance between classes of business and seeing how they vary from year to year.

REED's table is particularly useful because it shows, at a glance, the group's dramatic shift away from manufacturing; discontinued activities account for over half the 1988 turnover.

Note should also be taken of the chairman's statement or chief executive's report as, in a good set of accounts, these will contain comment on the reasons for marked changes in profitability, and

may indicate future trends.

Looking at the continuing activities in REED's table, together with comments from the report:

(a) capital employed has increased by 47%; a note on acquisitions showed that over half this increase was publishing rights acquired;

(b) overall margins (operating profit ÷ turnover) rose from 12.7% in 1988 to 14.9% in 1989, although return on capital employed (ROCE) was down from 17.0% to 16.5% and there were considerable variations between classes of business, as this table on ratios shows:

REED *Ratios by class of business*

	Margins		ROCE	
	1989	1988	1989	1988
Business publishing – Europe	20.3%	13.6%	60.3%	53.4%
Business publishing – USA	14.2%	13.9%	11.3%	13.1%
Books	14.7%	14.2%	9.6%	8.4%
Consumer publishing	11.0%	9.6%	26.9%	62.0%
Overall	14.9%	12.7%	16.5%	17.0%

(c) the enormous disparity between the ROCE in business publishing in Europe and in the USA is due to the difference in the book cost of titles the group has largely built up itself in the UK and the book cost of titles that have been bought recently in the USA as part of REED's new strategy.

(d) the most striking change is that the ROCE on Consumer publishing has more than halved, and the capital employed has more than trebled.

The chief executive's review of operations explains why:

'IPC magazines added to the number and range of its titles very significantly, with the acquisition of Stanbrook, the integration of Carlton and a very active launch programme . . . efficiency has been increased by the reorganisation of the wholesale trade and by the development of enhanced computer systems . . . closure costs of a lossmaking Carlton title.'

Vigorous expansion and modernisation has clearly been expensive, particularly the cost of buying titles (£63.9 million spent in 1989 in Consumer publishing) and is likely to continue to be so while new titles become established and unsuccessful ones are weeded out in a highly competitive market. Similar combing through the report can be made to find the underlying factors in the other business segments.

But one word of warning on the use of ratios: where companies have made acquisitions during the year and have written off large amounts of goodwill immediately against reserves (as recommended by SSAP 22, currently under review), the ROCE will be distorted unless the amount of goodwill written off can be identified by business segment and added back to the capital in the calculations.

TRADING PROFIT

Trading profit does not appear in the formats in the Companies Act 1985, but we have included it because it enables the analyst to calculate two important ratios, Trading profit/Turnover and Trading profit/Capital employed (see Chapter 24).

In Format 1 we define trading profit as turnover *less*:

cost of sales
distribution costs
administrative expenses

plus other operating income.

In Format 2 it is turnover *less* all deductions up to and including other operating charges, *plus* other operating income (see Example 12.2).

As already explained, companies have the choice under the Companies Act 1985 of analysing expenditure (called in the formats themselves 'charges') functionally, i.e. as cost of sales, distribution costs and administrative expenses, or by its nature, e.g. raw materials and consumables, staff costs and so on. Staff costs include wages and salaries, social security costs and pension costs (Sch. 4, para. 94).

The Act does not define cost of sales, distribution costs or administrative expenses.

Cost of sales will represent:
cost of materials consumed;
production wages (both directly on the product or service and those of an overhead nature);
depreciation of production machinery;
production expenses (e.g. rent and rates, light and heat).

Distribution costs will include:
distribution wages (i.e. staff costs of the distribution function);
distribution materials (packaging, etc.);
distribution expenses (e.g. depreciation of motor vans, freight, insurance).

Administrative expenses apparently cover all items not already included in the cost of sales or in distribution costs, and which are not separately disclosed (e.g. as interest) elsewhere in the standard format.

Other operating income will include income from normal operations which does not fall under any other heading, e.g. royalties and rents received. Net income from *rents of land* must be shown separately if it forms a substantial part of a company's revenue (CA 1985, Sch. 4, para. 53(5)).

Disclosure of supplementary information – statutory requirements

Schedule 4 of the 1989 Companies Act requires that the following be shown separately in the profit and loss account or in the notes annexed:

1. *Chairman's emoluments* for each person acting as chairman during the year, unless the duties were wholly or mainly discharged outside the United Kingdom (para. 3).

2. *Directors' emoluments*: the aggregate amount of

emoluments including pension contributions, other benefits, and sums paid for accepting office as a director, i.e. 'golden hellos' (para. 1); the number of directors who fall into each band of £5,000, i.e., up to £5,000, between £5,001 and £10,000 and so on and the emoluments of the highest-paid director if more than the chairman but excluding directors whose duties were wholly or mainly discharged outside the UK (para. 4); the number of directors who have waived rights to receive emoluments and the aggregate amount waived (para. 6).

3. *Particulars of staff*: the average number employed during the year, and the aggregate amounts of their (a) wages and salaries, (b) social security costs, (c) other pension costs (CA 1985, Sch. 4, para. 56), see below.

4. *Auditors' remuneration* in their capacity as such, including expenses; remuneration for services other than those of auditors should be shown separately (CA 1989, s. 121). A sharp increase in the auditors' renumeration (i.e. more than merely keeping pace with inflation) may be an indication of difficulties; for example SOCK SHOP paid their auditors £60,000 for the 17 months ended 28 February 1989 compared with £10,000 for the previous year, and went into receivership in 1990.

5. *Hire of plant and machinery*: to be shown if material (CA 1985, Sch. 4, para. 53(6)). There are basically two types of hiring or leasing: the first is where equipment is hired on a temporary basis and can be returned when no longer required (an *operating lease*); the second type is where equipment is leased for its useful life (a *finance lease*, which has to be capitalised in the balance sheet, see Chapter 11). Some companies incur substantial hire charges on finance leases as part of a deliberate policy to reduce the amount of capital tied up in fixed assets and to take advantage of the favourable terms a lessor offers. The lessor is able to offer favourable terms on finance leases because he receives the benefit of the capital allowances on the assets leased, which help to defer his Corporation Tax liability (see Chapter 13).

However, extensive finance leasing may also reflect a shortage of cash – the company resorts to leasing to avoid the immediate capital outlay.

6. *Depreciation* and diminution in value of fixed assets (see Chapter 6). In Format 1 depreciation is not shown as a separate item, but in all formats the amount provided during the year will be found in the balance sheet note on fixed assets.

PENSION COSTS

(Reference: SSAP 24 *Accounting for pension costs*.)

Until the introduction of SSAP 24, accounts simply showed the contributions paid during the year as 'Other pension costs' in a note to the accounts. This practice of 'cash accounting', showing what the company had paid into its pension funds rather than accounting for the increase in pension liabilities that had accrued during the year, enabled companies whose pension funds showed a surplus on actuarial valuation to reduce their contribution, and thus increase their reported profits, at will.

For example, in 1986 LUCAS reported pre-tax profit of £95.2 million compared with £57.8 million in the previous year, an increase of 64.7%. However, the accounts also showed that following actuarial valuations, the charge for Other pension costs fell from £38.8 million to £8.4 million, which accounted for more than 80% of the increase in pre-tax profit.

SSAP 24 aims at making the employer 'recognise the expected cost of providing pensions on a systematic and rational basis' over the period of employment. Cash accounting is no longer permitted, and companies are required to disclose detailed information on their pension arrangements.

Types of pension scheme

Pension schemes can be either funded or unfunded.

In a funded scheme, the company's contributions (and the employees' contributions if it is a 'contributory' rather than a 'non-contributory' scheme) are paid away to be invested externally to meet future pension liabilities, and the assets of the scheme are held in trust outside the company.

In an unfunded scheme, which is the norm in some foreign countries, the company makes a provision for future liabilities in its accounts, e.g. LUCAS:

LUCAS *Note on provisions*

Provisions for liabilities and charges

	Overseas pension obligations £m	Discontinuing business segments £m	Other £m	Total £m
At 1 August 1988	10.1	50.5	35.6	96.2
Exchange adjustments	0.1	—	0.2	0.6
Acquisitions	—	—	17.2	17.2
Utilised or paid in the year	(0.6)	(35.6)	(12.5)	(48.7)
Charged in the year	2.0	11.1	17.0	30.1
At 31 July 1989	11.9	26.0	57.5	95.4

Pension schemes in the UK are funded. There are three types of scheme:

1. SERPS, the State Earnings-Related Pension Scheme. Companies pay the employer contribution and have no further liability.
2. Defined contribution schemes.
3. Defined benefit schemes.

Defined contribution schemes

In a defined contribution or 'money purchase' scheme, the employer has no obligation beyond payment of the contributions he has agreed to make. The benefits may vary with the performance of the investments purchased by the contributions, but this risk is borne by the employees.

The cost of providing pensions is thus straightforward: it is the amount of contribution due for the period, and will be charged against profits, e.g. TESCO:

TESCO *Note on pension commitments*

The group operates a defined benefit scheme for all full-time employees . . .

The group also operates a defined contribution pension scheme for part-time employees which was introduced on 6 April 1988. The assets of the scheme are held separately from those of the group, being invested with an insurance company. The pension cost represents contributions payable by the group to the insurance company and amounted to £1.6m. (1988 – £Nil). There were no material amounts outstanding to the insurance company at the year end.

Smaller companies tend to run this type of scheme, or to contribute to SERPS or to employees' own Personal Pension Plans, in order to avoid taking on any open-ended future commitment.

Defined benefit schemes

In a defined benefit or 'final salary' scheme, the pensions to be paid depend on the employees' pay, normally the pay in the final year of employment, so the employer's liability is open-ended.

Because of the complexities of estimating the contributions needed to provide for pensions based on wages or salaries often many years hence, consulting actuaries are used to carry out periodic valuations, usually every three years, and to determine the contribution rate required.

Where an actuarial valuation reveals a material deficiency or surplus in a defined benefit scheme, SSAP 24 requires that it should normally be taken into account by adjusting the current and future costs in the accounts over the remaining service lives of the current employees, or over the average life. See SSAP 24 paras. 81 to 83 for exceptions.

Where there are changes to the actuarial assumptions, or to the valuation method or to the benefits of the scheme, their effect on pension costs should also be spread over the remaining service lives or average life.

The disclosure requirements of SSAP 24 are very extensive. Items of particular interest to the analyst are:

(i) the accounting policy and, if different, the funding policy and any resulting provisions or prepayments;
(ii) the pension cost charge and the reasons for any significant change from the previous year;
(iii) details of the expected effects on future costs of any material changes in pension arrangements.

In the example overleaf, SMITHS INDUSTRIES gives the reason for lower pension costs (adopting SSAP 24), the surplus in the pension schemes (a prepayment of £4.3m.), and the way in which the surplus is being used (spread over approximately ten years), so pension costs are unlikely to vary significantly in the future, at least until the next actuarial valuation. Under the old system of cash accounting, SMITHS INDUSTRIES could have paid nothing for 1989, eliminating the prepayment and reducing the pension cost not from £5.1m. to £4.2m., but to zero. In addition, with an actuarial surplus of 42%, it could have also taken a pension fund 'holiday' for the following year or two.

SMITHS INDUSTRIES *Note on pension commitments*

Smiths Industries operates a number of pension schemes throughout the world. The major schemes are of the defined benefit type with assets held in separate trust administered accounts.

Total pension costs for 1988/89 were £4.2m. (1988 £5.1m.). The reason for lower costs was the introduction of an accounting policy conforming to Statement of Standard Accounting Practice No. 24.

Contributions to pension schemes are made on the advice of independent qualified actuaries . . . The latest actuarial assessments were as at 5 April 1989 . . . The most significant assumptions were:

Investment return	9% per annum
Salary inflation	7% ,,
Dividend growth	4½% ,,
Pension increase	4% ,,

The variation from regular cost, which recognises the excess of assets over liabilities in the pension schemes existing at the time of initially adopting the present accounting policy, has been spread over approximately 10 years, being the average remaining working life.

The company's defined benefit schemes had assets with a market value of £278m. The actuarial value of the scheme assets represented 142% of the liabilities for benefits that had accrued to members, allowing for expected future increases in salaries.

A prepayment of £4.3m. is included in debtors, this being the excess of the amount funded over the accumulated pension cost.

OTHER PRE-TAX ITEMS

Investment income

Statutory requirements

Companies must distinguish in their profit and loss account (or in the notes) between income from listed investments and that from unlisted investments (CA 1985, Sch. 4, para. 53(4)). Until 1967 it was necessary to distinguish between income from trade investments and other investments, and some companies continue to do this. A *trade investment* is an investment made for a trade reason, rather than purely as a means of earning income. It might, for example, be an investment in a supplier (to help the supplier, to obtain information, or to act as a lever in dealing with him), in a competitor, or in a customer.

Franked and unfranked income

Investment income may be *franked* (dividends paid by another UK company out of profits which have already borne UK Corporation Tax) or *unfranked* (received from a source that has not borne UK Corporation Tax, which includes almost all types of interest received and any dividends from overseas companies). Under SSAP 8, incoming dividends from UK resident companies should be included before tax in the profit and loss account at the amount of cash received or receivable plus the tax credit (see Chapter 13).

Interest paid

The cost of servicing (paying the interest on) all

debt is normally allowed to be deducted before profits are assessed for Corporation Tax.

The Companies Act 1985 (Sch. 4, para. 53(2)) requires the disclosure of the interest paid on bank loans and overdrafts, on loans repayable within five years and on other loans. Most companies show a single figure in their profit and loss account, giving details in a note which may include some netting out of interest received or other adjustments, as, for example, in the note from RTZ's accounts shown here.

RTZ *Note on interest payable*

Interest payable	£ million 1988	£ million 1987
Interest paid on borrowings by the Group:		
Loans not wholly repayable within 5 years	49.2	59.6
Loans wholly repayable within 5 years	16.6	10.7
Bank overdrafts	20.0	16.3
Short-term borrowings	4.2	0.5
	90.0	87.1
Less: Amount capitalised relating to projects during construction	13.5	14.3
	76.5	72.8

Profit before taxation

As shown in Examples 12.1 and 12.2, trading profit *plus* income from interests in associated undertakings and from other participating interests (see Chapter 17), *plus* income from other investments and other interest receivable, *less* interest payable and any amounts written off investments, leaves the profit before taxation, or 'pre-tax profits'.

Chapter 13

TAXATION

(References: SSAP 8 *Taxation under the Imputation System*; SSAP 15 *Accounting for Deferred Taxation.*)

INTRODUCTION

A UK resident company is liable to Corporation Tax on its income and capital gains, and has to pay Advance Corporation Tax (ACT) when it distributes dividends. If it has income taxable abroad, it will also suffer overseas tax. All this appears in the profit and loss account under the heading 'Taxation'.

VAT, Excise Duty, employee PAYE and other forms of taxation that the company may bear or be involved in are not normally shown, though some companies give details of government charges peculiar to their business (e.g. LADBROKE shows that its operating profit is stated after charging so much 'betting duties and levy').

Schedule 4 of the Companies Act 1985 requires taxation to be shown in *the profit and loss account* under three headings:

1. Tax on profit or loss from ordinary activities
2. Tax on extraordinary profit or loss
3. Other taxes not shown under the above

with notes giving details of the basis of computation, any special circumstances affecting the tax liability, and:

(*a*)   the amount of UK corporation tax,
(*b*)   the extent of double taxation relief,
(*c*)   the amount of UK income tax, *and*
(*d*)   the amount of foreign tax charged to revenue.

The notes may also include details of:

(*e*)   irrecoverable ACT
(*f*)   over/under provision for prior years' taxation
(*g*)   deferred taxation
(*h*)   tax credit on UK dividends received (i.e. on franked investment income)
(*i*)   taxation on share of profit of associated companies (see Chapter 17).

Items (*e*), (*g*) and (*h*) are required by SSAP 8.

TRAFALGAR HOUSE's profit and loss account illustrates a typical presentation of a fairly complex tax charge:

TRAFALGAR HOUSE *Extract from 1989 accounts*

Profit and loss account

	Notes	Year ended 30 September 1989 £m	Year ended 30 September 1988 £m
Profit on ordinary activities before taxation		270.4	229.1
Taxation	6	54.1	45.8

Note 6   Taxation

	1989 £m.	1988 £m.
The charge for taxation based on the net profit is arrived at as follows:		
UK corporation tax at 35% (1988 35%)	55.4	9.6
Less: Double taxation relief	(.9)	(.1)
	54.5	9.5
Advance corporation tax written back	(2.3)	(5.0)
Transfer from UK deferred taxation	(8.0)	33.5
Tax credit on franked investment income	.7	.4
Overseas tax	8.6	4.3
Associated companies	.6	1.4
Petroleum Revenue Tax	—	1.7
	54.1	45.8

The UK corporation tax charge for the year has been reduced because of accelerated depreciation, tax losses brought forward and the utilisation of provisions previously disallowed for tax purposes.

In the *balance sheet* taxation will appear as follows:

1. Under creditors falling due within one year: the amount falling due within one year will normally include one year's mainstream Corporation Tax, ACT on any dividends recently paid, ACT on any proposed dividends, and any foreign tax due.

2. Under provisions: any provision for deferred taxation and any provision for other taxation, shown separately (CA 1989, Sch. 1, para. 7).

3. Under assets: ACT paid and payable which has not yet been offset against the company's CT liability (unrelieved ACT is normally offset against deferred tax, and only occasionally appears separately as an asset).

Corporation Tax – the imputation system

Corporation Tax was introduced by the Finance Act 1965 and was subsequently modified from 1 April 1973 by the introduction of the imputation system.

Under the imputation system, whenever a

Example 13.1   Corporation Tax: different levels of dividend distribution

	No dividend £m	Some dividend £m	Maximum dividend £m
The profit and loss account would show:			
Pre-tax profits	600	600	600
Total Corporation Tax (35%)	210	210	210
	390	390	390
Dividends (net;)	Nil	195	390
	390	195	Nil
Retentions			
Other information:			
Net dividend per share	Nil	39p	78p
Associated tax credit (25/75ths)	Nil	13p	26p
Gross dividend equivalent	Nil	52p	104p
Government receives:	£m.	£m.	£m.
Advance Corporation Tax	Nil	65	130
Mainstream tax	210	145	80
Total tax	210	210	210

company pays dividends to shareholders, it is required to hand over to the Inland Revenue what is termed *Advance Corporation Tax* (ACT), which is, *in effect*, the basic rate of Income Tax ($x\%$) that would be payable on the dividends if they were grossed up at the basic rate.

The amount of ACT payable is thus a given fraction, $x/(100-x)$ of the dividend actually paid, where $x\%$ is the basic rate of Income Tax. For example, if the basic rate of Income Tax is 25%, ACT will be 25/75ths of the actual dividend paid. ACT serves two purposes:

1. It is a part payment of the company's Corporation Tax liability for the period in which the dividend is paid. (The remaining Corporation Tax payable is known as *mainstream Corporation Tax*.)
2. In addition, it is 'imputed' to the shareholder as a *tax credit* which exactly discharges the basic rate UK Income Tax liability on the dividend. So far as the tax inspector is concerned, the shareholder's income from the company is the sum of the (net) dividend

plus the tax credit. This sum of the (net) dividend plus the tax credit is usually referred to as the 'gross equivalent', and it is on the gross equivalent that the dividend yield on a share is calculated.

The total amount of tax the government receives from a company operating mainly or solely in the United Kingdom is *normally* independent of the amount of dividends paid, as Example 13.1 shows.

Tax years and rates of tax

The *fiscal* (Income Tax) *year* runs from 6 April to 5 April and is referred to by stating both years, e.g. Income Tax year 1989/90 is the year from 6 April 1989 to 5 April 1990.

The *financial year* (FY) runs from 1 April to 31 March and is referred to by the year in which it *starts*, e.g. financial year 1989 is the year from 1 April 1989 to 31 March 1990. The rate of Corporation Tax for each financial year is normally set in the Budget in the March before the start of the financial year.

The tax rates since 1979 are shown below:

Financial year (FY)	Corporation Tax rate	Basic rate of Income Tax (6 April)	ACT as fraction of dividend
1979 to 1982	52%	30%	30/70ths
1983	50%	30%	30/70ths
1984	45%	30%	30/70ths
1985	40%	30%	30/70ths
1986	35%	29%	29/71sts
1987	35%	27%	27/73rds
1988 to 1990	35%	25%	25/75ths

Note: If a company's accounting year falls partly in one financial year and partly in the next, the profits are divided between the two financial years on a time basis and bear Corporation Tax at the appropriate rate for each financial year. The rate of ACT, however, is the rate of ACT at the date of dividend payment (*not* the rate at the date the dividend was declared *nor* the rate in force in the period in respect of which the dividend is being paid).

If a trading company's taxable profits (income and capital gains) do not exceed £200,000 in a year, its income is subject to a lower rate of Corporation Tax, the *small companies* rate, set at 25% for 1990. There is also marginal relief for companies with profits of between £200,000 and £1,000,000, (25% on the first £200,000 plus a marginal rate of 37.5% on the balance up to £1,000,000).

CORPORATION TAX WITH NO DISTRIBUTION OF DIVIDENDS

Before we get any further involved in the complications of ACT, let us first deal with how the amount of Corporation Tax chargeable to a company is worked out, assuming that the company pays no dividends. This is the calculation of tax and after-tax earnings on what is called the 'nil distribution' basis, i.e. no distribution of dividends.

Inland Revenue's assessment of Corporation Tax

There are several reasons why the tax charge shown in the profit and loss account may not be 'normal', i.e. may differ from what the layman might expect, namely, pre-tax profits × average rate of Corporation Tax during the company's accounting year. The amount of Corporation Tax payable depends not on the company's pre-tax profit figure, but on the assessment made by the Inland Revenue. The tax charge varies not only because of differences that arise between the taxable profit and the profit shown in the company's accounts (the 'book profit'), but because of differences in rate.

The differences fall into three categories:

1. *Permanent differences*, where expenses are disallowed or income is tax-free or is taxed at a rate other than that of UK Corporation Tax (see page 88).
2. *Timing differences*, where the company may be liable to pay the full rate of tax at some time, but not in the year being reported upon.
3. *Previous years*, where the effect of losses and/or unrelieved ACT carried forward can materially reduce the tax charge for the year (see page 90).

Easily the most important difference in most companies is the timing difference caused by depreciation (in the company's accounts) not being the same as the capital allowances applied by the tax inspector, although timing differences have been greatly reduced by the phasing out of first-year allowances.

Depreciation and capital allowances

Different classes of asset have long been treated quite differently for tax purposes. For some, like commercial buildings, there is no allowance for depreciation, or as the Revenue terms them 'capital allowances', except in Enterprise Zones. Others have been treated particularly generously (e.g. plant and machinery), or more harshly than similar assets (e.g. private motor cars costing over £8,000).

The rules and rates of allowance are subject to periodic change, depending on whether the government wishes to encourage, or discourage, capital expenditure.

Under reforms made by the Finance Act 1984 most first-year and initial allowances were phased out by 31 March 1986, except for business buildings in Enterprise Zones. From 1 April 1986 allowances are as follows:

Asset category	Allowance
Plant and machinery Aircraft Patent rights Know how	Writing down 25% p.a. on reducing balance
Industrial buildings Hotels	Writing down 4% p.a. on cost
Scientific research Commercial buildings in Enterprise Zones	Initial 100% on cost

New ships	'Free depreciation' Purchaser can choose the amount to be allowed in any period, up to the total value of the expenditure.

Example of a timing difference

A company will have a subnormal tax charge if the capital allowances received for the year are greater than the amount the company provides for depreciation, as Example 13.2 illustrates.

Example 13.2   Depreciation and capital allowances

If a company invested £1 million in plant and machinery in 1986 and used straight line depreciation spread over an anticipated ten-year life, the capital allowances and depreciation would be:

	Capital allowance £	Depreciation £
1986	250,000	100,000
1987	187,500	100,000
1988	140,625	100,000
1989	105,469	100,000
1990	79,102	100,000
1991	59,326	100,000
1992	44,495	100,000
1993	33,371	100,000
1994	25,028	100,000
1995	75,084	100,000
	1,000,000	1,000,000

Note: this assumes that trading ceased in 1995 and that the plant and machinery had no residual value. If the company continued trading, the allowances would continue *ad infinitum* at 25% p.a. on the declining balance, i.e. £18,771 in 1995, £14,078 in 1996 . . . £334 in the year 2009, and so on. The advantage of the declining balance method is that it simplifies accounting, see page 35.

If the company made taxable trading profits before capital allowances of £1 million in each of the ten years and we ignore all other allowances for the purpose of illustration, the Corporation Tax payable, assuming a 35% rate throughout, would have been:

	Taxable profit £	Corporation Tax liability £
1986	750,000	262,500
1987	812,500	284,375
1988	859,375	300,781
1989	894,531	313,086
1990	920,898	322,314
1991	940,674	329,236
1992	955,505	334,427
1993	966,629	338,320

1994	974,972	341,240
1995	924,916 (Note 1)	323,721
	9,000,000 (Note 2)	3,150,000 (Note 2)

Notes:

1. Assuming trading ceases in 1995 and the plant and machinery has no residual value, to give capital allowances of £75,084 that year.

2. The *reported* profit before tax each year would be £900,000 (£1 million less £100,000 depreciation), so the *total* taxable profit over the ten years would be the same as the total *reported* profit, and the total tax payable would be the same as a tax charge of 35% each year on reported profit.

Deferred taxation

In order to remove the effect of timing differences from the profit and loss account, i.e. to allow for deferred tax liability, companies transfer to a Deferred Tax Account a sum equal to the difference between the Corporation Tax actually payable on taxable trading profits and the tax that would have been payable if the capital allowances had equalled the depreciation shown in the company's accounts.

In Example 13.2, the deferred tax would *originate* between 1986 and 1989, when taxable profit each year is less than the reported profit of £900,000 p.a., and would be shown in the company's accounts for 1986 as:

Profit and loss account	£000
Pre-tax profits	900
Tax (see Note)	315
Profit after tax	585

Note	
Corporation Tax payable	262
Transfer to provision for deferred tax	53
Total tax charge	315

The deferred tax thus originated is then added to the accumulated figure for 'deferred tax' in the balance sheet.

In the years 1990 to 1994 the effect of the timing difference would be *reversed*, in that more tax would be payable than the tax charge shown in the profit and loss account; the transfer would have been from the deferred tax account.

Accounting for deferred taxation

In 1975 the Accounting Standards Committee proposed to make it obligatory for all companies to account for deferred taxation on all material timing differences, as this is quite clearly the prudent thing to do for two reasons:

(a) the system of capital allowances might change adversely (as it did in 1984);

(b) a company falling on hard times could find itself with an onerous tax charge if it has to cut back heavily on capital expenditure.

However, the proposal met with considerable opposition and, as the result of representations from the CBI and others, it was decided to allow *partial* provision, and this is now required: tax deferred by timing differences should *not* be accounted for if it is probable that it will not crystallise (SSAP 15, para. 26), but the amount of tax not provided for in the period should be disclosed in a note (SSAP 15, para. 35).

The SSAP goes on to say that the assessment of whether deferred tax will or will not crystallise should be based on reasonable assumptions, taking into account all relevant information available. But what is a reasonable assumption? The scope for differences of treatment from company to company is enormous.

Ignoring the concept of prudence eventually caught up with company accounts when, in the 1984 Budget, the timing of capital allowances was radically altered with the phasing out of first-year allowances. As a result most companies had to make a substantial extra provision for deferred tax, and in some cases these provisions were very large indeed, as the extracts from the ROYAL BANK OF SCOTLAND's 1984 accounts illustrate:

ROYAL BANK OF SCOTLAND GROUP *Effect of 1984 Budget on deferred tax provisions*

Consolidated profit and loss account

	1984 £m	1983 £m
Profit before extraordinary items	72.4	95.1
Extraordinary items		
Profits less losses on disposals	25.1	(1.6)
Provisions required for corporation tax changes	(177.7)	—
Transfer from reserves	177.7	—
Profit attributable to ordinary shareholders	97.5	93.5

Unfortunately these provisions were treated as extraordinary items (as SSAP 15 requires), leaving earnings per share unscathed, although providing less than fully for deferred tax had, in previous years, boosted e.p.s.

Analysts should be sceptical where after-tax profits have been increased by reducing or omitting provision for deferred taxation, and should normally apply a full tax charge in calculating earnings per share (see page 195).

Methods of accounting for deferred taxation

SSAP 11, which preceded SSAP 15, defined two permitted methods of accounting for deferred taxation:

1. *The deferral method*, where amounts taken to the deferred tax account at the rate of Corporation Tax at the time remain unchanged despite any subsequent changes, so that reversals take place at the same, original rate.
2. *The liability method*, where deferred balances are maintained at the current rate of tax, so that the balance has to be adjusted when the rate of Corporation Tax changes.

SSAP 11 called upon companies to state which method they were using for deferred tax in their note on accounting policies, and although SSAP 15 has since laid down that deferred tax should be computed under the *liability method* (SSAP 15, para. 26) some companies still state which method they use (as in MARKS & SPENCER's 1988 accounts, shown here).

MARKS & SPENCER *1988 accounts*

Deferred taxation is provided on the liability method, to the extent that it is probable that a liability will crystallise . . .

Adjustments due to changes in tax rates and tax allowances should normally be disclosed separately as part of the tax charge, but the effect of changes in the basis of taxation or of significant changes in Government fiscal policy should be treated as an extraordinary item (SSAP 15, para. 36).

Other uses of the deferred taxation account

In addition to differences between capital allowances and depreciation, timing differences requiring deferred tax treatment also arise over the following items.

Accruals
Certain items of expenditure or income (e.g. debenture interest) are accrued in the accounts but are not included for tax purposes until paid or received. SSAP 15 calls for the provision for deferred taxation on these.

Revaluation of assets
If the surplus on revaluation is written into the accounts, SSAP 15 requires that a provision for taxation should be made out of the revaluation surplus as soon as a liability is foreseen, usually at the time a company decides in principle to dispose of the asset. If a company's year end falls after the decision in principle but before the actual disposal, the provision for taxation would be included in deferred tax, but these circumstances rarely arise.

Asset sales

When an asset is sold and the proceeds exceed the original cost, Corporation Tax may be payable on the capital gain, but the gain arising before 31 March 1982 is not taxable, and relief is given to allow for the fall in the value of money since that date.

This relief, called indexation allowance, is calculated using the Retail Price Index (RPI) in the months of purchase and sale:

$$\frac{\text{Indexation}}{\text{allowance}} = \frac{\text{Original}}{\text{cost}} \times \frac{\text{RPI (sale)} - \text{RPI (purchase)}}{\text{RPI (purchase)}}$$

The chargeable capital gain is the proceeds of the sale minus the original cost, minus the indexation allowance:

Example 13.3   Sale proceeds exceed original cost

An industrial building which cost £1.2 million in April 1987 (when the RPI was 101.8, as shown in Appendix 3) was sold in December 1989 (when the RPI was 118.8) for £2 million:

$$\text{Indexation factor} = \frac{118.8 - 101.8}{101.8} = 0.167$$

Indexation allowance = £1.2m × 0.167 = £0.2m
Chargeable gain = £2m − £1.2m − £0.2m = £0.6m
Corporation tax = £0.6m × 35% = £0.21m

When an asset was bought before 31 March 1982, the value at that date is used instead of the original cost and the RPI for March 1982 is used instead of the RPI in the month of purchase.

Where an industrial building is sold, the proceeds of sale are compared with the tax written-down value; if the proceeds exceed the tax written-down value a balancing charge is made, or if they are less a balancing allowance is given. Balancing charges are added to taxable profits, and balancing allowances are deducted from taxable profits. The balancing charge (or balancing allowance) represents the difference between the sale proceeds (or cost if that is less) and the tax written-down value (see Example 13.4).

Example 13.4   Computation of balancing charge

If the building in Example 13.3 had a written-down value for tax purposes at the time of sale of £0.8 million, the balancing charge would be:

> (Proceeds of sale or cost, whichever is the less) − Tax written-down value = £1.2 million − £0.8 million = £0.4 million

and the company's taxable profits would be increased by £0.4 million. Tax on this £0.4 million would be in addition to the tax on the capital gain in Example 13.3.

In the case of plant and machinery (but not cars), a 'pool' is maintained of plant available for writing-down allowances. Where such assets are sold, the proceeds of sale (or their cost if less) are simply deducted from the pool; there is normally no balancing allowance or balancing charge.

If a company disposes of a building (or other qualifying assets, e.g. a ship or an aircraft) at a profit and purchases another, it can obtain what is known as 'rollover relief' by electing to have the gain arising on the disposal deducted from the cost of the new building rather than paying tax on it (Example 13.5).

Example 13.5   Rollover relief

If freehold premises costing £1.2 million were sold for £2 million, producing a chargeable capital gain of £0.6 million (as it did in Example 13.3) and new freehold premises were bought for £3.5 million, the company could defer payment of tax on the £0.6 million by electing to deduct the gain from the cost of the new premises. However, if the new premises were subsequently sold for, say, £5.0 million, tax would be assessed on the gain of £5.0 million less (£3.5m − £0.6m), i.e. on £2.9 million less indexation allowance based on £2.9m (not 3.5m).

The relief is subject to a number of conditions. SSAP 15 does not normally require provision for deferred tax where advantage has been taken of rollover relief.

Further reasons for 'abnormal' tax charges – permanent differences

Permanent differences, the effects of which are not of course offset by provisions for deferred tax, include the following items:

Disallowed expenses
Some items, such as the cost of entertaining customers, are charged by companies to their profit and loss account thus reducing pre-tax profits, but are not allowed as expenses by the Inland Revenue in calculating taxable profits. This causes the tax charge to appear higher than 'normal'.

Franked income
This is income that has already borne Corporation Tax, i.e. dividends received from other UK companies. Franked income is *not* subject to Corporation Tax a second time, which means that companies receiving dividends can pass them straight through to their shareholders, together with the tax credits, without incurring any further tax. Thus the gross value of franked income to a *company* is normally the dividend received grossed up at the Corporation Tax rate rather than at the basic rate of Income Tax.

SSAP 8 requires the sum of dividends plus tax credits to be brought in at the pre-tax level and an amount equal to the tax credits to be included in the taxation charge. For example, if a company's only taxable income was £750,000 in dividends from other companies, together with associated tax credits of £250,000, the profit and loss account would show:

Pre-tax profits	£1,000,000
Taxation	250,000
Profits after tax	750,000

and the apparent tax rate would be 25%.

Capital gains
Unless a company's capital gains are treated as an extraordinary item, the tax payable on them is included in the Corporation Tax charge. For example, if a company's sole taxable profit for the year arose from the £4 million sale of assets costing £3 million, and the indexation allowance was £400,000, the chargeable gain would be only £600,000. The profit and loss would show:

Pre-tax profit	£1,000,000
Taxation (35% on £600,000)	210,000
Profit after tax	790,000

and the apparent rate of tax would be 21%.

Gains and losses on loans
Gains on loans are not normally subject to Corporation Tax, and losses on loans are not deductible as expenses. For example, if a company issued a loan stock at £99% and subsequently bought it in for cancellation at £95%, neither the £1% loss on issue

nor the £5% gain on repurchase would be included in the calculation of the company's Corporation Tax charge. However, in 'deep discount' issues (see p. 24), the 'income element' is an allowable expense.

Losses

Where a company makes a loss, it may carry that loss back for up to two years to recover Corporation Tax previously paid or, failing that, can carry the loss forward indefinitely to offset against future profits. However:

(a) Capital losses, for example the loss on sale of investments, cannot normally be offset against trading profits.

(b) Losses by UK-resident subsidiaries cannot be offset against profits elsewhere in the group unless the subsidiary is at least 75% owned by the parent company. If the loss-making subsidiary is less than 75% owned, the group's tax charge will appear abnormally high, but the losses can be carried forward within the subsidiary and, if and when subsequently matched against future profits, the effect on the group's tax charge will be reversed.

(c) The losses of a subsidiary in one country cannot be offset against the profits of subsidiaries in other countries, and this can result in a tax charge well in excess of a group's pre-tax profit, as WATERFORD GLASS illustrates:

WATERFORD GLASS *1988 report and accounts*

Consolidated profit and loss account

	IR£000
Profit on ordinary activities before taxation	2,703
Taxation	(7,946)
Loss after taxation and before extraordinary items	(5,243)

Chairman's statement

The year 1988 proved to be difficult for the Group. Serious problems at the Waterford Crystal manufacturing operation (in Ireland) . . . Taxation amounting to IR£7.9 million arose primarily on the Wedgwood operations (in the UK), and was unrelieved by losses in the Waterford manufacturing operation.

Stock relief

Stock relief was introduced by the Finance Act 1975 as a temporary measure to stop companies being taxed both unfairly and penally on the increase in value of stocks caused by inflation, then running at over 20%. Subsequently, it was put on a more permanent basis, and in 1981 it was recast to relate the relief to increases in the All Stocks Index rather than to increases in the value of stocks held during a period of account.

With inflation falling to around 5% p.a., the Finance Act 1984 abolished stock relief for any period beginning after 12 March 1984, but if inflation were to return to double figures there would be pressure to reintroduce it.

Small companies rate

Small companies pay Corporation Tax on income at a lower rate, see page 84.

Under- or over-provision for prior years

SSAP 6 requires that normal adjustments of estimates made in prior years should be included in the profit and loss account (see Chapter 14).

Overseas income

1. Overseas income of non-resident subsidiaries is not generally liable to UK taxation; it bears only foreign tax. The foreign tax may be at a higher or lower rate than UK corporation tax. In particular some countries, such as Ireland, give foreign companies several years of tax holidays to encourage them to set up subsidiaries there.

2. Dividends, interest or royalties remitted to the United Kingdom from certain countries, including the United States, may bear a further 'withholding tax'.

3. Overseas income of a UK-resident company is liable to UK tax whether remitted or not.

4. Double taxation relief (DTR) is given for overseas tax on income liable to UK tax, so overseas earnings *that are remitted* to the United Kingdom by overseas subsidiaries normally bear no UK tax if the foreign tax has already been borne at a rate equal to or greater than UK Corporation Tax. If the foreign tax is lower, only the difference is payable in the United Kingdom, but in both cases this is only true for foreign taxes of an income nature (taxes of a capital nature do not qualify for relief). Example 13.6 illustrates the way in which double taxation relief is applied:

Example 13.6   Double taxation relief

A UK holding company which does not itself trade has one overseas subsidiary, whose profit and loss account shows:

	£000
Pre-tax profits	1,000
Tax paid at 25%	250
	750
Dividends	300
Retentions	450

The UK holding company's £300,000 dividends are subject to 10% withholding tax (£30,000) on remittance, so the UK company actually receives £270,000.

For UK tax purposes the holding company's dividend is grossed up:

	£000
Dividend from subsidiary	300
Associated foreign tax at 25%	100
Gross income from subsidiary	400

UK tax is then calculated:

	£000
Corporation Tax 35% on £400,000	140
less DTR, which is the *lesser* of	
(a) Tax paid on £270,000 net £100,000 + £30,000 = £130,000	130
(b) UK Corporation Tax liability of £140,000	
Tax payable in the UK	10

The UK holding company's profit and loss account would show:

	£000	£000
Pre-tax profits		1,000
UK Corporation Tax	140	
less DTR	130	
	10	
Overseas tax	250	
Withholding tax	30	290
Profit after tax		710

Effect of previous years

Not many listed companies have substantial accumulated losses and/or unrelieved ACT to carry forward, but when they have the effect on the tax charge can be dramatic. BLACKWOOD HODGE, for instance, paid only £124,000 UK corporation tax in 1988 on a UK operating profit of £3.2 million,

and the overall tax charge on a pre-tax profit of £15.5 million was only £3,375,000. The note on taxation gave details, including the amount of losses available for set-off in future years:

BLACKWOOD HODGE *Note on taxation*

	1988 £000	1987 £000
UK corporation tax at 35%		
Current	177	47
Less: double taxation relief	53	47
	124	—
Advance corporation tax written off	728	722
Overseas taxation	2,478	1,792
	3,330	2,514
Adjustment for prior years	45	20
	3,375	2,534

Cumulative losses of UK subsidiaries of approximately £2,800,000 (1987 – £4,597,000) are available for set-off against future profits of those companies. Cumulative advance corporation tax of £2,100,000 (1987 – £1,422,000) is available for set-off against future UK corporation tax liabilities . . .

Cumulative losses of overseas subsidiaries of £4,040,000 (1987 – £5,403,000) are available for set-off against future profits of those companies . . .

In the same year c. h. bailey's note on taxation was somewhat briefer: 'As a result of losses in previous accounting periods, no provision for corporation tax is necessary.'

However, tax reliefs brought forward will eventually get used up, so it is recommended that, in comparing companies like BLACKWOOD HODGE and c. h. bailey with other companies, the standard rate of Corporation Tax should normally be applied to UK profits.

CORPORATION TAX WITH DIVIDEND DISTRIBUTION

Advance Corporation Tax (ACT)

We have so far dealt with factors affecting the amount of tax a company pays if no dividends are paid.

The payment of dividends affects the company's overall tax liability if:

(a) the dividends are very high, or

(b) a large proportion of the company's earnings comes from overseas and bears foreign tax at anything more than a modest rate.

In either case some of the ACT paid on the distribution of dividends may be unrelieved, i.e., may not be able to be offset against the company's corporation tax liability.

Limitations on the use of ACT

ACT can be set off against Corporation Tax liability on profits (income and chargeable gains) and on unfranked investment income. But it cannot reduce the mainstream Corporation Tax (referred to from now on as 'mainstream tax') on income arising in the United Kingdom in any year below a minimum rate of (Corporation Tax rate – basic rate of Income Tax), as illustrated in Example 13.7.

Example 13.7   Unrelieved ACT due to high dividend distribution

In the financial year 1989 tax rates were as follows:

Corporation Tax rate	35%
Basic rate of Income Tax	25%
So, minimum rate of mainstream tax was	10%

In that year, if a company operating solely in the United Kingdom made £1 million pre-tax and distributed £900,000, considerably more than its profits after tax of £650,000 (perhaps to maintain its dividend in a poor year), it would suffer unrelieved ACT as follows:

	£
Pre-tax profit	1,000,000
Corporation Tax (35%)	350,000
	650,000
Dividends paid	900,000
ACT paid (25/75ths of 900,000)	300,000
Minimum mainstream tax (10%)	100,000
ACT set off	250,000
	350,000
Unrelieved ACT (£300,000 – £250,000)	50,000

ACT is normally set off against the Corporation Tax liability for the year in which the related dividend has been distributed, but any that cannot be used in that year (i.e. is unrelieved) can be carried back for six years, or carried forward indefinitely.

It can also be surrendered to other companies in a group, subject to certain restrictions, and offset against their tax liability.

Irrecoverable ACT

Although ACT can be carried forward indefinitely, SSAP 8 regards it as irrecoverable if its recoverability is not 'reasonably certain and foreseeable', i.e. the carry-forward should normally not extend beyond the next accounting period.

Alternatively, unrelieved ACT can be deducted from that proportion of the balance of deferred tax against which ACT can be set off in the future (*not* deferred tax representing future mainstream tax or tax on deferred chargeable gains). For example, with Corporation Tax at 35%, and an ACT rate of 25%, 10% must remain in charge to meet mainstream liability. Thus if a deferred tax account balance of, say, £70,000 represents tax on £200,000 chargeable profits at 35% then the minimum mainstream tax on the chargeable profits would be £200,000 at 10% = £20,000, leaving the balance of £50,000 (£70,000 – £20,000) as the maximum amount against which unrelieved ACT could be offset (£50,000 = £200,000 at 25%).

If unrelieved ACT is set off against deferred tax it will be deducted from deferred tax in the balance sheet rather than being charged to the profit and loss account, and so will *not* increase the profit and loss account figure for taxation.

Irrecoverable ACT, on the other hand, should be included as part of the tax charge, and the amount should be separately disclosed if material, as in BLACKWOOD HODGE's note on taxation on page 90.

ACT and relief for foreign tax

Relief for foreign tax, which is called Double Taxation Relief (DTR), is offset against a company's UK corporation tax liability before ACT offset. As Example 13.9 illustrates, if DTR plus ACT exceeds the corporation tax liability, the ACT is unrelieved. Unrelieved ACT can be carried back for up to six years and can be carried forward indefinitely.

Timing of payments of Corporation Tax

Advance Corporation Tax is payable within fourteen days of the end of the quarter in which the distribution is made, and is offset against the Corporation Tax liability for the company's accounting period in which the dividend is distributed (see Example 13.8).

The timing of payment of mainstream Corporation Tax used to depend on when the company started trading. For companies which started trading after the end of March 1965, Corporation Tax was and still is due nine months after the end of the company's accounting period. For companies which were trading before 1 April 1965 (the normal case for most listed companies), tax was payable on 1 January of the financial year following the financial year in which the company's accounting period ended, which could be up to 21 months later. In the 1987 Budget the payment interval was standardised to 9 months for all companies, with the change being phased in over a period of three years.

Example 13.8   Offset of ACT

A company whose year end is 31 December pays the following dividends for the year 1989:

Sept 89   Interim dividend of 1.5p per share
July 90   Final dividend of 3.0p per share

On the *interim dividend*, ACT of 0.5p per share will be payable within 14 days of 30 September 1989, and will be offset against Corporation Tax liability for the year 1989 (payable 1 October 1990).

On the *final dividend*, ACT of 1.0p per share will be payable within 14 days of 30 September 1990 and will be offset against Corporation Tax liability for the year 1990 (payable 1 October 1991).

In the *1989 accounts* the ACT of 1.0p per share on the final dividend will be provided for as a liability payable within one year, but the company will not be able to offset it against its Corporation Tax liability until 1990.

EARNINGS AND DIVIDEND COVER

Nil earnings

As we mentioned earlier in this chapter, nil earnings are the after-tax earnings that a company would report, assuming it paid no dividends.

Net earnings

Net earnings are the same as nil earnings unless the dividend distribution the company makes increases the company's overall tax liability.

In Example 13.9, earnings on a nil distribution basis would be £1,300,000, but with some dividend distribution the 'net' earnings would be only £1,200,000 because of £100,000 unrelieved ACT, if that ACT was deemed to be irrecoverable.

'Full distribution' earnings

These are the earnings that would be attributable to ordinary shareholders if they were all distributed as dividends; they are expressed at the gross level: dividends plus associated tax credits.

As foreign tax cannot be used as a credit against ACT, the maximum distribution a company can make at gross level (dividends plus tax credits) = Pre-tax profits − Minimum mainstream tax on UK earnings − Foreign tax.

In Example 13.9, 'full distribution' earnings are £2,000,000 − £0 (no UK earnings) − £600,000 foreign tax = £1,400,000, made up of £1,050,000 dividends and £350,000 ACT.

Dividend cover

Dividend cover is the maximum dividend that a company could pay out of profits divided by the dividend actually paid.

Dividend cover with mainly UK operations

The calculation of the cover presents no difficulty when distribution of all the profits does not increase a company's overall tax liability (i.e. when overseas earnings and foreign tax are not significant and the tax charge is reasonably

Example 13.9   The effect of double taxation relief on the offsetting of ACT

Suppose a UK company's earnings all arise overseas and bear foreign tax (including withholding tax on remission) at 30% UK Corporation Tax is 35% and all earnings are remitted, then with ACT at 25%:

	Nil distribution £000	Some distribution £000	Full distribution £000
Pre-tax profits	2,000	2,000	2,000
Dividends distributed	Nil	600	1,050
UK Corporation Tax liability	700	700	700
less Double Taxation Relief on foreign tax	600	600	600
CT liability against which ACT can be offset	100	100	100
ACT paid (25/75ths of dividends)	Nil	200	350
ACT offset	Nil	100	100
Unrelieved ACT	Nil	100	250
Total tax paid	700	800	950
Profits after tax (i.e. 'Earnings')	1,300	1,200	1,050
Retained earnings	1,300	600	None

normal). In these cases simply divide the profits after tax, minorities and preference dividends by the ordinary dividends distributed.

Dividend cover in these cases can also be calculated by dividing earnings per share (nil basis) by the dividend per share. (Earnings per share, e.p.s., = profit attributable to ordinary shareholders ÷ number of ordinary shares in issue; see Chapter 14.)

Dividend cover with overseas earnings and foreign tax

Where a large proportion of a company's earnings arises overseas and bears foreign tax (including withholding tax on remitted earnings) at or near to the UK rate of Corporation Tax, dividend cover becomes more complicated because 'full distribution' increases the company's overall tax liability. This is because there is insufficient UK tax liability after DTR against which to offset the ACT that would be payable on full distribution.

In Example 13.9 the dividend paid in *Some distribution* is only 1.75 times covered, in spite of retentions being equal to the dividends paid, because *Full distribution* would cause an increase of £150,000 in unrelieved ACT.

The maximum amount of dividend plus tax credit that a company can distribute out of profits (i.e. the 'gross' dividend under full distribution) is the *lesser* of:

(a) [Pre-tax earnings × (1 − CT rate) − minorities − pref. dividends] ÷ [1 − basic rate of Income Tax], (Note i)

(b) Pre-tax earnings *minus*:
   Minimum mainstream tax on UK earnings (Note ii)
   Foreign tax (Note iii)
   Minorities (grossed up at the standard rate of Corporation Tax)
   Preference dividends (grossed up at the basic rate of Income Tax)

Notes

(i) (a) produces the same answer as e.p.s. ÷ dividend per share.

(ii) Minimum mainstream tax on UK earnings = UK earnings × (Corporation Tax rate − ACT rate).

(iii) The foreign tax should include the withholding tax that would be payable if all overseas earnings were to be remitted to the United Kingdom.

(iv) Franked income plus associated tax credits should be excluded from pre-tax earnings, but should be added back afterwards in both (a) and (b).

Chapter 14

PROFITS AFTER TAX, EXCEPTIONAL AND EXTRAORDINARY ITEMS, DIVIDENDS AND EARNINGS PER SHARE

(References: SSAP 6 *Extraordinary Items and Prior Year Adjustments*.)

PROFITS AFTER TAX

The unsuspecting layman might think that, once a company had made a profit and deducted tax, all that remained to be done would be to decide how much to pay out to ordinary shareholders and how much of the profit to retain in the business. In some companies it is as simple as that, but, alas, not in many, due to the minor complications of minority and preference shareholders, the major complications of extraordinary items, prior year adjustments and transfers to/from reserves, and the legal restrictions on the distribution of profits (as well as any government dividend restraint in force at the time).

Example 14.1 shows how extraordinary items appear 'below the line' in a profit and loss account – i.e. below the figure for profit attributable to ordinary shareholders, on which earnings per share are calculated. The decision on whether to treat a large item as extraordinary or not can thus substantially affect the apparent profitability of the company and in some cases can actually turn a profit into a loss (or vice versa); extraordinary items are therefore the subject of considerable debate, as we will discuss shortly. The illustration also shows how any prior year adjustment arising from changes in accounting policies and from the correction of fundamental errors should be shown as an adjustment to the reserves brought forward at the beginning of the year (as required by SSAP 6, paras. 16 and 39).

Minorities

As explained in detail in Chapter 16, minorities

Example 14.1   Extraordinary items in the profit and loss account

Profit and loss account

	£000
Profit on ordinary activities after tax	1,231
less Minorities	68
Profit attributable to shareholders	1,163
Extraordinary items (less tax attributable)	247
Profit for the financial year	1,410
less Dividends	447
Retained profit	963

Earnings per share (see note)	11.16p
Extraordinary items per share	2.47p

Note: E.p.s. based on profits of £1,163,000 less preference dividends of £47,000, and 10,000,000 ordinary shares in issue throughout the year.

Note on reserves

	£000	£000
Reserves at beginning of year:		
As previously reported	2,742	
Prior year adjustment	(174)	
As restated		2,568
Retained profit for the year		963
Reserves at end of year		3,531

occur when a group has one or more subsidiaries which are only partially owned by the group. The other (minority) shareholders in the 'partially owned' subsidiary are entitled to a share in the profit or loss of that subsidiary; their share, called 'minorities' or 'minority interests', has to be deducted in arriving at the profit attributable to the group's shareholders.

Preference dividends

Preference dividends, like ordinary dividends, are paid net and carry an associated tax credit. When the imputation system of taxation was introduced the basic rate of Income Tax was set at 30% and the coupons (the rates of dividend) on all UK preference shares were adjusted by statute to 70% of their former value on a once-and-for-all basis.

Thus, for example, a 5% £1 preference share became a 3½% £1 preference share, receiving a dividend fixed at 3½p, plus an associated tax credit dependent on the basic rate of Income Tax at the time of payment of the dividend.

Preference dividends and any arrears of cumulative preference dividends have to be met before any ordinary dividends can be declared.

Profit attributable to shareholders

Profit attributable to shareholders (sometimes called 'profit attributable to the company') is what is left for the shareholders after tax and all other charges have been deducted, but *before* extraordinary items.

It is this figure of attributable profits, less any preference dividends, divided by the number of ordinary shares in issue which gives the earnings per share, i.e. the amount the holder of one share would normally receive if the company distributed all its profits as dividends.

As earnings per share (e.p.s.), which we will discuss in detail towards the end of this chapter, are a key measure of a company's profitability, the decision on what items should or should not be treated as extraordinary can often make a very significant difference to a company's attributable

profits and thus to the e.p.s., as, for example, in the case of KINGFISHER's 1989 accounts, illustrated here:

KINGFISHER *Consolidated profit and loss account*

£ millions	1989	1988
Profit before exceptional items	186.9	147.2
Exceptional items (Note 4)	37.2	29.8
Profit on ordinary activities before taxation	224.1	177.0
Taxation	(51.8)	(37.6)
Profit on ordinary activities after taxation	172.3	139.4
...		
Earnings per share	39.9p	33.9p

Note 4   Exceptional items

Profit on sale and leaseback of properties	44.7	35.2
Exceptional costs of reorganisation	(7.5)	(5.4)
	37.2	29.8

Had the profits on the sale and leaseback of properties been treated as an extraordinary item, i.e. below the line, and assuming these profits were taxed at 35% (i.e. no rollover relief), then profits on ordinary activities after taxation would have been reduced by £29.1m. (1988 – £22.9m.) and earnings per share would have been only 33.2p (28.3p).

The treatment of currency adjustments will be dealt with in Chapter 18. Let us now proceed to a detailed discussion of extraordinary items so that the reader can judge for himself whether it was reasonable for KINGFISHER to include the profit from sale and leaseback in its normal profits, i.e. 'above the line', or whether it should have been dealt with 'below the line', i.e. as an extraordinary item.

EXCEPTIONAL AND EXTRAORDINARY ITEMS

Conflicting concepts of profit

As the general idea of accounting is many hundreds of years old, one might expect that there would be fundamental agreement among users of accounts as to the basic purpose of the profit and loss account, or income statement as it is normally termed in the United States, but there is not. There are two conflicting views of the basic purpose of the profit and loss account:

(*a*)   the current operating performance concept;
(*b*)   the all-inclusive concept.

Current operating performance concept
Those who advocate the current operating performance concept believe that the profit and loss account should be designed to disclose the earnings of the business which arise from the normal operating activities during the period being reported upon. If this was followed to the extreme,

the profit and loss account would include only the ordinary activities of the business during the reporting period; anything extraordinary or relating to prior years, and the effects of accounting changes, would be excluded. A profit and loss account prepared in this way facilitates comparison both with those of the same business for earlier periods and with those of other companies for the current period.

All-inclusive concept

Advocates of the all-inclusive concept, on the other hand, believe that the profit and loss account should include all transactions which bring about a net increase or decrease in net tangible assets during the current period, apart from dividend distributions (which appear in the appropriation section) and transactions such as the issue of shares. The aggregate income shown by such income statements over the life of an enterprise then constitutes a complete historical summary of net income. Advocates of the all-inclusive concept warn that if extraordinary items, the effect of accounting changes and prior period adjustments are charged or credited directly to retained earnings, as they are under the current operating performance concept, there is a danger that they will be overlooked in a review of operating results of several periods.

There has been a shift of opinion towards the all-inclusive concept during the past few years, not only in the United Kingdom but also in the United States and Canada, although none of these countries adopts a pure all-inclusive basis.

SSAP 6 definition of exceptional and extraordinary items

SSAP 6 uses two confusingly similar terms: extraordinary items and exceptional items. The distinction between these two items can be very significant in the calculation of the profit a company reports, so it is important to note SSAP 6's definition of them:

'*Exceptional items* are material items which derive from events or transactions that fall within the ordinary activities of the company, and which need to be disclosed separately by virtue of their size or incidence if the financial statements are to give a true and fair view.'

'*Extraordinary items* are material items which derive from events or transactions that fall outside the ordinary activities of the company and which are therefore expected not to recur frequently or regularly. They do not include exceptional items nor do they include prior year items merely because they related to a prior year.'

The classification of items as extraordinary depends on the nature of the business. For example, most companies would regard the sale of land as an extraordinary item, but REDLAND, whose business involves the continual acquisition and disposal of land (e.g. gravel pits, sold off when worked out), states specifically in its accounts that 'profits and losses arising on the disposal of fixed assets, including land and property, are included in the profit before taxation'.

Presentation of extraordinary items

Extraordinary items (extraordinary income, extraordinary charges and attributable taxation) should be shown separately in the profit and loss account for the year, below the results derived from ordinary activities. If there are extraordinary items, the profit and loss account for the year should include the following elements:

(a) profit on ordinary activities after taxation;
(b) extraordinary items after taxation;
(c) profit for the financial year.

The detailed breakdown required by the formats in the Companies Act is normally given in a note, as in ALLIED LYONS' 1988 accounts, shown here:

ALLIED LYONS *Note to the profit and loss account*

Extraordinary items	1988 £m	1987 £m
Profit/(loss) on disposal of subsidiaries and related company and other investments	15.3	(6.7)
Bid defence costs	—	(7.5)
Cost of closures, redundancies and re-organisations	—	(40.0)
	15.3	(54.2)
Taxation (charge)/relief	(3.0)	14.4
	12.3	(39.8)

Importance of extraordinary items

Extraordinary items should be studied carefully for the following reasons:

(a) Treatment of ordinary items as extraordinary (or vice versa) can make a very significant difference to earnings per share.
(b) They may signal important changes in the nature of the business.
(c) They may also give important clues to the quality of management and to the future profitability of the company.

For example, terminal losses written off may indicate:

(a) the capacity of the management to admit their mistakes and/or to face up to changed economic circumstances, and their ability to take action to correct the situation once and for all, rather than devoting a disproportionate amount of management time and other resources into trying to revive dying ducks;

(b) the likelihood of higher future profits as the result of cutting out a loss-maker.

In addition, the chairman's or directors' report and other sources of information (e.g. press reports) should be checked to get a full picture of what lies behind an extraordinary item. For example, the extraordinary items in GRAND METROPOLITAN's 1989 accounts included 'Gaming £48m.' under business disposals and the chairman, in his statement, explained in some detail the reason for the disposal:

GRAND METROPOLITAN *Extract from chairman's statement*

As reported in my statement last year, William Hill was acquired in December 1988 and was combined with Mecca Bookmakers to establish a major force in the UK betting industry. At the time of the acquisition research was being undertaken to see whether a retail betting brand could be established across Europe and in the United States. The European off-track betting industry is highly controlled offering only restricted immediate opportunities. In the United States in-depth customer research showed that the perceived poor image of off-track betting would have had adverse implications for our US consumer branded food, drinks and retailing businesses. The decision was therefore made not to develop in the United States and to sell the UK business. The high sale price achieved (£685 million) reflected the benefits of combining Hills with Mecca Bookmakers.

It is worth emphasising that one of the main limitations of many companies is the availability of first-class management: if a large proportion of it is devoted to 'salvage operations', the rest of the business is less likely to be run to maximum advantage.

Exceptional items

Exceptional items, as defined on page 96, should be separately disclosed above the line (SSAP 6, para. 36). For example WATERFORD GLASS:

WATERFORD GLASS *Note to the profit and loss account*

Exceptional gains/(losses)

	1988 IR£000	1987 IR£000
Net gains on property disposals	7,001	—
Excess production costs during restructuring and stock provisions at Waterford manufacturing division	—	(14,802)
	7,001	(14,802)

It is very tempting for management to treat exceptional costs as extraordinary, in order to enhance earnings per share. A particular favourite is to treat closure, redundancy and re-organisation costs in a continuing activity of the company as extraordinary, although SSAP 6, paras. 14 and 32 make it quite clear that 'Programmes of reorganisation which, although involving redundancies and a reduction in the level of activities, do not amount to the discontinuance of a business segment (a material and separately identifiable component of the business operations of a company) are not extraordinary.'

For example, ICI in 1988 reported the cost of restructuring UK compound fertiliser production facilities, £44 million net of tax relief, as an extraordinary item. Had the cost been treated as an exceptional item rather than an extraordinary item, the earnings per share reported in 1988 would have shown an increase of less than 9% over the 1987 figure, rather than the 14% increase reported in the Chairman's statement.

Prior year items

Prior year items are items which relate to an earlier year or years. Those which represent the normal recurring corrections of accounting estimates made in prior years should be included in the normal calculation of pre-tax profits and, if material, should be stated separately in the published accounts.

Prior year adjustments
Only those prior year items which are the result of:

(a) changes in accounting policies, *or*
(b) the correction of fundamental errors,

and are material, are treated as 'prior year adjustments' for the purpose of SSAP 6. Prior year adjustments should not appear in the profit and loss account for the year being reported on, but in the statement of retained profits/reserves.

Restatement of accounts
Prior year adjustments (less attributable taxation) should be accounted for by adjusting the opening balance of retained profits accordingly. Where practicable, the effect of the prior year adjustment on the results for the preceding year should be disclosed, but restatement in any real sense is comparatively rare. The analyst should therefore

ensure that prior year adjustments are applied to the figures for the prior year or years concerned to obtain a true comparison of the company's results from year to year.

Examples of items needing special treatment (if material) (see also Example 14.2 opposite)

Prior year adjustments
(a) Change in accounting policy (e.g. change from a method of computing the cost of stock and work in progress including no overheads to one including all production overheads).
(b) Correction of fundamental errors (e.g. a major error in adding up stock figures); these are comparatively rare.

Extraordinary items
(a) Discontinuance of a significant part of a business.
(b) Sale of an investment not acquired with the intention of resale.

(c) Writing-off of goodwill or other intangibles because of unusual events or developments during the period.
(d) Expropriation of assets.
(e) Profit on sale and leaseback of property.

Exceptional items charge in current year – disclose separately
(a) Abnormal charges for bad debts.
(b) Abnormal write-offs of stock and work in progress.
(c) Abnormal expenditure on research and development.
(d) Abnormal losses on long-term contracts.
(e) Most adjustments of prior year tax provisions.
(f) Exchange differences (unless connected with an extraordinary item).
(g) Profit or loss on disposal of a fixed asset (unless the transaction itself is extraordinary for SSAP 6 purposes).

DIVIDENDS

Distribution of dividends

In deciding what profits to distribute the directors of a company should have in mind:

(a) the company's cash position;
(b) what is prudent from an accounting viewpoint;
(c) what is legally permissible.

Ideally, directors should choose the lowest of these three figures.

In deciding what is prudent in cash terms, directors should weigh up the cost of raising capital in various ways. Is it, for instance, better to borrow (i.e. increase the gearing) rather than ask equity shareholders to contribute more towards the net assets of the company? And, if equity shareholders are to be called upon to provide more, should they be asked to do so by means of a rights issue, in which case each shareholder has the choice of whether to take up, or sell, his rights; or should profits be 'retained', in which case the individual shareholder has no choice?

Unfortunately, the picture is confused by inflation and the present, historical cost, method of accounting. With no inflation (or an inflation accounting system recognised for tax purposes) a company would, in theory, be able to distribute all its profits and maintain its assets in real terms. With inflation most companies need to retain a proportion of their earnings as calculated by historical cost accounting in order to maintain their assets in real terms (but more of that in Chapter 23).

Having decided how much it is necessary to retain in order to continue the existing scale of operations, and how much should be retained out of profits in order to expand the scale of operations, the directors should look at what remains.

Ideally, a company should pay a regular, but somewhat increasing, dividend. For example, from a market point of view, it is preferable to pay: 8.0p; 9.0p; 9.0p; 9.0p; 9.5p; 10.0p; rather than 8.0p; 12.0p; 10.5p; 4.0p; 10.0p; 10.0p; though both represent the same total sum in dividends over the six years, because investors who need steady income will avoid erratic dividend payers, and because a cut in dividend undermines confidence in the company's future. In other words, the directors of a company should think twice before paying a dividend this year which they may not be able to maintain, or setting a pattern of growth in the rate of dividend which could not reasonably be continued for the foreseeable future. For if they do either of these things, they are liable to disappoint shareholder expectations, to damage their market rating and to see their share price slashed if their dividend has to be cut.

Legal restrictions on dividend distribution

Prior to the Companies Act 1980 companies could, in general, distribute profits arising in an accounting period without making good previous revenue or capital losses, and could also distribute unrealised surpluses on asset revaluations.

Companies are now allowed to distribute only the aggregate of accumulated realised profits not

Example 14.2   Flowchart of decisions on extraordinary items, exceptional items and prior year adjustments

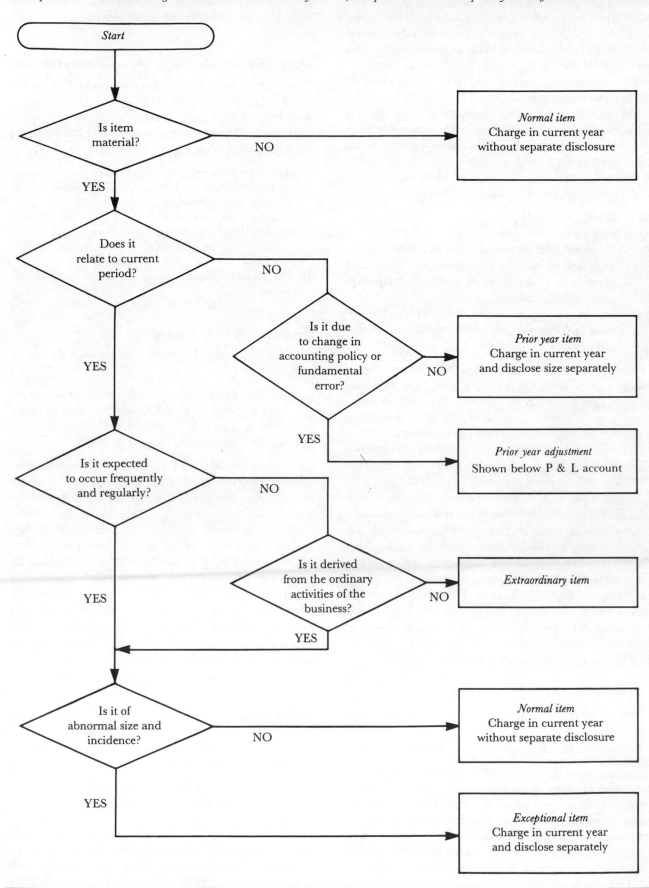

previously distributed or capitalised *less* accumulated realised losses not previously written off in a reduction or reorganisation of capital (CA 1985, S. 263). The word 'realised' is not defined in the Act, but SSAP 2 says that profits should be included in the profit and loss account 'only when realised in the form of cash or of other assets the ultimate cash realisation of which can be assessed with reasonable certainty'.

In addition, a *public* company may pay a dividend only if the net assets of the company after payment of the dividend are not less than the aggregate of its called-up share capital and undistributable reserves (S. 264(1)). Undistributable reserves are defined in Section 264(3) as:

(*a*) share premium account;
(*b*) capital redemption reserve;
(*c*) accumulated unrealised profits not capitalised *less* accumulated unrealised losses not previously written off in a capital reduction or reorganisation;
(*d*) any reserve which the company's Memorandum or Articles prohibit being distributed.

This requirement reflects the 'capital maintenance' principle of the EEC Second Directive and means that public companies will, in future, have to cover net losses (whether realised or not) from realised profits before paying a dividend.

Investment companies (a new class of company created by the Companies Act 1980 and defined in Section 266 of the Companies Act 1985 as a UK listed company investing mainly in securities with the aim of spreading investment risk and obtaining the benefit of specialist management *and* which has given notice to the Registrar of Companies) will have the option of paying dividends either on the basis of the capital maintenance section (S. 264) or on an asset ratio test (S. 265). This test requires the investment company's assets after the distribution to equal not less than one and a half times its aggregate liabilities.

Where any company's audit report has been qualified, the auditor must provide a statement in writing as to whether the qualification is material in deciding whether the distribution would be a breach of the Act, *before* any distribution can be made.

Company articles on dividend distribution

Most companies lay down their own rules for dividend distribution in their Articles by adopting Articles 114 to 116 of Table A (the model set of Company Articles given in the First Schedule to the Companies Act 1948); these Articles say:

114. The company in general meeting may declare dividends, but no dividend shall exceed the amount recommended by the directors.
115. The directors may from time to time pay to the members such interim dividends as appear to the directors to be justified by the profits of the company.
116. No dividend shall be paid otherwise than out of profits.

Declaration of dividends

Any dividends the directors recommend should be shown:

(*a*) in the profit and loss account, together with any interim dividend already paid (CA 1985, Sch. 4, para. 51(3));
(*b*) in the balance sheet as a liability.

Interim dividends can be declared by the directors without reference to the shareholders, but by convention they do not normally exceed half the anticipated total for the year. However, if the latest audited accounts disclose a 'non-distributable' position or if the level of accumulated profits has fallen significantly, interim accounts must be prepared to justify the payment of an interim dividend (CA 1985, S. 272). Interim dividends appear in the profit and loss account as a distribution, and also in the balance sheet if the company has not paid the interim dividend by the end of the accounting period.

EARNINGS PER SHARE

(Reference: SSAP 3 *Earnings per Share*.)

Earnings per share (e.p.s.) are the amount of profit on *ordinary* activities, after tax and all other charges, that has been earned for each ordinary share and, as such, are a much better measure of the company's performance than profits, which can be boosted by acquisitions paid for by the issue of new shares and by rights issues.

The e.p.s. depend, rather obviously, on the amount of attributable profits (*before* extraordinary items) and the number of shares in issue, thus:

$$\text{e.p.s.} = \frac{\text{Profit attributable to ordinary shareholders}}{\text{Number of ordinary shares in issue}}$$

(see page 194 for details of calculation on a fully taxed basis). What is a little less obvious is that a company's profits may rise without a corresponding rise in earnings per share, because of changes

Example 14.3   Comparison of growth in profits and e.p.s.

	1984	1985	1986	1987	1988	Growth p.a. 1984–88
	Year ending in					
HALMA						
Profit before taxation (£m.)	3.05	3.89	5.28	6.47	9.08	+31.4%
Earnings per share[1]	3.29p	4.45p	6.05p	7.20p	9.46p	+30.2%
HANSON						
Profit before tax (£m.)	169	253	464	741	880	+51.1%
Earnings per share[2]	5.7p	7.9p	10.7p	14.0p	15.9p	+29.2%
MAXWELL COMMUNICATION CORPORATION						
Profit before tax (£m.)	37.9	25.2	80.3	166.0	153.6[3]	+41.9%
Earnings per share	27.2p	17.0p	23.2p	26.7p	19.2p[3]	− 8.3%

Notes:
[1] Restated for scrip issues in 1985 and 1987.
[2] Fully diluted and adjusted for capitalisation issues.
[3] 15-month period ending 31 March 1989, annualised.

in the issued share capital, as Example 14.3 shows.

The issued share capital of HALMA was only marginally increased between 1984 and 1988; acquisitions were made, but they were paid for mostly in cash, so the growth in e.p.s. was only slightly less than that of profits. In the same period HANSON's profits grew at more than 50% per annum; this was achieved partly by organic growth in existing businesses and partly by a stream of acquisitions, several of which were for paper (i.e. new shares were issued as consideration rather than paying cash); as a result e.p.s. grew by less than 30%. Finally MAXWELL, where chairman Robert Maxwell's stated goal was to become 'a global information and communications corporation before the end of the decade, with annual revenues of £3–5 billion with profits growth to match'. Maxwell's sales in the period grew from £266.5 million to over £1 billion, at an annual rate of 42.9% with profits growth almost to match, but this was achieved by the profligate use of paper and earnings per share suffered accordingly.

It is interesting to compare the share price movement of these companies between 1984 and 1988:

Closing prices at:	01/01/84	01/01/89	Gain/loss on Market index
Halma	49.33p	123.33p	+26.94%
Hanson	63.21p	154.75p	+24.31%
Maxwell	128.43p	188.00p	−25.67%

Source: Datastream

The Market has not been impressed by Mr Maxwell's global aspirations.

The effect of acquisitions on earnings per share

The fact that an acquisition for paper makes e.p.s. grow at a slower rate than profits does not mean that acquisitions for paper are bad for e.p.s. It all depends on whether the e.p.s. are higher with the acquisition than they would have been without it (Example 14.4 overleaf).

Earnings growth by acquisition

Buying earnings cheaply enables a company to boost its e.p.s. when its own earnings are static, or even when they are falling. Suppose in Example 14.4 that the attributable profits of the company were expected to fall the following year to £912,000, despite the recently acquired business performing satisfactorily. The company finds another victim (Example 14.5).

'But,' you may say, 'how did the company in the example manage to get the shareholders of the second acquisition to accept 2.4 million shares for attributable earnings of £468,000, which is 19.5p per share, far higher than the e.p.s. of the acquiring company?' And well may you ask – the secret is in 'market rating'.

Market rating – the PER

The measure of a company's market rating is its Price/Earnings Ratio (P/E ratio or PER), which is the market price of the ordinary share divided by the earnings per share:

PER = Share price ÷ e.p.s.

101

Example 14.4   Acquisition for paper

	Existing company	Acquisition	Company post-acquisition
Attributable profits (£)	800,000	200,000	1,000,000
Issued equity (shares)	8,000,000		
Vendor consideration (shares)		1,600,000	
Resulting equity (shares)			9,600,000
e.p.s.	10p		10.4p

In this case 1.6 million shares are issued for a company bringing in £200,000 at the attributable profit level, or 12.5p for each new share, which is higher than the e.p.s. of the existing company, so the e.p.s. of the company, post-acquisition, are improved. Had the acquiring company paid more than 2 million shares for the acquisition, its earnings per share would have fallen.

Example 14.5   Further acquisition

	Present company	Second acquisition	Resulting company
Attributable profits (£)	912,000	468,000	1,380,000
Issued equity (shares)	9,600,000		
Vendor consideration (shares)		2,400,000	
Resulting equity (shares)			12,000,000
e.p.s.	9.5p	11.5p	

The PER depends mainly on four things: the overall level of the stock market, the industry in which the company operates, the company's record, and the markets' view on the company's prospects. In an average market the PER of the average company in an average sector might be around 10, with high-quality 'blue chips' like GLAXO or TRUSTHOUSE FORTE standing on a PER of around 15 and small glamour growth stocks on 20 or more, while companies in an unfashionable sector (e.g. the clearing banks, with their overhang of LDC debt) might be on a multiple of only 5.

Unfortunately, the introduction of SSAP 15 gives companies considerable scope for subjective judgement in the amount of deferred tax they provide, which, of course, directly affects their reported e.p.s. This makes PERs derived from reported e.p.s. (as published in the *Financial Times* and elsewhere) an unsatisfactory basis for inter-company comparisons, so that most analysts use e.p.s. calculated on a full tax charge to produce comparable PERs. They also estimate a company's profits and e.p.s. for the current year and will quote a *prospective* PER (P/PER) as well as a historic one (see Example 14.6); in fact it is the P/PER, based on the market's estimate of the current year's profits, which is normally the yardstick analysts use for comparison with other companies, rather than the published historic PER.

$$\text{Prospective PER} = \frac{\text{Ordinary share price}}{\text{Estimated e.p.s. for current year}}$$

Example 14.6   Historical and prospective PER

Suppose the fully taxed e.p.s. calculated from a company's latest report and accounts, published two to three months after the year has ended, are 8.0p. The analyst is expecting profits to rise by about 27% in the current year, and for there to be a proportionately higher charge for minorities (because one partly owned subsidiary is making a hefty contribution to the improved profits). He therefore estimates that e.p.s. will rise a little less than profits, to about 10.0p. The current share price is 88p, so

Last year's e.p.s.	= 8p	Historical PER	= 11.0
Current year e.p.s.	= 10p	Prospective PER	= 8.8

'Wonder growth' by acquisition

There is nothing fundamentally wrong with improving a company's earnings per share by acquisition, and it can be beneficial all round if there is some industrial or commercial logic involved, i.e. if the acquired company's business fits in with the acquiring company's existing activities or employs common skills and technology, or if the acquirer can provide improved management and financial resources. However, the practice is open to abuse, especially in bull markets.

Enter the 'whiz-kid' (known as a 'gunslinger' on the other side of the Atlantic), who might proceed as follows:

1. Acquire control of a company that has a listing on The Stock Exchange, but little else, e.g. the 'DEMISED TEA COMPANY', known in the jargon as a 'shell'.

2. Reverse the shell into an unlisted company, thus giving his victim the benefit of a ready market for his shares and himself the benefit of a company with real assets.

3. Sell off some of the assets, particularly property that is ripe for development. He doesn't lose any sleep over the fact that closing a factory throws 200 people out of work, as the office block that will replace it will house twice that number of civil servants in the department recently set up to encourage investment in industry; this 'asset-stripping' process is essential to provide the cash to gain control of his next victim.

4. By now the earnings per share of the 'Demised Tea Company', since renamed 'ANGLO-TRIUMPH ASSETS', have shown remarkable growth, albeit from a very low base (it's very easy to double profits of next-to-nothing), the bull market has conveniently started and the Press has noticed him.

    He projects a suitable image of dynamic young management, talking to them earnestly about the need for British industry to obtain a fair return on assets, and his photograph appears in the financial sections of the Sunday papers. He has arrived.

5. His share price responds to Press comment, putting his 'go-go' company on a PER of 15 or 20; he continues to acquire companies, but now uses shares rather than cash, thus continually boosting his e.p.s., as we have shown.

6. Following Press adulation, he broadens out into TV financial panels, seminar platforms, and after-dinner speeches; the bull market is now raging; Anglo-Triumph features regularly as an 'up stock' in the price changes table on the back page of the *FT* as the PER climbs towards 30. Deals follow apace, and Anglo-Triumph thrusts ahead, acquiring a huge conglomeration of businesses in an ever-widening range of mainly unrelated activities – it may be shoes, or ships or sealing-wax, but it's certainly Alice in Wonderland.

7. The moment of truth. The bull market, after a final glorious wave of euphoria, tops out. Profits in Anglo-Triumph's businesses turn

down as little or nothing has been done to improve their management. Asset-stripping becomes politically unacceptable, and the word 'conglomerate' is coined to describe hotchpotch outfits like Anglo-Triumph. Down goes Anglo-Triumph's share price, and with it the market rating; without a high PER the company can no longer boost profits by acquisition, and the game is up.

Whether the whole edifice of Anglo-Triumph collapses completely or becomes just another lowly rated ex-glamour stock depends on the financial structure of the company. If it has geared up (i.e. has built up debt, on which interest has to be paid), and hasn't the cash to service the debt, the company will probably be forced into liquidation unless some sympathetic banker (possibly embarrassed by the prospect of disclosing a huge loss if the company goes under) decides to tide things over until 'hopefully' better times. But we must return to earnings per share.

Adjustments to earnings per share – SSAP 3

If a company issues new shares during the year, the e.p.s. for *that year* have to be calculated using the time-weighted average number of shares in issue during the year, and the e.p.s. of *previous years* have to be adjusted to allow for any bonus element in the share issue. SSAP 3 describes in detail the method of adjustment to be used by companies for each type of issue, which are briefly described here.

Scrip (Bonus) issue or share split
Use the year-end figure for number of shares, and apply a factor to previous years' e.p.s. to put them on a comparable basis. For a scrip issue of y shares for every x shares held, the factor is $x \div (x + y)$ and for a split of 1 old share into z new shares it is $1 \div z$ (Example 14.7).

Example 14.7   Scrip issue and e.p.s.

Let us suppose that 'UNIVERSAL TRADERS PLC' is a company whose year ends on 31 December. At the end of 1986 the issued share capital was £4,000,000, of which £1,000,000 was in 3½% preference shares and £3,000,000 was the equity share capital of 12,000,000 ordinary shares of 25p each. No new shares were issued in 1987 and e.p.s. reported in 1987 were 8p: see tabulated accounts overleaf, showing adjustments to previous years' e.p.s. required by the issue of new shares in this and ensuing examples.

In 1988 the company made a 1-for-3 scrip issue and profits after tax increased from £1.255m to £1.525m. Earnings per share were 7.5p which, at first sight, appear to be down on the previous year, but 1987's figure of 8p has to be adjusted by a factor of $3 \div (3 + 1)$ to make it comparable with 1988: ¾ of 8p = 6p.

Shares issued in an acquisition

The shares are assumed to have been issued at market price (even if the shares issued, the 'vendor consideration', have been placed at a discount at the time). The weighted average number of shares in issue during the year is calculated and used for working out the e.p.s. (Example 14.8).

Example 14.8 Acquisition issue and e.p.s.

To continue Example 14.7, on 1 April 1989 Universal Traders acquired another company and issued 2 million new fully paid 25p ordinary shares in payment (an acquisition 'for paper').

At the year end, the profits of the new subsidiary for the period 1 April to 31 December 1989 were included in Universal Traders' consolidated profit and loss account and the weighted average number of shares in issue during the year was calculated:

$$\frac{16m.\ for\ 3\ months\ plus\ 18m.\ for\ 9\ months}{12\ months}$$

= 17.5m. on weighted average

Profits at the attributable level came out at £1,400,000 to give earnings per share of 8.0p.

Rights issue

A rights issue is regarded as being partly an issue at the market price and partly a scrip issue (the bonus element); the e.p.s. of previous years are adjusted by the factor appropriate to the bonus element in the same way as a scrip issue (Example 14.9).

Example 14.9 Rights issue (on first day of company's year) and e.p.s.

Let us suppose Universal Traders made a rights issue on 1 January 1990 on the basis of one new share for every 4 shares held at a price of 80p per share, against a market price of 100p on the last day the old shares were quoted cum-rights. The issue would have the same effect as a 1-for-5 at 100p, followed by a 1-for-24 scrip issue. The factor for adjusting the e.p.s. for previous years is thus $24 \div (1+24)$, which can be calculated in more complicated cases by the formula:

Theoretical ex-rights (xr) price ÷ actual cum-rights price on the last day of quotation cum-rights

where the Theoretical xr price is, in this case, 1 share at 80p plus 4 old shares at 100p each = 5 shares for 480p = 96p, and 96/100 = 24/25.

If, instead of being made on the first day of the company's year (as in Example 14.9), a rights issue is made during the company's year, the calculation of the bonus element and the factor for adjusting previous years' e.p.s. is just the same but, in

'UNIVERSAL TRADERS PLC' *Accounts*

Year end 31 December	1987	1988 Scrip issue	1989 Acquisition	1990 Rights issue
	£000	£000	£000	£000
Profit after tax	1,255	1,525	1,745	2,165
less Minorities	260	290	310	420
	995	1,235	1,435	1,745
less Preference dividends	35	35	35	35
Attributable profits	960	1,200	1,400	1,710
add Convertible interest (net)				72
fully diluted attributable				1,782
Ordinary shares in issue	12m.	16m.	18m.	22.5m.
1989 weighted average			17.5m.	
1990 fully diluted				23.75m.
e.p.s. reported in 1987	8p	—	—	—
e.p.s. in 1988 and 1989 with 1987 adjusted	6p	7.5p	8.0p	—
e.p.s. in 1990 with prior years adjusted	5.76p	7.2p	7.68p	7.6p
Fully diluted e.p.s.	—	—	—	7.5p

addition, the weighted average number of shares in issue during the year has to be calculated (see Example 14.10).

Example 14.10   Rights issue (during company's year) and e.p.s.

If Universal Traders had made its 1-for-4 rights issue on 1 September 1990, then the number of shares at the beginning of the year is adjusted by the reciprocal of the e.p.s. factor and the calculation to find the weighted average is:

$$\left[18m \times \frac{25}{24} \times \frac{8}{12}\right] + \left[22.5m \times \frac{4}{12}\right] = 20m \text{ shares}$$

which would give e.p.s. of 8.55p rather than 7.6p for 1990.

Adjusting the number of shares in issue during the first 8 months of 1990 by 25/24 allows for the bonus element of the rights issue, i.e. it puts the shares in issue at the beginning of the year on the same basis as the shares in issue at the end of the year.

Fully diluted earnings per share

Where a company has in issue any form of security that does not, at present, rank for ordinary dividends but may do so in the future, e.g. convertibles, deferred or partly paid shares, warrants or options granted, the effect on earnings per share of these securities becoming entitled to dividends is called 'full dilution' (see Example 14.11).

Example 14.11   Full dilution of e.p.s.

Suppose that Universal Traders had made a £2 million issue of 5½% convertible unsecured loan stock on 1 January 1990, entitling holders to convert into ordinary shares on the basis of 62½ ordinary shares per £100 nominal of CULS at any time between 1992 and 1997. The calculation of fully diluted e.p.s. allows for the extra 1.25 million shares that would be issued if all the CULS holders converted, and for the annual interest of £130,000 the company would save at the pre-tax level, which has to bear Corporation Tax before being attributable to shareholders. In our example, with Corporation Tax at 35%, fully diluted e.p.s.:

$$\frac{£1.71m + (£0.11m \times 0.65)}{22.5m + 1.25m} = 7.5p$$

SSAP 3 requires companies to show fully diluted earnings per share if dilution reduces the basic e.p.s. by 5% or more. In Example 14.11, 7.5p is less than a 5% drop on the basic e.p.s. of 7.6p, so Universal Traders would not need to report it. Where the dilution is 5% or more, details are usually given either in the profit and loss account and/or in a note. For example, AUTOMATED SECURITY (HOLDINGS) gave details of the calculations in a note and showed the result at the bottom of the profit and loss account:

AUTOMATED SECURITY (HOLDINGS) *Extract from 1988 profit and loss account*

Earnings per ordinary share – Basic	18.13p
– Fully diluted	16.58p

Where full dilution involves payments to the company, e.g. warrant-holders exercising their right to subscribe for shares at a given price (the exercise price), the calculation of fully diluted e.p.s. assumes that the company would invest the proceeds of subscription in 2½% Consols.

Net and nil basis

SSAP 3 requires companies to show net earnings per share in the profit and loss account and to state the amount of the earnings and the number of shares used in the calculation, which is usually done in an accompanying note. Where there is a material difference between earnings per share calculated on the net basis and on the nil distribution basis, because the distribution of dividends has increased the company's tax charge (as described in Chapter 13), the e.p.s. calculated on the nil distribution basis should also be shown on the face of the profit and loss account.

Earnings on more than one class of share

Where there is more than one class of equity share or where some shares are only partly paid, the earnings should be attributed to the different classes of share in accordance with their dividend rights or profit participation.

MOVEMENTS IN RESERVES

Although the effect of most transactions of a company should be reflected in the profit and loss account, there are a number of occasions where transfers are made direct to or from reserves. These include any premium on the issue of shares, unrealised surpluses arising on the revaluation of fixed assets, a general write-off of goodwill, and foreign exchange adjustments (see Chapter 18).

Schedule 4, para. 46 of the Companies Act 1985 requires the source of any increase and the application of any decrease in reserves to be disclosed; this information is sometimes given in a statement immediately following the profit and loss account, but is usually shown in a note to the accounts, as illustrated here:

REDLAND *Note on capital and reserves*

	Group £ million	Redland PLC £ million
Called up share capital		
. . .		
Share premium account		
Balance at 26 March 1988	233.8	233.8
Premium arising on shares allotted for cash	2.6	2.6
Balance at 31 December 1988	236.4	236.4
Revaluation reserve		
Balance at 26 March 1988	33.2	2.1
Foreign currency adjustments	0.6	—
Surplus arising on revaluation of properties	31.2	—
Transfer to profit and loss account	(0.9)	—
Balance at 31 December 1988	62.9	2.1
Profit and loss account		
Balance at 26 March 1988	176.8	83.9
Foreign currency adjustments	1.0	(0.7)
Goodwill arising on consolidation of new subsidiaries and associates	(22.0)	—
Transfer from revaluation reserve	0.9	—
Retained profit for the period	91.1	11.7
Balance at 31 December 1988	247.8	94.9

Chapter 15

ACQUISITIONS AND MERGERS

(References: SSAP 23 *Accounting for acquisitions and mergers*; ED 48 *Accounting for acquisitions and mergers*; *City Code on Take-overs and Mergers*)

PREFACE

There are two ways of accounting for an acquisition:

1. *Acquisition accounting, and*
2. *Merger accounting.*

The rules for acquisition and merger accounting are contained in SSAP 23. However, ED 48, published in February 1990, proposes that merger accounting should only be permitted if the combining of two or more businesses meet certain criteria. The key criteria proposed are:

1. None of the parties sees itself as acquiror or acquiree.
2. None of the parties dominates the management of the combined entity.
3. No party is more than 50% larger than any other party in the proportion of the equity share capital they own or control in the combined enterprise.

In other words, merger accounting will only be allowed for genuine mergers, and acquisitions will have to be acquisition accounted: at present, providing the consideration paid for an acquisition is mostly 'paper' (shares of the acquiror), SSAP 23 allows companies to choose which method to apply in *each* acquisition; i.e. they are free to choose the more flattering method, and choose they do, e.g. CRAY ELECTRONICS:

CRAY ELECTRONICS *Extract from note on accounting policies*

Basis of consolidation

. . .

The purchase of Executive Action Ltd on 1 July 1988, Ultranet Ltd and its subsidiaries Ultranet Marketing Ltd, Ultranet Services Ltd, Ultranet Manufacturing Ltd and Taunton Software Development Ltd on 8 February 1989 have been accounted for on an acquisition basis.

The acquisition of GRP Material Supplies Ltd on 11 January 1989; Beatcan Ltd and its subsidiary Peatgrange (IVD) Ltd on 10 March 1989 and Crown Graphics Sales Ltd on 28 April 1989 have been accounted for on a merger basis, and accordingly comparatives have been restated.

ACQUISITION ACCOUNTING

Because acquisition accounting is the usual method, and by far the more common method, we will begin by describing acquisition accounting.

Interests in another company

If a company, A, wishes to obtain an interest in the activities of another company, B, it may do so in three ways:

(a) by buying some or all of the assets of company B;
(b) by buying some shares in company B;
(c) by making a bid for company B.

Buying assets of company B
If company A only wishes to acquire some or all of the assets of company B, it may do so either by paying cash or by paying in shares of company A; the latter is an example of a vendor consideration issue of shares described in Chapter 4. Example 15.1 illustrates acquiring all the assets of a company, but not the company itself. Note that, in the example, Company B remains an independent company:

Example 15.1   Acquisition of assets by share issue

Let us suppose that, at 31 December 1989, the balance sheets of A and B were:

	A £000	B £000
Ordinary share capital	800	80
Reserves	100	340
	900	420
Net assets	900	420

Suppose A purchases the net assets of B by the issue to company B of 600,000 £1 ordinary shares (valued at par at the time) then *company A's balance sheet would become*:

	£000
Ordinary share capital	1,400
Reserves	100
	1,500
Net assets (£900,000 + £420,000)	1,320
Goodwill (£600,000 − £420,000)	180
	1,500

Goodwill represents the *excess* of the purchase consideration (i.e. the value of the shares that A issued to B) over the book value of the net assets purchased.

Company B's balance sheet after A's purchase would show:

	£000
Ordinary share capital	80
Reserves (£340,000 + £180,000 profit on realisation of net assets)	520
	600
Investment at cost	600

Company B would not automatically cease to exist; it would become an investment holding company.

Had A's shares been listed and had they been standing at, say, 300p at the time, A would only have needed to issue 200,000 £1 ordinary shares, and A's balance sheet after the purchase would have been:

	£000
Ordinary share capital	1,000
Share premium account	400
Other reserves	100
	1,500
Net assets	1,320
Goodwill	180
	1,500

Where goodwill does arise, most companies write it off against reserves (see page 33), but doing so distorts some ratios (see page 178).

Buying some shares in company B
(a) If A acquires 3% or less of the equity of B, A's balance sheet would show the purchase as an *investment* (see Chapter 7).
(b) If A acquires 3% or more of the equity of B, the purchaser would still show the purchase as an *investment*, but would be obliged by Section 134 of the Companies Act 1989 to declare its interest.
(c) If A acquires 20% or more of the equity of B, and is allowed by B to participate in the major policy decisions of B, usually by holding a seat on B's board, then A should treat B as an *associated company* (see Chapter 17).
(d) If A acquires 30% or more of the voting rights of B, or if A in any period of 12 months adds more than 2% to an existing holding of between 30% and 50% in B, then Rules 9.1 and 9.5 of the Takeover Code oblige A to make a bid for the remainder of the equity of B at a price not less than the highest price A paid for any B shares within the preceding 12 months.

Making a takeover bid for company B
Company A may offer the shareholders of B either cash or 'paper' (i.e. shares and/or loan stock and/or warrants of A). If A has already gone over

the 30% limit or has added more than 2% in 12 months to a holding of 30–50%, the offer must be in cash or be accompanied by a cash alternative. If the bid results in A acquiring 90% or more of the shares of B that it did not already own, A may force the remaining B shareholders to accept the bid using the procedure laid down in Section 428 of the Companies Act 1985.

Acquisition of a subsidiary: revaluation of assets

Under acquisition accounting, SSAP 14, para. 29 requires that the purchase consideration should be allocated between the underlying net tangible and intangible assets other than goodwill on the basis of *fair value to the acquiring company*, rather than simply adopting the value placed on them in the accounts of the subsidiary.

Any excess of the purchase consideration over the *fair value* ascribed to the net tangible and identifiable intangible assets, such as trade marks, patents and development expenditure, will represent the premium on acquisition, and will be shown in the consolidated accounts as goodwill.

Example 15.2 shows the acquisition accounting of company A's successful bid for company B, where the assets of B have been revalued to a fair value of £480,000 and the excess of the value of the shares issued over that value (£600,000 – £480,000) appears in the consolidated balance sheet as goodwill.

Example 15.2   Acquisition of the entire share capital

Continuing with our example of companies A and B (whose balance sheets were shown at the beginning of Example 15.1), let us suppose that A made a successful bid of 2 shares in A for each share of B (with no cash alternative or with the cash alternative underwritten to ensure that A did not have to provide any cash). Thus A acquires the entire share capital of B by the issue of 200,000 £1 ordinary shares in A (standing at 300p each) to the *shareholders* of B, and the *balance sheet of A* will become:

	£000
Ordinary share capital	1,000
Share premium account	400
Other reserves	100
	1,500
Net assets	900
Shares in subsidiary at cost	600
	1,500

The balance sheet of A does not disclose the underlying net assets of B, simply A's investment in B but, to comply with the provisions of the Companies Act 1989 de-

scribed in the next chapter, company A must also produce consolidated accounts.

The consolidated balance sheet of the group (A and its subsidiary B) simply substitutes the net assets of B (which have been revalued from £420,000 to a fair value of £480,000) for the item 'Shares in subsidiary at cost':

	£000
Ordinary share capital	1,000
Share premium account	400
Other reserves	100
	1,500
Net assets	1,380
Goodwill on consolidation (£600,000 – £480,000)	120
	1,500

Had the market value of the shares exactly equalled the net assets of B after revaluation, there would have been no goodwill.

Capital reserve on consolidation

As Example 15.2 illustrates, goodwill on consolidation (or 'cost of control') represents the excess of the purchase price over the net assets acquired.

Where the net assets acquired exceed the purchase price, the difference is shown as a 'capital reserve', or 'negative consolidation difference' (CA 1989, Sch. 2, para. 9(5)). For example, when BRITISH AEROSPACE acquired ROVER in 1988, the £849 million surplus arising on the acquisition was added to the capital reserve in the group balance sheet. Details of the cost of subsidiaries acquired during the year were shown in the source and application of funds statement:

BRITISH AEROSPACE *Extracts from 1988 accounts*

Source and application of funds

	£m
Cost of subsidiaries acquired:	
Fixed assets	1,118
(Capital reserve)/goodwill	(849)
Stocks	502
Debtors	616
Creditors	(939)
Advances	—
Provisions	(416)
Purchase of net assets (excluding cash and loans)	32
Net cash/(loans) acquired	133
Consideration paid	165

109

Group balance sheet

	£m.
Capital and reserves:	
Called up share capital	128
Share premium account	231
Statutory reserve	202
Revaluation reserve	234
Capital reserve	894
Profit and loss account	425
	2,114

Where goodwill on consolidation arises from an acquisition in a group that already has a capital reserve, the goodwill can be offset against that capital reserve, and vice versa.

Subsidiary's profits in year of acquisition or disposal

In acquisition accounting, when a subsidiary is acquired (or disposed of) during the accounting period, the results of the subsidiary are included from the effective date of acquisition (or to the effective date of disposal), e.g. CADBURY SCHWEPPES:

CADBURY SCHWEPPES *Note on accounting policies*

Acquisition and disposal of subsidiaries

Results of subsidiary companies acquired during the financial year are included in group profit from the effective date of acquisition and those of companies disposed of up to the effective date of disposal. For this purpose the net tangible assets of newly acquired subsidiaries are incorporated into the accounts on the basis of the fair value to the group as at the effective date of acquisition . . .

The effective date of acquisition (or disposal) of a subsidiary is defined as the *earlier* of the date on which consideration passes, *or* the date on which an offer becomes or is declared unconditional (SSAP 14, para. 32). At one time unscrupulous companies sometimes backdated an acquisition made towards the end of an accounting period (or excluded the pre-disposal losses of a subsidiary sold during the year), so as to increase the apparent profits in the consolidated accounts, but this is no longer permissible in *acquisition accounting*.

However, in *merger accounting*, as we will describe in the second part of this chapter, when an acquisition made during an accounting period is merger accounted its profit for the entire period is consolidated, rather than its profit since the effective date of acquisition.

Acquisition accounting: scope for enhancing profits

In acquisition accounting companies sometimes exploit the lack of rules on attributing 'fair values' to assets acquired by attributing the lowest possible values to them, so that future depreciation charges on fixed assets are minimised and undervalued stock reduces future cost of sales; both enhance profits.

It is also tempting for management to take excessive advantage of para. 14 of SSAP 22, which allows provision to be made for anticipated future losses or costs of reorganisation of an acquisition; any provision subsequently found to be excessive can then be released to the profit and loss account.

A third way in which profits can be enhanced is by the subsequent sale of part or all of an acquisition at a price above the 'fair value' ascribed: the profit is taken into the profit and loss account without any adjustment for the cost of goodwill in the acquisition: the excess of goodwill over fair value is (normally) written off straight away against reserves, but the excess of the subsequent sale over fair value is taken into the profit and loss account.

However, the Accounting Standards Committee has recognised these loopholes, and has produced ED44, *Accounting for goodwill, additional disclosures*, which, if accepted, will require companies to disclose details of adjustments and provisions made on acquisitions. In addition, if any significant disposal occurs within 3 years of acquisition the company will have to disclose 'the amount of purchased goodwill attributable to a disposal which has previously been written off to reserves, to the extent that it was not taken into account in determining the profit or loss on disposal'.

MERGER ACCOUNTING

When two companies, A and B, come together in a merger effected by a share for share exchange, it was argued that the *acquisition method* of accounting, as illustrated in Example 15.2, did not satisfactorily reflect a true amalgamation of interests: the assets of B are adjusted to fair value, any excess of consideration over net asset value appearing as goodwill; the distributable reserves of B are frozen;

and any excess of the market value of company A's shares issued over their nominal value has to go into a share premium account.

To overcome these difficulties, the *merger method* of accounting was developed, and was used in several major mergers at the end of the 1960s, including CADBURY with SCHWEPPES and TRUST HOUSE with FORTE. Under merger accounting, aptly called 'pooling of interests' in the United States, the following occur:

1. The assets and liabilities of both companies are incorporated into the group accounts at book value.
2. The pre-acquisition reserves of Company B are not capitalised, but are available to the group.
3. The shares issued as consideration are recorded at their *nominal* value (so there is no share premium and no goodwill arises on consolidation).
4. If the total nominal value of the shares issued by Company A is more than the total nominal value of the shares of Company B, the difference is deducted from group reserves. If the total value is less, the shortfall becomes a non-distributable reserve.
5. At the subsequent year end, the consolidated profit and loss account of A takes in the profits of B for a full year, rather than for the period since acquisition.

Although an early Exposure Draft (ED 3, issued in 1971) advocated merger accounting in certain limited circumstances (e.g. where the merging companies were not too dissimilar in size), the ruling in a subsequent test case, *Shearer* v. *Bercain Limited*, held that, because of Section 56 of the Companies Act 1948, the merger method of accounting was not lawful.

However, the situation was changed by the Companies Act 1981, which contained provisions allowing merger accounting where at least 90% of the cost of the acquisition is paid for by the issue of shares in the acquiring company (see CA 1989, Sch. 2, para. 10).

Example 15.3 shows how the acquisition of company B in Example 15.2 would have been treated under merger accounting, compared with acquisition accounting:

Example 15.3   Merger accounting of an acquisition

At 31 December 1989 the balance sheets of companies A and B were:

	A £000	B £000
Ordinary share capital	800	80
Reserves	100	340
	900	420
Net assets	900	420

A made a successful bid for B, acquiring the entire share capital of B by the issue of 200,000 new A £1 ordinary shares (standing at 300p each). The consolidated balance sheet of A would then show:

	Merger accounting £000	Acquisition accounting £000
Ordinary share capital	1,000	1,000
Share premium account	—	400
Distributable reserves	320[1]	100
	1,320	1,500
Net assets	1,320	1,380[2]
Goodwill	—	120
	1,320	1,500

[1] Computed as follows:	£000
Distributable reserves of A	100
Distributable reserves of B	340
	440
Less the excess of the nominal value of the shares A issued (£200,000) over the nominal value of the share in B (£80,000)	120
	320

[2] Under acquisition accounting, the net assets of B were taken at fair value £480,000, rather than at book value £420,000.

Pre-acquisition profits

Although the consolidated profit and loss account should include the profits (or losses) of acquisitions for the entire period, i.e. without adjustment for that part of the period prior to the merger, and corresponding amounts should be presented as if the companies had been combined throughout the previous period, SSAP 23 also requires a breakdown of the profits prior to the merger and in the previous year, e.g. MICROGEN merger accounted the acquisition of MPCS in 1988 and showed details of the profits in a note:

MICROGEN *Note on the acquisition of MPCS*

The results of MPCS have been incorporated on merger accounting principles. The table below sets out the effect of the merger on the profits of the Group for years ending 31 October on a time apportionment basis.

Profit on ordinary activities before taxation:

	1988 £000	1987 £000
Prior to effective date of merger:		
Group excluding MPCS	7,432	7,166
MPCS	147	74
	7,579	7,240
After effective date of merger:		
Group excluding MPCS	2,282	2,347
MPCS	178	21
	2,460	2,368
	10,039	9,608

Criticisms of merger accounting

Although permitted by company law and by accounting standards in certain defined circumstances (SSAP 23, para. 11), merger accounting is criticised for:

1. *The creation of instant earnings.* Companies making acquisitions close to their year end and applying merger accounting can boost their earnings per share to a misleading degree.
2. *The creation of instant distributable reserves.* By applying merger accounting a company may acquire distributable reserves, which it can pay out as dividends, as illustrated by PINEAPPLE GROUP's accounts. Pineapple decided, in retrospect, to merger account rather than acquisition account their purchase of two subsidiaries, and restated the previous year to reflect this change of treatment:

PINEAPPLE GROUP *Note to the profit and loss account*

	£000
Balance as previously stated at 1 August 1986	(575)
Adjustment for merger accounting of Premium Pen PLC and Keymark Out & About Limited	420
Balance as restated at 1 August 1986	(155)
Profit for the year	619
Exchange loss on retranslation of investment in subsidiary companies	(62)
Transfer from revaluation reserve	5
Balance at 31 July 1987	407

---

3. *Lack of a size test.* ED 3, which remained an ED for many years before it was withdrawn, suggested that merger accounting was only appropriate when there was a genuine pooling of interests by shareholders of two companies of similar size, resulting in a common

ownership of the combined entity. Many people still take this view, although the currently accepted view, reflected by SSAP 23, is that provided an acquisition is effected by a share for share exchange the companies are essentially amalgamating, so merger accounting is appropriate.

4. *Understating assets.* The assets of the acquired company are brought into the consolidated balance sheet of the group at book value rather than at fair value. If the book value is below the fair value, as it was in Example 15.3, profits in subsequent years will be enhanced by a lower depreciation charge and net asset value will be understated. Both of these will increase the apparent return on assets.

Avoidance of share premium in acquisition accounting

The merger relief provisions contained in CA 1989, Sch. 2, para. 10 allow companies using acquisition accounting to take advantge of the provisions to show shares issued in an acquisition at their nominal value, i.e. excluding any share premium. Any surplus of net assets acquired over the consideration becomes a *merger reserve* and any goodwill arising on consolidation is written off against this reserve.

For example, TESCO in its 1988 accounts noted that the acquisition of HILLARDS 'has been consolidated by the means of acquisition accounting, adopting the merger relief provisions of the Companies Act 1985', and gave details in a note on merger reserve:

TESCO *Extract from note on merger reserve*

Merger reserve:

	£m
Net assets/(liabilities) acquired	
Goodwill on acquisition	193.9
Fixed assets . . .	
Total net assets acquired	248.3
Reorganisation costs, net of taxation[1]	(10.3)
	238.0
Consideration paid	
Ordinary shares issued[2] (at nominal value)[2]	2.1
Cash	2.4
Merger reserve on consolidation	233.5
Less: Goodwill written-off	193.9
Merger reserve (shown in note on reserves)	39.6

Notes:
[1] Reorganisation costs, net of taxation
The costs of reorganising Hillards' retailing, distribution, marketing and administration operations include principally head office and depot closure costs

£3.6m, store conversion costs £4.2m, and other items including alignment of accounting policies £2.5m.

[2] Ordinary shares issued
In accordance with Section 131 of the Comapnies Act 1985, the company has recorded the ordinary shares issued in respect of the acquisition at their nominal value excluding the share premium, and expenses of the share issue of £6.9m. have been offset against share premium account.

Note that TESCO made a provision of £10.3 million for reorganisation costs. It also showed an upward adjustment of £6.4 million on fixed assets and a £2.7 million write-down of stock.

Chapter 16

SUBSIDIARIES AND GROUP ACCOUNTS

(References: SSAP 14 *Group Accounts*; SSAP 22 *Accounting for goodwill*.)

HOLDING COMPANIES, SUBSIDIARIES AND GROUPS

Definitions

(Reference: CA 1989, S. 144)

A *holding company* is a company which exercises control over another company, its subsidiary company, and is often referred to as the *parent* company.

A company is a *subsidiary* of another company, its *holding company*, if that other company:

(*a*)   holds a majority of the voting rights, *or*
(*b*)   has the right to appoint or remove directors holding a majority of voting rights at board meetings, *or*
(*c*)   controls, by agreement, a majority of the voting rights.

A *group* is a holding company, together with its subsidiary company or companies.

A *wholly owned subsidiary* is one in which all the share capital is owned either by the holding company or by other wholly owned subsidiaries.

A *partially owned subsidiary* is one in which some of the share capital is owned outside the group. The outside shareholdings are called minority interests.

For an illustration of the use of these terms, see Example 16.1.

Example 16.1   Partially and wholly owned subsidiaries

H is the holding company of a group of companies, and is incorporated in Great Britain.

H holds 100,000 of the 100,000 ordinary shares of S
H holds   7,500 of the   10,000 ordinary shares of T
S holds   5,100 of the   10,000 ordinary shares of U
T holds   1,000 of the   1,000 ordinary shares of V

The H group may be depicted thus:

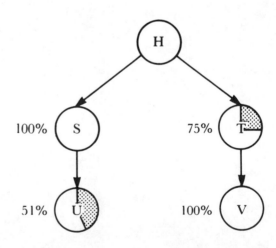

The group consists of:
H's wholly owned subsidiary S
H's partially owned listed subsidiary T (in which there is a 25% minority)
T's wholly owned subsidiary V (which in law is also a subsidiary of H, but colloquially a partially owned sub-subsidiary of H)
S's partially owned subsidiary U (in which there is a 49% minority).

Statutory requirements for group accounts

The term 'holding company' and 'subsidiary' apply for general purposes. For accounting purposes, and in particular to reduce the scope for off-balance-sheet finance, the Companies Act 1989, S. 21, introduced a new pair of terms, 'parent undertaking' and 'subsidiary undertaking', with wider definitions than holding company and subsidiary. *Undertakings* include partnerships and unincorporated associations as well as companies.

Parent undertaking. An undertaking is a parent undertaking if it is a holding company and, in addition, if:

(*a*) the memorandum or articles of association of another undertaking or a control contract give it the right to exercise a dominant influence over that undertaking, *or*

(*b*) it actually exercises a dominant influence over that undertaking, *or*

(*c*) it and the subsidiary are managed on a unified basis.

If, at the end of a financial year, a company is a parent company, group accounts have to be prepared as well as individual accounts for the parent company (CA 1989 S. 5), although small and medium-sized private groups are exempt from this (CA 1989, S. 13). Group accounts comprise a consolidated balance sheet and profit and loss account dealing with the parent company and its subsidiary undertakings. However, as we shall discuss, subsidiary undertakings may be excluded in certain circumstances (see page 119).

Additional information

If the matters required to be included in group or individual company accounts would not be sufficient to give a true and fair view, the Act requires that 'the necessary additional information shall be given'.

This requirement should force the disclosure of activities that have deliberately been structured to get them off balance sheet in order to conceal high gearing and high risk. For example, it should prevent a repetition of the celebrated case of BURNETT & HALLAMSHIRE, where trusts were used to hide the extent of its property development activities in the United States, which eventually led to a £50 million write-off that nearly brought the company down.

CONSOLIDATED ACCOUNTS

The consolidated balance sheet

In simple terms a consolidated balance sheet shows all the assets and all the liabilities of all group companies whether wholly owned or partially owned. Where a partially owned subsidiary exists, its shareholders' funds are provided partly by the holding company and partly by the minority interests.

To illustrate the basic principles of consolidated accounts let us take the case of a holding company, 'H LTD', with a partially owned subsidiary, 'S LTD', and imagine that we wish to prepare the consolidated balance sheet for the H Group at 31 December 1989. H paid £340,000 cash for 200,000 of the 250,000 £1 ordinary shares of S Ltd on 1 January 1986, when the balance sheet of S was as shown on p. 116.

There are six steps to consolidating the two companies' balance sheets at 31 December 1989, which are also shown below.

1. *Ascertain the goodwill cost of control* by comparing the cost to H Ltd of its investment in S Ltd with H Ltd's share of the equity shareholders' funds of S Ltd at the date of acquisition. The goodwill cost of control will be:

	£000	£000
Purchase consideration		340
Holding company's share of ordinary shareholders' funds at date of acquisition:		

4/5ths of Ordinary share capital	200	
4/5ths of Reserves	68	268
Goodwill cost of control		72

Note the following:

(*a*) Any *pre-acquisition profits* of S Ltd which have not already been distributed will form part of that company's reserves, and are thus represented by equity shareholders' funds taken into account in computing goodwill cost of control.

(*b*) Any distribution by S Ltd after it is acquired by H Ltd which is made out of pre-acquisition profits (i.e. reserves existing at acquisition) must be credited not to the profit and loss account of H Ltd as income, but to the asset account 'Investment in S Ltd' as a reduction of the purchase price of that investment. The goodwill cost of control does not change.

2. *Compute the holding company's share of the undistributed post-acquisition profits of the subsidiary.* This equals the holding company's proportion of the change in reserves since the date of acquisition:

$$\frac{200,000}{250,000} \times (£150,000 - 85,000)$$

$$= (£120,000 - £68,000)$$

$$= £52,000.$$

115

This, added to the holding company's own reserves, represents the reserves of the group which will appear in the consolidated balance sheet:

£52,000 + £480,000 = £532,000.

3. *Compute minority interests in the net assets of S Ltd:*

Minority interests =

$$\text{Minority proportion} \times \text{Net assets (capital + reserves) of S Ltd at balance sheet date.}$$

The minority interest in the equity shareholders' funds of S Ltd is:

$$\text{Minority proportion} \times \text{Equity shareholders' funds of S Ltd at balance sheet date (31 December 1989)}$$

$$= \frac{50,000}{250,000} \times £400,000 = £80,000.$$

4. *Draw up the consolidated balance sheet:*
   (a) insert as share capital the share capital of the holding company;
   (b) insert the figures already computed for (i) goodwill (cost of control) (see 1 above) and (ii) minority interests (see 3 above);
   (c) show as 'reserves' the total of the reserves of the holding company and the post-acquisition reserves of the subsidiary applicable to the holding company (see 2 above).

5. *Cancel out any inter-company balances:* the aim of the consolidated balance sheet is to show a true and fair view of the state of affairs of the group as a whole. Inter-company balances (where an item represents an asset of one group company and a liability of another) must be cancelled out since they do not

---

'S LTD' *Balance sheet at 1 January 1986*

	£000		£000
Ordinary share capital	250	Fixed assets:	
Reserves	85	Freehold land and buildings	120
		Plant and machinery	146
Ordinary shareholders' funds	335		266
7% Debenture	100		
		Net current assets	169
	435		435

'H LTD' *and* 'S LTD' *Balance sheets at 31 December 1989*

	H Ltd £000	S Ltd £000		H Ltd £000	S Ltd £000
Ordinary share capital	500	250	Fixed assets:		
Reserves	480	150	Freehold land and buildings	150	120
			Plant and machinery	250	180
Ordinary shareholders' funds	980	400		400	300
10% Unsecured loan stock	120	—	Shares in S Ltd	340	—
7% Debenture	—	100	Net current assets	360	200
	1,100	500		1,100	500

'H GROUP' *Consolidated balance sheet at 31 December 1989*

	£000		£000
Ordinary share capital	500	Fixed assets:	
Reserves	532	Freehold land and buildings	270
		Plant and machinery	430
Ordinary shareholders' funds	1,032		700
Minority interests	80		
H Ltd's 10% ULS	120	Net current assets	560
S Ltd's 7% Debenture	100	Goodwill – cost of control	72
	1,332		1,332

concern outsiders. Thus, if S Ltd owes H Ltd on current account £10,000, this £10,000 will appear as an asset in H Ltd's own balance sheet, and as a liability in that of S Ltd, but it will not appear at all in the consolidated balance sheet.

6. *Consolidate:* add together like items (e.g. add freehold land and buildings of the holding company and freehold land and buildings of the subsidiary) and show the group totals in the consolidated balance sheet. Omit, in so doing, the share capital of the subsidiary, reserves, and the investment in the subsidiary, which have already been taken into account in steps 1 to 3.

It will be seen that only the share capital of the holding company appears in the consolidated balance sheet. The share capital of the subsidiary has disappeared, one-fifth of it becoming part of 'minority interests' while the other four-fifths (£200,000), together with H's share of S's reserves on acquisition (£68,000) and the 'goodwill – cost of control' (£72,000) balance out the removal of H's balance sheet item 'shares in S Ltd' (£340,000).

Goodwill on consolidation (purchased goodwill)

As mentioned in the previous chapter, when goodwill on consolidation does arise, most companies write it off straight away against reserves, and this is the treatment recommended by SSAP 22: 'Purchased goodwill should normally be eliminated from the accounts immediately on acquisition against reserves ('immediate write-off')', although ED 47 proposes to change this: see page 146.

But immediate write-off distorts some ratios; for example in 1987 UNILEVER with the acquisition of Chesebrough-Pond's wrote off £1.288 billion of purchased goodwill; then, as a 'key ratio' in its annual report's financial highlights, it showed the return on shareholders' equity (ordinary share capital plus reserves) increasing from 17.8% in

1986 to 25.4% in 1987. If the purchased goodwill had not been written off against reserves, the return in 1987 would have been only 17.7%, marginally down on the previous year.

The alternative treatment allowed by SSAP 22 is to amortise purchased goodwill through the profit and loss account over its useful economic life. But this method, which is the only method allowed in the United States, is not popular in the UK because it reduces profits in future years, which immediate write-off does not.

The problem was well described by the chairman of ERSKINE HOUSE, a leading company in the distribution and servicing of office equipment:

ERSKINE HOUSE *Extract from chairman's 1986 statement*

In almost all of our acquisitions of service businesses the total value which we are obliged to pay includes a significant amount of goodwill. A new accounting standard now makes it necessary to write off this goodwill either through the profit and loss account or against reserves. Such a write-off against profit appears to your board to be quite artificial and misleading . . . fails to reflect the fact that most of the companies we have acquired have increased their profits and their customer base. The value of these businesses, and hence the goodwill associated with them, has not diminished.

The alternative of writing it off against reserves has the effect of appearing to reduce the shareholders' funds. This results in a return on capital which appears to be very high and which is quite unrelated to reality. In the current year, for example, the group's pre-tax return on capital on this basis would appear to be 88%.

Erskine House's solution is to adopt SSAP 22's preferred treatment, immediate write-off, but to recognise the goodwill written off by presenting the cumulative amount in its accounts as a separate 'goodwill reserve'. Several companies, including IMI and TI, have followed ERSKINE HOUSE's example, and PEARSON now shows it in the historical summary:

PEARSON *Extract from seven-year summary*

	1982 £m	1983 £m	1984 £m	1985 £m	1986 £m	1987 £m	1988 £m
Capital employed	490.3	477.8	570.8	572.5	598.4	620.6	877.4
Cumulative goodwill written off since 1981	4.5	13.3	39.8	71.4	102.5	156.1	612.1

Other companies, like GUINNESS shown below, have incorporated a goodwill reserve in their accounts. Goodwill is then set off against this reserve, producing a negative reserve which reduces the total reserves by the total amount of goodwill written off. GUINNESS has complicated it further by deciding, retrospectively, to recognise the value of brands acquired in acquisitions as intangible fixed assets, thus reducing the negative figure in the goodwill reserve:

GUINNESS *Extract from note on reserves*

Goodwill reserve	£m
At 1 January 1988	—
Prior year adjustment	1,375
Transfers	(1,869)
As restated	(494)
Goodwill during the year	(60)
At 31 December 1988	(554)

The prior year adjustment relates to the cost of acquired brands recognised as an intangible fixed asset.

The consolidated profit and loss account

Consolidated profit and loss accounts follow the same pattern as described for single companies at the beginning of Chapter 12, except that if the group contains partially owned subsidiaries, the minority interests in the profits of those subsidiaries have to be deducted at the after-tax level.

Continuing with our example of H Ltd owning four-fifths of the £250,000 ordinary share capital of S Ltd, let us suppose that at the beginning of 1990, S Ltd issued 30,000 £1 7% preference shares to a third party as part payment for an acquisition, and that the pre-tax profits and tax charges of H Ltd and S Ltd for that year were:

	H Ltd £	S Ltd £	Total £
Profit before tax	72,000	51,200	123,200
Corporation Tax at 25%	18,000	12,800	30,800
Profit after tax	54,000	38,400	92,400

The combined pre-tax profit, tax and profit after tax will be shown in the group's consolidated profit and loss account.

Calculation of minority interests
The minority interests in the profits after tax of S Ltd will then be computed as follows:

	S Ltd £	Minority interests £
Profit before tax	51,200	
less Corporation Tax	12,800	
Profit after tax	38,400	
less Preference dividends	2,100	2,100
Attributable to ordinary shareholders	36,300 $\times \frac{1}{5}$ = 7,260
Minority interests total		9,360

It is this sum of £9,360 which will be deducted as 'minority interests' from the profit after tax in the consolidated profit and loss account.

Appropriations of the subsidiary
Suppose, for instance, that S Ltd proposed a single ordinary dividend of 4p for 1990. Then the profit attributable to S Ltd's ordinary shareholders would be appropriated as follows:

	Total £	Minorities £	H Ltd £
Attributable	36,300	7,260	29,040
Proposed dividend of 4.0p per share	10,000	2,000	8,000
Retentions	26,300	5,260	21,040

H Ltd's share of the proposed dividend (£8,000) would also appear, as dividends receivable, in the holding company's accounts, and the two figures would cancel out on consolidation. The dividends payable to minority shareholders (£2,000) would be charged (behind the scenes) against the minority interests deducted on consolidation, and the minorities' share of the retentions (£9,360 − £2,100 preference dividends − £2,000 ordinary dividends = £5,260) added to the consolidated *balance sheet* item 'minority interests'.

The group profit and loss account
Suppose H Group declared dividends of £25,000 for the year. The group profit and loss account would then show:

	£
Profit before tax	123,200
less Tax	30,800
Profit after tax	92,400
less Minority interests	9,360
	83,040
less Dividends	25,000
Retentions	58,040

Retained profit
The group's retained profit of £58,040 would be carried forward partly in the holding company's accounts:

	£
H Ltd profit after tax	54,000
H Ltd's dividends from S Ltd	8,000
less Dividends paid by H Group	25,000
	37,000

The remainder, £21,040, would be carried forward in S Ltd's accounts, being H Ltd's share of S Ltd's retentions.

Some companies show where the retained profits of the group are being carried forward in a statement of retained profit/reserves below their profit and loss account, e.g. ICI, illustrated below, or in a note to the accounts.

ICI *Statement of retained profit/reserves*

Group reserves attributable to parent company

	1988 £m	1987 £m
At beginning of year	2,769	3,008
Profit retained for year:		
Company	170	389
Subsidiaries	260	38
Related companies	66	56
	496	483
Amounts taken direct to reserves	(23)	(722)
At end of year	3,242	2,769

Unrealised profits on stocks

It frequently happens that one group company supplies another company within the group with goods in the ordinary course of trade; indeed, this sort of trading link may often be at the very heart of the existence of the group in the first place. But where one group company has made a profit on the supply of goods to another group company and those goods, or some of them, remain in stock at the end of the accounting year, a problem arises and, although nothing can normally be gleaned from the accounts, the procedure for consolidation is designed to prevent a group's profits being artificially inflated by sales within the group.

Exceptions to consolidation of subsidiaries

Under Section 5 of the Companies Act 1989, a subsidiary undertaking *may* be excluded from consolidation on the following grounds: not material, severe long-term restrictions, disproportionate expense or undue delay or held solely for resale, and shall be excluded where the activities are so different that their inclusion would be incompatible with a true and fair view.

In contrast, SSAP 14, para. 21, requires that a subsidiary *should be* excluded from consolidation in the following circumstances (there is no discretion):

1. *Dissimilar activities*: if its activities are so dissimilar from those of other companies within the group that consolidation would be misleading and that it would be better to present separate financial statements, e.g. NEXT does not consolidate its credit card services subsidiary Club 24, and explains why in its accounting policies:

NEXT *Extract from accounting policies*

Basis of consolidation

The Group consolidates the accounts of the Company and its subsidiaries with the exception of Club 24 Limited, which is accounted for on the equity basis. The Directors consider that comprehension of the accounts is improved by not consolidating Club 24 because its activity is significantly different from that of the rest of the Group.

The profits of Club 24 are shown as a separate item in NEXT's consolidated profit and loss account.

2. *Lack of control*: if the group does not own share capital carrying more than half the votes, or is restricted in its ability to appoint the majority of directors. With the new definition of subsidiary in the Companies Act 1989, this situation is less likely to arise in the future.

3. *Severe restrictions*: if the subsidiary operates under severe restrictions which significantly impair control by the holding company. For example, the group accounts of BOOKER do not consolidate the results of some of its overseas subsidiaries, and they explain why in the statement of accounting policies: 'Certain subsidiary and associated companies operate in countries overseas where the amount of profit that may be remitted is restricted or where freedom of action may be limited. In the opinion of the directors, it would be misleading to consolidate these companies and the group share of their results is therefore included in profit only to the extent of remittances received.' Other companies consolidate subsidiaries operating in areas of economic and political uncertainty, but make provisions, e.g. BOC:

BOC *Extract from accounting policies*

Economic uncertainty

Certain subsidiary and related companies operate in countries subject to severe economic uncertainty. Provision is made against profits earned in cases where the ability to repatriate dividends or capital is doubtful.

4.   *Temporary control*: if control is intended to be temporary.

Where subsidiaries are not consolidated for any of these four reasons, SSAP 14 describes the accounting treatment that should be used in each case (see SSAP 14, paras. 23 to 27).

Group accounts are not required where the company is, at the end of its financial year, the wholly owned subsidiary of a parent undertaking (CA 1989, S. 5). In Example 16.1, S would not need to produce consolidated accounts, but T would.

The parent company's own balance sheet

Subsidiaries are normally shown at cost less any amounts written off, but some companies show them at their underlying net asset value, i.e. they use the equity method of accounting, which includes them at cost plus the parent company's share of the post-acquisition retained profits and reserves.

The parent company's own profit and loss account

Under Section 5 of the Companies Act 1989, the parent company's profit and loss account may be omitted from the consolidated accounts providing the parent company's balance sheet shows the parent company's profit or loss for the year. In practice one seldom if ever sees the parent company's own profit and loss account.

The company's financial (accounting) year end

Under Section 3 of the Companies Act 1989 a parent company's directors must ensure that the financial year of each of its subsidiaries coincides with the holding company's own financial year, unless in their opinion there are good reasons against it. If the financial year of a subsidiary undertaking ends no more than 3 months beforehand, its annual accounts may be used. If more than 3 months, interim accounts must be used for the subsidiary, made up to the parent company's year end (CA 1989, Sch. 2, Para. 2(2)).

Unfortunately, the Companies Act uses the term 'financial year' here to mean the company's accounting year; the term is normally used to describe the Corporation Tax year, which runs from 1 April to 31 March, as described in Chapter 13. Many companies nowadays arrange for their overseas subsidiaries to end their accounting year, say, three months before that of the holding company, in order to make the task of preparing group accounts easier.

Further statutory requirements in consolidated accounts

Emoluments of directors

Chairman's and directors' emoluments, pensions and other details required by Schedule 4 of the Companies Act 1989 and described on page 77, only have to be shown for the parent company, but all their remuneration from the group should be included (e.g. fees they may receive for being directors of subsidiaries).

However, all these requirements have to be met by each subsidiary in its own accounts, which are not normally published but do have to be filed eventually at Companies House.

Information on subsidiaries

Schedule 3 of the Companies Act 1989 requires that where a company has a subsidiary, its accounts must show:

(*a*)   the subsidiary's name;

(*b*)   if incorporated in Great Britain, the subsidiary's country of registration (England or Scotland) if different from that of the holding company; if incorporated outside Great Britain, the subsidiary's country of incorporation;

(*c*)   the proportion of the nominal value of each class of the subsidiary's share capital held by the holding company.

But information about a subsidiary either incorporated, or carrying on business, outside the United Kingdom, which would be harmful to the business of the company or any of its subsidiaries if made public, need not be disclosed if the Department of Trade and Industry agrees.

Where the required information would be of excessive length, details need be given only of subsidiaries principally affecting the profits or losses and the assets of the group, but in this case full particulars must be annexed to the annual return.

Holdings in subsidiaries held directly by the holding company must be distinguished from those held by another subsidiary.

Subsidiary's holding of holding company's shares

With certain minor exceptions a subsidiary cannot be a member of its holding company (i.e. cannot hold shares in its holding company, either directly or through a nominee), and any allotment or transfer of shares in a company to its subsidiary is void (CA 1989, S. 129).

Where a group acquires a subsidiary that holds shares in the group, the group may cancel or retain them. If it retains them, it may not exercise any voting rights on them (CA 1989, S. 129). Alternatively the shares can be offered to existing shareholders; this is what FEEDEX AGRICULTURAL INDUSTRIES did in a reverse takeover by USBORNE, when Usborne held a 28% stake in Feedex:

FEEDEX AGRICULTURAL INDUSTRIES *Circular to shareholders*

The 5,172,000 Feedex Ordinary shares presently owned by Usborne are being sold to raise additional capital for the Enlarged Group. Hambros, as agents for Usborne, is offering these shares at 45p per share to Qualifying shareholders by way of rights, on the basis of 38 Rights shares for every 100 Feedex Ordinary shares held on 30 October 1987 . . . The Rights Offer is being underwritten by Hambros.

THE INTERPRETATION OF CONSOLIDATED ACCOUNTS

Profitability of subsidiaries

Some listed companies are not particularly forthcoming about the profitability of the various component parts of their organisation, and many do not file the reports and accounts of their subsidiaries at Companies House at the same time as they publish their consolidated accounts.

Thus, while in theory it is possible to deconsolidate strategic parts of the group in order to find out just where the profits are being made, this may not be easy, nor may it be possible at the time the report and accounts of the holding company become available; but the effort involved can be very rewarding, as Example 16.2 shows.

Example 16.2 Analysing subsidiaries' performance:
GEORGE WIMPEY

The 1988 accounts of the housebuilding and construction company GEORGE WIMPEY showed:

Operating profit by activity	1987 £m	1988 £m
Construction related	89.6	160.2
Property	20.0	0.6
	109.6	160.8

The chairman in his statement mentioned that Wimpey's strong regional presence in housebuilding had paid off handsomely, while construction had a busy year, but there was no indication of the relative importance of these two main activities.

A leading stockbroker's analyst, who had done his homework at Companies House, produced a much more informative breakdown:

	1987 £m	1988 £m
Housing	66.0	112.0
Construction	12.6	27.0
Minerals	11.0	18.0
Property	20.0	0.6
Miscellaneous	—	3.2
Operating profits	109.6	160.8

As the housing market had peaked, and was turning down sharply in 1989, the fact that almost 70% of WIMPEY's 1988 operating profits came from housebuilding was particularly significant.

Leaving aside the possibilities of devilling at Companies House, the analyst should look carefully at the group's published accounts to see if there are any clues as to the spread of profitability (in addition to those already gleaned from the geographical analysis, discussed in Chapter 12). Worthy of special note are the effect on profitability of acquisitions and disposals and figures for minority interests.

Acquisitions and disposals

Where an acquisition is merger accounted, its profits are included for the entire period, and a breakdown of profits prior to the merger has to be shown, as we described in the previous chapter.

With acquisition accounting, the profits of the subsidiary are included from the date of acquisition or to the date of disposal but, although SSAP 14 requires disclosure of 'sufficient information about the results of the subsidiaries acquired or sold to enable shareholders to appreciate the effect on the consolidated results', the manner and extent to which this is done varies considerably.

Information can appear in a separate note, or in a note on operating profit, e.g. TESCO in 1988: 'Operating profit includes £13m in respect of incremental contribution from the stores acquired with Hillards plc', or in the segmental analysis. For example BET:

BET *Note on activity analysis*

	Revenue 1989 £m	Operating profit 1989 £m
Support services	2,061.0	266.2
Thames Television	92.3	8.8
Discontinued operations[1]	71.1	16.4
	2,224.4	291.4

[1] Discontinued operations comprise broadcasting and publishing operations.

Minority interests

Where a group has subsidiaries that are partially owned, an indication of their profitability will be given by minority interests. For example, in 1988 RTZ's minority interests, shown in the group profit and loss accounts as 'Attributable to outside shareholders', jumped from £72 million to £130.9 million. RTZ has three major subsidiaries that are partially owned: Rio Algom in Canada (51.5% owned), Rossing Uranium in Namibia (53%) and Palabora in South Africa (64.9%), and a table of 'Contribution to net profit attributable to RTZ shareholders' gave details of the significant improvement in all these companies.

Transfer prices

A further hazard we should mention in assessing the profitability of individual subsidiaries is that of 'transfer pricing'. When two subsidiaries of a holding company trade substantially with each other or with the holding company (e.g. a manufacturing subsidiary wholesaling through a trading subsidiary), the transfer prices may not always be arm's length prices, and thus the profitability of the business transacted may be slanted towards one subsidiary at the expense of the other. This may be done deliberately to minimise taxation overall, to maximise profits in currencies the group most needs (e.g. for the servicing and repayment of foreign loans), and possibly to hide highly lucrative activities from the jealous eyes of potential competitors.

Chapter 17

ASSOCIATED UNDERTAKINGS AND PARTICIPATING INTERESTS

(Reference: SSAP 1 *Accounting for the results of associated companies*.)

New terminology

The Companies Act 1989 abolished the term 'related company' and introduced two new terms: a *participating interest* in an undertaking, and an *associated undertaking*, which includes associated companies.

The main changes from 'related company' and 'associated company' are that *undertakings* include partnerships and unincorporated associations carrying on a trade or business as well as companies, CA 1989, S. 22, and an *interest* now includes convertible securities and options as well as shares.

A *participating interest* is an interest held by the investing group or company on a long-term basis to secure a contribution to its activities by the exercise of control or influence. A holding of 20% or more of the shares of an undertaking shall be presumed to be a participating interest unless the contrary is shown. An *interest* includes convertible securities and options (CA 1989, S. 22).

An *associated undertaking* is an undertaking (other than a subsidiary or a proportionally consolidated joint venture) in which the investing group or company has a participating interest and over whose operating and financial policy it exercises a significant influence. (CA 1989, Sch. 2, para. 20.) Associated undertakings are accounted for by the 'equity method' of accounting.

Equity method of accounting

This is the treatment prescribed by SSAP 1. In summary:

Consolidated profit and loss account
Turnover: nothing included from associates.

Pre-tax profit: share of associates, shown separately.
Tax: share of associates, shown separately.
Extraordinary items: share of associates, included in the group figure unless material.
Net profit retained: share of associates, shown separately.

Consolidated balance sheet
Unless shown at valuation, the investing group's interest should be shown at *cost*, less amounts written off, plus share of the associated companies' subsequent *retained profits and reserves*.

SSAP 1 also requires separate disclosure of the goodwill element of the cost of associates, loans to and from associates, and any balances representing normal trading transactions (if material).

Example of equity method

BET's accounts provide a good example of the treatment of associated companies using the equity method of accounting, see page 124.

The *holding company's share* of the associated companies' turnover (revenue) and the *holding company's share* of the associated companies' profits appear on the face of the consolidated profit and loss account as separate items [A] and [B], but the share of the tax charge appears only in a note [D].

In the group balance sheet, BET follows the normal practice of including the group's interest in associated companies in a single figure for investments [E], with a breakdown between investments in associated companies and other investments in a note [F], which gives details of cost [G] and post acquisition reserves [I].

From this information we can work out what happened to BET's £10.3m. share of associated companies' profits in 1989:

BET *Extract from 1989 accounts*

	Text ref.	1989 £m	1988 £m
Consolidated profit and loss account			
Revenue			
Subsidiaries		2,106.2	2,015.1
Share of associated companies	[A]	118.2	114.2
		2,224.4	2,129.3
Operating profit		281,1	228.3
Share of results of associated companies (Note 3)	[B]	10.3	11.7
Investment income		0.8	1.0
Interest		(21.6)	(24.6)
Profit on ordinary activities before taxation		270.6	216.4
Taxation (Note 6)		(84.4)	(64.6)
Profit on ordinary activities after taxation		186.2	151.8

Note 3 Associated companies

Dividends receivable		
Listed company		2.1
Unlisted companies		0.3
	[C]	2.4

Note 6   Taxation

UK corporation tax at 35%		66.9
Overseas tax . . .		
		80.7
Associated companies	[D]	3.7
		84.4

Consolidated balance sheet

Tangible fixed assets		773.4
Investments (Note 14)	[E]	51.6
		825.0

Note 14   Investments   [F]

		Associated companies £m	Other investments £m
Cost			
Beginning of year		13.2	10.6
Additions		0.8	16.7
Disposals		(4.8)	(5.7)
End of year	[G]	9.2	21.6
Post-acquisition reserves			
Beginning of year		16.7	—
Currency adjustments		0.2	—
Retained for year	[H]	4.2	—
Other movements		(0.3)	—
End of year	[I]	20.8	—
Balance sheet value		30.0	21.6
Balance sheet value 1988		29.9	10.6

The balance sheet value of the above investments includes a listed associated company, Thames Television PLC ('Thames'), with a book value of £19.9 million and a market value of £62.7 million. BET holds 28.24% of Thames and this investment is not listed: the market value of £62.7 million is based on the mid-market price of the listed shares in Thames as at 1 April 1989.

		£m
Taxation	[D]	3.7
Dividends	[C]	2.4
Retained earnings	[H]	4.2
		10.3

Information on associated undertakings

The Companies Act 1989 requires that the following information shall be given on associated undertakings: name, country of incorporation or address if unincorporated, identity of each class of share held and the proportion held (CA 1989, Sch. 3, para. 22), e.g. CHLORIDE shown below.

Information also has to be given on other significant holdings, including participating interests in undertakings that are not associated undertakings, as described in Chapter 7.

Misuse of SSAP 1

Although companies now disclose much more information on substantial and influential investments in other companies than they did before SSAP 1, the equity method of accounting does give the more imaginative members of the business community a great deal of scope for 'dressing up' their accounts. They do so by making marginal adjustments to their holdings; see Example 17.1.

Similar manoeuvres can take place at the 50% level in order, for instance, to turn a 51%-owned subsidiary that is heavily borrowed into a 49%-owned associated company whose borrowings don't appear on the investing group's balance sheet (although they will appear as a contingent liability of the group if the holding company has guaranteed them). This trick can do wonders for the investing group's gearing, but it is only 'fair' if

Example 17.1   Dressing up accounts under SSAP 1

Year 1:   Holding Company A holds 19.95% of the voting equity of Company B. Company B makes pre-tax profits of £10m., but distributes only £1m. of dividends.

Result: Contribution to Group A's pre-tax profits is £266,000 (£199,500 dividends and £66,500 associated tax credits).

Year 2:   Group A has increased its holding in Company B to 20.1%, has obtained board representation, and has adopted equity accounting. Company B's profits and dividends are the same as in Year 1.

Result: Group A will include its share of the now associated Company B's pre-tax profits of £2,010,000, an increase of more than 600%!

Year 3:   In a rising market, Company B's shares are now standing at twice 'cost plus share of subsequent retained profits and reserves'. Group A wants to dress up its balance sheet, so it changes its accounting policy to show its holding in Company B at valuation (i.e. market price).

Result: The balance sheet amount shown for Group A's investment in associated companies doubles.

Year 4:   Company B makes losses. Group A wants to avoid including its share of these losses in its profit and loss account, so the holding company either sells a shade more than 0.1% of the voting shares of Company B or takes its man off Company B's board.

Result: Group A's profit and loss account includes only dividends (if any) received from Company B, as B is no longer an associated company.

CHLORIDE *Principal associated companies*

	Country of incorporation	Class of capital	Currency	Total issued capital 000	Sterling equivalent £000	Group interest %
Associated Battery Manufacturers (Ceylon) Ltd	Sri Lanka	Ordinary shares	Sri Lankan rupees	31,680	537	49
Dexel Battery Makers Ltd	Cyprus	Ordinary shares	Cyprus £	250	298	33
P.T. Chloride Battieres Indonesia	Indonesia	Ordinary shares	Rupiahs	3,639,271	1,199	49
West African Batteries Ltd	Nigeria	Ordinary shares	Nigerian naira	4,000	483	40

the group is no longer responsible for the borrowings of its former subsidiary, i.e. if it hasn't guaranteed them.

In order to bowl out this sort of window dressing, the analyst should check:

(a) for any changes in the group's accounting policy on associated companies;

(b) for any companies that have either become or ceased to be associated companies during the year;

(c) under Contingent Liabilities, for any guarantees of associated company borrowings.

If you find this sort of thing going on, ask yourself whether there are good commercial reasons for the changes. If there are none, be wary of the accounts.

Chapter 18

FOREIGN EXCHANGE

(Reference: SSAP 20 *Foreign Currency Translation*.)

The problem of variable exchange rates

The advent of floating exchange rates has produced both accounting problems and operating problems. This chapter will deal with the accounting problems first, and then look at what companies do to mitigate the adverse effects that currency fluctuations may have on their operations.

The main accounting problem is the rate (or rates) of exchange to be used in translating the accounts of foreign subsidiaries, associates and branches, which are kept in foreign currencies, into sterling when producing the consolidated accounts of a group. The choice lies between:

(a) the *closing rate*: the spot rate of exchange at the balance sheet date;
(b) the *average rate* of exchange during the period; *and*
(c) the *historical rate*: the spot rate of exchange at the date of the transaction.

Various methods of translation use different combinations of these rates.

The UK accounting standard

SSAP 20, *Foreign Currency Translation*, is concerned with:

(a) *individual companies* which enter directly into business transactions denominated in foreign currencies, *and*
(b) *groups* which conduct foreign operations through subsidiaries, associated companies or branches whose operations are based in a country other than that of the investing company, and whose accounting records are maintained in a currency other than that of the investing company.

Individual companies

When a company enters into transactions denominated in a foreign currency (i.e. a currency other than that in which the company's accounts are kept), SSAP 20 requires that they should normally be translated at the rate ruling at the date of each transaction, i.e. at the spot rate.

In the annual accounts of the individual company:

(a) non-monetary assets, e.g. plant and machinery, will already be carried in the accounts in the company's reporting currency, having been translated at the time of acquisition;
(b) foreign equity investments, being non-monetary assets, are normally shown at the rate of exchange ruling at the time the investment was made but, where financed by foreign currency borrowings, they may be translated at the closing rate. Any exchange differences on the investments are then taken to reserves, where the exchange differences on the foreign borrowings may be offset against them (SSAP 20, para. 51).
(c) monetary assets and liabilities denominated in foreign currencies should be translated at the closing rate;
(d) all exchange differences, except those in (b) above, should be reported as part of the profit or loss for the year (unless resulting from extraordinary items), e.g. differences arising from variations in exchange rates between the dates of invoicing in a foreign currency and the dates of payment.

Example 18.1 illustrates the treatment of four simple transactions involving foreign currency:

Example 18.1   Treatment of foreign transactions by an individual company

Able PLC is a UK company whose accounting year ends on 31 December. During the year, ABLE:

		Rate of exchange
(i)	Purchases hock from a West German company, Weinburger GmbH, on 31 October for DM40,000	£1 = DM3.20
	Pays Weinburger GmbH on 30 November	£1 = DM3.04
	Goods remain in stock at 31 December	
(ii)	Sells cider to Pomme et cie, a French company, for FFr105,000.	£1 = FFr10.50
	Debt remains unpaid at 31 December	
(iii)	Borrows on long-term loan from a Swiss bank SFr 750,000 on 1 April	£1 = SFr3.0
(iv)	Purchases plant and machinery from a US company for $480,000 on 15 August	£1 = US$1.50
	Pays on 30 September	£1 = US$1.60

On 31 December exchange rates are:

£1 = DM2.95
£1 = FFr10.00
£1 = SFr2.50
£1 = US$1.55

The company maintains its bank account in sterling and buys or sells foreign exchange as needed on the spot market.

Under SSAP 20 the transactions of Able will be treated as follows:

(i) The purchase will be recorded at the rate ruling on 31 October, £1 = DM3.2. The hock will appear in stock at a book cost of £12,500 and the eventual cost of sales will also be £12,500.
When the account is paid, the rate has fallen to £1 = DM3.04, so it is necessary to pay £13,158 to buy the necessary currency.
An exchange loss of £658 will be charged to the profit and loss account for the year.

(ii) The sale is translated at the rate ruling at the date of the transaction, £1 = FFr10.50 = £10,000. At the end of the year, the debtor is a monetary item and translated at the closing rate, £1 = FFr10.00 = £10,500.
The resulting exchange gain of £500 will be credited to the profit and loss account for the year.

(iii) The loan will initially be translated at the transaction rate of £1 = SFr3.00, i.e. as £250,000.

At the year end the loan will be translated at the closing rate £1 = SFr2.50, i.e. as £300,000.
The exchange loss of £50,000 may be treated as 'financing' and disclosed separately as part of 'other interest receivable/payable and similar income/expense'.

(iv) The fixed asset will be translated at the transaction rate of £1 = $1.50, i.e. as £320,000. The asset will continue to appear at this cost unless it is revalued. Depreciation will be charged on £320,000. Payment for the machine will take (at £1 = $1.60) £300,000. The gain of £20,000 will be credited to the profit and loss account for the year.

In Able PLC's statement of accounting policies, the treatment of these purchases and sale would be explained in a note similar to that in CHURCH's accounts, illustrated below.

CHURCH *Extract from note on accounting policies*

Foreign Currencies

Assets and liabilities at the balance sheet date . . . are translated to sterling at the rates of exchange ruling at the balance sheet date.
Exchange differences arising on trading during the year are taken into account in arriving at the profit before taxation.

Group accounts

Where a company has foreign subsidiaries, associated companies or branches, the *'closing rate net investment method'* is normally used in translating local currency financial statements, (SSAP 20, para. 52). Under this method:

(a) *Balance sheet* items should be translated into the currency of the holding company at the 'closing rate' (the spot rate on the balance sheet date). Where this year's closing rate differs from the previous year's closing rate, the differences arising from the retranslation of the opening *net investment* at this year's closing rate should be taken to reserves.
    The *net investment* is the holding company's proportion of the subsidiary or associated company's share capital and reserves. (Long-term indebtedness between members of the group should be treated as part of the net investment.) The translation process is illustrated in Example 18.2.

(b) *Profit and loss account* items should be translated using either the average rate for the accounting period or the closing rate and the method chosen should be applied consistently. Any difference between translation at the average rate and the closing rate should be taken to reserves.

The rate used can make a considerable difference to the reported profit; for example, if a West German subsidiary made a profit of DM27 million during a year in which the rate of exchange fell from DM3.1=£1 at the beginning of the year to DM2.7=£1 at the end of the year, averaging DM3.0=£1 because most of the fall occurred in the last three months, on an average basis the group accounts would include West German profits of £9 million; on a closing rate basis they would include £10 million.

If the closing rate method is used, no difference will arise between the profit or loss in sterling terms used for profit and loss account purposes, and the result of translation for balance sheet purposes. If the average rate is used there will be a difference, which should be recorded as a movement on reserves, (SSAP 20, para. 54). The method used should be stated in the accounts, as BLACKWOOD HODGE illustrates here:

BLACKWOOD HODGE *Extract from note on accounting policies*

Foreign Currencies

Profits and losses of overseas subsidiaries are translated into sterling at the average rates ruling during the year. Assets and liabilities are translated into sterling at the rates ruling at the balance sheet date. The resultant exchange differences are shown as movements on reserves.

(c)   *Foreign exchange borrowings*: where borrowings have been used to finance equity investment in foreign subsidiaries or associates, differences arising on their translation (at the closing rate) due to currency movements during the period may be offset against differences arising from the retranslation of the opening net investment in (*a*) above.

Example 18.2   Translation of an overseas subsidiary's accounts

On 31 December 19X0, Injection Moulders PLC acquired a small foreign manufacturing company, Ruritania Plastics, to expand its operations into Ruritania, and paid asset value, 60 million Ruritanian dollars, for it. At the time the exchange rate was R$10=£1, so the sterling cost was £6 million.

During the first year of operation as a subsidiary Ruritanian Plastics made a profit after tax of R$10 million, and the R$ fell to R$12.5=£1. Ruritanian Plastics' actual and translated balance sheets for 19X0 (R$10=£1) and 19X1 (R$12.5=£1) were:

Year ended 31 December	19X0		19X1	
	R$	£	R$	£
	m	000s	m	000s
Fixed assets	100	10,000	100	8,000
Current assets	20	2,000	32	2,560
	120	12,000	132	10,560
5 year State loan	50	5,000	50	4,000
Current liabilities	10	1,000	12	960
	60	6,000	62	4,960
Shareholders' funds	60	6,000	70	5,600

The difference between the opening net equity of R$60 million translated at R$10=£1 (the closing rate in the 19X0 accounts) and at R$12.5=£1 (the 19X1 closing rate) is £6m.−£4.8=£1.2m., which would be taken from group reserves at 31 December 19X1 as an exchange translation difference.

The profit of R$10 million (represented in the absence of any capital input or dividends by the difference between opening and closing shareholders funds) has been translated in the group accounts at the closing rate of R$12.5=£1 to produce £0.8 million.

The fall in sterling terms in the net equity of Ruritanian Plastics from £6 million to £5.6 million is made up of the exchange translation loss of £1.2 million less the £0.8 million profit for 19X1, i.e. £0.4 million.

In countries with hyper-inflation companies can use different methods of translation to cope with the huge changes in exchange rates, as the accounts of RECKETT & COLMAN illustrate:

RECKITT & COLMAN *Extract from accounting policies*

Foreign currency translation

. . . fixed assets of companies operating in countries where hyper-inflation exists are translated at historical rates of exchange. Profit and loss account . . . an inflation adjustment is charged in arriving at local currency profits of companies operating in hyper-inflation countries to reflect the impact of hyper-inflation on the companies' working capital requirements.

The temporal method

Where, and only where, the trade of a subsidiary is a direct extension of the trade of a holding company, e.g. a subsidiary acting purely as a selling agency in a foreign country, the temporal method of translation should be used in consolidation:

(a) all transactions should be translated at the rate ruling on the transaction date or at an average rate for a period if this is not materially different;

(b) *non-monetary assets should not normally be retranslated* at the balance sheet date;

(c) monetary assets and liabilities should be retranslated at the closing rate; and

(d) all exchange gains and losses should be taken to the profit and loss account as part of the profit and loss from ordinary activities.

Current UK practice

Most companies follow the requirements of SSAP 20. About 60% use the average rate rather than the closing rate in translating overseas profits, and state which method is used in their accounting policies, e.g. ALLIED LYONS:

ALLIED LYONS *Accounting policies*

Foreign currencies

The profits of overseas subsidiary companies are translated at the weighted average of month end rates and the difference in relation to closing rates is dealt with through reserves.

Taxation

The position with regard to overseas activities is complicated by the problems of taxation. Unless a profit or loss item falls within the scope of a tax schedule dealing with income subject to UK Corporation Tax, or arises from the disposal of an asset in such a way as to be within the computation of a capital gain, then the profit is not taxable, and no relief is available in respect of any loss.

In particular, losses on repayment of foreign borrowings are not allowable for UK tax purposes. Some companies, including ICI, have overcome this difficulty by channelling foreign currency borrowings through a separate finance company subsidiary; there is no distinction between capital and revenue losses in a banking-type operation so foreign exchange losses show up as revenue losses and qualify for full tax relief.

Mitigating the effect of foreign currency fluctuations

In the last ten years the US dollar has fluctuated between US$2.4/£1 and almost parity, see Example 18.3, while the Deutschmark has almost doubled in value against sterling, see Example 18.4.

Companies have sought to protect themselves against the effect of these and other currency fluctuations, both on their earnings and on their balance sheets. For example JAGUAR, with a high proportion of sales in the United States, protects its earnings with forward cover:

JAGUAR *Accounting policies*

Foreign currencies

It is the Group's policy to protect the sterling value of overseas income, where appropriate, by means of forward currency sales contracts entered into to fix the exchange rates applicable to estimated future overseas sales revenue. Profits or losses arising from these arrangements are accounted for through cost of sales in the financial period in which the contracts mature. Accordingly, no account is taken of unrealised profits or losses arising on such forward exchange contracts, except to the extent that foreign exchange contracts match debtors in foreign currency.

Although selling currency forward does protect the sterling value of future foreign income, doing so can have adverse effects if the foreign currency then strengthens rather than weakens. For example, if Jaguar's European competitors do not cover forward and the US dollar strengthens, they will have scope for cutting their prices in the United States, while Jaguar will not. So much for earnings.

Protecting the balance sheet can be done in a

Example 18.3   Sterling–US dollar exchange rate

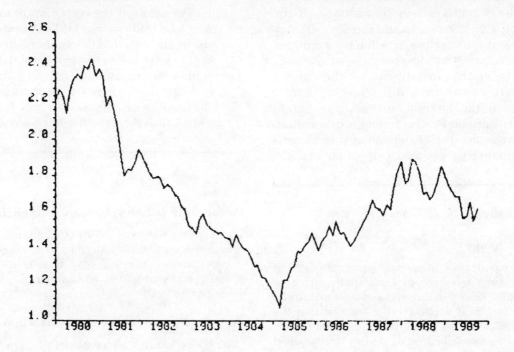

Example 18.4   Sterling–DM exchange rate

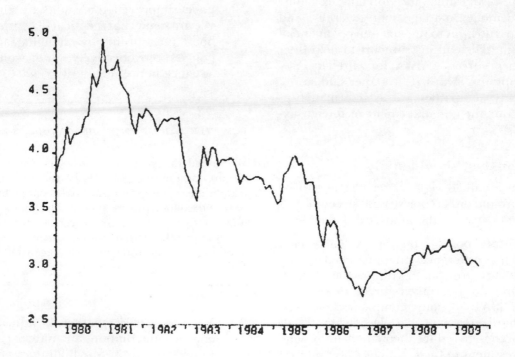

Source: Datastream

variety of ways, the most obvious one being to borrow in the foreign currency. If the foreign subsidiary does the borrowing, the net equity investment in the subsidiary will be reduced. If the parent company borrows in the foreign currency and switches it into sterling, it will have a gain (or loss) to offset against any loss (or gain) on translating the net equity investment of the foreign subsidiary. If interest rates in sterling are higher than those in the foreign currency the parent company will also make a profit on the differential.

Some companies disclose when they are protecting their balance sheets; for example BOWATER:

BOWATER *Extract from 1988 financial review*

Foreign exchange

The Group's policy for managing its assets has been proactive against a background of rapidly changing exchange rates. Equity in Bowater Industries Australia was not hedged as it was correctly assumed that the Australian dollar would strengthen. Conversely European investments were hedged as sterling strengthened against currencies of the European Monetary System. The Group's assets in the United States were fully hedged throughout the year due to the uncertain prospects for the dollar.

Most large companies have a separate Treasury department responsible for foreign exchange (Forex) and money management generally, and there is almost no limit to the ingenuity of financial advisers in thinking up instruments to help their clients reduce currency risks: forward currency contracts, options, swaps, Europaper and so on, but not many companies are as informative as Bowater about their management of foreign exchange risks.

What the analyst should study

Information about foreign currency tends to be scattered around in reports and accounts. A suggested sequence for the analyst to follow is:

1. Accounting policies on foreign currencies. Check that differences on unmatched foreign borrowings are dealt with in the P & L account and not taken direct to reserves. Before SSAP 20, some companies borrowed in a hard currency, e.g. Deutschmarks or Swiss francs, to reduce their cost of borrowing for investment in the UK. The lower interest rates (broadly reflecting the lower expectations of inflation) increased the companies' profits and, when the foreign currency inevitably strengthened, they debited the increase

in the sterling value of their borrowings direct to reserves. This method of enhancing the profits was short-sighted and often very costly. For example the WEIR Group managed to lose £3.6 million on a DM denominated loan originally worth £6.3 million, and the loss would have been even greater if the company hadn't arranged early repayment.

Note also if there has been any change in accounting policy, as this can be a way of enhancing the year's results, e.g. BUNZL:

BUNZL *1987 accounts*

Accounting policies; Foreign currencies

The trading results of overseas companies have been translated into pounds sterling at average exchange rates, whereas in previous years these results have been translated at year-end rates. Comparative figures have been restated . . .

Note 2   Foreign currency translation

Average exchange rates have been adopted . . . Had the former accounting policy of translating at year-end rates been continued, the 1987 profit before taxation would have been £80.9m. . . .

Bunzl's reported pre-tax profit was, in fact, £85.7 million, so the change of accounting policy improved the results by almost 6%. We are somewhat sceptical of companies that boost their profits by changing accounting policies retrospectively, and would prefer advance notice, e.g. BOWATER:

BOWATER *Extract from chairman's statement*

We intend this year to make a change in one of the Group's accounting policies. To the end of 1988, the translation of the profit and loss account has been at year-end exchange rates. We consider that with today's fluctuating movements in currencies the Group can better plan its forward operating currency exposures by adopting average rates of exchange from 1 January 1989.

---

2. Reserves. Check whether the adjustments for currency fluctuations are material in relation to pre-tax profit. SSAP 20 does not state to which reserves exchange differences should be taken. A few companies, like BTR, set up a special 'Currency Equalisation Account' or similarly named reserve, which give a useful

total of differences that have accumulated over the years, but most take differences straight to the balance of the profit and loss account, although some give a breakdown of the differences either in a separate note or in the note on reserves, e.g. GLAXO:

GLAXO *Note on reserves*

	Share premium account £m	Holding company £m	Other reserves		Total £m
			Subsidiaries £m	Associated companies £m	
At 1 July 1988	1	347	1,035	31	1,413
Exchange adjustments relating to net assets of subsidiary and associated companies:					
– tangible fixed assets		—	24	—	24
– stocks and work in progress		—	2	—	2
– net liquid funds		—	18	—	18
– other net liabilities		—	(3)	—	(3)
Premium on shares issued . . .					

3. If the exchange adjustments are large, look for further information elsewhere. Any comments will usually appear in the 'Financial Review', if there is one, or in the chairman's statement or possibly in the directors' report.

Where exchange adjustments are significant, further information may include tables of exchange rates and, as in RTZ, an analysis by currency of borrowings and assets:

RTZ *Extracts from 1988 accounts*

Financial Review

RTZ's shareholders' funds rose by £447 million to £2,052 million as a result of the improvement in earnings, the gain on disposals, translation gains, particularly from the Australian dollar . . .

Exchange rates to the pound sterling	Year end		% change to sterling	Annual average		% change to sterling
	1988	1987		1988	1987	
US dollar	1.81	1.88	+4	1.78	1.64	−9
Canadian dollar	2.15	2.44	+12	2.19	2.17	−1
Australian dollar	2.11	2.60	+19	2.28	2.34	+3
South African rand[1]	4.30	3.63	−18	4.05	3.33	−22
PNG kina	1.48	1.64	+10	1.54	1.49	−3

[1]Commercial rand

Note on medium and long-term loans

Analysis of borrowings	RTZ parent	Wholly owned subsidiaries	Partly owned subsidiaries	1988 Total £m	1987 Total £m
Total outstanding indebtedness is repayable in the following currencies:					
Sterling	173.2	11.2	26.5	210.9	325.9
United States dollar	—	174.5	29.4	203.9	198.2
Canadian dollar	—	76.5	124.6	201.1	179.2
South African rand	—	—	31.3	31.3	6.7
Other currencies	—	9.8	0.3	10.1	1.2
	173.2	272.0	212.1	657.3	711.2

Geographical analysis

	1988 £m	1988 %	1987 £m	1987 %
	Group assets			
United Kingdom	548.9	17.3	349.4	10.8
United States of America	610.6	19.2	530.3	16.5
Australia and New Zealand	566.3	17.8	528.4	16.4
Africa	280.3	8.8	279.2	8.7
Canada	795.0	25.0	648.1	20.1
Papua New Guinea	85.5	2.7	77.8	2.4
Mainland Europe	186.8	5.9	195.7	6.1
Other countries	107.3	3.3	69.9	2.2
Discontinued businesses			543.0	16.8
	3,180.7		3,221.8	

In 1988 RTZ reported net profit attributable to shareholders of £427.5 million and Adjustment on currency translation of £98.5 million positive compared with £194.9 million negative the previous year. As the Financial Review pointed out, the movement of the Australian dollar was particularly helpful: it strengthened 19% against sterling during the year with assets in Australia and New Zealand, mainly the former, standing at £566.3 million at the year end, with little or no Australian or New Zealand borrowings.

Extensive overseas assets with little or no matched borrowings will mean large fluctuations in currency adjustments on the balance sheet. Some companies accept this as part of the scenario in overseas operations, while others match their overseas assets with overseas borrowings as closely as possible within the constraints of overall group gearing.

The effect of currency movements on profits is harder to analyse, as all trading gains or losses are taken direct to the P & L account, but chairmen often comment if turnover and profits have been affected, e.g. GLAXO:

GLAXO *Extract from chairman's 1989 statement*

About half the Group's total sales are denominated in US dollars and related currencies and these results, expressed in sterling, were favourably affected by the appreciation of the dollar. If exchange rates had remained unchanged from the corresponding period last year, this year's sales of £2,570 million would have been £140 million lower at £2,430 million, and the trading profit of £876 million would have been £45 million lower at £831 million. As a result, the recorded rate of sales growth over last year would have been about 20% instead of the 25% shown in the Accounts.

But probably equally if not more important for the profitability of foreign operations than a weak exchange rate is the state of the economy in the foreign country concerned. If the weak exchange rate reflects a weak economy, then adverse trading conditions may be more damaging for profits than translation.

Chapter 19

SOURCE AND APPLICATION OF FUNDS STATEMENTS

(Reference: SSAP 10 *Statements of Source and Application of Funds*.)

Purpose

Traditionally, published accounts have comprised:

(*a*) a balance sheet providing a statement of the financial position at the end of a company's accounting year, together with 'corresponding figures' showing the position at the end of the previous year (which is, of course, the same as the position at the beginning of the year being reported upon);

(*b*) a profit and loss account showing, in particular, the amount of profit retained in the business from that year.

A comparatively recent introduction is a third statement known in the UK as a statement of source and application of funds.

It is today widely accepted that, apart from share capital issued or redeemed and any revaluation of fixed assets, the profit and loss account (together with the statement of retained profits/reserves) should explain all changes in shareholders' funds between one balance sheet date and the next, including prior year adjustments and items such as preliminary expenses which are allowed to be charged direct to reserves. It thus provides a link between successive balance sheets.

The profit and loss account does not, however, bridge the gap between each item in successive balance sheets, which can only be done by a note on the individual item (e.g. fixed assets) or by a source and application of funds statement, sometimes called a funds flow statement or more simply a funds statement. In the United States such a

statement is called a statement of changes in financial position, which is precisely what it is: a statement explaining the balance sheet changes which occurred during the period.

In this chapter we will look at three aspects of funds statements:

(*a*) the requirements of SSAP 10;

(*b*) the interpretation of source and application statements, including how to estimate the likely requirements for funds in the future.

(*c*) the limitations of source and application of funds statements.

The requirements of SSAP 10

Companies with a turnover of £25,000 or more per annum must include a statement of source and application of funds both for the period under review and for the corresponding previous period.

The objective of the statement is to show how the operations of a company have been financed and how its financial resources have been used (SSAP 10, para. 2). It should:

(*a*) identify the movement in assets, liabilities and capital which have taken place during the year, and the resultant effect on *net liquid funds* (cash at bank and in hand and cash equivalents e.g. investments held as current assets), less bank overdrafts and other borrowings repayable within one year), (SSAP 10, paras. 1 and 8).

(*b*) show clearly the funds generated or absorbed by the operations of the business (SSAP 10, para. 3).

Layout

Although SSAP 10 gives examples in appendices, it only requires the layout to 'be so framed as to reflect the operations of the group'. No standard format is prescribed, and so the formats companies adopt can and do vary widely. SSAP 10's examples of group statements show:

Source of funds
Funds generated from operations
Funds from other sources
Application of funds
Dividends paid
Tax paid
Purchase of fixed assets
. . .
Increase/decrease in working capital
Increase (decrease) in stocks
Increase (decrease) in debtors
(Increase) decrease in creditors

Movement in net liquid funds
SSAP 10's examples do, in fact, include 'Movement in net liquid funds' as part of 'Increase/decrease in working capital', but most companies show it separately, as we have done above.

Arithmetically, the movement in net liquid funds equals sources minus applications minus (plus) the increase (decrease) in working capital.

This is the format adopted by IMI, shown opposite, and is the one followed by the majority of companies, but there are many variations which an analyst needs to watch out for.

Starting point
The normal starting point, as in IMI, is 'Profit before taxation', but some companies begin with 'Trading profit', showing Investment income and Interest paid in the statement, while one or two, e.g. BP, start with 'Profit after taxation'. Starting at trading profit affects the treatment of associates, as we will describe, while companies starting with profit after tax omit the item 'Tax paid'.

Associated undertakings
As the holding company does not control the funds of associated undertakings, they are not treated as part of the holding company's funds. However, 'Profit before taxation' does include the holding company's share of the profit of associates; some of this may have been remitted by way of dividends paid to the holding company (and thus is a source), and some may have been retained by the associates. This latter part has to be deducted as an adjustment not involving the movement of funds:

Profit retained in associated undertakings   £xxx

Where a company starts its statement with 'Trading profit' it normally shows an item 'Dividends from associated undertakings', so that profit retained by associates never gets into the statement.

Treatment of minorities
The examples in SSAP 10 deal with minorities by beginning with the item:

Profit before tax and extraordinary items,
  less minority interests   £xxx

and then adding back, as an item not involving the movement of funds:

Minority interests in the retained profits
  of the year   £xxx

However, some companies do not deduct minority interests from profit before tax, but show 'Dividends paid to minorities' as an application of funds. The net effect is just the same: retentions on the part of minorities are left in as a source of funds.

'Netting off'
SSAP 10 recommends (though does not specifically require) that there should be a minimum of 'netting off', since netting off tends to mask the significance of individually important figures.

For example, if two companies A and B start the period with a portfolio of investments of £468,100 and, during the period, carry out the following transactions:

	Company A £	Company B £
Purchase of investments	56,000	488,000
less Sales of investments	4,200	436,200
	51,800	51,800

there is a vast difference between the two companies' investment activities. A has made a minor addition to its portfolio, while B has traded actively and could have made almost a 100% change in its investments. But if reported on a 'netting off' basis, both companies would show an application of £51,800.

Profit on disposals
The accounting standard does not specifically require the profit or loss on the sale of an asset to be shown. Logically it is the proceeds of the sale that are important in analysing funds flow, but if the proceeds are shown then any profit (loss) which has already been included in pre-tax profit has to be deducted (added back); e.g. TARMAC:

TARMAC *Extract from Group source and application of funds statement, 1988*

	£m
Items not involving the movement of funds:	
Depreciation	54.1
. . .	
Profit from the sale of fixed assets	(4.4)
. . .	
Proceeds from the sale of fixed assets	21.9
. . .	

IMI *Group source and application of funds statement*

	1988 £m	1988 £m	1987 £m	1987 £m
Source of funds:				
Profit before taxation		108.1		92.3
Extraordinary profit before taxation		0.3		—
		108.4		92.3
Adjustments for items not involving the movement of funds:				
Depreciation	23.6		23.4	
Other items	(3.6)	20.0	(3.0)	20.4
Total generated from operations		128.4		112.7
Funds from other sources:				
Disposal of tangible fixed assets	3.9		2.9	
Disposal of fixed asset investments and loan repayments	3.1		1.7	
Proceeds from issue of shares	2.1		0.3	
Disposal of subsidiary companies	12.4	21.5	7.2	12.1
		149.9		124.8
Application of funds:				
Purchase of fixed assets	(35.3)		(39.6)	
Fixed asset investments	—		(0.3)	
Acquisition of subsidiary companies	(53.1)		—	
Goodwill purchased	—		(0.7)	
Provisions utilised	(8.6)		(6.8)	
Taxation paid	(20.9)		(21.9)	
Dividends paid	(23.7)	(141.6)	(20.0)	(89.3)
		8.3		35.5
(Increase)/decrease in working capital:				
Stocks	(21.4)		(13.6)	
Debtors	(24.2)		(3.7)	
Creditors	15.2	(30.4)	11.4	(5.9)
Movement in net liquid resources		(22.1)		29.6
Made up of changes in:				
Short term investments and bank balances		3.4		33.3
Bank overdrafts and borrowings		(25.5)		(3.7)
(Increase)/Decrease in net borrowings		(22.1)		29.6

The effect of the acquisition and disposal of subsidiary companies is summarised below:

	1988 *Acquisitions* £m	1988 *Disposals* £m	1987 *Disposals* £m
Net assets acquired/(sold):			
Fixed assets	8.3	(3.4)	(2.6)
Goodwill	36.5	—	—
Working capital	8.3	(2.2)	(5.9)
	53.1	(5.6)	(8.5)
Represented by:			
Cash consideration	52.4	(13.3)	(5.5)
Borrowings/cash at date of disposals/acquisitions	0.7	0.9	(1.7)
Reduction in minority interest	—	—	(1.3)
Profit on sale of subsidiaries	—	6.8	—
	53.1	(5.6)	(8.5)

Other companies, e.g. RMC, show 'Disposal of fixed assets (net book value)', but it is often not clear whether the item is the proceeds or the net book value. It can be checked by referring to the note on fixed assets, e.g. MARKS & SPENCER:

MARKS & SPENCER *Disposal of fixed assets*

	£m
Source and application of funds:	
Sale of fixed assets	8.0
Note on tangible fixed assets	
Cost or valuation	
. . .	
Disposals	(48.6)
. . .	
Accumulated depreciation	
. . .	
Disposals	(40.6)

Net book value of disposals = 48.6m − 40.6m = £8.0m, the figure shown in the funds statement.

MARKS & SPENCER also showed 'Loss on sale of tangible fixed assets £4.6m.' in a note on 'Other expenses', but some companies bury any profit or loss in their depreciation charge.

Acquisitions and disposals

SSAP 10 requires any purchases or disposals of subsidiaries to be shown either as separate items or to be reflected in each item in the statement, and suggests that, in either case, the details should be shown in a footnote. The former method is more helpful to the analyst, as it separates the effect on each item; e.g. in the IMI example on page 137 the change in working capital due to acquisitions, plus £8.3m, and disposals, minus £2.2m, are shown separately from the change in the remainder of the group's working capital, an increase of £30.4m.

IMI's presentation is also helpful in that it shows the effect of acquisitions and the effect of disposals separately. Some companies net off disposals against acquisitions, despite SSAP 10's request that 'a minimum of "netting off" should take place' in statements. Unfortunately the samples in SSAP 10 only show groups making acquisitions.

The interpretation of source and application statements

A funds statement may be useful to a chairman at an annual general meeting, or to an analyst when confronted by an investor asking embarrassing questions such as:

> Where did all the profits go?
> If those are the profits, why wasn't it possible to pay a larger dividend?

> How come, when there has been a loss, that a dividend can still be paid?
> What happened to the proceeds of the recent rights issue?
> What happened to the proceeds of disposal of a major fixed asset (e.g. freehold property)?
> In the case of a group growing rapidly by takeovers for paper (shares or loan stock), how did the company pay for these new subsidiaries?

A funds statement, or a series of funds statements, may also be of use to an analyst trying to trace movements over several years, to identify the trends in liquidity and to estimate the likely need for funds in the future.

Interpreting an imaginary funds statement

Example 19.1 shows the funds statement from an imaginary set of accounts for 1989, together with a projected statement for the year ending 31 December 1990. Each line is numbered for ease of reference (S for source, A for application, while the line numbers in the table on 'Other information' at the bottom refer to other pro-formas in Chapter 25).

Let us look at this information in conjunction with comments gleaned from the chairman's report.

Changes in net liquid funds (Line A 12)

The improvement in 1988 was due mainly to the sale of a subsidiary (Line S 21) and to the low tax paid (Line A 1).

In 1989 the fall in net liquid assets was due mainly to the purchase of a subsidiary for £4 million in February 1989 (Line A 5) being paid for in cash (no new shares were issued, Line S 15), only part of which was financed by an increase in loans of £3 million (Line S 17), the remainder being funded by deferred tax and an increase in overdraft.

Chairman's comments as an aid to forecasting liquidity

IEC's turnover went up by more than £10 million in 1989, but pre-tax profits increased by only £377,000. The chairman commented in his report that turnover in the first three months of the current year was 27% up on the corresponding period in 1989 but that, although all divisions are currently trading profitably, increased costs and strong competition are continuing to put pressure on margins. Despite currently adverse trading conditions, the board of IEC has every confidence in the future prosperity of the company, and is continuing the capital investment programme initiated in 1988 so as to be ready to take maximum advantage of the economic upturn when it comes. In addition, the chairman announced that, since the year end, a further acquisition

Example 19.1   *Funds statement:* 'IMAGINARY ENGINEERING COMPANY' ('IEC')

Line[1]	Year ending 31 December	1988	1989	1990 Projected
	Source	£000	£000	£000
S 1	Profit before tax *less* minorities	6,247	6,624	7,000
S 2	Extraordinary items	(203)	—	
S 4	Depreciation	3,650	3,741	3,800
S 6	Minority retentions	298	327	330
S 14	**Generated from operations**	9,992	10,692	11,130
S 15	Issue of shares	—	—	
S 17	Increase in Loans	—	3,000	
S 18	(Decrease in Loans)	—	—	(650)
S 19	Disposal of fixed assets	802	758	775
S 21	Sale of subsidiaries	740	—	
S 23	**Source total**	11,534	14,450	11,255
	Application			
A 1	Tax paid	1,947	2,299	2,438
A 2	Dividends	1,780	1,958	2,154
A 4	Purchase of fixed assets	4,890	3,880	4,380
A 5	Purchase of subsidiary	—	4,000	500
A 11	Increase (Decrease) in Working Capital	1,277	2,263	2,545
A 12	Increase (Decrease) in Net Liquid Funds	1,640	50	(762)
	Application total	11,534	14,450	11,255
	Other information			
112	Debt/Equity ratio	64.1%	82.8%	
106	Acid test	0.82	0.61	
1	Turnover (£000)	32,705	42,857	
110	Working capital ratio	21.7%	22.3%	
	Capital commitments:			
	Authorised (£000)	5,186	5,801	
	Contracted (£000)	1,296	1,480	

[1] For an explanation of the line numbers, see the pro-forma analysis charts in Chapter 25.

had been made, the consideration being £500,000 in cash.

Using last year's figures, current trading conditions and anything we can glean from the chairman's comments on this year's prospects, let us now try to project 1990's sources and applications for the IMAGINARY ENGINEERING COMPANY. Of course, any attempt to project the future financial position of a company without the detailed and up-to-date information available within that company is bound to be rough and ready, but it will indicate whether the company is growing healthily, remaining static or heading for cash problems.

IEC's projected funds statement for 1990
Line S 1 1989's improvement included 11 months' contribution from the £4m. acquisition; as margins are still under pressure there is little scope for further improvement, say £7.0m. at most for 1990.

Lines S 4, 6 and 19 No evidence of marked change.
Line S 17 High Debt/Equity ratio (line 112) leaves little scope for further borrowing.
Line S 18 £650,000 convertible unsecured loan stock remaining unconverted at last date for conversion 31 December 1989, is due for redemption on 31 December 1990.
Line A 1 Assuming tax paid in 1989 represented tax at 36.8% on 1988 profits, and that tax paid in 1990 will be at a similar rate on 1989 profits.
Line A 2 The company is likely to increase dividends by the same amount as last year, i.e. by 10%.
Line A 4 The expenditure on fixed assets in past years has been roughly equal to the capital commitment that has been let to contract plus half the authorised expenditure. The chairman has said that the investment programme is continuing, so using the same lead time, £1.48m plus ½ × £5.801m = £4.380m.

Line A 5 The cost of the current year acquisition announced by the chairman.

Line A 11 A 27% increase in turnover and a normal working capital ratio of 22% will mean an increase in working capital in 1990 of $0.27 \times £42.857m. \times 0.22 = £2.545m.$

These figures require a balancing item of £0.762 million in Line A 12 to make the 1990 Application total equal the Source total, meaning that the company is likely to have a decrease in net liquid funds in 1990 of around £0.7 million to £0.8 million on the present evidence.

However, as the 'Acid test' ratio (Line 106) has already fallen to a very low level, a further increase in the overdraft looks undesirable. The most likely solution, to restore the imbalance caused by the £4 million acquisition made for cash in 1989, aggravated by substantial increases in the working capital requirement, is for IEC to make a rights issue (Line S 15) in 1990, and one might well ask why part of the consideration for the £4 million acquisition was not made in paper.

Limitations of funds statements

A source and application statement is a record of historical facts. It will record expenditure upon additional plant and machinery, but can express no opinion upon whether the expenditure was necessary, or will be profitable. Similarly, it may show an expansion of stocks (or debtors), but it will not tell us whether this was due to:

(a) poor stock or production control;
(b) inability to sell the finished product; *or*
(c) a deliberate act of policy, because of a feared shortage of supply, a potential price rise, or the need to build up stocks of a new model (or product) before it is launched.

And, in the case of increased debtors, it will not tell us whether it is the debtors who are slow to pay, or the credit policy which has changed; or whether they merely represent the expansion of turnover. It will show how new capital was raised, but not whether it was raised in the best way, nor indeed whether it really needed to have been raised at all or if it could have been avoided by better asset control.

Source and application of funds statements do not usually tell us the following:

(a) Where the money is. In the case of a multinational group, exchange controls or the tax situation may make it impossible or undesirable to remit some funds to the United Kingdom.
(b) How much more the company can borrow from its bankers. A fall in liquidity may be perfectly in order where a company has made

arrangements with its bankers to cover just that eventuality. On the other hand, a company compelled by its bankers to reduce the scale of its operations may show a satisfactory improvement in liquidity, while being crippled by its inability to expand, or possibly being unable to maintain its existing plant properly.

One of the drawbacks of the layouts shown in SSAP 10 is that they do not achieve the stated purpose 'to show clearly the funds generated or absorbed by the business'. Some analysts rearrange the figures to show whether the business is cash generative or cash hungry, and then add funds from other sources and show how they have been used. For example, recasting the IMI example on page 137 for 1988·

IMI *Recast funds statement*

	£m
Operational sources	
Profit before taxation	108.1
Depreciation and other items	20.0
Operational applications	
Provisions utilised	(8.6)
Taxation paid	(20.9)
Dividends paid	(23.7)
Increase in working capital	(30.4)
Purchase of fixed assets	(35.3)
Disposal of tangible fixed assets	3.9
Net inflow(outflow) from operations	13.1
Other sources	
Disposal of fixed asset investments	3.1
Proceeds from issue of shares	2.1
Disposal of subsidiary companies	12.4
Increase in net borrowings	22.1
Extraordinary items	0.3
	53.1
Other applications	
Acquisition of subsidiary companies	(53.1)

In our view this shows more clearly that the existing business generated £13.1m net which, together with funds from other sources, primarily disposal of subsidiaries £12.4m and increase in net borrowings £22.1m, paid for £53.1m of acquisitions. FISONS follow a similar format to show 'Net inflow (outflow) of funds from operations'.

Cash flow statements

In the United States, despite years of experience with funds statements, termed in the US 'Statements of changes in financial position', a recent

SFAS (Statement of Financial Accounting Standards) calls for a statement of *cash flows*, classifying receipts and payments by operating, investing and financial activities, and reconciling their effect on beginning and end cash positions, as shown by the opening and closing balance sheets.

In the UK there is pressure to revise SSAP 10 to clarify the purpose of funds statements, to prescribe the format, and to move in the same direction as the US. Some major international companies have already moved to the production of statements of cash flows. For example, ROYAL DUTCH/SHELL replaced its 'Statement of source and use of funds' with a 'Statement of cash flows':

ROYAL DUTCH/SHELL *Statement of cash flows*

	1989	1988
		£ million
Cash flow provided by operating activities		
Net income for the year	**3,954**	2,941
Adjustments to reconcile net income to cash flow provided by operating activities:		
Depreciation, depletion and amortisation	**3,048**	2,858
Movements in: inventories	**(577)**	276
accounts receivable *debtors*	**(1,354)**	(281)
accounts payable and accrued liabilities *creditors*	**981**	237
taxes payable	**119**	129
Associated companies: dividends less than net income	**(39)**	(42)
Deferred taxation and other provisions	**421**	(18)
Other	**(331)**	85
Income applicable to minority interests	**60**	58
Cash flow provided by operating activities	**6,282**	6,243
Cash flow used in investing activities		
Capital expenditure (including capitalised leases)	**(4,353)**	(4,245)
Acquisition of new Group companies and additional joint venture interests	**(647)**	(308)
Proceeds from sale of assets	**551**	292
New investments in associated companies	**(597)**	(348)
Disposals of investments in associated companies	**167**	189
Other investments	**(41)**	(74)
Cash flow used in investing activities	**(4,920)**	(4,494)
Cash flow used in financing activities		
Long-term debt (including short-term part):		
new borrowings	**823**	904
repayments	**(1,154)**	(836)
	(331)	68
Net increase/(decrease) in short-term debt	**52**	(390)
Dividends paid: to Parent Companies	**(1,743)**	(1,642)
to minority interests	**(21)**	(17)
Redemption of preference shares held by minority interests	**—**	(66)
Cash flow used in financing activities	**(2,043)**	(2,047)
Increase in cash on aggregation of certain companies previously accounted for as associated companies and on aggregation of new Group companies	**—**	54
Currency translation differences relating to cash and cash equivalents	**221**	(2)
Decrease in cash and cash equivalents	**(460)**	(246)

Chapter 20

HISTORICAL SUMMARIES

Variations in form and content

In 1964 the Chairman of The Stock Exchange wrote to the chairmen of all listed companies asking for various items of information to be included in their reports and accounts. One of the items which 'might be included' was 'Tables of relevant comparative figures for the past ten years'.

Apart from this request, listed companies are under no obligation to provide any form of historical summary: there is no Accounting Standard (SSAP) on the subject, and no uniformity of content, layout, or period covered.

The majority of companies give a five-year summary; most of the remainder show ten years, although a few choose a different period, usually for a specific reason; e.g. LONRHO's 'Financial Record' goes right back to 1961, the year their chief executive, Tiny Rowland, joined the company.

Because there is, as yet, no standard on historical summaries, the content varies enormously. AARONSON BROS., for example, show only five basic items in their 'Five-year record', illustrated below, but many companies give much more information than this. CADBURY SCHWEPPES, for instance, devotes three pages to its five-year record, including a page of financial ratios, see opposite, while some companies include information on their particular type of business; e.g. TESCO, in their ten-year record, shows the number of stores, sales area opened during the year and total sales area, while BP includes statistics on refinery throughput, crude oil and natural gas reserves in its six pages of historical information.

But there is a growing tendency for companies to omit the normal table of historical information in favour of colourful diagrams of a few salient items; for example SAATCHI & SAATCHI took up two whole pages with bar charts of revenue, pre-tax profit, e.p.s. and dividends per share, until 1989 when it

AARONSON BROS *Group 5-year record*

	1984 £000	1985 £000	1986 £000	1987 £000	**1988** £000
Turnover	89,390	82,300	88,546	107,070	100,913
Shareholders' funds	17,684	23,786	22,808	24,077	24,431
Net profit before taxation and minority interest	3,818	3,739	1,919	5,578	5,823
Earnings per ordinary 10p share	10.03p	9.50p	3.70p	12.06p	12.17p
Dividend per ordinary 10p share	4.06p	4.20p	4.20p	5.45p	5.75p

CADBURY SCHWEPPES *Extract from Group 5-year summary: Financial Ratios*

			1988	1987	1986	1985	1984
Profitability							
Margin	$\dfrac{Trading\ profit}{Sales}$	%	**9.6**	8.9	7.6	6.0	7.7
Return on assets	$\dfrac{Trading\ profit}{Operating\ assets^1}$	%	**33.8**	23.6	21.1	14.6	18.5
Return on equity	$\dfrac{Earnings}{Ordinary\ shareholders'\ funds}$	%	**29.1[2]**	23.1	16.5	10.2	14.0
Interest and dividend cover							
Interest cover	$\dfrac{Trading\ profit}{Net\ interest\ charge}$	times	**13.1**	21.5	9.8	4.1	4.1
Dividend cover	$\dfrac{Earnings\ per\ ordinary\ share}{Dividend\ per\ ordinary\ share}$	times	**2.5[2]**	2.4	2.1	1.6	2.7
Gearing ratio							
	$\dfrac{Net\ borrowings}{Shareholders'\ funds + minority\ interests}$	%	**(0.6)**	24.6	17.1	42.6	39.9
Asset ratios							
Operating asset turnover	$\dfrac{Sales}{Operating\ assets^1}$	times	**3.5**	2.6	2.8	2.4	2.4
Working capital turnover	$\dfrac{Sales}{Working\ capital}$	times	**31.9**	11.3	14.6	9.2	8.6
Per share							
Earnings per share – net basis		p	**23.47[2]**	19.05	14.28	9.31	15.65
Dividends per share		p	**9.20**	8.00	6.70	5.90	5.90
Net tangible assets per share		p	**80.22**	79.72	82.36	90.18	102.1

[1] Operating assets represent tangible fixed assets, stock, debtors and creditors after excluding borrowings, taxation and dividends.

[2] These figures include a non-recurring adjustment to Advance Corporation Tax. Excluding this, the corresponding ratios are:

Return on equity	%	**26.4**
Dividend cover	times	**2.3**
Earnings per share	p	**21.26**

reported a pre-tax loss and dropped the historical information altogether.

An Accounting Standard is certainly needed on historical summaries.

Difficulties of interpretation

Among the difficulties facing the shareholder or analyst who tries to interpret a five- or ten-year summary are the following:

Inflation

Whereas pre-war it was reasonable in Britain to suppose that a pound today was the same as a pound last year and would be the same as a pound next year, rapid inflation has made this concept of a stable currency (referred to in the United States as the 'uniform dollar concept') unsustainable. A pound in 1989 was not the same as a pound in 1988, 1987, 1986 or 1979. To read a ten-year record as though it was is to obtain a false picture, and can be just as misleading as the company chairman who makes much of yet another year of record profits when they have advanced a mere 5% compared with a 15% or 20% rate of inflation.

Changes in accounting bases

Changes in accounting practices can make a significant difference to the figures a company publishes; e.g. SSAP 22, Accounting for goodwill, published in December 1984, recommended that purchased goodwill should normally be written off immediately against reserves; this sharply reduced shareholders' funds in some companies.

In addition, most companies change their accounting ideas, either expressly or unknowingly, over a long period. Unless the figures for earlier years are revised, or a note drawing attention to the change in basis is included in the five- or ten-year statistical summary, readers may be misled. Thus, a company may in earlier years have operated on the basis that research and development expenditure should be written off in the year in which it was incurred, but may now capitalise it, i.e. carry it forward as an asset whenever the benefits of the expenditure can reasonably be foreseen. Clearly, neither the figures in the profit and loss account in earlier years, nor those in the balance sheet, are comparable with the figures of later years.

Changes in basis may arise without any positive decision having to be made on the part of the company. For instance, the abolition of 100% first year allowances and the fall in the standard rate of Corporation Tax from 50% in 1983 to 35% in 1986 makes the year-on-year comparisons of after-tax items very difficult. Some companies, for example, RANK ORGANISATION shown below, do state what adjustments they have made in a footnote, but they are in the minority.

RANK ORGANISATION *Footnote to 1988 five-year review*

Figures for 1984 and 1985 have been restated for the change in 1986 to an immediate write off basis for goodwill. Figures for 1985 only have been restated for the change made in 1986 by a subsidiary in its basis for depreciating certain tangible fixed assets and by the Rank Xerox companies in their basis of providing deferred taxation.

Changes in the composition of the group

Where a group either grows or contracts, comparability is bound to be affected. Most groups do not strip out the effect of companies no longer being part of the group, and additions to the group are only included from the date of acquisition, or year of acquisition if merger accounted.

Goodwill written off

As we have mentioned SSAP 22 says that purchased goodwill (the excess of the cost of an acquisition over the value of the tangible assets acquired) should normally be written off immediately against reserves, which reduces ordinary shareholders' funds (OSF); this can make a nonsense of some ratios, as we illustrate with CADBURY SCHWEPPES on page 146.

Use of ratios

Thus, while a five- or ten-year summary can be very helpful, its limitations in times of high inflation and the adjustments which need to be made because of changes in accounting bases and in the composition of the group mean that it should be treated with caution. However, as we have said, some companies do go to considerable trouble to make the figures as comparable as possible, and explain adjustments in footnotes.

It is sometimes possible to avoid some of these difficulties by using ratios in which both the denominator and the numerator are in pounds of the same year; the current ratio and quick ratio and the collection period (Debtors/turnover) are comparable year by year, for example. But this is not true of all ratios. For instance, profit margin (Trading profit to sales ratio) is affected in historical cost accounts by stockholding gains and by the charging of depreciation only on the basis of historical cost, while Earnings per share are, of course, directly affected by inflation, since earnings are expressed from year to year in pounds of different vintages, while the number of shares in issue is unaffected by inflation.

The key ratios

Despite all the difficulties we have discussed, the company's own historical summary does provide a readily accessible picture of the company's progress over past years, and should therefore be used when the analyst cannot afford the time and effort involved in preparing the detailed summary we advocate in Chapter 25; two key ratios to look at are Earnings per share and Shareholders' funds per share.

Earnings per share

E.p.s. are of prime interest to the investor. Very few companies are as helpful as BP in providing e.p.s. and other key items expressed in 'constant pounds' (see extract from BP's 'Information on price changes' page 146, where the lower part shows items in 1988 pounds), but a crude adjustment can quite easily be made to allow for the

Example 20.1   Adjustment of e.p.s. for inflation: CADBURY SCHWEPPES

	1988	1987	1986	1985	1984
Reported earnings per share	23.47	19.05	14.28	9.31	15.65
Average RPI for the year	106.9	101.9	97.8	94.6	89.2
E.p.s. adjusted by the RPI	23.47	19.98	15.61	10.52	18.76

Note: Where a company's accounting year is not the calendar year, the RPI for the month in which the company's half year ends can be used as an approximation for the average RPI for the year.

effect of inflation by the use of the Retail Price Index (see Appendix 3). The method is as follows:

(a)   Place the average RPI for the period below each reported e.p.s. figure.

(b)   Multiply the reported e.p.s. figure for each earlier year by the average RPI for the year being reported upon, and divide by the average RPI for the earlier year.

Example 20.1 above shows this method in practice, using the e.p.s. from CADBURY SCHWEPPES' summary on page 143. The calculation for 1984 is:

$15.65 \times 106.9 \div 89.2 = 18.76$

The reported figures show an encouraging increase in e.p.s. of about 50% between 1984 and 1988, despite a nasty fall in 1985; but in real terms the e.p.s. went up by only 25%. Where companies report *static* earnings per share they are, in fact, falling by the rate of inflation.

The fall in the value of money has a diabolical effect on e.p.s. in times of high inflation: not only are profits each year overstated due to the historical cost method of accounting, but the e.p.s. can appear to rise encouragingly when, in real terms, they may actually be falling.

Net tangible assets per share (n.t.a.)
The n.t.a., or 'Shareholders' funds per share', is the ordinary shareholders' funds (excluding goodwill and any other intangible assets) divided by the number of ordinary shares in issue (see Example 20.2 below).

Example 20.2   Calculation of net tangible assets per share: CADBURY SCHWEPPES

		£m
(a)	Issued *ordinary* share capital at 31 December 1988 (Note 1)	150.4
	Reserves	332.3
(b)	Ordinary shareholders' funds (OSF)	482.7

(c)   Number of 25p ordinary shares in issue
$= (a) \times 4$ (Note 2) $= 601.6$ million
Net tangible assets per ordinary share (n.a.v.) $= \dfrac{(b)}{(c)} = 80.2$p (Note 3).

Notes:
1.   Issued ordinary share capital = issued share capital *minus* any issued preference capital (£3.3 million in CADBURY SCHWEPPES' case).
2.   To obtain the number of ordinary shares in issue at the end of the year (*not* the average number given in the accounts for calculating e.p.s.), multiply the issued ordinary share capital by 100p and divide by the nominal value of the ordinary shares.
3.   A quick way to calculate n.t.a. straight off the balance sheet is:

$$\frac{(b)}{(a)} \times \text{nominal value of ordinary share,}$$

but make sure that the issued share capital does not include any preference capital and that any intangible assets are deducted from ordinary shareholders' funds.

The progression over the years shows how much profit is being ploughed back into the company to help earnings grow, and is a much better indicator than overall figures for assets employed or for shareholders' funds, which can be boosted by acquisitions for paper. The n.t.a. can, of course, be boosted by upward revaluation of assets, particularly of property, which is usually the cause of any sharp jump in n.t.a. that is larger than the year's e.p.s. less the dividend per share, i.e. is larger than any change that could be caused by retained earnings. Unless a company is making losses, any fall in the n.t.a. is almost always due to extraordinary items, i.e. amounts written off below the line or to the writing off of goodwill (the difference between the cost of an acquisition and the value of the tangible assets acquired). For example, in the 5-year summary on page 143, CADBURY SCHWEPPES shows a fall in n.t.a. from 102.1p to 80.22p between 1984 and 1988; but for the write-off of goodwill it would have *increased* to 131.2p:

145

CADBURY SCHWEPPES *Effect of writing off goodwill on net tangible assets*

	Year ended December		1984	1985	1986	1987	1988
(a)	Ordinary shareholders' funds £m						
	(Capital + reserves − £3.3m pref.)		515.4	467.7	459.9	473.4	482.7
	Goodwill written off £m			26.6	115.0	60.0	105.3
	Cumulative goodwill written off £m			26.6	141.6	201.6	306.9
(b)	OSF plus goodwill written off since end of 1984 £m		515.4	493.3	601.5	675.0	789.6
(c)	Net tangible assets per share, as reported		102.1p	90.18p	82.36p	79.72p	80.22p
(d)	Net tangible assets + goodwill written off, per ordinary share	$=\dfrac{(c) \times (b)}{(a)}$	102.1p	95.1p	107.7p	113.7p	131.2p

The writing off of goodwill also distorts other ratios. For example CADBURY SCHWEPPES' return on equity appears to have risen from 14.0% in 1984 to 26.4% in 1988. But for the write-off of goodwill in 1985–88, the return on equity in 1988 would have been only 17.8%.

It is interesting to note that, although CADBURY SCHWEPPES writes off goodwill immediately, the company's new borrowing powers proposed in the 1988 accounts recognised purchased goodwill. The practice of 'immediate write-off' is clearly confusing, and ED 47, *Accounting for Goodwill*, published in February 1990, proposes that 'Purchased goodwill should be recognised as a fixed asset and recorded in the balance sheet', i.e.

no immediate write-off, and that it should be amortised through the profit and loss account over a maximum of 20 years (or in rare circumstances 40 years).

This is a complete reversal of SSAP 22, where immediate write-off is the preferred method, and it is meeting considerable opposition, even though the ED does not *require* purchased goodwill previously written off direct to reserves to be reinstated in the balance sheet. Had Cadbury Schweppes taken purchased goodwill on the balance sheet since 1984 and amortised it over 20 years, reported pre-tax profits of £215.7 million would have been reduced by £14.4 million.

BRITISH PETROLEUM *Extract from Information on price changes*

As reported

	1984	1985	1986	1987	£ million 1988
Turnover	38,645	41,929	27,269	28,328	25,922
Historical cost profit before extraordinary items	1,402	1,598	817	1,391	1,210
Earnings per ordinary share	25.6p	29.1p	14.9p	24.9p	20.0p
Dividends per ordinary share	10.00p	11.33p	11.67p	12.50p	13.50p
Adjusted for the average UK retail price index of:	89.2	94.6	97.8	101.9	106.9
					£ million
Turnover	46,313	47,381	29,806	29,718	25,922
Historical cost profit before extraordinary items	1,680	1,806	893	1,459	1,210
Earnings per ordinary share	30.7p	32.9p	16.3p	26.1p	20.0p
Dividends per ordinary share	11.98p	12.80p	12.75p	13.11p	13.50p

Chapter 21

DIRECTORS' REPORT, CHAIRMAN'S STATEMENT AND AUDITORS' REPORT

THE DIRECTORS' REPORT

Contents

The contents of the directors' report fall broadly into three categories:

1. *Information required by law* – the statutory requirements – a mass of information some of which is obvious from the accounts anyway, some of which is of comparatively little interest to the analyst (but appears to have been motivated by political considerations, e.g. contributions for political purposes), but some of which may be of vital interest and importance to anyone interpreting the accounts, e.g. the review of the year and likely future developments.
2. *Information required by The Stock Exchange*, which we described in Chapter 3, some of which overlaps the statutory requirements.
3. *Voluntary information* – additional information and commentary which the company wants to include: this is usually concerned with the events of the past year, current trading and future plans and prospects.

The voluntary information is normally contained mainly or wholly in the chairman's statement or review of the year, leaving the directors' report chiefly a catalogue of compulsory details; but if there is no chairman's statement, and there is no compulsion for a chairman to report separately from the board of directors, any voluntary information will be included in the directors' report. In this chapter we will assume that there is a chairman's statement, and we will deal with voluntary information under that heading later in the chapter.

Statutory requirements

Under the Companies Acts, a directors' report must give the following information:

(a) a *fair review* of the development of the business during the year, together with an indication of likely *future developments* and of *research and development* activities (CA 1989 S. 8 and CA 1985, Sch. 7, paras 6(b) and (c));
(b) the names of the *directors* and details of their interests (shareholdings) (CA 1989, Sch. 5);
(c) particulars of significant changes in *fixed assets* (CA 1985, Sch. 7, para. 1);
(d) details of company's *own shares* acquired by the company during the year (CA 1985, Sch. 7, Part II);
(e) *important events* affecting the company which have occurred *since the end of the year* (CA 1985, Sch. 7, para. 6(a); see also post balance sheet events, page 152);
(f) details of *political or charitable contributions*, if over £200 in the year (CA 1985, Sch. 7, para. 3).

Listing requirements

As described in Chapter 3, the Continuing Obligations of listed companies require them to circulate certain information with the annual report; this information is usually contained in the directors' report, but may appear separately or in notes to the accounts. Items of particular interest are:

(a) a geographical analysis of turnover of operations outside the United Kingdom and Ireland, and of their contribution to the *trading results* if 'abnormal';

(b) holdings, other than by directors, of 5% or more of any class of voting capital;

(c) whether or not the company is a 'close company'.

Control of the company

It is always worth checking whether a company is a 'bid prospect'. If an acquisition-minded company has a substantial holding, this can explain why the company's share is looking overrated or 'expensive' in comparison with other similar companies.

On the other hand, if the company is a close company (i.e. under the control of its directors or of five or fewer persons – see Chapter 2), or if the directors' interests are substantial although not controlling, the dividend policy is likely to be conservative. In addition, growth will probably be limited to ploughing back profits, because directors or the controlling shareholders are unlikely to be in a position to take up their entitlement in a rights issue, and because acquisitions for paper would also dilute their control.

However, if the principal director shareholder is nearing retirement, with no obvious successor (check list of shareholders for family names of the next generation, and remember that new issue prospectuses give directors' ages), then an agreed bid could well be in store.

The board of directors

Although many companies are built up primarily through the efforts of a single person, a one-man band is a potentially dangerous situation. He's going to present a succession problem in due course, and what would happen if he had a heart attack tomorrow? And, if he's egocentric, he may surround himself with yes-men and come an awful cropper with his company.

We would therefore prefer a top management team: it is, for example, preferable not to combine the posts of chairman and managing director, and to have a separate finance director, and to have at least five board members. We would be unhappy, for instance, with the statement of one chairman/MD: 'Apart from overall control of the Group's affairs, I shall have particular responsibility for financial control, and investigating possible acquisitions by the company.'

We like the inclusion of a few non-executive directors, provided they are of a healthily independent disposition, devote sufficient time to the company to have a good grasp of its affairs (i.e. they must know what's going on), are prepared to make a stand/resign if they disagree on important issues, and bring some relevant experience to the boardroom.

Where a company has been in difficulties or has become complacent, a change in the top management should be watched closely, because it can often mark the turn in a company's fortunes; for example the appointment of Eugene Anderson as chief executive of JOHNSON MATTHEY after its disastrous foray into banking and the appointment of Derek Birkin as chief executive of RTZ after several years of little or no *real* growth in e.p.s. It is well worth checking on the track record of new management and, if you can, going to the AGM to meet them.

Having checked the composition of the board and the management structure, let us now have a look at the chairman's statement, not only for what it says but also for what we can read between the lines.

THE CHAIRMAN'S STATEMENT

Sequence of study

It is difficult to lay down a set of rules as to the best order in which to study a report and accounts, and each individual will develop his own method (one stockbroker tells us he always goes straight to the directors' holdings to see if they are reducing their holdings!), but we think it is useful to start by glancing at the chairman's statement and the directors' report to see whether anything has occurred which would invalidate a straightforward comparison between one year and another. If, for instance, a major acquisition took place at the beginning of the year under review, almost all operating and financial ratios are likely to have been affected. This does not mean that the ratios are useless: simply that the analyst must bear in mind the change in composition of the group every time he compares one ratio with another.

Having then studied the accounts (a process we will discuss in detail in Chapters 24 and 25) and having examined any analysis given of turnover and pre-tax profits between classes of business and any geographical analysis of turnover and trading results outside the United Kingdom, the reader will now have a good idea of how the company has fared in the past year, but little idea why (except in the context of happening to know that it was a good, average or bad year for the industry or industries in which the company operates), and little idea of how the company is likely to do in the current year and beyond. It is to the chairman's statement that we should look for this information.

Example 21.1   Estimating current year profits: 'POLYGON HOLDINGS PLC'

Activity	Industrial climate	Chairman's remarks	Previous year £m	Reported year £m	Estimate of current year £m
Building	Continued recession	'Further decline inevitable'	1.0	0.8	0.5–0.6
Paper	Cyclical upturn	'Marked improvement'	2.2	1.8	2.4–2.8
Bookmaking	One of the UK's few growth industries	'Continued progress'	1.0	1.2	1.4–1.5
Plastic extrusions	Demand flat	'Market share increasing but lower margins'	0.6	0.75	0.6–0.8
Interest charges	Rates down 2%	'Improvement in liquidity likely'	−0.8	−1.0	−0.8
Pre-tax total			4.0	3.55	4.1–4.9

Contents

In companies which believe in keeping share-holders well informed, the chairman's statement will usually contain comment on:

(a) overall trading conditions during the period, current climate and general outlook;
(b) the performance achieved by each activity, current trading and future prospects;
(c) special items of interest (e.g. closures and new ventures);
(d) company strategy and plans for the future.

We find it's useful to read through the whole statement highlighting key phrases and points of interest as we go, before getting down to any detailed analysis.

Estimating current year profits

A rough estimate of profits for the current year can be constructed (by each activity separately reported) by quantifying the chairman's comments, bearing in mind prevailing conditions and prospects for the industry concerned; for example, 'POLYGON HOLDING PLC' (Example 21.1).

The chairman may also give some overall view, e.g. Polygon Holding's turnover in the first three months of the current year has been 22% higher than the same period last year, the paper division's order-book is now four months, compared with one month last year, and, despite constant pressure on margins and the increasing ineptitude of government, the outlook for the group is encouraging. 'Outlook encouraging' sounds to us like a 20–25% increase in pre-tax profits, i.e. to £4.3–£4.5 million, pointing to the middle of the range we constructed division by division.

Other points to bear in mind in making a profits estimate are these:

1. Loss-makers discontinued will not only eliminate the loss but should, in addition, improve liquidity (and thus reduce interest charges, assuming there is an overdraft). But have all terminal losses been provided for?
2. Most new ventures, branches, factories, depots, etc., are doing well if they break even in their second year of operation.
3. What is the chairman's previous record? Has he been accurate – cautious – unduly optimistic – erratic? Have past assurances of better times ahead been unfulfilled?
4. Remember, too, that one of the chairman's most important jobs is to maintain general confidence in the company, so he is likely to concentrate on the good points and only dwell briefly or remain silent on the weaker aspects of the company. Here it is a good idea to jot down questions, even if the analyst or shareholder is unlikely to have the opportunity of putting them to the company, because it helps to establish what the chairman hasn't revealed and whether any unexplained area is likely to be significant. A good question to ask oneself is 'What are the company's main problems, and what is being done about them?'
5. Beware of vague statements, such as:
   (a) 'Turnover in the first ten weeks of the current year has exceeded the corresponding figure for last year.' It may be 1% ahead in value because of inflation, but a 4% drop has occurred in volume.
   (b) 'Unforeseen difficulties have occurred

in . . . and a provision of £1.3 million has been made.' Unless there is some indication of the likely overall cost of overcoming these difficulties, or of abandoning the activity altogether, the company should be assumed to have an open-ended loss-maker on its hands.

Longer-term prospects

The chairman of a company should be continually looking to the future and, unless he and his board have good sound ideas on where the future growth in profits is likely to come from, and are steering the company in that direction, then above-average profits growth is unlikely. Although there must, of course, be some restrictions on what a chairman discloses about plans for the future, because of competition, he will usually include some indication of where he thinks the company is going in his annual statement.

A good past growth record is clearly encouraging (a no-growth company is likely to stay a no-growth company unless the management or the management's attitude changes), but what indications are there of future growth? Possibilities to look for are the following:

1. *Better margins on existing business.* This is an unreliable source of growth unless the company *either*

    (*a*) has some very strong competitive advantage, such as patents or lucrative long-term contracts, *or*

    (*b*) has spent large sums of money building up brand images and carving out market share, and is now beginning to reap the benefits,

    and even then the profits growth will only last until the patents expire, the long-term contracts run out and the brand images tarnish.

2. *Further expansion of existing activities within the United Kingdom.* Is there any scope for this, or is the company in a position like BOOTS or W. H. SMITH, with a store in every town of any size, or like PILKINGTON, with 90% of the UK glass market?

3. *Diversification within the United Kingdom.* This was BOOTS' answer to its saturation problem with chemist shops: it widened the range of goods sold to include records and tapes, hi-fi, cameras, binoculars, even sandwiches. BOOTS was using its retailing expertise in wider product ranges, rather than going into some totally unrelated activity, and there does need to be some logic in diversifications or they can come very badly unstuck.

4. *Acquisition within the United Kingdom.* Has the company got a successful record of acqui-

sitions, or would this method of growth be new to it (and therefore more risky)? This was part of W. H. SMITH's solution for further growth: in 1986 it took over the recorded music chain OUR PRICE, with 130 outlets, added 40 music outlets it already had and by 1990, with further acquisitions, had built the chain up to around 300 outlets.

5. *Exports.* Is the product suitable for export, or would transport costs make competitiveness overseas unlikely or impossible (e.g. bricks)? Does the company export already, is it a significant amount, and is it growing? The chairman may report that 'exports are 80% up on last year', but if this is an increase from 0.1% to 0.18% of turnover, it is hardly thrilling, and one should be wary of the chairman whose efforts to paint a rosy picture involve misleading statements like that, which should in honesty be qualified by some phrase like 'albeit from a very low base'.

6. *Are there opportunities for overseas growth,* like W.H. SMITH's acquisition of the US news and gifts chain ELSON, specialising in shops in hotels and airports, or PILKINGTON putting down float glass plants overseas, either on its own or in joint ventures, or by licensing the process to foreign glass manufacturers? There are, however, a good many hazards in opening up operations abroad, apart from the initial expense: different business ethics and practices, language, law, accounting and tax systems, and so on. For manufacturing abroad, cost levels and exchange rates may change over time, so that what today looks a good investment may prove otherwise in years to come if the cost of living rises faster in that country than elsewhere.

7. *Is the company spending money on, and attaching importance to, developing new products?* This is particularly important for pharmaceutical companies; GLAXO, for instance, in 1989 reported £323 million spent on research and development, representing over 12% of the pharmaceutical product group's turnover.

    Although any manufacturing company that *isn't* developing new products is almost certainly going downhill, it is also bad news if the chairman is always eulogising about new products that never come to anything: the company's track record on product development should be checked.

8. *Is the company ploughing profits back?* Profits in most industries cannot expand beyond a given point unless the asset base (needed to support the trading needed to generate the profits) is also expanded. There is a limit to gearing up, while acquisitions and rights

issues don't necessarily enhance e.p.s.: only steady ploughback gives scope for steady growth in e.p.s.

In the context of future growth, it is also worth checking press cuttings for stories on the company, which often contain glimpses of the company's thoughts on the future (see Chapter 22 on McCarthy's press cutting service).

Information on the quality of management

Returning to the business of assessing the strength of the management, perhaps the most encouraging facet is when the chairman admits to a mistake or to being caught wrong-footed, and reports what is being or has been done about it. A classic example comes from the 'rag trade': the chairman's statement for WEARWELL in 1976, a year in which trading results had fallen from £1 million profit to £28,000 loss on turnover down from £7.1 million to £6.2 million and with over £½ million in terminal losses, contained the following comments:

WEARWELL *Extracts from chairman's report, 1976*

... in 1973 we operated what was basically a cash and carry operation. [In 1974 and 1975 the company made two acquisitions for cash and we] found ourselves in the business of building up stock and financing customers for considerable periods ... sales not as buoyant as expected ... liquidity difficulties in the opening weeks of 1976 ... instituted immediate measures, namely:

1. Closure of the mail order supply business which has required the financing of substantial stocks.
2. Cutting out much of the credit business with chain stores.
3. The waiver by directors of a substantial part of their salary entitlement together with a waiver of between 94.0% and 99.9% of their total entitlement to the interim dividend.
4. Strenuous efforts were made to liquidate stocks.

... your company operates now only in the cash and carry type business which is where your management has proved its expertise.

We are glad to say that Wearwell's drastic action paid off. The company just managed to get out of the red in 1977, and from then on pre-tax profits grew steadily; five years later the chairman, Asil Nadir (of POLLY PECK fame, the group which Wearwell subsequently joined) was able to report pre-tax profits in excess of £4 million.

Wearwell's shareholders also had a bumpy ride: from an Offer for Sale price of 30p (adjusted for subsequent scrip and rights issues) in July 1973 they saw the ordinary share price fall to a low of 8p in November 1976, and received no dividends at all in 1977 and 1978. But in the longer run they were amply rewarded: in 1984 Wearwell merged with POLLY PECK, whose chairman was also Mr Asil Nadir. The deal gave WEARWELL shareholders 53 POLLY PECK shares for every 100 WEARWELL, valuing WEARWELL's ordinary shares at 164p each: twenty times the 1976 level.

In contrast, the chairman of a housebuilding company reported proudly in 1974 that 'notwithstanding all these problems [the three-day week, the shortage of mortgage funds, rising interest rates and increases in building costs] your company increased its turnover to a new record level'. The turnover had risen from £25.4 million to almost £44 million on an equity base of less than £2 million net of goodwill and after writing £8.7 million off the value of the land bank, now in the books at a mere £24.4 million plus £23.4 million work in progress. Apart from the feeling that the chairman was steering his company straight for the eye of a financial typhoon, and his avoidance of mentioning the year's pre-tax loss of £6.3 million in his statement, there were a number of fairly conspicuous danger signals scattered around the report:

(a) The notice of the AGM included a resolution to appoint a top London firm of accountants to be joint auditors with the existing provincial firm of auditors.

(b) The directors' report contained a little paragraph on 'financial arrangements', which revealed that the group's bankers had agreed to 'roll up' interest on group borrowings.

But perhaps the most telling fact was an omission: the group's habit of including a historical summary (which in the previous year's accounts had shown a seven-year progression in pre-tax profits from £142,000 to over £7 million) had been discontinued! The fall into loss was too painful to face. Liquidation followed quite shortly afterwards.

It is hoped that the same fate will not befall SAATCHI & SAATCHI which, in 1989, omitted its two-page 'Financial Record' when profits after tax fell from £87.6 million in the previous year to a loss of £15.4 million. SAATCHI & SAATCHI is, however, taking strenuous steps to reverse its disastrous expansion into management consultancy and to refocus on its core advertising business; a new chief executive and a new finance director have been appointed and at the AGM the chairman, Maurice Saatchi, announced a 30% cut in his salary.

POST BALANCE SHEET EVENTS

(Reference: SSAP 17 *Accounting for Post Balance Sheet Events*.)

It might be thought that, since a company's report and accounts reflect the state of affairs at the balance sheet date, events arising after that date would be excluded, but this is not entirely the case: post balance sheet events (events occurring between the balance sheet date and the date the accounts are approved by the board) should be reflected or disclosed if they are important (CA 1985, Sch. 7, para. 6).

Types of post balance sheet event

SSAP 17 distinguishes between two types of post balance sheet event:

(*a*) *Adjusting events*, which provide additional evidence of conditions existing at the balance sheet date, e.g. the insolvency of a debtor. The accounts should be adjusted accordingly, but separate disclosure is not normally required.

Where any subsequent events indicate that the 'going concern' concept should not have been applied to the company or to a material part of it, the accounts should also be adjusted accordingly.

(*b*) *Non-adjusting events*, which concern conditions which did *not* exist at the balance sheet date. The events should be disclosed together, if practicable, with an estimate of the financial effect.

Disclosure is usually made in the directors' report (e.g. MAXWELL COMMUNICATION CORPORATION's disclosure of an acquisition, shown below), or in a note to the accounts (e.g. ICELAND FROZEN FOODS' acquisition of BEJAM, illustrated below), and if the event is of major importance, further details will be given elsewhere; for example the chairman of ICELAND devoted half a page of his annual statement to the acquisition of BEJAM.

MAXWELL COMMUNICATION CORPORATION *Extract from Directors' report for year ended 31 March 1989*

Post balance sheet events

Disposals

On 19 June 1989 the Company sold the British Newspaper Printing Corporation Group ('BNPC') to Mirror Group Newspapers Limited.

The basic consideration was £270.3 million, subject to adjustment for changes in BNPC's net assets between 1 January 1989 and 19 June 1989. An initial payment of £206.2 million was made on 19 June 1989 with the balance of moneys to follow . . .

Acquisitions

In April 1989 the Group acquired 100% of the issued share capital of Sphere Books Limited for a cash consideration of £13.8 million . . .

ICELAND FROZEN FOODS *Note to the 1988 accounts and extract from chairman's statement*

Post balance sheet event

On 4 January 1989 the Company acquired control of Bejam Group PLC. The new Iceland ordinary shares issued as part of the consideration are entitled to participate in the proposed final ordinary dividend. The cost of the dividend in respect of these shares is estimated to amount to £1,835,000.

Chairman's statement

Acquisition

The geographical fit of Iceland and Bejam is excellent and the commercial logic of putting them together is overwhelming. Rationalisation will permit substantial cost savings . . . We gained effective control of Bejam on 4 January 1989, and have already made great progress in its integration with Iceland . . . A new management structure has been created and a major rationalisation programme is being implemented . . . Bejam's sales were down 10%. We are confident this trend will be reversed . . . We have started a two-year programme of refits and conversions to the Iceland format . . . All stores will share a common format by the end of May 1989.

Window dressing

One method of improving the appearance of a company's accounts is to borrow short-term money, perhaps just overnight, in order to bump up liquidity at the balance sheet date, a trick that was particularly popular amongst fringe bankers in the early 1970s.

SSAP 17 endeavours to preclude this and similar types of cosmetic operation by requiring the disclosure of 'the reversal or maturity after the year end of transactions entered into before the year end, the substance of which was primarily to alter the appearance of the company's balance sheet'.

This requirement may not prevent this type of window dressing, but it should discourage auditors from being party to deliberate deceptions.

THE AUDITORS' REPORT

(References: Companies Act 1989, S. 9; *Auditing Standards and Guidelines*.)

Appointment of auditors

Every company is required to appoint at each annual general meeting an auditor or auditors to hold office from the conclusion of that meeting until the conclusion of the next AGM.

Auditors' access to information

Under the Companies Act 1985 it is an offence for a director or company secretary to give false or misleading information to auditors, and auditors of holding companies have the right to obtain information about subsidiary companies which they themselves do not audit.

The auditor has a right of access at all times to the books and accounts and vouchers of the company and to require from the officers of the company such information and explanations as he thinks necessary for the performance of his duty. He has the right to attend any general meeting, and to be heard thereat on any part of the business of the meeting which concerns him as auditor.

Scope of the report

The auditors are required to report to the members (i.e. to the shareholders) whether in their opinion the profit and loss account and the balance sheet, and any group accounts, have been properly prepared in accordance with the Companies Acts and all relevant SSAPs, and give a true and fair view of the profit and state of affairs of the company or group.

If they are of the opinion that proper accounting records have not been kept, or that the accounts are not in agreement with the books, or if they are unable to obtain all the information and explanations necessary for their audit, they must state the fact in their report; i.e. they must qualify their report.

Qualified auditors' reports

Auditing Standards and Guidelines (published by the Institutes of Chartered Accountants and the Chartered Association of Certified Accountants) distinguishes between what may be termed a 'clean' audit report and one which is 'qualified', and recommends the form of words to be used in qualified reports in different circumstances.

This can be very helpful to the reader in interpreting the significance of an audit report, provided he or she understands the 'standard jargon', so it is well worth explaining the auditing rules in some detail:

Clean report In a 'clean' report the auditors will say in an 'opinion paragraph' that, in their opinion, the financial statements give a *true and fair view*, without any qualification. (*Financial statements* embrace the balance sheets, profit and loss accounts, statement of source and application of funds, notes and other statements, which collectively are intended to give a true and fair view of the financial position and profit or loss – SSAP 14, para. 10.)

Qualified report If the auditor is unable to give a clean report 'he should qualify his report by referring to all *material* matters about which he has reservations. All reasons for the qualification should be given, together with a quantification of its effect on the financial statements if this is both relevant and practicable.' The Standard goes on to emphasise that 'a qualified audit report should leave the reader in no doubt as to its meaning and its implications for an understanding of the financial statements' – although whether this always happens, or whether it is always possible, is open to question.

In addition, when a report is qualified, Section 271(4) of the Companies Act 1985 requires the auditors to state in writing whether the qualification is material for the purpose of determining whether the dividend distribution contravenes other sections of the Act.

Categories of qualified report

There are two categories:

(*a*) *uncertainty* – where there is an uncertainty which prevents the auditor from forming an opinion on a matter; *and*

(*b*) *disagreement* – where the auditor is able to form an opinion on the matter but this conflicts with the view given by the financial statements.

Each category is then further subdivided according to whether the subject matter of the uncertainty or disagreement is *fundamental* (so important and significant 'as to undermine the view given by the financial statements taken as a whole'), or is only *material*. In each case recommended wording is given for the *opinion paragraph*, as shown in Example 21.2.

Example 21.2 Recommended wording for the opinion paragraph

Material uncertainty	: 'subject to'
Fundamental uncertainty	: 'unable to form an opinion as to' (called a 'disclaimer of opinion')

Material disagreement : 'except for'
Fundamental disagreement : 'do not give a true
and fair view'
(called an
'adverse opinion')

Examples of qualified reports

Uncertainty qualifications include:

(*a*) limitations in the scope of the audit due to lack of information; and

(*b*) inherent uncertainties, e.g. events which have not yet been concluded, such as major litigation and investigation and closures being carried out but not yet completed, and uncertainty over the continued support of the company's bankers.

Where an auditors' report refers to specific paragraphs or notes in the financial statements, these should also be checked, as they can often be more revealing than a tactful auditors' report.

Where continued financial support is in doubt, the key words to watch for are *going concern*. For example CENTRAL & SHERWOOD:

CENTRAL & SHERWOOD *Auditors' report and notes to the 1985 accounts*

To the members of Central & Sherwood PLC

We have audited the financial statements on pages 14 to 27 in accordance with approved auditing standards.

The financial statements have been prepared on the going concern basis on the assumption of the continuing support of the principal bankers and on the basis of accounting set out on page 18.

Subject to the Group's principal bankers continuing to provide finance, in our opinion the financial statements, which have been prepared on the basis of the accounting policies set out on page 18, give a true and fair view of the state of affairs of the Company and the Group at 31 December 1985 and of the loss and source and application of funds of the Group for the year then ended and comply with the Companies Act 1985.

Binder Hamlyn
Chartered Accountants

Page 18   Accounting policies

Basis of accounting

The financial statements have been prepared on the basis that the Group's principal bankers will continue to provide finance towards the implementation of the Group's operational plan for 1986 and that the Group will be able to realise such plan (see Note 20).

Note 20   Bank and other borrowings repayable in less than one year

Bank overdrafts . . .

During September 1986 the Group's principal Bankers confirmed that they will continue to provide finance, conditional upon the continuing achievement of the Group's operational plan. The bankers will continue to monitor the Group's performance on a regular basis against this plan.

Disagreement qualifications cover:

(*a*) unjustified non-compliance with SSAPs and/or inappropriate accounting policies

(*b*) disagreement on facts or amounts, or on the way in which they have (or haven't!) been disclosed; *and*

(*c*) non-compliance with legislation.

Where SSAPs have not been complied with, it is interesting to check the effect of non-compliance on reported profits and e.p.s., and whether the company is being consistent. For example FARNELL ELECTRONICS' accounts to 31 January 1988 (a few months after the stockmarket crash of October 1987) were qualified by auditors Sagar Croudson because 'The company has treated the loss on its equity portfolio as an extraordinary item rather than as an exceptional item as required by SSAP 6' and a note to the accounts, to which the auditors drew attention, showed that 'The effect of this treatment is to increase the profit on ordinary activities before tax by £2,268,000.' Had the SSAP been complied with, the pre-tax profit would have been marginally down on the previous year, rather than 9% up, and e.p.s. would have been 12.0p rather than 13.1p, against the previous year's 11.9p.

But non-compliance with SSAP 6 would not have been such a blatant attempt to massage the profits if the company, in previous years when the market was rising, had not taken *profits* on its equity portfolio above the line. We are glad to say that the Press picked it up, and gave FARNELL a good deal of well-deserved flack.

Fundamental qualifications

A fundamental qualification – the 'unable to form an opinion as to' where there is uncertainty, and the 'do not give a true and fair view' where there is disagreement – is the extreme form of qualification, and should be regarded as the measure of last resort.

In the case of FEEDEX AGRICULTURAL INDUSTRIES, it was the last resort: the auditors were in fundamental disagreement with the chairman, and used the words 'do not give a true and fair view' in their report:

FEEDEX AGRICULTURAL INDUSTRIES *Qualified auditors' report*

To the members of Feedex Agricultural Industries plc

We have audited the accounts on pages 6 to 19 in accordance with approved auditing standards.

An unrealised profit on the sale of development land held as stock to a related company has been credited in full to the consolidated profit and loss account of the Group because the directors consider this accounting treatment best presents a true and fair view of the transaction. In our opinion an adjustment should be made to exclude such unrealised profit as required by Statement of Standard Accounting Practice No. 1. If such an adjustment was made, the effect would be to reduce the consolidated profit on ordinary activities before taxation by £945,000, the consolidated profit on ordinary activities after taxation by £614,000 and to turn the consolidated profit for the year of £119,000 into a loss for the year of £495,000.

In view of the impact of the failure to adjust for the unrealised profit referred to above, in our opinion the accounts do not give a true and fair view of the state of affairs of the Group at 31 December 1988 or of the profit or loss and source and application of funds of the Group for the year then ended. In all other respects . . .

Hodgson Impey
Chartered Accountants

In FEEDEX's directors' report there was a special paragraph about auditors:

'Following the merger with the Usborne Group of Companies in 1987 the Group audits have been conducted by two firms of auditors. The directors felt that this added unnecessarily to the complication and expense of the audit. Last year they therefore invited Hodgson Impey the Group auditors and Baker Tilly who audit some of the subsidiary companies, along with three other firms, to tender for the audit of all the companies in the Group . . .'

and, surprise, surprise, Hodgson Impey got the push.

Although the auditors are technically elected by the members (shareholders), we know of no case where the members have done anything other than confirm the directors' choice. Auditors will therefore avoid fundamental qualifications whenever humanly possible, so the reader should be on the lookout for 'borderline cases'.

Materiality

The explanatory note in the auditing standard on qualifications is pretty woolly: 'In general terms a matter should be judged to be material if knowledge of the matter would be likely to influence the user of the financial statements . . . materiality may be considered in relative or absolute terms.' However, in a similar context, SSAP 3 (earnings per share) is rather more specific: 'the fully diluted earnings per share need not be given unless the dilution is material. Dilution amounting to 5% or more of the basic earnings per share is regarded as material for this purpose.'

It might therefore be argued that an auditor need not qualify his report if the amount involved would not alter the bottom line of the profit and loss account by 5% or more.

Emphasis of matter

In general a clean report should not make reference to specific aspects of the financial statements, in case it is misconstrued as a qualification. If, however, the auditor wishes to draw attention to anything he considers important, he should do so in a *separate* paragraph, using suitable wording, e.g. 'We draw attention to . . .', and should *not* refer to it in the opinion paragraph, e.g. Price Waterhouse's audit report on GUINNESS, which drew attention to Note 27 'Disputes following the acquisition of DISTILLERS':

GUINNESS *Auditors' report: emphasis of matter*

Report of the auditors to the members of Guinness PLC

We have audited the financial statements on pages 32 to 55 in accordance with approved Auditing Standards.

We draw attention to Note 27 referring to possible legal and other actions which may involve the Company.

In our opinion the financial statements give a true and fair view of the state of affairs of the Company and of the Group at 31 December 1988 and of the profit and source and application of funds of the Group for the year then ended and comply with the Companies Act 1985.

Price Waterhouse
Chartered Accountants

Delay in publication

One final and rather obvious point about auditing: it often takes longer if the company is in difficulties, so any delay in publishing the annual report and accounts is usually a bad sign; The Stock Exchange likes to see them issued within six months of a company's year end, and failure to do so is comparatively rare among listed companies (see page 159 for details of the period currently allowed by the Companies Act 1989 for laying and delivering accounts).

Chapter 22

OTHER SOURCES OF INFORMATION

Investors and analysts should recognise that the annual report and accounts of a company represent only a part, albeit a key part, of the total information available to them, and they should not neglect other sources. For convenience the other sources can be divided into:

(a) information the company provides, *and*
(b) external information.

INFORMATION PROVIDED BY THE COMPANY

The main sources of information from the company itself, apart from the annual report and accounts, are:

(a) half-yearly (and in a few cases quarterly) reports;
(b) prospectuses;
(c) circulars;
(d) form 20-F (if listed in the US);
(e) company newsletters and magazines;
(f) catalogues and sales information literature;
(g) annual meetings;
(h) company visits.

Interim reports

The EEC directive on Interim Reports requires each listed company to prepare a report on its activities and profit and loss for the first six months of each financial year. This report must *either* be sent to shareholders *or* be inserted in two national daily newspapers not later than four months after the end of the period (see The Stock Exchange's *Admission of Securities to Listing*, Section 5, Chapter 2, paras. 24 and 25).

In addition to providing information on the first six months, interim figures can and should be used subsequently in conjunction with the full year's figures to detect changes in trends in the second half. For example MCCARTHY & STONES's annual report to 31 August 1989 made no mention of the loss the group incurred in the second half, but the figure can easily be deduced:

MCCARTHY & STONE *Second-half results*

Pre-tax profit reported

	£m
Six months to 28 February 1989	11.5
Year ended 31 August 1989	7.1
Pre-tax loss in second half, deduced	(4.4)

Interim statements are not audited and it is possible that the stringent look which is given to the balance sheet at the end of the year, and the consequent making of adequate provisions, does not occur at the half-year. This tends to means that adverse exceptional and extraordinary items are somewhat more likely to be included in the second half of a year than in the first half.

Prospectuses and listing particulars

When a company offers shares or debentures for sale to the general public it is obliged in law to issue a prospectus; the Third Schedule to the Com-

156

panies Act 1985 lays down the items which a prospectus must contain.

When a company 'goes public' – that is, when its shares gain a listing on The Stock Exchange (see Chapter 3) – its prospectus has to include all the information required for listing (see The Stock Exchange's *Admission of Securities to Listing*, Section 3, Chapter 2: 'Contents of Listing Particulars'), and so the prospectus is about the most comprehensive document a company ever produces about itself. The normal layout used is as follows:

1. Details of the offer, share capital and indebtedness.
2. Details of the company's directors, secretary, auditors, financial advisers, solicitors, bankers and stockbrokers.
3. Description of the company, giving:
   (*a*) an introduction and a brief history;
   (*b*) a comprehensive description of its business;
   (*c*) information on the management and staff;
   (*d*) details of the company's premises;
   (*e*) use of the proceeds of the issue (where any new shares are being issued);
   (*f*) the earnings record, with a forecast for the current year's profits and intended dividends;
   (*g*) the company's plans and prospects for the future.
4. The accountants' report, containing a table of the last three years' profit and loss accounts and source and application of funds statements and the latest balance sheet.
5. Various statutory and general information on share capital and options, on the Articles of Association, on subsidiary and associated companies, directors' interests and service agreements, taxation clearances, material contracts, and any pending litigation.

On other occasions of shares being offered to the general public either directly, as in a secondary offer for sale of existing shares already listed (e.g. the government's £550 million sale of BRITISH AEROSPACE shares in May 1985), or indirectly, as in a rights issue of new shares of a company whose existing securities are already listed, much less information is required; nevertheless, the prospectus of a secondary offer or the circular letter to shareholders produced for a rights issue can be a useful source of up-to-date information on a company.

Circulars on acquisitions and disposals

Section 6 of The Yellow Book divides transactions into four classes, as shown in Example 22.1.

When a listed company makes a Class 1 transaction (i.e. equivalent to 15% or more of the existing company), shareholders have to be sent a circular giving full details; alternatively, if the company is making a takeover bid, they can be sent a copy of the offer document, provided the offer document includes all the information required for circulars on acquisitions (as contained in Section 6 of The Yellow Book). In either case the information provides the analyst with useful details of any major additions to or realisations of the company's assets.

Circulars also have to be sent to shareholders for Class 4 transactions (those involving a director or substantial shareholder, past or present); these can be of considerable interest if the transactions are large and/or if there is any question of sharp practice, but the majority are fairly mundane, produced mainly to ensure that shareholders' interests are scrupulously protected.

Where there is a very substantial acquisition or reverse takeover, it must be subject to shareholders' approval, and the acquiring company will normally be treated as a new applicant for listing (see para. 7 of Chapter 1 of Section 6 of The Yellow Book).

Documents issued in a contested bid

When the management of a company defends a bid, it has to make the best possible case for the company's continued independence and, in doing so, it will often be rather more forthcoming about the company's future plans and prospects than it normally is in the annual report. Analysts may therefore find it worth reading any documents that a company has issued in successfully contesting a bid. It is also interesting to see whether a company subsequently lives up to any rosy picture it may have painted of its future at the time of the bid.

Form 20–F

This is the annual report that UK and other 'foreign' companies have to file with the Securities and Exchange Commission (SEC) if their shares are listed in the United States. Most companies are prepared to supply copies to shareholders on request and some, e.g. BP, actually offer to do so in their annual report.

Form 20–F contains extensive information, some of which may not be included in the annual report and accounts: it is well worth getting a copy to study.

Company newsletters and magazines

An increasing number of companies now produce a house magazine or newsletter for employees, and many produce a 'report to employees' summarising the company's results for the year, often presenting the information in charts or diagrams.

Example 22.1 Criteria for classification of transactions

Class	Size of acquisition or disposal	Criteria in relation to the company which is acquiring or disposing	Stock Exchange requirements
1	Value of assets *or* Net profit before tax *or* Consideration given *or* Equity capital issued	15% or more of company's assets 15% or more of company's net profit before tax 15% or more of company's assets 15% or more of equity capital previously in issue	Company must make an announcement to the Company Announcements Office and to the Press *and* send circular to shareholders (obtaining their consent if it is a 'Super Class I' transaction i.e. if any of the criteria are 25% or more) *or* publish listing particulars (only if the company is increasing its issued share capital by 10 per cent or more)
2	As above	5% or more of the above but not Class 1	Company must make an announcement to the Company Announcement Office and to the Press
3	As above	All less than 5%	No announcement required unless listing is being sought for securities given in consideration
4	Transactions which involve, or involve an associate of, a director, past director, substantial shareholder or past substantial shareholder		Quotations Department must be consulted beforehand; a circular to shareholders and their consent in general meeting normally required unless transaction is very small

These publications can be very helpful in giving the analyst (as well as the employee) a better feel for the company, and they may contain information that is *not* included in the accounts.

Companies producing an annual newsletter or report to employees may also send copies to shareholders to ensure that information given to employees is also made available to the shareholders, but where newsletters are published more frequently or where a large group has several subsidiaries, each of which has its own separate newsletter, they are unlikely to be distributed to investors. If the analyst can lay his hands on them he may gain a better insight into the various activities of the company and pick up facts that are not generally available.

Catalogues and sales information literature

The shareholder or analyst who really wants to know a company should study its catalogues and sales literature for evidence of pricing policy, marketing ability, and changes in product range, quality or design.

Failure to adapt to changing circumstances is an early sign of sleepy management. Innovation may be essential if the company is to keep moving – but not every management is capable of thinking up new ideas and of putting them into practice. Promotional literature on new products can sometimes indicate the potential for success.

Annual General Meeting

When all is going well, annual meetings tend to be sparsely attended. This is a pity, because they provide an opportunity for investors and analysts to seek and obtain further information about the company.

The routine business of an AGM is:

(a) to receive the report and accounts;
(b) to declare a dividend;
(c) to elect directors;
(d) to appoint auditors;
(e) to transact any other ordinary business.

The chairman will often take the opportunity to make a statement on current trading and/or to amplify the statement he made in the annual report. This is usually done before the routine business, sometimes to pre-empt hostile questions, the classic example being BURTON chairman Ralph Halpern's statement at the AGM following extensive publicity in the Sunday tabloids on his extra-marital activities, which successfully forestalled any further discussion of the matter, although it did inspire one shareholder to get up and say 'If you want to enjoy yourself, then good luck to you, Sir!'

Any ordinary shareholder may attend the AGM and speak. Normally his best opportunity to obtain information is upon the motion considering the accounts. If the information he seeks is reasonable (e.g. not of a confidential nature or likely to be of more value to the competition than to members) and he does not obtain a satisfactory answer, he should press the point and state publicly his dissatisfaction. He may find he has more support than he expects.

Generally, directors are prepared to answer all reasonable questions when times are good, but become guarded when the situation is unsatisfactory. If this occurs, the individual shareholder may find that he can obtain the information during informal discussion after the meeting.

Company visits

Companies differ widely in their attitude to company visits by analysts and/or shareholders. Most major companies welcome the interest of both and arrange from time to time group visits at which plans and prospects are discussed in depth, and those interested are able to seek further information.

Those actually making visits should ask themselves the following:

(a) Is there any evidence of cut-back, of falling sales and growing stocks or of maintenance delayed to save cash?
(b) Is the workforce contented – or are labour relations uneasy?
(c) Do they look efficient – or is there a general atmosphere of chaos?
(d) Do they appear forthcoming, or are they hiding something?

It is also worth asking management whether it is experiencing any difficulties: good management is usually prepared to talk about the problems facing the company, and to explain the action being taken to overcome them.

Finally, always ask about the competition: the replies will help to show whether the management has a practical and realistic attitude to the business environment in which it operates, and may well provide the analyst with useful information about other companies in the industry. We well remember on one company visit, in reply to a question about a competitor, the chairman simply remarked 'that company is structured for disaster'. The competitor went bust a year later.

EXTERNAL INFORMATION

There is a vast range of external information useful to the analyst who wishes to make a study in depth of a particular company, group or industrial sector. Useful sources include:

(a) the Registrar of Companies;
(b) Extel Cards;
(c) ICC Datacards;
(d) *The Hambro Company Guide*;
(e) Macmillan's;
(f) McCarthy Information Services;
(g) Finsbury Data Services;
(h) Datastream;
(i) Key Notes;
(j) the Economist Intelligence Unit;
(k) government statistical publications;
(l) other government publications – NEDO;
(m) specialist and trade publications.

The Registrar of Companies

The Registration Department of the Department of Trade and Industry has offices at Companies House, 55 City Road, London EC1Y 1BB, and at Crown Way, Maindy, Cardiff CF4 3UZ; and, for Scotland, at Exchequer Chambers, 102 George Street, Edinburgh.

Rules for filing accounts
Section 11 of the Companies Act 1989 requires a company to lay its annual report and accounts before its members in general meeting and to deliver them to the Registrar of Companies within certain time limits fixed by reference to its accounting year end. The limit for a UK public company is seven months, which can be extended by three months if the company has interests outside the United Kingdom.

The Stock Exchange requires listed companies to issue an annual report and accounts within six months of the end of the financial year being reported on (The Yellow Book, Section 5, Chapter 2, para. 20), but this may be extended for companies with significant overseas interests.

Other information to be filed

Companies are also required to file with the Registrar:

(a)   copies of their Memorandum and Articles of Association, and details of any subsequent changes;

(b)   address of the registered office, and the place at which the company's registers are kept, if not at the registered office;

(c)   details of the company's share capital and debentures;

(d)   details of each mortgage and charge on the assets of the company;

(e)   a list of the directors and secretary and any changes.

In addition, Section 363 of the Companies Act 1985 requires a company to file an *annual return*, which contains a summary of (b) to (e) above and a list of past and present members. Every third year the list must be a complete list of persons holding shares or stock in the company; in the intervening years only changes need be given, but in each year the return must show anyone whose name has appeared on the register as holding shares or stock in the company at any time since the last return. It is therefore possible to find out from Companies House if anyone has been a registered shareholder at any time, however short the period of ownership, although nominee names may hide the beneficial owner.

Inspecting a company's files

Companies' files are now maintained at Cardiff, and can be inspected either at Cardiff or at City Road, on payment of a fee of £2.50 per company. For this fee the searcher is provided with a microfiche of the company's file, which can be examined on their viewing equipment; hard copy can also be obtained at an additional 10p per page. The microfiche belongs to and may be taken away by the searcher, so anyone with suitable microfiche equipment can consult the file at leisure in his own office.

A search can also be made by post, to the Cardiff office. The fee for a microfiche by post is £4.00, and hard copy is £5.50 per document. There are also a number of search agents who will provide the service on payment of a suitable fee, for example Jordan & Sons Ltd, Jordan House, 47 Brunswick Place, London N1 6EE.

The microfiche facilities available at City Road, London and at Cardiff are virtually identical, and there is no significant time difference in the recording of information at the two offices. For instance, information on charges registered in London is available on the microfiche file in Cardiff within the hour.

Analysing a group

Most group accounts contain a general breakdown of their activities, but much more detail can often be obtained by examining the accounts which each subsidiary and associated company has to file at Companies House.

Extel Cards

Extel (Extel Financial Ltd, 13–17 Epworth Street, London EC2A 4DL, part of the United Newspapers group) is the leading UK provider of financial information services, both on data tape and in printed form. The best known printed services are Extel Cards, which provide information on companies in the United Kingdom and overseas. Extel's card services in the United Kingdom include the following:

1.   The *UK Listed Companies* service, covering every company listed on the British and Irish Stock Exchanges. Two individual cards are issued for each company:

(a)   An Annual Card, which summarises the company's activities and lists its subsidiaries and associated companies, its board members, its share and its loan capital (with history). Tables of profit and loss items, dividend payment details, and balance sheet items are given for the last 5 years, together with a summary of the chairman's most recent statement and a whole host of other information ranging from the company's registered number to its net asset value.

(b)   A Cumulative News Card, issued as and when dividends are announced and when other major items of news justify.

2.   The *Analyst's* service, which complements the *UK Listed Companies* service and covers over 1,000 leading listed companies, giving a ten-year record (analysed and adjusted) of capital changes, balance sheets, profit and loss accounts, share prices, dividends, etc.

3.   The *Unlisted Securities Market* (USM) service, which includes cards for all companies whose shares are traded on The Stock Exchange's Unlisted Securities Market.

4.   The *Matched Bargain* service, which gives details of over 100 UK companies whose shares are traded on a matched bargain basis.

5.   The *Unquoted Companies* service, which is an

extension of the other UK services. It contains similar information on more than 1,700 unquoted companies, on the same system of continuous updating year after year.

The *UK Listed Companies* service, which is an essential part of any stockbroker's or professional investor's office, costs £1,500 per annum for the basic service, takes up about eight cubic feet of filing cabinets and needs two or three hours' clerical effort per week to cope with the steady stream of new cards; but copies of individual cards can be purchased from Extel's extra card department for a few pounds.

A less expensive and more condensed form of information on listed companies is provided by Extel's *Handbook of Market Leaders*, which is published twice a year at £120 per annum. It covers all the companies in the *FT* Actuaries All-share Index, and gives a share price graph as well as other information covering a five-year period. Extel also publishes an annual *Secondary Markets Handbook* at £50 per annum.

ICC Datacards

This recently started service can provide a single-page computer printout on any limited company trading in the United Kingdom, providing its accounts have been filed at Companies House. The page contains basic information on the company, the balance sheets and profit and loss accounts for four years, and a large number of ratios calculated for those years. ICC Company Information Services Ltd, 16/26 Banner Street, London EC1Y 8QE.

The Hambro Company Guide

This is a popular alternative to Extel's *Handbook of Market Leaders*; it gives less information on each company, and only includes a share price graph on some of them. It does, however, cover a much wider range: every UK Listed, USM and OTC company, a total of more than 2,200. It also carries further information on some of the companies, provided and paid for by each company (e.g. the summary of the chairman's statement and annual results as advertised in the financial press); this enables it to be sold at a very reasonable price: £89.50 per annum for four quarterly editions. Published by Hemmington Scott Publishing Ltd, 26–31 Whiskin Street, London EC1R 0PB.

Hemmington Scott also publish the *Hambro Performance Rankings Guide* twice a year at £135.00 per annum, and the *Hambro Corporate Register*, also twice a year at £135.00 per annum.

Macmillan's

Macmillan's Unquoted Companies, a book compiled by the ICC Information Group, contains financial information on the top 20,000 unquoted companies in Britain (those with a turnover in excess of £3 million). The January 1990 edition cost £195. Macmillan Publishers Ltd, 1 Melbourne Place, London WC2B 4LF.

McCarthy Information Services

The Press provides a major source of news and information on companies, but keeping track of what appears on any particular company is a time-consuming and somewhat hit-and-miss affair. Fortunately McCarthy's (McCarthy Information Ltd, The Manor House, Ash Walk, Warminster, Wiltshire BA12 8PY) provides an excellent *Quoted Company* service, the reading list for which includes:

Birmingham Post	*Lloyds List*
Daily Express	*Mail on Sunday*
Daily Mail	*Marketing Week*
The Daily Telegraph	*The Observer*
The Economist	*Private Eye*
Euromoney	*The Scotsman*
Financial Times	*Evening Standard*
Financial Weekly	*Sunday Express*
Glasgow Herald	*Sunday Telegraph*
The Guardian	*Sunday Times*
Investors Chronicle	*The Times*
Irish Independent	*Yorkshire Post*
The Irish Times	

All relevant news, comment and articles on a company are cut out and reproduced on information sheets and a new sheet is circulated to subscribers, on a daily basis. In addition, McCarthy's provides a range of other services, including services on Australian and European companies, on USM and UK unquoted companies, and on industries, banking and property; the company services are also available on line. McCarthy's also runs a service called *Mirac,* which provides the reports and accounts of all listed and USM companies and of all nationalised industries on microfiche.

Datastream

Datastream is a brilliantly conceived computer-based system which provides detailed information both on individual companies and on companies within a specified sector of the market. Analysis of individual company accounts can be obtained on a five-year basis, covering profit and loss account, balance sheet and financing table, together with key accounting ratios, while the same information for a single year can be displayed on up to five companies at a time.

The system is accessed from remote visual display units (VDUs) situated in subscribers' offices and, once the initial programme has been selected, a series of questions is displayed on the VDU to enable the user to specify exactly what he requires. The information is then displayed on the VDU and can be printed out on a Datastream printer if hard copy is required.

Datastream also provides a chart plotting facility, macro-economic data, price monitoring and performance measurement, a portfolio performance program and a news channel.

The Datastream system, pioneered by stockbrokers Hoare & Co. Govett, is now run by Datastream International Ltd, 58–64 City Road, London EC1Y 2AL, part of the Dun & Bradstreet Corporation.

Datastream serves over 1,000 financial and investment institutions in the UK, Europe, the United States and the Far East, including Japan and Australia. The annual charge for the full service is £25,000, £11,000 for company accounts data only or alternatively, for a small monthly subscription, access to the Datastream system can be obtained on a metered dial-up basis.

Other on-line services

Finsbury Data Services, part of Reuters, 85 Fleet Street, London EC3N 1DY, provides four electronic business information systems over the public telephone network: a press abstracts service called *Textline*, a news headlines service called *Newsline*, a company financial data service called *Dataline*, which includes a forecasting model facility, and a company annual accounts service, *Accountline*. All four services are charged on a 'connect hour' basis at £1.75 per minute.

The Analysis Corporation, 42–47 The Minories, London EC3N 1DY, provide similar services on all UK listed and USM companies.

Key Notes

Each Key Note provides a concise introduction to a sector of British industry. The series covers more than 220 sectors, and each note includes:

(a) a summary and interpretation of the latest production and trade statistics from government, industry and market sources;

(b) an appraisal of the market background, highlighting recent developments and future prospects;

(c) financial data on the sector and ratio analysis of the major companies in the sector; *and*

(d) sources of information: an index of recent press articles and a list of trade associations, trade publications and statistical studies.

Key Notes cost £155 each, or £9,300 p.a., to subscribe to the entire service; they are available from Key Note Publications Ltd, 72 Oldfield Road, Hampton, Middlesex TW12 2HQ.

The Economist Intelligence Unit (EIU)

The EIU produces a wide range of business as well as economic publications, including special reports (e.g. *The World Car Industry to the year 2000*, published in 1988 at £175), and periodical reviews (e.g. *Paper and Packaging Bulletin* quarterly, which cost £300 or so per annum). The EIU's London headquarters are at 40 Duke Street, London W1A 1DW.

Government statistical publications

The best overall presentation of the huge range of statistics prepared by government departments is given in the *Monthly Digest of Statistics*, published by the Central Statistical Office (CSO).

Other statistical publications include:

Financial Statistics (monthly) – gives the key financial and monetary statistics of the United Kingdom.

Economic Trends (monthly) – commentary and a selection of tables and charts providing a broad background to trends in the UK economy.

Annual Abstract of Statistics – contains many more series than the monthly digest and provides a longer run of years.

United Kingdom National Accounts – known as the 'Blue Book', which is published annually and gives detailed estimates of the national accounts including consumers' expenditure over the previous ten years.

United Kingdom Balance of Payments – known as the 'Pink Book'.

Business Monitors – monthly, quarterly and annual publications produced by the CSO, giving statistical information from various government departments on a wide range of subjects, e.g., Motor vehicle production, published quarterly, and the monthly overseas trade figures.

A useful booklet *Government Statistics – a brief guide to sources* is available free from the Public Inquiry Unit, Central Statistical Office, Great George Street, London SW1P 3AQ.

Other government publications – NEDO

Government departments produce a wide range of publications on individual industries, in particular National Economic Development Committee reports from the National Economic Development Office, NEDO. All NEDO publications are listed in the *Nedo Catalogue*, obtainable free from NEDO Books, Millbank Tower, Millbank, London SW1P 4QX.

Specialist and trade publications

Trade magazines published by trade associations may contain useful statistical information compiled from the association's own members, as well as general news about the industry, while independent specialist magazines provide useful background information in their particular sphere. Some independent periodicals are published on a private subscription-only basis, for example the market intelligence reports on consumer goods, retailing, leisure and personal finance in the United Kingdom, published by Mintel International, 18–19 Long Lane, London EC1A 2HE.

Finally, on a broader note, an independent view and forecasts on the UK and world economy are contained in the *National Institute Economic Review*, published quarterly by the National Institute of Economic and Social Research, NIESR. The NIESR, 2 Dean Trench Street, Smith Square, London SW1P 3HE, is an independent non-profit-making body, which conducts research by its own staff and in co-operation with the universities and other academic bodies.

Chapter 23

INFLATION ACCOUNTING

INTRODUCTION

Some people think that company accounts should make allowance for the effects of inflation, while others think it's too difficult: 'don't let's bother'. The latter tend to predominate unless the rate of inflation is high.

In the 1970s and early 1980s, when inflation in the UK was running in double figures, efforts were made to introduce inflation accounting, but the accountancy profession was split between two methods: Current Purchasing Power (CPP), which simply adjusts figures for the rise in the Retail Price Index (RPI), and Current Cost Accounting (CCA), which allows for changes in relative prices.

Because both these methods have been tried and abandoned, there is a temptation to treat the subject as irrelevant. This attitude is like the ostrich burying its head in the sand: even a single-figure rate of inflation has an insidious effect on reported profits. For example, if a company reports steady earnings per share in a period when inflation is running at $7\frac{1}{2}\%$ per annum, and the reported e.p.s. are adjusted for inflation, the result is:

Year	0	5	10
Reported	10p	10p	10p
E.p.s. in constant pounds	10p	6.96p	4.85p

This adjustment only allows for the effect of inflation on reported e.p.s. If inflation was allowed for in the accounts themselves, i.e. in calculating the e.p.s., then the earnings per share by Year 10 would probably be nearer two or three Year 0 pence for the majority of companies.

If the Chancellor fails to curb the current rising trend in the rate of inflation, or a future government resorts to Harold Wilson's old trick of promising the earth, and pays for it by printing money, then the whole subject will be back at the top of the agenda.

We will therefore examine the shortcomings of historical cost accounts in a bit more detail, give a brief history and description of CPP and CCA, and end the chapter with some suggestions on where we should go from here.

THE SHORTCOMINGS OF HISTORICAL COST ACCOUNTING

In attempting to present a true and fair view of a company's affairs, accounting systems have two principal enemies: inflation and subjective judgement.

Historical cost (HC) accounting

In a time of stable prices, the historical cost system works well. What an asset cost is seldom in dispute, and although the directors have to assess the expected useful lives of fixed assets, and their likely disposal values, there is limited scope for subjective judgement. Furthermore, the quality of historical cost accounts has steadily improved over the years, largely thanks to the efforts of the Accounting Standards Committee. SSAPs have considerably reduced the number of options available to company directors and, though problems do still remain, not many people other than accounting theorists would seriously suggest that historical cost be abandoned as the basis of accounting in a period of zero inflation.

HC accounting with inflation

In a period of substantial price rises (i.e. inflation), historical cost accounting has five main weaknesses:

1. *Depreciation inadequate for the replacement of fixed assets.* Historical cost accounting seeks to write off the cost of fixed assets over their effective lives. It does not set out to provide a fund from which the fixed assets can be replaced at the end of their lives. Nevertheless, in a period of stable prices, sufficient cash could be set aside over the life of an asset to replace it at its original cost. In times of inflation, insufficient is provided in this way to enable the business to replace its assets. For example, where an asset is written off on a straight line basis over ten years, the total provisions for depreciation as a percentage of cost are:

Inflation rate	Depreciation as % of cost (*Constant pounds*)
5%	79.1%
10%	64.4%
15%	53.8%

2. *Cost of sales understated.* In historical cost accounts, stock consumed and sold is charged against sales at its original cost, rather than at the cost of replacing it. But, in order to retain the same stock level, the company has to finance the difference (and has to do so entirely out of profits after tax since the abolition of stock relief). This is perhaps most easily understood if we add a few figures. Assume that the company has in stock items which cost £4,000. It sells the items for £6,000, incurring overheads of £1,600, and replaces them at a cost of £4,300. Corporation tax is payable at, say, 35%.

HC accounts will say that the company has made a profit of £400 but, to maintain its original stock level, it has to use £300 of the 'profit' of £400 simply in order to stand still and, with no stock relief, the tax man would want a further £140, leaving a 'net profit' of minus £40.

3. *Need for increase in other working capital not recognised.* In most companies, debtors are greater than creditors, so, on an unchanged volume of business, 'debtors minus creditors' increases with inflation, requiring extra money to be provided for working capital. Historical cost accounts fail to recognise that this extra working capital is necessary to maintain the operating capacity of a business and that it has to be provided for the business to remain a going concern.

4. *Borrowing benefits not shown.* Borrowings are shown in monetary terms, and if nothing is repaid, and nothing further is borrowed, borrowings appear stable. This is a distortion of the picture, because a gain has been made at the expense of the lender (since in real terms the value of the loan has declined): some people feel that this gain ought to be reflected in the accounts.

5. *Year-on-year figures not comparable.* In addition to being overstated due to:
    (a) inadequate provision for depreciation,
    (b) understated cost of sales, and
    (c) no provision for increase in other working capital,

profits are stated in terms of money which has itself declined in value. Similarly, sales and dividends are not comparable with those of other years, because they are expressed in pounds of different purchasing power. For example RTZ, illustrated below, reported e.p.s. rising from 25.55p in 1980 to 35.79p in 1987; but if the reported e.p.s. are adjusted for the rise in the Retail Price Index in that period to show all the e.p.s. figures in December 1987 pence, then in real terms e.p.s. have fallen by about 5% between 1980 and 1987.

The reporting of profits in inflated pounds gives a far too rosy impression of growth in profitability. This tends to lull both managers and shareholders into thinking that their company is doing very much better than it really is, it encourages unions and employees to expect wage increases that are

RTZ *e.p.s. as reported, and after adjustment by the Retail Price Index*

Year ended 31 December	1980	1981	1982	1983	1984	1985	1986	1987
Reported e.p.s. (pence)	25.55	18.42	20.31	27.98	31.87	33.22	31.56	35.79
RPI for December	69.9	78.3	82.5	86.9	90.9	96.0	99.6	103.3
E.p.s. in December 1987 pence	37.76	24.30	25.43	33.26	36.22	35.75	32.73	35.79

unmatched by real (as opposed to reported) profit growth, and it also can and does encourage government measures that are very harmful to the long-term prosperity of a company, e.g. the imposition of price controls or excess profits tax made on a completely false impression of profitability.

Before going on to discuss how inflation accounting has developed over the last few years, it is worth looking in more detail at the impact that even quite modest rates of inflation can have on the value of money if they persist for several years.

The staggering impact of inflation

As Example 23.1 shows, the effect of inflation on the value of money over a number of years is staggering.

To give a more general example of the effects of inflation, anyone who bought £100 of Government irredeemable 3½% War Loan when it was issued at par in the 1940s now sees it standing at about

Example 23.1   Effect of inflation on the value of £1

Annual rate of inflation	After 5 years	After 10 years	After 20 Years
2½%	88.3p	78.1p	61.0p
5%	78.3p	61.3p	37.6p
7½%	69.6p	48.5p	23.5p
10%	62.0p	38.5p	14.8p
15%	49.7p	24.7p	6.1p
20%	40.1p	16.1p	2.6p

£30 per cent, because of current high interest rates, which reflect inflationary expectations.

If you adjust the original £100 by the subsequent movement in the RPI, to express its value in today's pounds, you get about £1,600. In real terms the investor has lost about 98% of his capital: horrifying! See Appendix 3 for table showing the effect of inflation in the United Kingdom on the Retail Price Index.

THE DEVELOPMENT OF INFLATION ACCOUNTING SYSTEMS

Current purchasing power accounting (CPP)

An Exposure Draft, ED 8 – *Accounting for changes in the purchasing power of money* – was issued in 1973 recommending that companies adopt what came to be known as current purchasing power accounting (CPP). The main features of ED 8 were that, in addition to HC accounts, listed companies would show a *supplementary statement* in terms of the value of the pound at the end of the period being reported on, and that the RPI should be used in making the adjustments.

CPP accounting was concerned solely with removing the distorting effects of changes in the general purchasing power of money on accounts prepared in accordance with established practice (i.e. on a historical cost basis). It did not deal with changes in the *relative* values of non-monetary items (which can and do occur in the absence of inflation).

CPP accounts were criticised on a number of grounds. Among these were the following:

1. Shareholders were faced with a choice between two sets of figures which frequently gave very different results. Both could not be correct.

2. CPP accounting enhanced the profits of companies which were heavily borrowed, particularly those showing low profits on a historical cost basis, and could even turn a loss into a profit. This was because assets on

which perhaps little or no profit was being made were shown by CPP to be increasing in value in line with inflation (i.e. maintaining their real value), while money borrowed to acquire them was treated as declining in real value. The more heavily borrowed the company, the more the profits became boosted by CPP, as for example in GRAND METRO-POLITAN's 1974 accounts, illustrated here.

GRAND METROPOLITAN *Extracts from 1974 accounts*

	£000
Ordinary shareholders' funds	429,436
less Goodwill	295,361
OSF net of goodwill	134,075
10% CULS 1991/96	121,114
Other loan capital	281,219
Bank overdrafts and short-term borrowings	130,396
Total debt	532,729
Earnings per share (historical)	7.3p
Earnings per share (CPP basis)	35.2p

3. The Retail Price Index is not a true index of general purchasing power: it may quite badly represent the effects of inflation upon some groups of individuals, and it is not *designed* to reflect the effects of inflation on companies.

In the event, in spite of being adopted by quite a large number of public companies, CPP accounting was overtaken by the appointment of the Sandilands Committee, which was set up in 1974 under the chairmanship of Mr (now Sir) Francis Sandilands.

Current cost accounting (CCA)

The Sandilands Report
The Sandilands Committee reported to the Chancellor of the Exchequer and the Secretary for Trade in June 1975: the Committee rejected the proposals contained in PSSAP 7 (a provisional SSAP on CPP, which had been issued as a follow-up to ED 8 pending the Sandilands findings), and recommended instead the development of a system to be known as current cost accounting (CCA), in which:

(a) no adjustment is made for inflation (i.e. for changes in the 'purchasing power' of money);
(b) assets and liabilities are shown in the balance sheet at their 'value to the business', which can be very much a matter of subjective judgement;
(c) 'operating profit' is struck after charging the value to the business of assets consumed during the period, thus excluding holding gains from profit and showing them separately.

The Sandilands report also recommended that current cost accounting should become the basic published accounts of companies as soon as practicable.

In response to the Sandilands recommendations there followed much debate and a special committee, which produced an Exposure Draft (ED 18) in November 1976. ED 18 met with considerable opposition – the members of the Institute of Chartered Accountants in England and Wales actually voted at an extraordinary general meeting that current cost accounting should not be made compulsory – so a new committee was appointed, leading to the eventual publication of a Standard on CCA (SSAP 16) in March 1980.

SSAP 16
SSAP 16 required larger companies to produce a separate current cost P & L account and balance sheet, to recognise two basic concepts:

1. that the profitability of a company should be assessed after deducting the amount of money it needs in order to stand still in real terms, *and*
2. that the assets of a company should be shown at their value to the business.

The SSAP 16 system of CCA calculates the profit of a business by making adjustments to the HC profit and loss account.

Three *operating adjustments* were made to the HC trading profit to allow for the impact of price changes:

1. the *depreciation adjustment*,
2. the *cost of sales adjustment*,
3. the *monetary working capital adjustment*;

and a fourth adjustment, the *gearing adjustment*, was then made to allow for the proportion of assets financed by borrowings.

Price indices are used in calculating the operating adjustments, to reflect relative price changes and, for a time, the Government Statistical Service produced a special book each year, *Price Index Numbers for Current Cost Accounting*, containing a myriad of industry-specific and asset-specific indices, updating it by a monthly supplement.

But, in spite of the enormous effort put into developing CCA, the system had some major shortcomings:

1. It was very complicated: even the Accounting Standards Committee's step-by-step guide *CCA the Easy Way* ran to 145 pages of A4.
2. There was so much scope for discretion that similar companies produced wildly different figures for individual adjustments.
3. The figures produced each year were not comparable with figures for the previous year.
4. The system was irrelevant for tax purposes.

Attempts were made to modify the system (ED 35), but CCA failed to gain sufficient acceptance to become the basic published accounts of companies, as Sandilands had recommended.

When inflation eased, SSAP 16 was gradually abandoned, and some companies gave their reasons for doing so:

CADBURY SCHWEPPES – '. . . the CCA approach produced fluctuations in the profit figures, which were a consequence of the method of accounting rather than of changes in the fortunes of the Company.'

EUROTHERM – 'The Directors consider it inappropriate to prepare current cost accounts given . . . the currently confused state of the accounting profession regarding a suitable method for the preparation of such accounts.'

WATTS BLAKE BEARNE – 'Following the expiration of the three years' trial period for SSAP 16 and the subsequent publication and apparent rejection of ED 35 as a modified version of this Standard, it appears that there is now even less consensus over how the effects of inflation should be demonstrated in Financial Statements.

Your Directors have therefore decided to discontinue

the annual publication of the Group's inflation-adjusted figures until a consensus is reached whereby their presentation will serve some practical and meaningful purpose.'

However a few companies do still include supplementary CCA information in their accounts, although BRITISH GAS is the only one we know of that produces CCA accounts with supplementary HC information. For example, BAT shows how much of its HC profit needs to be retained to allow for inflation:

BAT *Note to the HC accounts*

Accounting for inflation

	1988	1987
	£ millions	
Cost of sales adjustment	161	106
Depreciation adjustment	89	81
Monetary working capital adjustment	(80)	(49)
	170	138
Gearing adjustment: net other monetary items	78	82
Commercial activities	248	220
Associated companies	6	4
	254	224
Attributable to minority shareholders	(53)	(44)
Required inflation retention	201	180

The figures shown above have been calculated as follows:

(*a*) Cost of sales adjustment represents the difference between the cost of sales charged in the profit and loss account and their replacement cost at the time of sale.
(*b*) Depreciation adjustment is the excess of the depreciation charge based on the current cost of fixed assets over the depreciation charge on their costs.
(*c*) Monetary working capital adjustment represents that part of the inflation adjustments which is not borne by the business as a result of the financing benefit derived from the excess of trade creditors over trade debtors.
(*d*) Gearing adjustment is calculated by reference to price indices on monetary items not included in the monetary working capital adjustment.

Replacement cost accounting

Some companies which, by the nature of their business, carry large stocks of commodities, e.g. oil companies, use replacement costs to iron out the effect of widely fluctuating commodity prices, and show stock holding gains or losses separately. For example BRITISH PETROLEUM:

BRITISH PETROLEUM *Accounting for replacement cost*

Accounting policies

Replacement cost

The results of individual businesses and geographical areas are presented on a replacement cost basis. Replacement cost operating results exclude stock holding gains or losses and reflect the average cost of supplies incurred during the year. Stock holding gains or losses represent the difference between the replacement cost of sales and the historical cost of sales calculated using the first-in first-out method.

Profit and loss account

		£ million
	1988	1987
Turnover	25,922	28,328
Replacement cost of sales	19,330	21,515
Production taxes	566	901
Gross profit	6,026	5,912
Distribution and administration expenses	3,333	3,416
Exploration expenditure written off	495	469
	2,198	2,027
Other income	693	784
Replacement cost operating profit	2,891	2,811
Stock holding gain (loss)	(232)	133
Historical cost operating profit	2,659	2,944

. . .

A similar method is used by COOKSON for valuing the 'base stock' in its metal and mineral processing companies, so that the P & L account is charged with the current cost of materials consumed.

WHERE DO WE GO FROM HERE?

The nub of the matter is whether we are trying to achieve:

(*a*) a system that allows for the general effect of inflation, *or*

(*b*) what the Sandilands Committee was asked to produce, a system to 'allow for changes (including relative changes) in costs and prices'.

We believe that PSSAP 7, *Accounting for changes in the purchasing power of money*, was along the right lines, and that the root cause of the present disarray is the attempt to allow for relative changes, rather than for inflation.

Measuring inflation

The Sandilands Committee took the view that inflation was 'not a phenomenon capable of independent and objective measurement' and, in line with government thinking at the time, rejected the concept of using the Retail Price Index (RPI) to index accounts.

As the RPI has since been used satisfactorily by government to index personal tax allowances, for Index-linked gilt-edged securities and SAYE schemes and, most recently, for the indexation of acquisition cost in CGT calculations, the Sandilands view, from which we believe all the problems of CCA stemmed, now seems absurd (as it did to some at the time). The RPI *is* the generally accepted measure of inflation in the United Kingdom.

What inflation accounts should achieve

The first point is that if the cost of a fixed asset is written off in pounds of falling value, the provision for depreciation is inadequate. In order that the total amount written off over the useful life of a fixed asset should be its cost (less residual value) expressed in *pounds at the date of purchase*, each annual depreciation charge needs to be adjusted by the movement in the RPI since the asset was acquired. Fixed assets should therefore appear in the balance sheet at cost less accumulated depreciation, adjusted for inflation into balance sheet date pounds.

The second point is that, in calculating the cost of goods sold, the opening stock should be adjusted for the RPI movement during the year so as to eliminate stock profits due to general inflation.

Thirdly, the amount of additional working capital required by a company due to the effects of inflation should be deducted in calculating distributable profits.

Fourthly, the benefit of inflation in reducing the real value of borrowings and the adverse effect of inflation on holdings of cash should be taken into account.

Finally, figures for previous years should be adjusted to balance sheet date pounds, so that like can be compared with like, a point well recognised by the Central Statistical Office (imagine how misleading their financial statistics would be if they weren't expressed in constant pounds!).

Because inflation accounting would allow for the general effect of inflation but not for any relative change in price levels, inflation accounts would, in a long period of zero inflation, produce the same figures as historical cost accounts.

The future

Until the purpose of inflation accounting is agreed and a system of inflation accounting is introduced accordingly, we believe that the accountancy profession will continue in disarray and that HC accounts will continue to lull many managers and shareholders into thinking that their companies are doing considerably better than they really are, and will continue to encourage unions and employees to seek wage increases that are not justified by real (as opposed to reported) profits.

We also believe that unless the system so developed is acceptable to the Inland Revenue (for tax purposes) and can therefore become the *only* accounts a company produces, the production of *two* sets of accounts will always pose the problem of 'Which one is to be believed?'.

Chapter 24

TRENDS AND RATIOS

This chapter deals with the calculation of trends and ratios, describing each ratio in turn with an indication of the size of ratio one would expect, while the following chapter, Chapter 25, contains a suggested pro-forma for analysis, with a line-by-line explanation of each item.

How to tackle the analysis

Now that we have been right through the balance sheet and profit and loss account explaining each component in detail, we come to the heart of the matter: how to set about analysing a report and accounts. We suggest this is best tackled in stages:

1. Take a quick look at the balance sheet and profit and loss account to get a general idea of the size of the company, its capital structure and its profitability. Also look at the historical summary (if provided) to see if the company is growing, cyclical, stagnant or declining, and look at the breakdown of turnover by activity and geographically if one is given. It is also worth while reading any 'report to employees' that may be enclosed with the accounts, to help get a general picture of the company before getting down to any detail.

2. Read carefully through the chairman's statement and the directors' report, highlighting any interesting points, and then go through the balance sheet and profit and loss account item by item, reading each accompanying 'Note' as you go, highlighting anything unusual. In particular, check the 'statement of accounting policies' for any changes or anything abnormal and the auditors' report for any qualification or reservation.

3. The trends and ratios should now be cal-

culated. In doing so the analyst should remain on the *qui vive* for interesting points and not allow himself to get mesmerised by number-crunching, because the figures produced at this stage are not an end in themselves. They are merely a means of helping the analyst assimilate what is happening in the company, providing him with pointers to the reasons behind good or poor performance, and they will often give warning of increasing risk or even of impending disaster.

4. The final stage is the interpretation of the trends and ratios, and the assessment of likely current profits and future prospects. Here the analyst should compare performance with that of similar companies (allowing for any differences in accounting policies) and/or with the industry's averages (using ratios), and should consult other sources of information on the company and on the industry or industries in which the company operates.

The use of percentages and ratios

Any assessment of a company is likely to include a look at:

(a) the company's performance in previous years, *and*

(b) a comparison with other companies.

The use of percentages and of various ratios helps in the assessment of trends and in comparisons with other companies, and in particular may highlight aspects of a company that merit closer scrutiny.

Methods of relating items of information

There are four basic ways in which one item of financial information can be related to another:

1. A line-by-line comparison can be made of the current year's accounts with those of the previous year. This is sometimes called *horizontal analysis*.
2. The horizontal analysis can be extended over several years, usually by giving the figure for an item in the first year of the series a value of 100 and relating subsequent years' figures to base 100. This is sometimes termed *trend analysis*.
3. 'Common size' balance sheets or income statements can be prepared, each balance sheet item being expressed as a percentage of the balance sheet total and each profit and loss account item as a percentage of sales or earnings. This is sometimes called *vertical analysis*.
4. *Ratios* can be produced by comparing one item in a balance sheet or profit and loss account with another for the same period, or with the current price of the company's shares.

TRENDS

Horizontal analysis – comparison with the previous year

This is possibly the simplest method of comparing one year's figures with another and involves working out the percentage change from the previous year of each main component of the accounts, as in Example 24.1 (CADBURY SCHWEPPES' 1988 profit and loss account).

Percentage changes in themselves may reveal a certain amount about a company's performance, but they are of most value in prompting further enquiry. The horizontal analysis in Example 24.1 might, for instance, prompt the following questions (letters in brackets refer to lines marked in the example):

[A] 17.3% is a good increase in *turnover*: was it uniform throughout the group? (The note on Sales showed that half the increase came from Australasia, up 46.2%, while North America was marginally down.)

[B] Why did *administration expenses* go up faster than turnover? (The note on Provisions showed £33.1 million charged to the P & L account in 1988 for rationalisation with expenditure of £24.4 million: how much was charged to Administration?)

[C] Did *net interest* more than double because of higher borrowings or higher interest rates? (The notes showed borrowings slightly down, but interest on Bank and other loans up from

---

Example 24.1   Horizontal analysis of profit and loss account: CADBURY SCHWEPPES

	1987 £m	1988 £m	% change	
Turnover	2,031.0	2,381.6	+17.3	[A]
Cost of sales	(1,177.2)	(1,365.0)	+16.0	
Gross profit	853.8	1,016.6	+19.1	
Distribution costs	(514.4)	(580.6)	+12.9	
Administration expenses	(167.2)	(207.1)	+23.9	[B]
Other operating income (charges)	8.4	(0.1)	−101.2	
Trading profit	180.6	228.8	+26.7	
Associates	3.9	4.4	+12.8	
Net interest	(8.4)	(17.5)	+108.3	[C]
Profit before taxation	176.1	215.7	+22.5	
Taxation	(53.4)	(52.0)	−2.6	
Profits after taxation	122.7	163.7	+33.4	
Minorities	(13.4)	(23.2)	+73.1	[D]
	109.3	140.5	+28.5	
Extraordinary items	1.4	28.4	+1,928.6	[E]
Profit attributable to shareholders	110.7	168.9	+52.6	
Dividends	(47.3)	(55.6)	+17.5	
Retained profit	63.4	113.3	+78.7	

Interpreting Company Reports and Accounts

£20.6 million to £27.9 million, i.e., higher interest rates.)

[D] Why did *minorities* increase by over 70%? Minority interests in the balance sheet were only up 20%. Which partially owned subsidiaries did particularly well during the year?

[E] What were the *extraordinary* items, and did they include reorganisation costs or the closure of loss-makers (which will help to improve profits in the future)?

These are the sort of questions that should be asked, and answered, by an alert analyst.

Horizontal analysis – half-yearly comparison

The fact that a company's annual figures for sales and profits show an increase on the previous year doesn't always mean that the company's performance is on a rising trend: it may have peaked out *during* the year.

This can be checked quite quickly by looking at the separately published interim results. If the increase over the previous year's first half is larger than the increase for the year as a whole, then there must have been a slowdown in the second half (Example 24.2), and vice versa.

Notice that in Example 24.2 we have compared each half-year in 1989 with the *corresponding* period in the previous year. This is because most businesses are to some extent seasonal, i.e. sales and profits are not evenly distributed between the first and second half. (For example, building materials suffer in the winter, and non-food retailers benefit

Example 24.2   Horizontal analysis and comparison of interim figures: 'IMAGINARY PLC'

	1988 £000	1989 £000	Change
Year's sales	3,425	3,764	+9.9%
Year's pre-tax profits	595	651	+9.4%

but the *interim* figures showed:

1st-half sales	1,470	1,880	+21.2%
1st-half pre-tax profits	213	316	+48.3%

Few companies show their second-half figures, so they have to be obtained by subtracting the interim figures from the full year's figures. In this case:

2nd-half sales	1,955	1,884	−3.6%
2nd-half pre-tax profits	382	335	−12.3%

heavily from Christmas.) Comparison of the second half of a year with the first half can therefore be misleading: in our example the improvement in the first half was clearly not maintained in the second half, although the results for the two half-years of 1989 were very similar.

Trend analysis – comparison over several years

Where comparison of a single company's figures is made over more than two years, the normal method is to take the earliest year's figures as a base of 100 and scale subsequent years accordingly, i.e. divide each year's figure by that for the first year, and multiply the result by 100 (Example 24.3).

Example 24.3   Trend analysis: CADBURY SCHWEPPES

	1984	1985	1986	1987	1988
Sales (£m)	2,016.2	1,873.8	1,839.9	2,031.0	2,381.6
Index (1984 base=100)	100.0	92.9	91.3	100.7	118.1
Trading profit (£m)	154.4	113.0	140.1	180.6	228.8
Index (1984 base=100)	100.0	73.2	90.9	117.0	148.2

Trading profit fell much more sharply than sales in 1985 (due to a disastrous year in North America, where sales were down 26% and trading profit plunged from £36.9 million into a loss of £5.6 million). Trading profit recovered in 1986 and then drew ahead of sales in 1987 and 1988, i.e., margins improved. How did earnings per share compare?

	1984	1985	1986	1987	1988
Earnings per share (pence)	15.6	9.3	14.3	19.0	23.4
Index (1984 base=100)	100.0	59.6	91.7	121.8	150.0

Earnings per share took a real hammering in 1985, aggravated by a 6% higher tax rate and 11% more shares in issue. They then recovered about in line with the trading profit.

The use of published historical summaries

Although the five- or ten-year summaries usually included in companies' reports and accounts need to be approached with caution, as we discussed in Chapter 20, most companies go to a good deal of trouble to present as fair a picture *as is possible on a historical cost basis*, and so the published summary can be very useful for a quick analysis of trends, even if slower and more detailed research is subsequently needed.

However, the main drawback to any analysis of trends over several years in times of high inflation is that the figures can be very misleading, with static or even declining performances in *real* terms appearing to have an upward trend in the reported figures.

A rough idea of the effects of inflation over the years can be gained by comparing the trend of turnover and trading profit with the trend in the Retail Price Index (RPI – see Appendix 3). Continuing with CADBURY SCHWEPPES in Example 24.4, we have adjusted the average RPI for 1984 to 100, with subsequent years scaled pro rata.

This admittedly is a very crude adjustment, but it certainly brings the figures much closer to the real state of affairs than no adjustments at all: in real terms, sales in 1988 were still less than in 1984.

We will be discussing ratios later in this chapter, but it is perhaps worth pointing out here that where both the items in a ratio are expressed in terms of the currency at the time of reporting, dividing one by the other removes the direct effect of inflation. For example, the ratio of CADBURY SCHWEPPES' trading profit to turnover in Example 24.5 gives a fair picture of how profit margins overall had recovered since 1985. However, Cadbury Schweppes gives a geographical analysis of sales and trading profits in its 'Group Financial Record', and the margins are well worth calculating for each area; they show, in particular, North America's painfully slow recovery from the débâcle of 1985, and Australasia and Other's consistently good margins.

Trends in rates of growth

One last point before we leave horizontal analysis: the question of growth rates. If the rate of growth is fast, the figures reported year by year can give the impression that the company's growth is accelerating when it is, in fact, slowing down. Consider, for example, the figures of 'MIRACLE GROWTH PLC' in Example 24.6.

Example 24.4 Trend analysis adjusted for inflation by the RPI: CADBURY SCHWEPPES

	1984	1985	1986	1987	1988
Sales (1984 = 100)	100	92.9	91.3	100.7	118.1
Trading profit (1984 = 100)	100	73.2	90.9	117.0	148.2
December RPI adjusted	100	105.6	109.6	113.6	121.3
Sales/Adjusted RPI	100	88.0	83.3	88.6	97.4
Trading profit/Adjusted RPI	100	69.3	82.9	103.0	122.2

Example 24.5 Trading profit/sales ratio: CADBURY SCHWEPPES

	1984	1985	1986	1987	1988
Sales (£m.)	2,016.2	1,873.8	1,839.9	2,013.0	2,381.6
Trading profit (£m.)	154.4	113.0	140.4	180.6	228.8
Trading profit/Sales overall	7.7%	6.0%	7.6%	9.0%	9.6%
United Kingdom	6.8%	6.9%	9.9%	8.8%	10.0%
Europe	7.1%	8.1%	8.0%	11.3%	10.4%
North America	7.6%	−1.6%	1.4%	5.1%	5.8%
Australasia and Other	10.3%	10.4%	9.5%	10.9%	10.8%

Example 24.6 Horizontal analysis of fast growth: 'MIRACLE GROWTH PLC'

	1986	1987	1988	1989	1990
Pre-tax profits (£000)	100	130	166	206	248
Year's increase (£000)		30	36	40	42
Percentage increase over previous year		30.0%	27.7%	24.1%	20.4%

Example 24.7   Vertical analysis of a balance sheet: CADBURY SCHWEPPES

	1987 £m	1988 £m	Common size statements 1987 %	1988 %
Assets employed				
Fixed assets	603.5	622.9	70.3	70.7
Stock	257.4	253.4	30.0	28.7
Debtors	398.2	434.5	46.4	49.3
Other creditors	(541.0)	(671.0)	(63.0)	(76.1)
Cash, loans, deposits	139.9	242.0	16.3	27.4
	858.0	881.8	100.0	100.0
Financed by				
Share capital and reserves	476.7	486.0	55.5	55.1
Long-term loans	112.9	124.7	13.2	14.2
Short-term borrowings	163.1	114.1	19.0	12.9
Provisions	28.9	65.8	3.4	7.5
Minority interests	76.4	91.2	8.9	10.3
	858.0	881.8	100.0	100.0

Example 24.8   Five-year review of capital employed: CADBURY SCHWEPPES

		1984 £m	%	1985 £m	%	1986 £m	%	1987 £m	%	1988 £m	%
Ordinary share capital	[A]	126.2		129.6		139.6		148.4		150.4	
Reserves	[B]	389.2		338.1		320.3		325.0		332.3	
Purchased goodwill	[C]	—		26.6		141.6		201.6		306.9	
Ordinary shareholders' funds	[D]	515.4	60.3	494.3	60.3	601.5	64.0	675.0	63.7	789.6	66.4
Preference capital		3.3	0.4	3.3	0.4	3.3	0.4	3.3	0.3	3.3	0.3
Minorities	[E]	48.8	5.7	41.4	5.1	53.0	5.6	76.4	7.2	91.2	7.7
Provisions	[F]	24.5	2.8	14.8	1.8	16.5	1.8	28.9	2.7	65.8	5.5
Borrowings over 1 year	[G]	198.5	23.2	195.4	23.8	185.6	19.7	112.9	10.7	124.7	10.5
Borrowings under 1 year	[H]	64.5	7.6	70.2	8.6	79.9	8.5	163.1	15.4	114.1	9.6
Funds employed	[I]	855.0	100	819.4	100	939.8	100	1,059.6	100	1,188.7	100
Extraordinary items	[J]	−7.4		−5.9		25.9		1.4		28.4	
Retained profits	[K]	36.2		11.2		64.4		63.4		113.3	
RPI for December		90.9		96.0		99.6		103.3		110.3	
Adjusted capital employed	[L]	1,037.5		941.5		1,040.8		1,131.4		1,188.7	

It is true that the increase in profits each year has been greater than the increase in the previous year in simple or absolute terms, but the compound or percentage growth rate has actually been slowing down each year.

Vertical analysis

So far we have discussed only working across the page, comparing each item with the previous year to get the percentage change, or looking at several years to see the trend of an item. If we work vertically, calling the total 100, we can construct 'common size' statements giving a percentage breakdown of the account items, as in Example 24.7.

The advantages of this method are, firstly, that the items are reduced to a common scale for inter-company comparisons and, secondly, that changes in the financial structure of a company stand out more clearly. For example the biggest changes in CADBURY SCHWEPPES between 1987 and 1988 were a 13.1% increase in Other creditors and an 11.1% increase in Cash, loans, deposits. Had these year-on-year changes been expressed in absolute terms, Other creditors would have increased by 21% and Cash, etc. would have been up 68%, figures that give no idea of their relationship to the overall capital.

The use of vertical analysis over several years helps to show how the financial structure of a company is changing.

Taking Cadbury Schweppes' capital structure over five years (Example 24.8), one can see that there was no major jump in the Ordinary share capital [A], i.e. no rights issues; the £10 million increase in 1986 included the issue of 35 million 25p ordinary shares in the acquisition of CANADA DRY, and the £8.8 million increase in 1987 was due almost entirely to the conversion of about 90% of the 8% Convertible Bonds 2000, which reduced long-term borrowings [G] by about £45 million.

The movement in Reserves [B] looks decidedly odd at first sight; a fall of more than £50 million between 1984 and 1989, although Retained profits [K] in that period amount to over £250 million pounds. The reason, as we described earlier (see page 146), was the immediate write-off of purchased goodwill arising from acquisitions.

In 1990 Cadbury Schweppes announced that it was placing a value of £307 million on its balance sheet to represent the major brands it had acquired since 1985 (but did not intend to amortise this value!). We have therefore included a line for Purchased goodwill [C] that the company has written off immediately to reserves.

The inclusion of purchased goodwill gives a much truer picture of Ordinary shareholders' funds, OSF, [D] growing by £274 million, mostly due to retained profits. The fall in 1985, a poor year for profits, was due to adverse exchange rate adjustments of £48.9 million.

In 1988 OSF accounted for 6% more of Funds employed [I] than in 1984, and Borrowings [G + H] for 10% less, a very healthy trend since the set-back in 1985.

Looking for further points of interest:

Minorities [E] increased sharply in 1987 and 1988. Details of principal operating companies given in the accounts show the setting up of Coca-Cola & Schweppes Beverages Ltd in the UK (51% owned), and the acquisition of Beatrice Australia Ltd (66% owned) and of Bromor Foods (Pty) Ltd in South Africa (53% owned).

Provisions [F] more than doubled in 1988. This included an increase of £17.9 million for deferred taxation and provisions for rationalisation, £33.1 million, exceeding £24.4 million of rationalisation expenditure.

The large favourable Extraordinary items [J] in 1986 and 1988 were both profits on disposals less closure costs and tax.

One general point before leaving the five-year review: Funds employed appear to have increased by nearly 40%. However, a more modest picture emerges if a simple adjustment is made to allow for inflation by *dividing* the funds employed at the end of each year by the Retail Price Index for December each year (taken from Appendix 3) and *multiplying* them by the RPI for December 1988, to show each year's funds employed in December 1988 pounds. Although this is admittedly very crude, the adjusted figures [L] show that, in real terms, the company's capital employed has increased by only about 15%, although retained profits have more than made up for the effects of inflation.

THE USE OF RATIOS

Choice of ratios

With both a balance sheet and a profit and loss account each containing a minimum of 10 to 20 items, the scope for comparing one item with another is enormous, so it is important to be selective, both to limit the calculations required and, more importantly, to make the presentation of the selected ratios simple and readily understandable. No decision-maker wants a jungle of figures, so the ratios chosen should be the key ones, logically grouped.

Logical grouping

Ratios can conveniently be divided into three main groups:

1. *Operating ratios*, which are concerned with how the company is trading, and take no account of how the company is financed.
2. *Financial ratios*, which measure the financial structure of the company and show how it relates to the trading activities.
3. *Investment ratios*, which relate the number of ordinary shares and their market price to the profits, dividends and assets of the company.

In describing these ratios we give what we regard as the most useful and practical definition of each component. Although there is an increasing trend towards standardisation, individual analysts do not always agree on definitions, while companies do not all define ratio components in the same way.

Some companies include a table of key ratios in their report and accounts, e.g. MARLEY in its five-year review, shown here.

MARLEY *Extract from five-year review*

Ratios

	1988	1987	1986	1985	1984
Net borrowings as % of capital employed	18.4%	22.5%	25.8%	36.2%	35.2%
Return on capital employed	27.3%	22.6%	16.1%	15.1%	17.3%

These can be useful for looking at trends within the company concerned, but it is preferable to work out one's own ratios by a standard method, so that they form a fair basis for inter-company comparisons. Marley, for example, wrote off almost £35 million of goodwill arising on NOTTINGHAM BRICK and other acquisitions in 1987; doing so enhanced the return on capital employed in 1987 and 1988 by about three percentage points.

Typical ratio values

Useful general guidance on the ratio values one might expect to find in various sectors of UK industry is contained in a book called *Industrial Performance Analysis* published annually by ICC (Inter Company Comparisons), 72 Oldfield Road, Hampton, Middlesex TW12 2HQ. Example 24.9 shows extracts from the aggregated balance sheet and profit and loss account data it gives, together with key ratios calculated from the data. Analysts using this book should be careful to note the definitions of each ratio component, and in particular that 'total assets' include intangible assets and that 'capital employed' does not include overdraft.

The ICC Information Group also publishes *Business Ratio Reports* on each of more than 190 sectors, giving detailed information on companies in the sector, and *Sector Trends in the UK*, a book showing upper quartile, median and lower quartile figures for various ratios in each sector, and provides a variety of on-line services.

Another source of information on ratios is the book *Key Business Ratios*, published annually by Dun & Bradstreet Ltd., Holmers Farm Way, High Wycombe, Bucks HP12 3BR.

Ratios and inflation

As we mentioned earlier, when discussing published historical summaries, where *both* items in a ratio are *monetary* and are expressed in terms of pounds of approximately the same date, dividing one term by the other removes the direct effect of inflation.

For example, Wages/Turnover can fairly be compared from year to year, but Trading profit/Capital employed is distorted to some extent unless fixed assets are revalued or adjusted annually.

OPERATING RATIOS

Most well-run companies of any size make extensive use of ratios internally, to monitor and ensure the efficient running of each division or activity.

However, companies are obliged to publish only a limited range of profit and loss account information, and a geographical analysis of turnover and trading results of operations, which limits the scope for analysis, although the amount of information will increase if and when ED 45 *Segmental reporting* becomes an SSAP (see Chapter 12).

In addition to the published report and accounts of a group, resort can be made to Companies House for accounts filed by subsidiaries, although these can be misleading if goods and services have been transferred within the group at unrealistic prices or if major adjustments have been made on consolidation. In any case, the accounts of subsidiaries are often not filed at Companies House until some considerable time after the group accounts have been published.

Main operating ratios

1.

$$\frac{\textbf{Trading profit}}{\textbf{Sales (Turnover)}}$$

= **Profit margin**, expressed as a percentage.

where *Trading profit* = profit before interest charges and tax; investment income and the company's share of the profits of associates are not included

and *Sales (Turnover)* = sales (excluding transactions within the group).

Example 24.9 Extracts from Industrial Performance Analysis

SUPERMARKETS

Period of accounts	87/88	86/87	85/86
Number of weeks	52	52	52
	£000	£000	£000

PROFIT & LOSS DATA

Sales	**23,239,441**	**21,152,518**	**18,810,811**
Net profit			
before tax	**1,541,166**	**1,322,949**	**1,048,837**
Interest paid	106,981	74,549	67,941
Depreciation	333,433	294,270	238,578

BALANCE SHEET

Fixed assets	8,015,961	6,228,739	5,172,286
Intangible assets	707	734	2,760
Intermediate assets	261,674	224,094	165,042
Stocks	1,562,652	1,458,664	1,353,352
Trade debtors	73,644	61,554	64,149
Other current assets	1,219,543	681,166	826,443
Total current assets	2,855,839	2,201,384	2,243,944
Creditors	1,835,970	1,690,963	1,535,495
Short term loans	501,933	168,179	400,490
Other current liabl.	1,524,222	1,413,754	1,120,077
Total current liabl.	3,862,125	3,272,896	3,056,062
Net assets	**7,272,056**	**5,382,055**	**4,527,970**
Shareholders funds	6,066,640	4,532,048	4,084,692
Long term loans	1,005,371	672,654	266,751
Other long term liabl.	200,045	177,353	176,527
Capital employed	**7,272,056**	**5,382,055**	**4,527,970**

KEY RATIOS

Profitability ratios			
Return on capital	21.2	24.6	23.2
Return on assets	13.8	15.3	13.8
Return on shrhldrs funds	25.4	29.2	25.7
Pre-tax profit margin	6.6	6.3	5.6
Turnover ratios			
Asset utilisation	208.7	244.4	248.0
Sales/fixed assets	2.9	3.4	3.6
Stock turnover	14.9	14.5	13.9
Credit period	1	1	1
Liquidity ratios			
Liquidity	0.7	0.7	0.7
Quick ratio	0.3	0.2	0.3
Gearing ratios			
Borrowing ratio	24.8	18.6	16.3
Equity gearing	0.5	0.5	0.5
Income gearing	6.5	5.3	6.1

CONSTRUCTION EQPT. DISTRS.

Period of accounts	87/88	86/87	85/86
Number of weeks	52	52	52
	£000	£000	£000

PROFIT & LOSS DATA

Sales	**1,086,340**	**848,456**	**907,870**
Net profit			
before tax	**35,570**	**19,994**	**13,456**
Interest paid	41,115	37,352	41,230
Depreciation	14,522	13,631	13,577

BALANCE SHEET

Fixed assets	90,112	76,004	76,977
Intangible assets	0	0	0
Intermediate assets	13,761	16,534	14,537
Stocks	211,909	142,484	114,626
Trade debtors	148,289	107,575	114,886
Other current assets	267,990	249,510	222,486
Total current assets	628,188	499,569	451,998
Creditors	150,546	90,138	57,925
Short term loans	104,330	77,047	102,346
Other current liabl.	64,624	47,418	42,241
Total current liabl.	319,500	214,603	202,512
Net assets	**412,561**	**377,504**	**341,000**
Shareholders funds	95,718	75,661	60,658
Long term loans	301,636	284,047	259,445
Other long term liabl.	15,207	17,796	20,897
Capital employed	**412,561**	**377,504**	**341,000**

KEY RATIOS

Profitability ratios			
Return on capital	8.6	5.3	3.9
Return on assets	4.9	3.4	2.5
Return on shrhldrs funds	37.2	26.4	22.2
Pre-tax profit margin	3.3	2.4	1.5
Turnover ratios			
Asset utilisation	148.4	143.3	167.0
Sales/fixed assets	12.1	11.2	11.8
Stock turnover	5.1	6.0	7.9
Credit period	50	46	46
Liquidity ratios			
Liquidity	2.0	2.3	2.2
Quick ratio	1.3	1.7	1.7
Gearing ratios			
Borrowing ratio	424.1	477.3	596.4
Equity gearing	0.1	0.1	0.1
Income gearing	53.6	65.1	75.4

This ratio gives what analysts term the profit margin on sales; a normal figure for a manufacturing industry would be between 8% and 10%, while high volume/low margin activities like food retailing can run very satisfactorily at around 3%. This profit margin is not the same thing as the gross profit margin (the difference between selling price and the cost of sales, expressed as a percentage of selling price), which can be obtained only if the company reports cost of sales.

Unusually low margins can be set deliberately by management to increase market share or can be caused by expansion costs, e.g. new product launching, but in general depressed margins suggest poor performance.

Somewhat better than average margins are normally a sign of good management, but unusually high margins may means that the company is 'making a packet' and will attract more competition unless there are barriers to entry (e.g. huge initial capital costs, high technology, patents or other special advantages enjoyed by the company).

The converse also applies: if a company has lower margins than others in the same sector, there is scope for improvement. For example, in the past few years TESCO has managed to more than double its margins as it shifted away from the 'pile it high and sell it cheap' philosophy of its founder, the late Sir Jack Cohen, towards SAINSBURY's quality image and better margins:

Example 24.10   Comparison of margins

Year ended	1985	1986	1987	1988	1989
TESCO	2.7%	3.1%	4.1%	5.2%	5.9%
SAINSBURY	5.1%	5.4%	6.2%	6.6%	7.2%

Trading profit margins are also important in that both management and investment analysts usually base their forecasts of future profitability on projected turnover figures multiplied by estimated future margins.

An alternative definition of trading profit, used by Datastream and some analysts, is *before* deducting depreciation, the argument being that different depreciation policies distort inter-company comparisons. If this approach is used, then trading profit should also be *before* deducting hire charges, to bring a company that leases rather than owns plant and machinery on to a comparable basis. Our view is that depreciation is a cost and should be deducted in any calculation of profit; we therefore prefer to deal with cases where a company's depreciation charge seems unduly low

(or high) by making an adjustment, rather than by adding back every company's depreciation charge. Datastream also excludes exceptional items.

2. $$\dfrac{\textbf{Trading profit}}{\textbf{Capital employed}}$$

= **Return on Capital Employed** (ROCE), expressed as a percentage.

This is a most important measure of profitability, for several reasons:

(a)   A low return on capital employed can easily be wiped out in a downturn.

(b)   If the figure is lower than the cost of borrowing, increased borrowings will reduce earnings per share (e.p.s.) unless the extra money can be used in areas where the ROCE is higher than the cost of borrowing.

(c)   It serves as a guide to the company in assessing possible acquisitions and in starting up new activities – if their *potential* ROCE isn't attractive, they should be avoided.

(d)   Similarly, a persistently low ROCE for any part of the business suggests it could be a candidate for disposal if it isn't an integral part of the business.

ROCE can be calculated either for the company overall or for its trading activities:

Capital employed (in trading) = Share capital + reserves + all borrowing including obligations under finance leases, bank overdraft + minority interests + provisions − associates and investments. Government grants are not included.

Capital employed (overall) Associates and investments are not deducted, while the *overall profit* figure includes income from investments and the company's share of the profits of associated companies, in addition to trading profit.

There are also the problems of Intangible fixed assets, and Purchased goodwill that has been written off directly to reserves (immediate write-off). As we described with CADBURY SCHWEPPES on page 146, adding back purchased goodwill gives a much truer picture.

ED 47 is attempting to solve the problem by proposing that 'Purchased goodwill should be recognised as a fixed asset and recorded in the balance sheet' and that it 'should be amortised through the P & L account', i.e. no more immediate write-off. But ED 47 also proposes that purchased goodwill previously written off immediately *need not* be reinstated. We hope that companies will have the common sense to reinstate it, at least for the last five years; meanwhile we recommend adding back cumulative purchased goodwill that has been written off direct to reserves.

We would also suggest that Intangible items shown in the balance sheet should be included in Capital Employed at their cost less any subsequent amortisation; e.g., Patents, newspaper titles and brand names that have been purchased, but *not* newspaper titles and brand names that have been built up internally. As Sir Adrian Cadbury said, after RHM had put £678 million of brands at valuation in its balance sheet: 'The market value of a company's brands can only be established objectively when their ownership is transferred. Any other form of valuation is by definition subjective.'

The figure for capital employed should, strictly speaking, be the average capital employed during the year, but for simplicity's sake it is normally satisfactory to use the capital employed at the end of the year unless there have been major changes. Some companies label the total at the bottom of their balance sheet as 'capital employed', but using this figure can be deceptive, in that bank overdrafts and loans repayable within 12 months are netted out against current assets, giving a company that has perhaps an embarrassingly large short-term debt a better ROCE than a company whose debt is more prudently funded long-term.

Another variation used by some analysts is to deduct any cash from the overdraft or, where a company has a net cash position, to deduct net cash in calculating capital employed. Netting out cash against overdraft can be justified where cash and overdraft are both with the same bank and the bank is known to calculate interest on the net figure (overdraft − cash), but in general our view is that if a company feels it prudent to operate with a large cash margin it should be measured accordingly, and that if the company's cash is locked up somewhere (for example, if it has arisen from retaining profits overseas to avoid UK taxation) the situation should be reflected in the ratio.

For example, the RUGBY GROUP showed the following details in its consolidated balance sheet in 1988:

	£000
Bank balances and short term deposits	112,471
Creditors falling due within 1 year:	
Bank loans and overdrafts	95,257

but did not disclose the whereabouts of the amounts involved; we would therefore think it wrong to net out the bank loans and overdraft in this case.

Any upward revaluation of property is likely to reduce ROCE in two ways:

(*a*) it will increase capital employed (the surplus on revaluation being credited to capital reserve), *and*

(*b*) it will probably increase the depreciation charge, and thus reduce profits.

Similarly, a company that shows government grants as a liability and uses them to offset against the depreciation charges over the life of the assets concerned will show a poorer return on capital employed than a company which shows assets net of any government grants. We recommend that government grants should *not* be included in capital employed, on the grounds that the original investment decision to purchase any asset was (or should have been) made on a net-of-grants basis.

3. $$\frac{\text{Sales (Turnover)}}{\text{Capital employed (in trading)}}$$

expressed as a multiple.

A rising ratio usually indicates an improvement in performance, i.e. the amount of business being done is increasing in relation to the capital base, but beware of an improvement in the ratio achieved when a company fails to keep its plant and machinery up to date; depreciation will steadily reduce the capital base and improve the ratio without any improvement in sales. Beware, too, of any rapid increase in the ratio, which may well be a warning signal of overtrading, i.e. trying to do too much business with too little capital.

In inter-company comparisons care should be taken to compare like with like: the ratio can be misleading unless the operations of the companies concerned are similar in their activities as well as in their products. For example, a television manufacturing group which is vertically integrated (makes the tubes, electronic circuits and the cabinets and then puts them together) will have much more capital employed than a company which merely assembles bought-in components.

A better measure of performance is that of value added compared with capital employed, but value added is not always included in published information. Because of the difference in operations that can occur in apparently similar companies we would place more importance on our previous ratio (Trading profit/Capital employed) than on the ratio of Sales/Capital employed.

Our first three ratios are, of course, interrelated:

$$\frac{\text{Trading profit}}{\text{Sales (Turnover)}} \times \frac{\text{Sales (Turnover)}}{\text{Capital employed}}$$
$$= \frac{\text{Trading profit}}{\text{Capital employed}}$$

and the equation helps to illustrate the four ways in which management can increase trading profit in relation to capital employed:

by increasing the first factor by

(a) reducing costs }
(b) raising prices } by higher profit margins

by increasing the second factor by

(c) increasing sales volume }
(d) reducing capital employed } by higher output per £1 of capital

The healthy way of reducing capital employed is to dispose of low profitability/high capital parts of the business when this can be done without adversely affecting the remainder. There was another way of producing the same optical effect other than by running down capital investment: by leasing rather than buying plant and machinery (or by selling and leasing back fixed assets already owned), but this loophole has largely been closed by SSAP 21, which requires companies to capitalise *financial leases* and include them in the balance sheet (see Chapter 11).

Two other ways in which companies may reduce capital employed are by the factoring of debtors, and by the off-balance-sheet financing of stock, providing the cash realised is used to reduce borrowings.

Further operating ratios

The choice of further operating ratios depends on what aspect is being examined and the information available. We have chosen four which deal with the size of working capital items (Stocks, Debtors, Creditors and Working capital itself) in relation to Sales, and finally one measuring trading profit as a percentage of wages and salaries.

4. $$\frac{\text{Stocks}}{\text{Sales (Turnover)}}$$

expressed as a percentage.

Stocks comprise stocks of raw materials and consumables, purchased components, work in progress (net of progress payments), finished goods, goods for resale, and payments on account (shown under stocks).

Except when stocks are built up in anticipation of sharp price rises, well-run companies usually try to carry the minimum stock needed for the satisfactory running of their business: they do so to minimise interest charges on the money tied up in stocks, to save the costs of extensive storage and to reduce the risk of being left with goods that can't be sold due to deterioration, becoming obsolete or going out of fashion. Although some distortion can occur with accelerating growth, because stock is a year-end figure while sales occur throughout the year (on average several months earlier), a rising

stock ratio without any special reason is regarded as bad news, reflecting lack of demand for goods and/or poor stock control. A high ratio in comparison to similar companies is undesirable, although Stocks/Turnover ratios vary enormously with the nature of a business. At one end of the scale, and apart from advertising agencies and other service industries, ready-mixed concrete companies probably have one of the lowest Stocks/Turnover figures of any industry: aggregates are extracted from the ground when required and the product is delivered the same day, so all that is needed in stock is a supply of fresh cement and fuel, giving a typical Stocks/Turnover figure of 5%. At the other end of the scale a company which maintains depots of finished goods and replacement parts worldwide, like a power transmission and mechanical handling systems manufacturer, can reasonably be expected to have a ratio as high as 35% in order to maintain a first-class service to its customers all over the world.

For an average manufacturing company a Stocks/Turnover ratio of around 15–20% would be reasonable, increasing the larger and more complex the goods made; for instance, an aircraft manufacturer might have stocks and WIP representing 30–35% of turnover and this level could be subject to sharp fluctuations, depending on whether completed aircraft had been delivered to clients just before or just after the end of the year; in contrast, a company making a limited range of nuts and bolts could probably run on a few weeks' stock, though if supplies were subject to interruption and/or shortages it might be prudent to carry more raw materials, and if orders tended to be erratic a higher stock of finished goods would be needed.

Where the *Cost of sales* is available, i.e. Format 1, it can be used instead of the sales figure and, taking the stock of *finished goods* (for a manufacturer) or *goods for resale* (for a distribution or retail business), the ratio Stocks/Cost of sales can be expressed as so many days or months of stock, or as stock turned over so many times a year. Many analysts take the average of the opening and closing stocks, as in Example 24.11, which has a smoothing effect, but doing so does dampen the effect of a major change in stocks over the period.

Example 24.11   Calculation of Stocks/Cost of sales

	1988 £000	1989 £000	1990 £000
Year-end stock	1,758	2,272	3,008
Average stock		2,015	2,640
Sales		10,830	12,490
Cost of goods sold		6,270	7,130

Stocks/Sales	18.6%	21.1%
Stocks/Cost of sales	32.1%	37.0%
Days of stock	117 days	135 days
Stock turned over p.a.	3.12×	2.70×

5. $$\frac{\textbf{Trade debtors}}{\textbf{Sales (Turnover)}}$$

expressed either as a percentage or, multiplied by 365, as the collection period in days.

For example, given Trade debtors of £820,000 and Sales (Turnover) of £5 million:

$$\frac{\text{Trade debtors}}{\text{Sales (Turnover)}}=\frac{£820,000}{£5,000,000}=16.4\% \ or$$

$$\text{Collection period}=\frac{£820,000}{£5,000,000}\times 365 \text{ days}$$

$$=60 \text{ days.}$$

Apart from 'strictly cash' businesses like supermarkets, with virtually zero debtors (e.g. TESCO's debtors average about 0.5% of sales), normal terms are payment at the end of the month following delivery, so with 100% prompt payment the average credit given would be between 6 and 7 weeks, making debtors about 12% of turnover. In practice, a figure of 15–20% is quite normal although some companies may, as a matter of policy, give more generous credit in order to give themselves a competitive edge, while others may factor their debts and thus show abnormally low debtors.

A falling collection period is generally a good sign – an indication of effective financial control – but it could show a desperate need for cash, involving extra discounts for cash and undue pressure on customers (see also page 55).

Where extended credit is given by hire-purchase facilities provided by the company itself, rather than through a finance company, the HP amount outstanding is usually shown separately, but unless the turnover figure is also broken down it isn't possible to calculate the ratios of HP debtors/HP turnover and Other debtors/Non-HP turnover separately, which is a pity.

6. $$\frac{\textbf{Trade creditors}}{\textbf{Sales}}$$

expressed as a percentage.

This gives some indication of the amount of credit a company is allowed by its suppliers, and quite a good indication, provided stock levels and profit margins are reasonably steady and the business is not highly seasonal.

A better measure would be Trade creditors/Cost of goods purchased, but the cost of goods purchased during the year is seldom disclosed, so the analyst has to content himself with Trade creditors/Sales. This ratio will still show up any change in credit allowed, so it is the *trend* which needs to be watched.

A company that is short of cash will be forced to try to get as much credit as it can, despite losing discounts for prompt payment. (*En passant*, any indications of change of suppliers or refusal of credit by suppliers can be an excellent early warning of trouble, because suppliers are usually in very much closer personal day-to-day contact with a company than an analyst or the company's shareholders. Similar warning can be given by the refusal of major factoring companies to offer further credit: because they act for so many individual creditors, factors often have a much clearer picture of a company's overall position.)

An alternative ratio to use here is Trade creditors/Stocks, to see what proportion of the stocks is financed by the company's suppliers. This is of particular interest in retailing businesses, where 160% is a normal figure for an efficient food retailer like SAINSBURY.

In addition, bankers often study movements in the ratio Debtors/Trade creditors. When things are normal this tends to be stable. Violent change in either direction is a warning signal.

7. $$\frac{\textbf{Working capital}}{\textbf{Sales}}$$

expressed as a percentage
where *Working capital* = Stocks + Trade debtors − Trade creditors.

This shows how much capital is required to finance operations in addition to capital invested in fixed assets. It can vary from a tiny 1%, or even negative for a food retailer, to 30% or more for a heavy engineering company, and gives some indication of the likely additional cash needed with increased turnover. A falling ratio indicates the possibility of overtrading.

It is also interesting to compare this ratio with our first ratio, Trading profit to Sales, to see whether increased sales will generate sufficient extra profit to provide the extra working capital required. Allowing for Corporation Tax on the extra profit, Trading profit to Sales must be higher than Working capital to Sales for a company to be 'self-financing' in working capital terms.

8. $$\frac{\textbf{Trading profit}}{\textbf{Wages}}$$

expressed as a percentage.

Trading profit/Wages gives a direct indication of the effect of wage increases on profits. For example, a company whose trading profit is only 15% of wages is likely to be much more adversely affected by a wage increase of 10% than a company with a ratio of 50%.

Finally, Sales per Employee and Trading profit per Employee are also useful ratios: their trend gives some indication of changing productivity.

FINANCIAL RATIOS

Financial ratios fall into two broad groups, gearing ratios and liquidity ratios. Gearing is concerned with the proportion of capital employed that is borrowed, the proportion provided by shareholders' funds and the relationship between the two, while liquidity ratios are concerned with the company's cash position.

Gearing

Financial gearing can be defined in a multiplicity of ways, the two most common being:

(a)   the Debt/Equity ratio, shown as Borrowings/Shareholders' funds in the *Investors Chronicle*, and called 'leverage' in the United States and elsewhere, *and*

(b)   the percentage of capital employed represented by borrowings.

Whatever method is used to compute gearing, a company with 'low gearing' is one financed predominantly by equity, whereas a 'highly geared' company is one which relies on borrowings for a significant proportion of its capital.

To illustrate (see Example 24.12), let us take the bottom half of three different companies' balance sheets, adjusting them to include the bank overdraft and any other borrowings falling due within one year (these are normally netted out against current assets in a company's balance sheet, but are just as much a part of capital employed as long-term borrowings are). As you can see, the Debt/Equity ratio is a more sensitive measurement of gearing than Debt/Capital employed, and it also gives a better indication of the effect of gearing on equity income, known across the Atlantic as the 'leverage effect', but it can be distorted by the treatment of deferred tax under Provisions varying from company to company, or varying within a company from year to year.

Leverage effect

The effect of leverage can be expressed as a ratio: percentage change in earnings available to ordinary shareholders brought about by a 1% change in earnings before interest and tax (EBIT).

Suppose each of the three companies in Example 24.12 has a return on capital employed (ROCE) of 10%, and that the rate of Corporation

Example 24.12   Calculation of gearing and Debt/Equity ratios

		Company A £000	Company B £000	Company C £000
Ordinary share capital		600	500	250
Reserves		850	550	300
Ordinary shareholders' funds	[A]	1,450	1,050	550
Redeemable preference capital (3.5%)	[B]	—	100	—
Minorities	[C]	150	150	150
Provisions		400	400	400
Loan stock (10%)	[D]	—	150	400
Overdraft (currently 12%)	[E]	—	150	500
Capital employed	[F]	2,000	2,000	2,000
Debt/Equity (Leverage) $\left(\dfrac{B+D+E}{A+C}\right)$		0%	33%	128%
Debt/Capital employed $\left(\dfrac{B+D+E}{F}\right)$		0%	20%	45%
Gearing		None	Low	High

Notes:

[B]   The treatment of preference shares is a problem: although they are not debt they do carry a *fixed* rate of dividend that is payable ahead of ordinary dividends. On balance we favour treating them as debt if redeemable in the reasonably near future, say in less than 10 years, but otherwise as equity when looking at capital (because it would be misleading to ascribe the same Debt/Equity ratio to a company with, say, 60 debt/40 equity as one with 60 pref/40 equity).

[C] Minorities have been included as equity in the calculation of Debt/Equity ratios, on the assumption that minority interests in subsidiaries are all pure (non-redeemable) equity.

Example 24.13   Calculation of leverage effect

	Company A	Company B	Company C
	£000	£000	£000
EBIT	200	200	200
less			
Loan stock interest	—	−15	−40
Interest on overdraft	—	−18	−60
Pre-tax profits	200	167	100
Tax at 35%	70	58.5	35
Profits after tax	130	108.5	65
Preference dividends	—	3.5	—
Available for minorities and ordinary shareholders [G]	130	105	65
1% change in EBIT	2	2	2
Tax	0.7	0.7	0.7
Available for minorities and ordinary shareholders [H]	+1.3	+1.3	+1.3
Leverage ratio			
$\dfrac{H}{G} \times 100$	1.0	1.24	2.0

Tax is 35%; then earnings before interest and tax (EBIT) will be as shown in Example 24.13.

Leverage, of course, works both ways; if EBIT fell by 50% then earnings available to ordinary shareholders would fall to £65,000 (Company A); £40,000 (Company B); and Company C would be on the verge of making a loss.

Interest rate sensitivity

A simple calculation can be made to see the sensitivity of a company's profits to interest rates: if, in Example 24.13, the rate charged on overdrafts rose to 16% (or fell to 8%), Company C's pre-tax profit would be reduced (or increased) by 20%.

Operational gearing

In assessing what level of financial gearing might be reasonable for a company, we must first look at the volatility of profits. This depends to a large extent on the sensitivity of profits to turnover, which we will call operational gearing (although the term operational gearing is sometimes used in the sense of overall gearing to include the effects of financial gearing as well).

The operational gearing of a company can be described as the ratio of the percentage change of trading profit which results from 1% change in turnover, and depends on the relationship between fixed costs, variable costs and net profit, where fixed costs are costs that are incurred regardless of turnover, and variable costs are directly proportional to turnover:

Operational gearing =
(Turnover − Variable costs) : Trading profit
or (Trading profit + Fixed costs) : Trading profit

Example 24.14 demonstrates this.

Example 24.14   Effects of operational gearing

	Turn-over	Fixed costs	Vari-able costs	Trad-ing profit	Operational gearing
	£m	£m	£m	£m	
Company D	100	20	70	10	3:1 (100−70:10)
Company E	100	70	20	10	8:1 (100−20:10)

If turnover increases by 10%:

	£m	£m	£m	£m	Change in profits
Company D	110	20	77	13	+30%
Company E	110	70	22	18	+80%

This is fine for both D and E, especially for E, which is much more highly geared operationally than D. But, as with high financial gearing, high operational gearing works against a company when turnover falls. Assume a 10% fall in turnover:

	£m	£m	£m	£m	
Company D	90	20	63	7	−30%
Company E	90	70	18	2	−80%

The effect of gearing can also be illustrated graphically on a 'profit/volume chart', as shown in Example 24.15.

A profit/volume chart is constructed by plotting two points:

(a)   trading profit against actual turnover
(b)   fixed costs against zero turnover

and joining the two points together. The point where this line crosses the horizontal 'zero profit' line represents the level of turnover at which the company 'breaks even', i.e. makes neither a profit nor a loss. The steeper the gradient of the line the higher the operational gearing of the company. The break-even point can also be calculated:

Example 24.15   Profit/Volume chart

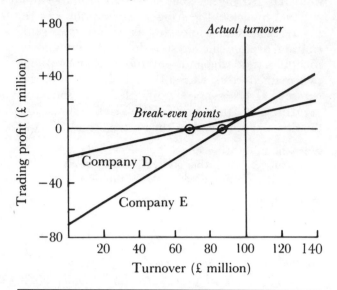

Break-even turnover

$$= \text{Fixed costs} \times \frac{\text{Turnover}}{\text{Turnover} - \text{variable costs}}$$

e.g. Company D $= 20 \times \dfrac{100}{100-70} = £66.67\text{m}.$

Company E $= 70 \times \dfrac{100}{100-80} = £87.5\text{m}.$

It is fairly obvious that a company with high operational gearing aggravates the problem by gearing up financially. Suppose, for instance, that Company E has borrowings that incurred interest charges of £3 million p.a.; Example 24.16 shows the effect on profits.

A company that illustrates the danger of high financial gearing on top of high operational gearing is BLACKWOOD HODGE, which is in the notoriously volatile subsector of Construction Equipment Distributors (see details of subsector ratios on page 177):

Example 24.16   Effect of high financial gearing coupled with high operational gearing

Turnover	Net trading profit	Interest charges	Pre-tax profits
£m.	£m.	£m.	£m.
100	10	3	7
110	18	3	15
90	2	3	−1

It was probably only the drastic action taken in 1983, which incurred extraordinary items of £13,778,000 in addition to the exceptional items shown below, which enabled the company to survive.

Conversely, the directors of a property company with mainly completed developments let to substantial clients know that they have an assured rental income coming in each quarter, and they would not be considered imprudent to borrow heavily (i.e. gear up) provided the level of interest payments plus running expenses could not exceed the stream of rental income. We say 'could not exceed', because one of the ways property companies get into trouble is by borrowing short-term with a variable interest rate (e.g. on bank overdraft), rather than at a fixed rate; they then get caught out when interest rates go up faster than rental income.

Liquidity ratios

The two ratios most commonly used in assessing a company's liquidity are concerned with current assets (stocks and WIP, debtors and cash) and current liabilities (creditors, bank overdraft and any debts due to be settled within the next 12 months):

1.   **Current ratio**

$$= \frac{\text{Current assets}}{\text{Current liabilities}}$$

BLACKWOOD HODGE *Profit record*

(£000)	1981	1982	1983	1984	1985	1986	1987
Profit before interest	20,187	14,147	3,003	12,836	14,899	14,433	19,181
Interest payable	18,070	17,835	14,497	9,796	7,736	5,613	6,620
Profit (loss)	2,117	(3,688)	(11,494)	3,040	7,163	8,820	12,561
Exceptional items	(1,100)	—	(9,123)	—	—	—	(56)
Pre-tax profit	1,017	(3,688)	(20,617)	3,040	7,163	8,820	12,505

2. **Quick ratio** (*or* 'Acid test')

$$= \frac{\text{Current assets} - \text{Stock}}{\text{Current liabilities}}$$

Note that the Companies Act 1985 requires all amounts owing by the company to be included under creditors, with amounts due within one year and after one year being shown separately. We regard creditors falling due within one year as being synonymous with current liabilities, but the Companies Act 1985 does not require provisions for amounts expected to fall due within one year to be shown separately: they are included under the general heading of provisions. When they can be identified, provisions for amounts due within one year should be included in current liabilities.

Current ratio

The Current ratio is a broad indicator of a company's short-term financial position: a ratio of more than 1 indicates a surplus of current assets over current liabilities. A current ratio of 2 or more used to be regarded as prudent in order to maintain creditworthiness, but in recent years a figure of about 1.5 has become quite normal, and a higher figure isn't necessarily a good sign: it may be due to excessive stocks or debtors, or it may mean that the directors are sitting on an unduly large amount of cash which could be more profitably invested.

When looking at an individual company's current ratio, there is no simple rule of thumb on what the company's ratio 'ought' to be, because it so much depends on a number of different factors, including the following:

1. *The nature of the company's business.* If large stocks and the giving of generous credit terms are normal to the business, the current ratio needs to be higher than the general average, whereas a retail business with only cash sales, no work in progress and with stocks financed mainly by suppliers (i.e. creditors a large item) may be expected to have a lower than average current ratio.

2. *The quality of the current assets.* Stocks, for example, may be readily saleable, e.g. gold, or virtually unsaleable, e.g. half-completed houses in a property slump.

3. *The imminence of current liabilities.* A large loan due for repayment very soon could be embarrassing. It would be acutely embarrassing if gearing was already very high, there was no scope for an equity issue and neither cash nor further overdraft facilities were available. Even that is not perhaps as embarrassing as being unable to pay the wages next week, and next week's wages do not, of course, appear in the balance sheet.

The key factor is whether a company has scope for further borrowings or is right up against its limits, but facilities available (as opposed to facilities being used) are not normally revealed in annual reports.

4. *The volatility of working capital requirements.* A company with a highly seasonal business pattern, for instance a Christmas card manufacturer or a UK holiday camp operator, may well make use of a much higher average level of borrowings during the year than the balance sheet shows, particularly as companies usually arrange their year end to coincide with low stocks and/or a low level of activity. When the interest charge in the P & L account is disproportionately large in comparison to the borrowings shown in the balance sheet, this is a clear indication that borrowings during the year have been significantly higher than at the year end.

Because of these individual factors, the most informative feature of a current ratio is its normal level and any *trend* from year to year. A drop below normal levels is worth investigating, and a continuing decline is a warning signal that should not be ignored.

For example the current ratio of the ECC GROUP (formerly English China Clays) remained very steady at around 1.35 between 1983 and 1985 (see below), but jumped to 1.70 in 1986, which was due entirely to the sale of the Leisure division for £37.5 million cash and a couple of minor disposals. The current ratio then declined sharply for two years as short-term borrowings increased to finance expansion in the United States. It was clear that this trend could not be allowed to continue, and it was reversed in 1989 by an issue of US $ preference shares raising £121.3 million. Without

---

ECC GROUP *Current ratio*

Year ended 30 September	1983	1984	1985	1986	1987	1988	1989
Current assets (£m)	213.0	256.1	307.4	303.3	335.4	413.2	456.5
Current liabilities (£m)	156.4	187.0	229.4	178.2	265.6	381.7	333.3
Current ratio	1.36	1.37	1.34	1.70	1.26	1.08	1.37

this issue, the current ratio would have fallen further to 1.00.

Quick ratio or acid test

As we have said, not all current assets are readily convertible into cash to meet debts; in particular stocks and work in progress may be able to be run down a certain amount, but not eliminated if the business is to continue. The quick ratio recognises this by excluding stocks from current assets and applies the 'acid test' of what would happen if the company had to settle up with all its creditors and debtors straight away: if the quick ratio is less than 1 it would be unable to do so.

Some companies whose normal terms of trade allow them to sell goods for cash before paying for them habitually operate with a quick ratio of well under 1 (0.2 is typical for a supermarket); so it is a poorer than average figure compared with other companies in the same industry, coupled with a declining trend, that signals possible trouble ahead. A feature that a low and declining ratio often highlights is a rising overdraft: the question then is, 'Are their bankers happy?' Fears in this direction may be allayed by a statement in the annual report about operating well within the facilities available, or by a statement at the time that new money is raised confirming that working capital will be adequate.

A large difference between the current ratio and the quick ratio is an indication of large stocks:

$$\text{Current ratio} - \text{Quick ratio} = \frac{\text{Stocks}}{\text{Current liabilities}}$$

Cash flow

If there is any doubt about the company's liquidity, the cash flow should be examined in as much detail as possible (see Chapter 19). There are two common definitions of cash flow:

Gross cash flow = depreciation plus profit after tax plus increase (less decrease) in deferred tax.
Net cash flow = gross cash flow minus dividends.

The question we need to ask is whether net cash flow in the current year will cover the company's cash requirements.

Cash requirements

There are three main areas to look at in identifying cash requirements:

1. *Repayment of existing loans* due in the next year or two, including convertible loans whose conversion rights are unlikely to be exercised. Loans repayable within 12 months should be shown under current liabilities.

2. *Increase in working capital.* Working capital tends, in an inflationary period and/or when a business expands, to rise roughly in line with turnover. It is useful therefore to use the Working capital/Sales ratio described earlier in this chapter to establish the relationship between working capital and sales (Example 24.17).

Example 24.17   Calculation of the Working capital/Sales ratio

Sales £26m; Stocks £6m; Trade debtors £4m; Trade creditors £3.5m. Calculate the Working capital/Sales ratio:

$$\frac{\text{Stocks} + \text{Debtors} - \text{Creditors}}{\text{Sales}} = \frac{£6.5m}{£26m} = 25\%$$

Thus if the turnover of this company was expected to increase by 20% in the current year, it would be reasonable to assume that unless stocks were unusually high at the last year end or unless the increase in turnover is not going to follow the company's normal trading pattern, the company is likely to need an increase in working capital of £1.3 million (£26m. × 20% × 25%).

---

3. *Capital expenditure requirements.* Companies are required to report the amount of capital expenditure that has been contracted for and the amount that has been approved by the directors but not yet put out to contract.

The flexibility of the company's capital expenditure programme is important; there is much more risk in building one large process plant than in adding 50 outlets to a retail chain at about the same total cost over, say, 2½ years, because the former, once embarked upon, is a complete liability unless and until it comes on stream while the retail chain's expansion could be curtailed if, say, the economic trends turned downwards and capital expenditure had to be cut a year later, leaving 20 new outlets trading profitably. In general, 'great leaps forward' are more risky than step-by-step progress, especially in areas of high technology.

The size of a single project in relation to the overall size of the company is another important factor to watch: a new £25 million process plant that fails to come on stream as planned and loses £5–6 million a year for several years might break a smaller company but would cause no more than mild embarrassment to BRITISH PETROLEUM, and would be regarded as normal in government-financed nuclear power projects.

186

Cash shortfall

If the net cash flow looks like falling short of the cash requirements we have identified, then the company may have to take one or more of the following steps:

(a) increase its overdraft (but is it at the limit of its facilities? – we probably don't know);

(b) borrow longer term (can it do so within its borrowing limits?);

(c) make a rights issue (is its share price at least 20% above par, is it at least a year and preferably two years since its last rights issue, and are market conditions suitable?);

(d) acquire a more liquid and/or less highly geared company for paper (i.e. bid for another company using shares);

(e) sell some assets (has it any listed investments which could be sold, or has it any activities which could be sold off without seriously affecting the business?);

(f) sell and lease back some of the properties used in the business (has it any unmortgaged properties?);

(g) cut back on capital expenditure that has not already been put out to contract;

(h) tighten credit and stock control;

(i) reduce or omit the ordinary dividend, and possibly even the preference dividend too.

If the company takes none of these steps it will run into an overtrading situation, which is likely to precipitate a cash crisis unless, as a last resort, it:

(j) reduces its level of trading.

Contingent liabilities: Ordinary shareholders' funds

Contingent liabilities which are large in relation to Ordinary shareholders' Funds (OSF) can, with a run of bad luck (or bad judgement), be a serious threat to the financial stability of a business, and although the great majority of contingent liabilities never materialise, it is prudent to monitor what is going on. In group accounts, contingent liabilities of the parent company in respect of guarantees of borrowings by subsidiaries can, of course, be ignored, because the borrowings concerned are incorporated in the consolidated accounts, but all guarantees for associates and third parties should be included. Leasing commitments, if material, should also be monitored, and the particular points to watch for are guarantees and commitments outside the normal course of business and sharp increases in the amounts involved, as reflected by the ratio Contingent liabilities/OSF. COLOROLL's accounts for the year to 31 March 1989, illustrated below, provide a good example.

Coloroll's accounts in the previous year had shown contingent liabilities of £1.141 million, only 1.5% of OSF, but in June 1988 Coloroll had acquired JOHN CROWTHER and, in order to expedite the swift disposal of unwanted parts of Crowther, had given guarantees of £21.75 million to assist the management buy-out of Crowther's clothing interests. It had also given two other new guarantees, (b) and (c) in the illustration, and as a result contingent liabilities in 1989 amounted to a total of £40.48 million, almost 40% of OSF.

In the following 12 months consumer demand turned down sharply and the RESPONSE GROUP (the management buy-out vehicle) called in the receivers. This happened shortly after Coloroll had announced interim results in which pre-tax profits were down by 51% reflecting, as the Chairman reported 'the extremely difficult and rapidly deteriorating climate in the markets in which your Group operates'. The market reacted accordingly, see the graph overleaf.

Contingent liabilities that come home to roost are more likely to do so in an economic downturn, just when the guarantor least wants to have to foot the bill! Coloroll soon followed into receivership.

COLOROLL *Extract from 1989 accounts*

Contingent liabilities

At 31 March 1989 the group had contingent liabilities in connection with the following matters:

(a) the sale with recourse of £7,500,000 of redeemable preference shares and £14,250,000 senior and subordinated loan notes in Response Group Limited which were received as part consideration for the sale of the clothing interests of John Crowther Group plc;

(b) the guarantee of borrowings and other bank facilities of Homfray Carpets Australia Pty Limited equivalent to £13,000,000 following the sale of the group's majority interest in that company. The guarantee provides for recourse by the group to the assets of Homfray Carpets Australia Pty Limited by way of a second charge;

(c) the guarantee of borrowings of £4,580,000 of the purchaser of land for development from the group;

(d) the guarantee of borrowings of the owners of properties occupied by a subsidiary which at 31 March 1989 amounted to £1,150,000 (1988: £1,141,000).

COLOROLL *Graph of share price 1 January 1988 to 31 March 1990*

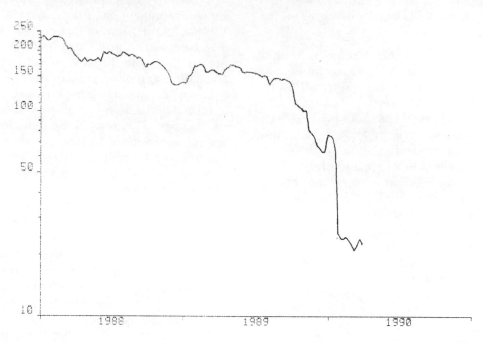

Source: Datastream

INVESTMENT RATIOS

These are the ratios used by investors when deciding whether a share should be bought, sold or held. Most of them relate to the current price of the share, and therefore vary from day to day. The two most popular ones are the Price Earnings Ratio (PER) and the dividend yield.

Price earnings ratio (PER)

$$PER = \frac{\text{Share price}}{\text{Earnings per share (e.p.s.)}}$$

where *share price* = the middle market price, which is the average of the prices at which shares can be sold or bought on an investor's behalf (the marketmaker's bid and offer prices respectively), and *e.p.s* = Profit attributable to ordinary shareholders ÷ Average number of ordinary shares in issue during year.

The calculation of earnings per share is described in detail in Chapter 14. The analyst will normally calculate two price earnings ratios: the 'historical PER', using last year's e.p.s., and the 'prospective PER', using his estimate of e.p.s. for the current year; he may also project his earnings estimates ahead to produce a PER based on possible earnings for the following year.

What the PER represents

One way of looking at the PER is to regard it as the number of years' earnings per share represented by the share price, i.e. *x* years' purchase of e.p.s., but this assumes static e.p.s., while in practice the PER reflects the market's view of the company's growth potential, the business risks involved and the dividend policy. For example, a company recovering from a break-even situation, with zero e.p.s. last year, will have a historical PER of infinity but may have a prospective PER of 12 based on expectations of modest profits for the current year, falling to 6 next year if a full recovery is achieved.

The PER of a company also depends not only on the company itself, but on the industry in which it operates and, of course, on the level of the stock market, which tends to rise more than reported profits when the business cycle swings up and to fall more than profits in a downturn. The level of the PER of the *Financial Times* 500 Index shows this very clearly:

	500 PER
Top of the bull market, 19 May 1972	19.88
Bottom of the bear market, 13 December 1974	3.71
Top of the bull market, 16 July 1987	21.03

The Actuaries Share Indices table published in the *Financial Times* every day except Mondays also gives the PER for each industry group and subsection, so any historical PER calculated for a company can be compared with its sector and with the market as a whole. The result of comparing it with the market as a whole (usually with the *FT* 500's PER) is called the *PER Relative*:

$$\text{PER Relative} = \frac{\text{PER of the company}}{\text{PER of the Market}}$$

This provides a quick indication of whether a company is highly or lowly rated, although differences in the treatment of tax by individual companies do cause some distortion here, so most analysts use e.p.s. calculated on a full tax charge to compare PERs within a sector.

In general a high historic PER compared with the industry group suggests either that the company is a leader in its sector or that the share is overvalued, while a low PER suggests a poor company or an undervalued share. In each case check to see if the prospective PER is moving back into line with the sector, as a historic PER that is out of line may be due to expectations of an above-average rise in profits for the current year (in which case the historic PER will be higher than average), or to poor results being expected (which would be consistent with a low PER). In addition, if Datastream is available (see Chatper 22), it is worth checking the company's PER history to see where it lies in relation to its historical range and to the sector PER: all Datastream's PERs are calculated using fully taxed e.p.s.

Another useful rule of thumb is to be wary when a PER goes much above 20. The company may well be a glamour stock due for a tumble or, if it is the PER of a very sound high-quality company, the market itself may be in for a fall. One exception here is the property sector, where PERs are normally very high because property companies tend to be highly geared and use most of their rental income to service their debt, leaving tiny e.p.s.; investors normally buy property company shares more for their prospects of capital appreciation than for their current earnings.

Dividend policy and the PER

As the price of a share is influenced both by the e.p.s. and the dividend, a company's dividend policy affects the PER.

Some companies pay tiny dividends and plough back most of their profits to finance further growth. Shares in these companies may enjoy a glamour rating while everything is going well, but the rating is vulnerable to any serious setback in profits, as there is little yield to support the price. Blue chip companies like to pay a reasonable

dividend and to increase it each year to counteract the effects of inflation and reflect long-term growth; and it is what the shareholders expect, particularly those who are retired and need income from their investments. This usually means that major companies pay out between 30% and 40% of attributable profits, retaining a substantial amount to reinvest for future growth and to allow some increase in the dividend in lean years. For example, BRITISH PETROLEUM increased its dividend by 8% in 1988, even though profits were down 13%.

If a company pays out much more than 50% in dividends it suggests it has gone ex-growth; it also runs a higher risk of having to cut its dividend in hard times (which tends to be *very* unpopular with investors) and, in times of high inflation, a company distributing a large proportion of its reported profits (calculated on a historical cost basis) will tend to lose credibility if dividends are believed to exceed real earnings.

Dividend yield

As described in Chapter 13, dividends under the imputation system are actually paid net of tax at the basic personal rate, and carry an associated tax credit. Dividend yields are based on *gross* dividends per share, that is, on the dividends actually paid plus the associated tax credit; if the gross equivalent of a net dividend paid is not given in the report and accounts, it can be obtained by grossing up, i.e. by dividing the net dividend by $(1 - \text{basic tax rate expressed as a decimal})$:

Gross dividend yield (%) =

$$\frac{\text{Net dividend in pence per share} \times 100}{(1 - \text{basic tax rate}) \times \text{Ordinary share price in pence}}$$

e.g. Net dividend = 6p; basic rate of income tax = 25%; share price = 200p:

$$\text{Gross dividend yield} = \frac{6 \times 100}{0.75 \times 200} = 4.0\%$$

The associated tax credit depends on the basic rate of tax at the time the dividend was paid (not the rate in the year it was earned).

Dividend cover

Provided the company is in a normal tax position with reasonably steady and mainly UK earnings, so that all the profits after tax can be distributed net with full tax credit, then, as Example 24.18 shows:

$$\text{Dividend cover} = \frac{\text{Earnings per share}}{\text{Net dividend per share}}$$

Example 24.18 is very straightforward, but when foreign tax on overseas earnings becomes

Example 24.18   Calculation of dividend cover

With a basic rate of personal tax of 25% and a Corporation Tax rate of 35%:

	Modest dividend £000	Maximum dividend £000
Pre-tax profits	3,000	3,000
Corporation Tax	1,050	1,050
Profits after tax	1,950	1,950
Ordinary dividends	600	1,950
Retained earnings	1,350	Nil

Tax payable

ACT: 25/75ths of net dividends	200	650
Mainstream tax	850	400
Total tax	1,050	1,050

Issued equity = 10m shares

Earnings per share $= \dfrac{£1.97m}{10m}$	19.5p	19.5p
Net dividend	6p	19.5p
Dividend cover	3.25 ×	1.0 ×

Example 24.19   Calculation of dividend cover: full distribution

Taking our previous Example 24.18, but assuming that half the profits are earned overseas and bear foreign tax (including any withholding tax on remission) at 50%, then the maximum distributable gross is:

Pre-tax profits	£3,000,000
less UK minimum mainstream tax	− 150,000
Foreign tax	− 750,000
Full distribution	2,100,000

75/100ths of this full distribution figure will be distributed as net dividends (£1,575,000), together with 25/100ths as the associated tax credit (£525,000).

With 10 million shares the full distribution (i.e. gross) earnings per share = 21p, while the modest 6p net dividend's gross equivalent, with a 25% basic rate of personal tax = 6 × 100/75 = 8p and

$$\text{dividend cover} = \frac{21}{8} = 2.625 \text{ times}$$

The overall tax position would be:

	Modest dividend £000	Maximum dividend (i.e. full distribution) £000
Net dividend	600	1,575
Tax credit (equal to ACT payable to company)	200	525
UK pre-tax profits	1,500	1,500
CT liability	525	525
less ACT (max. 25% of UK pre-tax)	200[a]	375 [A]
Mainstream tax (minimum 35%–25% = 10%)	325[b]	150 [B]
Overseas pre-tax profits	1,500	1,500
UK CT liability	525	525
Max. credit for overseas tax	525	525
Overseas tax	750[c]	750 [C]
Unrelieved overseas tax	225	225
Unrelieved ACT	—	150 [D]
Total tax	1,275 (a+b+c)	1,425 (A+B+C+D)
Profits after tax	1,725	1,575
Issued equity = 10m. shares		
Gross dividends	800	2,100
Gross dividends per share	8p	21p
Dividend cover	2.625	1.0

significant, the maximum net dividend a company can distribute out of a year's profits is no longer the e.p.s. but something less, and the cover has to be worked out at a gross level.

Full distribution

Example 24.19 illustrates the dividend cover calculated on a 'full distribution' basis.

As explained more fully in Chapter 13, the maximum distributable gross dividends ('full distribution earnings') are the lesser of:

(*a*) 'nil distribution' after-tax profits, grossed up;

or

(*b*) total pre-tax profits, *less*

    (i) Minimum mainstream tax on UK pre-tax profits, charged at (CT rate — basic tax rate) and

    (ii) Foreign tax payable if all overseas profits are remitted to the United Kingdom;

and dividend cover $= \dfrac{\text{Full distribution e.p.s.}}{\text{Actual gross dividend}}$

Payout ratio

Before the introduction of the imputation system this ratio could be defined as the dividends distributed (gross) expressed as a percentage of the profits after tax, or as the reciprocal of the dividend cover, which gave the same answer.

Under the imputation system the payout ratio is less straightforward. Provided the company would not incur any extra tax liability on full distribution, the payout ratio is still the reciprocal of the dividend cover, but if full distribution increases the tax charge a difference arises. Taking the 'modest dividend' situation in Example 24.19:

(*a*) Payout ratio $= \dfrac{\text{Net dividends}}{\text{Profits after tax}} = \dfrac{600}{1,725} = 34.8\%$

(*b*) Reciprocal of dividend cover $= \dfrac{1}{2.625} = 38.1\%$

As the payout ratio reflects, by implication, the amount retained by the company, (*a*) seems the better definition as the company does, in fact, retain 65.2% of attributable profits if it pays out 34.8% in dividends.

Net asset value (n.a.v.)

This shows the book value of assets attributable to each ordinary share:

n.a.v. $= \dfrac{\text{Ordinary shareholders funds' (OSF)}}{\text{Number of ordinary shares in issue}}$

Although the n.a.v. figure is *very* dependent on the balance sheet values of assets being realistic, it does give some indication of how much the price of a share depends on the ability of the company to generate profits and how much is backed by assets.

The net asset value is one reference point used in deciding on terms for an acquisition, assuming the potential biddee's assets are fairly valued or are adjusted for the purpose of the calculation. Where property has been revalued but the new value is only shown in a note to the accounts, i.e. the surpluses have not been credited to reserves, analysts will often show two figures, e.g. 'n.a.v. = 73p (94p including property revaluation)'.

Market capitalisation

The market capitalisation of a company is the market price of a company's ordinary shares multiplied by the number of shares in issue. The 'market cap' is a useful measure of the relative size of companies. For example, in the food retailing sector at 31 March 1990:

SAINSBURY	£3,878m.
KWIKSAVE	810m.
NORMANS GROUP	24m.

Chapter 25

PRO-FORMA GUIDE TO ANALYSIS

Although historical information summaries and analyses of company accounts are readily available from Extel Cards and Datastream, for those fortunate enough to enjoy these excellent services, there really is no substitute for poking around the accounts to spot, for example, when a company decides to include profits on the sale and leaseback of property above the line (because pre-tax profits would otherwise be down on last year?), or where a company has guaranteed extensive liabilities outside its normal business activities.

This chapter provides a pro-forma to help you poke round systematically and to work out key ratios. The first three sheets are designed for the analysis of a single year's accounts, and the remaining five sheets present a summary of a company's record over five years, to show the long-term trends of key ratios and percentages.

Analysts' views on the treatment of some items do vary and, under the Companies Act 1985, companies are given a choice of two balance sheet formats and four profit and loss account formats (CA 1985, Sch. 4). This pro-forma is only one way of tackling the figures; it should be modified, adapted and extended to cater for the company's choice of reporting formats and to suit the analyst's individual tastes, provided users are consistent in their treatment of items so that figures produced are on a fair basis for inter-company comparisons.

The following line-by-line notes, which provide cross-references to the relevant sections in earlier chapters, should be read in conjunction with the pro-forma. (It should be noted that some of the pro-formas have lines which are numbered but left blank: these are to accommodate any special items which may occur in individual cases.)

ANALYSIS SHEET 1 – PROFIT AND LOSS ACCOUNT

The main purpose of this sheet is twofold: to see if reported profits are distorted in any way and to examine the effect of an abnormal tax charge. This is done by 'normalising' profits and applying a 'full' tax charge (by deducting the potential liability for deferred tax as well as the reported tax charge) to produce 'normalised' e.p.s. The difference between normalised and reported e.p.s. then serves as a crude indication of the effect of SSAP 15 and other factors on the tax charge and, possibly, that something is abnormal about the way in which the company reports its pre-tax profits.

Line 1. Turnover or Sales
This figure should be after the deduction of trade

discounts, and should not include transactions within the group, VAT or other sales-based taxes.

Calculation of normalised trading profit

The method of calculating trading profit will depend on the profit and loss account format chosen by the company (see page 72). The pro-forma is designed for Format 1, and also includes 'Adjustments' to remove the effect of variations in accounting practices.

Line 2. Cost of sales
Distribution costs
Administrative expenses
These are described on page 72. If the company has chosen Format 2 or 4, the total of all deduc-

tions up to and including *Other operating charges* can be inserted in Line 2, unless a detailed breakdown is required (as in Example 2 in Chapter 12).

Line 3. Other operating income
Income from normal operations, not shown under any other heading (e.g. royalties).

Line 4. Adjustments
Although SSAPs have done much towards standardising the treatment and presentation of accounts, a number of companies include variations from normal practice which can make a significant difference to reported profits. These may arise in a number of ways:

(a) The provision of *depreciation* on intangible assets should be added back, to produce a fair comparison with the great majority of companies that write intangible assets off straight away against reserves, but see ED 47, latest proposals on treatment of purchased good will, described on page 178.

(b) *Capitalising expenses* and amortising them over the years in which benefits are expected to accrue, rather than charging the expenses at the time they were incurred. It may look fair, for example, to capitalise the cost of relocating a factory and to spread the charge over several subsequent years when the relocation will be saving rent, transport costs, etc., but the move may not turn out to be a success financially.

The standard accounting practice on research and development, SSAP 13, requires expenditure on research and development to be written off in the year of expenditure, except for specific projects where commercial success is reasonably assured (see page 74). We would also favour writing off all expenditure on relocation, start-up costs, etc. and any expenditure a company has capitalised in this way during the year should be deducted from pre-tax profits.

(c) *Capitalising interest.* When a company builds a new factory it is reasonable to capitalise interest on money borrowed for the project during construction as this would be included in the capital cost if the project was put out to contract or a newly completed factory was purchased, but if completion is delayed or the start of production is postponed because of lack of demand, then interest on the investment should be written off as an expense (see page 74).

Another variation of capitalising interest is on land banks and on sites awaiting development or redevelopment; the risk here is that the original cost plus subsequent interest may easily exceed the market value of the asset in its present condition, although some might argue that if the company has succeeded in 'rolling up' the interest on the associated debt (has been allowed to add the interest to the capital sum borrowed, rather than paying it when due), then it is reasonable to capitalise the interest on the other side of the balance sheet (i.e. add it to the book value of the asset concerned).

We feel that the capitalising of interest before construction has started or after planned completion should be treated with suspicion, and we recommend that any interest that has been capitalised in these circumstances should be deducted from pre-tax profits; see REGENTCREST on page 75.

(d) *Extraordinary expenses and losses.* As we have already discussed, the definition of extraordinary items as opposed to exceptional items (see page 96) leaves a certain amount of scope for differences of opinion. For example, the treatment of losses on unmatched foreign currency borrowings (see page 132), and the details of items the company has treated as extraordinary, need careful examination: any 'non-extraordinary' items should be deducted from reported profits.

(e) *Extraordinary profits.* The converse to (d) may apply when a company makes profits other than in the normal course of business and does *not* treat them as extraordinary. The profits on any extraordinary items, for example on the sale and leaseback of properties or on the redemption of debt, should be excluded from pre-tax profits.

All these variations, except depreciation, tend to boost the reported profits of the company and should be viewed with healthy scepticism. In many cases they are genuine differences in practice, consistently and openly applied, in which case the analyst should adjust the profits to avoid getting an unduly optimistic view of the company, but there is also an unfortunate tendency for companies to adopt 'expediency accounting' to paper over the cracks when profits are crumbling. If there is any suspicion of this, a fine-tooth comb is needed to check:

(a) the auditors' report for qualifications;
(b) the statement or note on accounting policies (usually Note 1 to the accounts) for any changes;
(c) extraordinary items;
(d) movements to and from reserves.

Calculation of normalised pre-tax profit

The next four lines contain items of income and

expenditure which are added to and deducted from Line 5, Normalised trading profit, to produce Normalised pre-tax profit in Line 10.

Line 6. Associates
This is the group's share of the pre-tax profits of associated undertakings and participating interests (page 123).

Line 7. Investment and other income
This includes the Companies Act 1985 format items Income from other fixed asset investments, and Other interest receivable, *less* Amounts written off investments. Dividends are shown gross, i.e. plus associated tax credits (page 88).

Line 8. Earnings before interest and tax (EBIT)
This figure is used in the calculation of return on capital employed (ROCE) in Line 103 at the bottom of this sheet.

Line 9. Interest paid
This is on all borrowings (page 80) including overdraft; shown in the CA 1985 formats as Interest payable and similar charges.

Line 10. 'Normalised' pre-tax profit
This is the reported pre-tax profit adjusted by Line 4 to correct for any variations in accounting practices.

Calculation of normalised earnings per share

As discussed in Chapter 13, there are many factors that can make a company's tax charge differ from pre-tax profits multiplied by the standard rate of Corporation Tax; for example, non-offsettable losses where the actual tax charge is higher, and franked income and the non-remission of overseas profits where the actual tax charge is lower. However, the main cause of any difference, resulting in a lower tax charge, is, under SSAP 15, the amount of deferred taxation *not* provided because the company does not expect it to be payable in the foreseeable future.

Because SSAP 15 gives companies so much discretion over the provision, or non-provision, of deferred tax, we recommend that e.p.s. should be calculated on a fully taxed basis, i.e. after the deduction of the 'potential amount of deferred taxation' the company would also have provided for if it had provided for *all* timing differences regardless of whether payable in the near future.

SSAP 15 requires this 'potential amount' to be disclosed, but if the information is not available a rough-and-ready practical rule is to deduct Corporation Tax at the standard rate from 'normalised pre-tax profits'.

Many analysts calculate a company's e.p.s. and PER on both an *actual* and a *full* tax basis, and

some very sensibly started using 35% as the full rate in advance of financial year 1986 (the first year in which the 35% rate applies) in order to make year-on-year comparisons on a uniform basis.

Line 11. Taxation reported
The amount of taxation on ordinary activities shown in the company's profit and loss account.

Line 12. Potential deferred tax
The additional amount of deferred tax had the company provided for *all* timing differences.

Line 13. Estimated tax
Where insufficient information is given on potential deferred tax, omit Lines 11 and 12, and insert in Line 13 *either* the estimated tax = 'normalised pre-tax profits' × standard rate of Corporation Tax *or*, if higher, the reported tax charge.

Line 15. Minorities
This is the share of profits of the minority shareholders in subsidiaries not wholly owned by the company. In theory the profits attributable to minorities should be adjusted here to reflect a 'full' tax charge in the subsidiaries concerned, but this usually involves extensive research at Companies House. A crude adjustment can be made by grossing up minorities at the reported rate of tax and then applying a tax charge at the standard rate.

Line 17. Preference dividends
Actual amount paid, i.e. net of tax credit (page 95).

Line 18. Normalised profits attributable to ordinary shareholders
This is the attributable profit, having adjusted pre-tax profits to conform to normal reporting practices and having applied a standard tax charge.

Line 19. Ordinary dividends
Ordinary dividends paid and proposed for the year; net of tax credit.

Line 20. Extraordinary items, as reported
Extraordinary items are items not arising in the ordinary course of business, and in a company's accounts are added or subtracted below the line, i.e. after the profit on which earnings per share are calculated. They include extraordinary income, charges and tax.

Line 22. Ordinary shares in issue
This is the average number of ordinary shares in issue during the year, i.e. the number of ordinary shares which a company should use in its e.p.s. calculations; it normally appears in the accounts in a note on e.p.s.

Line 23. Normalised earnings per share
Line 18 divided by Line 22. The difference between this figure and the reported e.p.s. is, as we have said, a measure of the difference between a 'full' tax charge and the actual tax charge and of any variations from normal practice in reporting pre-tax profits.

Line 25. Reported fully diluted earnings per share
Companies are not obliged to report fully diluted e.p.s. unless dilution is material, but they can easily be calculated if required, as we describe on page 105. A similar calculation can be made using normalised profits attributable to ordinary shareholders to obtain normalised fully diluted e.p.s., but in practice the effect will be very similar to the effect on reported e.p.s., unless normalised profits differ widely from reported profits.

Line 26. Extraordinary items per share
This is just a convenient way of expressing extraordinary items to see if they are significant in relation to earnings per share.

Line 27. Dividend per share
As reported (i.e. net of tax), expressed in pence.

Lines 27 and 28. Dividend cover and Normalised cover
In straightforward cases where Corporation Tax liability is not affected by the proportion of profits distributed (i.e. where ACT on full distribution can be entirely offset against Corporation Tax, without penalty, see page 92) the covers can be obtained by dividing the reported e.p.s. or normalised e.p.s. by the dividend. If full distribution increases the tax liability, usually owing to overseas earnings, the dividend cover becomes complicated and, if not shown in the accounts, can only be calculated approximately (page 190).

Profitability ratios

The ratios in Lines 101 and 102 are measures of trading performance, and thus are based on capital employed in trading (see page 178), while ROCE (return on capital employed) in Line 103 is for the overall performance of the company, and is therefore based on the overall capital employed.

ANALYSIS SHEET 2 – ASSETS EMPLOYED

This page contains two key ratios, the current ratio and the acid test, both of which can be seriously distorted if current assets are overstated and/or current liabilities are understated. Care should therefore be taken to adjust for any incorrect classification: for example, the inclusion of a housebuilder's land bank as a current asset if it comprises more than a year's supply of building land.

Line 29. Land and buildings
The accounts will give the net book value (cost or valuation less accumulated depreciation). Unfortunately the figure for capital employed and thus the return on capital employed can be very much distorted by the assets being shown at unrealistically low values, and this distortion is most likely to occur when a high proportion of land and buildings has not been revalued in the last few years; so the details of revaluations, contained in the notes to the accounts, should be checked to see if valuations are reasonably up to date.

Line 30. Surplus on revaluation
Companies sometimes report that they have had revaluations of land and buildings carried out, but have not written up the assets accordingly in their books. In these cases the surplus arising on revaluation can be added separately in Line 30 to produce a more accurate figure for capital employed, with a balancing entry on Analysis Sheet 3. Alternatively, Line 30 may be renamed to show

a more detailed breakdown of fixed assets, e.g. where a company shows an unusual category of assets peculiar to the nature of its business, for example 'keg cider installations' in the case of H. P. BULMER. If this is done, a balancing entry is not, of course, required on Analysis Sheet 3.

Line 31. Plant and equipment
This includes Plant and machinery, and Fixtures, fitting, tools and equipment. It is normally shown at cost less accumulated depreciation.

Payments on account
Where payments on account and assets in course of construction are shown under tangible assets in CA 1985 formats, amounts in respect of land and buildings should be included in Line 29 and for plant and equipment in Line 31.

Line 32. Investment grants
If investment grants are shown separately (as opposed to being deducted from the cost of an asset when it is acquired, see page 41), they should be deducted from the book value of fixed assets. If they have been included in the figure for reserves, they should also be deducted on Analysis Sheet 3 in calculating net assets attributable.

Line 32A. Intangibles
Pending decisions on the current proposals in ED 47, we would recommend including, in the calculation of capital employed, both Intangible fixed

assets whose *cost* can be clearly identified and Cumulative purchased goodwill that has been written off directly to reserves. We would not include Intangibles that have been 'valued' e.g. RHM Brand Names. See page 179.

Line 34. Associates
This figure is the cost of any investment in associated undertakings and participating interests less any amounts written off, plus the investing group's share of the post-acquisition retained profits and reserves of the associated undertakings and participating interests in both places (see Chapter 17).

Line 35. Other investments
These are long-term investments, and may include Loans made by the company and Own shares. In our view this figure should include all investments that cannot readily be converted into cash at a price guaranteed within narrow limits; see comments on Line 39, and Chapter 7.

Line 36. Stocks and WIP
See Chapter 8.

Line 37. Trade debtors
Where trade debts to the company have been settled by bills of exchange which the company is holding to maturity, and the amount involved is shown as 'bills receivable' (page 64), this may be included in the figure for Trade debtors.

Line 38. Other debtors
Include prepayments and accrued income, and any other item shown under debtors (other than trade debtors).

Line 39. Cash and other liquid assets
See comments on cash on Line 46. Other liquid assets are near-cash items such as government securities and local authority bonds due for redemption or repayment within 12 months. Longer-dated gilt-edged securities may be included on the grounds that they are easily saleable although prices may fluctuate, but holdings of ordinary shares should not be included in current assets as their value can easily fall and, even if quoted, the shares may not be marketable in any quantity.

Line 41. Trade creditors
This item is the amount owing to trade creditors falling due for payment within one year. Where amounts due to trade creditors have been settled by bills of exchange which have not yet fallen due, the amount outstanding may be shown in the accounts under 'bills of exchange payable' (page 64). Trade bills may be included on this line, but all other bills payable should be included on Line 47.

Line 42. Taxation
This is the taxation and social security payable within the next 12 months, and includes the ACT payable on proposed dividends.

Line 44. Other short-term creditors
This includes payments received on account, accruals and deferred income, and other creditors falling due within one year. It does not include debentures, loans, overdraft and bills of exchange (see Lines 46 and 47).

Line 45. Subtotal
This subtotal is struck before the inclusion of Loans and overdraft (Line 46) and Bills of exchange payable (Line 47) so as to avoid these two items being deducted from assets in the calculation of capital employed (see page 178). Both items are types of debt and are included in Analysis Sheet 3 as methods of financing.

Line 46. Loans (under one year) and overdraft
This includes debentures, bank and any other loans falling due within one year, plus overdraft. Some analysts net out any cash against the overdraft (that is, deduct cash from the overdraft), thus showing a lower figure for overdraft and reducing the figure for capital employed. Where it is known that a company's bank nets out cash balances in calculating interest charges on overdraft, netting out can be justified. On the other hand, if cash balances are retained in overseas subsidiaries, or if the management chooses to maintain cash balances that are independent of overdrafts elsewhere in the group, it is not realistic to net them out (page 179).

Line 47. Bills of exchange payable
Bills of exchange issued under an acceptance credit facility are only another method of borrowing (page 64) and can be treated in the same way as an overdraft; that is, by adding them in the Financing table on Analysis Sheet 3, rather than netting them out against assets in calculating capital employed on Analysis Sheet 2. Bills clearly identified as Trade bills should be included on Line 41.

Line 49. Trading capital employed
This is the sum of all assets except Associated undertakings and participating interests and Other investments, less all current liabilities except Loans and overdraft (Line 46) and Bills of exchange payable (Line 47).

Line 50. Overall capital employed
Associates on Line 34 and Other investments on Line 35 are added to Line 49.

Lines 105 to 110. Ratios
Each of these ratios is described in Chapter 24.

ANALYSIS SHEET 3 – FINANCING

Line 51. Ordinary capital
The total nominal value of both ordinary and deferred shares issued.

Line 52. Share premium account
The details of premiums paid on the issue of shares for more than their nominal value (see page 19) is usually the first item in the note on Reserves.

Line 54. Intangibles
Purchased goodwill that has been added back in Line 33A should also be added here, to make Lines 50 and 69 balance.

Line 55. Net assets attributable
These are the net tangible assets attributable to the ordinary shareholders.

Line 30. Surplus on revaluation
This is the balancing entry for any surplus on revaluation shown in Line 30 on Analysis Sheet 2.

Line 56. Redeemable preference shares
Redeemable preference shares that are redeemable within 10 years need listing separately from *Other preference shares*, as we count them as debt in the capital structure of the company because they eventually have to be repaid.

Line 58. Minorities
This represents the interest of minority shareholders in partially owned subsidiary companies.

Line 59. Deferred taxation and other provisions
Deferred tax is mainly due to capital allowances being given to the company for tax purposes faster than the company applies depreciation in its accounts (page 86). Other provisions may include provisions made for pensions and product guarantees.

Line 60. Long-term creditors
Amounts falling due after more than one year, excluding loans, overdraft, bills of exchange and amounts owed to associated and related companies.

Lines 62 to 67. Debenture and other loans (over one year)
The best way of presenting information on loan capital and other loans depends very much on the debt structure of the company; it may be useful to show:

(a) the division between loans repayable in less than five years and more than five years, which Schedule 4, para. 48 of the Companies Act 1985 requires to be reported;
(b) debenture, unsecured loan stock, convertible loan stock, bank loans and other loans separately;

(c) the breakdown between sterling denominated and foreign currency loans.

Lines 46 and 47. Loans (under one year) and overdraft, and bills of exchange payable
As already discussed, these current liabilities are *not* netted out against assets in Sheet 2, but are included here in Sheet 3 as part of a company's financing.

Line 68. Total debt
This includes Redeemable preference shares (Line 56), Loans (over one year) (Lines 62 to 67), Loans (under one year) and bank overdraft (Line 46), and Bills of exchange payable (Line 47).

Line 69. Capital employed
This figure should be the same as Line 50, Overall capital employed, on Analysis Sheet 2. The cause of any discrepancy should be found and corrected.

Line 70. Net asset value
This is the book value of the assets attributable to each ordinary share:

$$\frac{\text{Line 55}}{\text{Line 51}} \times \text{nominal value of ordinary share}$$

Further calculations can be made to obtain a fully diluted net asset value (i.e. allowing for paying up partly paid shares, for converting convertibles and for exercising warrants), but in practice the difference this makes is seldom significant.

Line 71. Net asset value plus revaluation
Line 30 from Analysis Sheet 2, any surplus on revaluation that has not been written into the books, is added to Line 55 in calculating the net asset value.

Line 72. Contingent liabilities
This is an item all on its own, usually to be found tucked away near the end of the notes to the accounts; it is easily overlooked but can be very important (see page 68). The figure that is required is the total of commitments and contingencies *outside* the group; that is, not including guarantees of borrowings by subsidiaries but including, for example, guarantees on behalf of associates.

Line 114. Contingent liabilities/n.t.a.
This ratio shows the extent of contingent liabilities outside the company or group in relation to the net tangible assets attributable to the ordinary shareholders. (A figure of more than 2–3% is unusual, and worth further investigation.)

Analysis Sheet 1 Profit and loss account

Line		19 . . . £ . . .	19 . . . £ . . .	% Change	Remarks
	Company:	Year to			
1	**Turnover or sales**				
2	− Cost of sales				
	− Distribution costs				
	− Administrative expenses				
3	+ Other operating income				
4	± Adjustments				
5	= **'Normalised' trading profit**				Sum of 1 to 4
6	+ Associates				
7	Investment and other income				
8	= Earnings before interest and tax				5 + 6 + 7
9	− Interest paid				
10	= **'Normalised' pre-tax profit**				8 − 9

Calculation of 'normalised' earnings per share

Line		19 . . .	19 . . .	% Change	Remarks
10	'Normalised' pre-tax profit				From 10 above
11	− Taxation reported				Lines 11 + 12, *or*
12	− Potential deferred tax				Line 13 on its
13	− Estimated tax				own
14	= **Normalised profit after tax**				10 − 11 − 12 − 13
15	− Minorities				
16	= Profits attrib. to company				14 − 15
17	− Preference dividends				
18	= **Norm. profit attrib. to ord.**				16 − 17
19	− Ordinary dividends				
20	± Extraordinary items				
21	= **Normalised retentions**				18 − 19 ± 20
22	Ordinary shares in issue				Average for year
23	Normalised e.p.s.				18 ÷ 22
24	Reported e.p.s.				
25	Reported fully diluted e.p.s.				
26	Extraordinary items per share				20 ÷ 22
27	Dividend per share (Div. cover)				
28	Normalised cover				

Profitability ratios

Line		19 . . .	19 . . .	% Change	Remarks
100	Trading profit/Sales				5 ÷ 1 as %
101	Trading profit/Capital employed				5 ÷ 49 as %
102	Sales/Capital employed				1 ÷ 49 as %
103	ROCE				8 ÷ 50 as %
104					
105	Interest cover				8 ÷ 9

198

Analysis Sheet 2 Assets employed

Line		19 . . .	19 . . .	% Change	Remarks
Company:		Year to			
		£ . . .	£ . . .		
Fixed assets					
29	Land and buildings				
30	+ Surplus on revaluation				
31	+ Plant and equipment				
32	− Investment grants				
32A	+ Intangible fixed assets				
33	= Total tangible fixed assets				Sum of 29 to 32A
34	Associates				
35	Other investments				
Current assets					
36	Stocks and WIP				
37	+ Trade debtors				
38	+ Other debtors				
39	+ Cash and other liquid assets				
40	= Total current assets				Sum of 36 to 39
Current liabilities					
41	Trade creditors				
42	+ Taxation				
43	+ Dividends				
44	+ Other short-term creditors				
45	= Subtotal				Sum of 41 to 44
46	+ Loans (under 1 year) and overdraft				
47	+ Bills of exchange payable				
48	= Total current liabilities				45 + 46 + 47
49	Trading capital employed				33 + 40 − 45
50	**Overall capital employed**				34 + 35 + 49
Ratios					
105	Current ratio				40 ÷ 48
106	Acid test ratio				(40 − 36) ÷ 48
107	Stocks/Sales				36 ÷ 1 as %
108	Trade debtors/Sales				37 ÷ 1 as %
109	Trade creditors/Sales				41 ÷ 1 as %
110	Working capital/Sales				(36 + 37 − 41) ÷ 1 as %

Analysis Sheet 3 Financing

Line	Company:	Year to 19 . . . £ . . .	19 . . . £ . . .	% Change	Remarks
51	Ordinary capital (Nominal value each:)				
52	+ Share premium a/c				
53	+ Other reserves				
32	− Investment grants				Only if in reserves
54	+ Intangible assets				
55	= Net assets attributable				51 + 52 + 53 − 32 + 54
30	Surplus on revaluation				From Analysis Sheet 2 (if any)
56	Redeemable preference shares				Under 10 years
57	Other preference shares				
58	+ Minorities				
59	+ Deferred tax and other provisions				
60	+ Long-term creditors				
61	= **Subtotal**				Sum of 57 to 60
Debenture and other loans					
62					
63	+				
64	+				
65	+				
66	+				
67	+				
46	+ Loans (under 1 year) and overdraft				From Analysis Sheet 2
47	+ Bills of exchange payable				
68	= **Total debt**				56 + (62 to 67) + 46 + 47
69	**Capital employed**				55 + 30 + 61 + 68
70	Net asset value (n.a.v.)				(55 ÷ 51) × Nominal value
71	n.a.v. plus revaluation				[(55 + 30) ÷ 51] × Nominal value
72	Contingent liabilities				
Ratios					
112	Debt/Equity				68 ÷ (55 + 58) as %
113	Debt/Capital employed				68 ÷ 69 as %
114	Contingent liabilities/net assets				72 ÷ 55 as %

SUMMARY SHEET 1 – SUMMARY OF PROFIT AND LOSS ACCOUNTS

In practice it can be confusing to show normalised figures mixed in with figures actually reported, so the only special figures shown in the profit and loss summary sheet are:

(*a*) 'normalised' trading profit;
(*b*) adjustments – to indicate reporting variations;
(*c*) normalised e.p.s. – to show the effect of (*b*) and the application of a 'full' tax charge.

Where a company's reported profits do not require adjustment it may be found satisfactory to dispense with Analysis Sheet 1 and the calculation of normalised e.p.s.: the summary can then be compiled direct from the accounts, as the figure for percentage of pre-tax profits taken by taxation will show up any abnormal tax charge.

Summary Sheet 1 does not, however, allow each item's percentage change from the previous year to be shown unless the % column provided is used for that purpose instead of showing each item as a percentage of reported pre-tax profits.

SUMMARY SHEET 2 – SUMMARY OF ASSETS EMPLOYED

This summary sheet gives a slightly compressed version of the information in Analysis Sheet 2, and shows each item as a percentage of capital employed instead of the percentage change from the previous year. Here again the summary sheet can, with practice, be compiled straight from a company's accounts.

SUMMARY SHEET 3 – SUMMARY OF FINANCING

This is the counterpart to Summary Sheet 2 and similarly, with practice, can be completed straight from a company's balance sheet without using Analysis Sheet 3.

SUMMARY SHEETS 4 AND 5 – SUMMARY OF SOURCES AND APPLICATIONS

As discussed in Chapter 19, the contents and the presentation of source and application statements vary considerably from company to company, so it can be useful to put the information provided into a standard format. It may also be useful to look at the pattern over the years, in particular at the use of external financing (funds from other sources), the growth in working capital and the trends in liquidity. As with earlier sheets, these formats should be adjusted to taste and to cater for any special features of the company being examined.

In general our formats follow those in the Examples in SSAP 10, except that Applications of funds are shown as positive amounts on Summary Sheet 5, rather than negative amounts on the same sheet as Sources, and changes in Working capital and changes in Liquidity are shown separately.

Note, in particular, that Line S1 on the Sources page is Profit before tax *less* minorities. If minorities have not been deducted by the company then dividends paid to minorities should be inserted as an application (Line A3) and there will be no minority retentions on Line S6. As the treatment of minorities illustrates, the Sources and Applications pro-formas will often need modification to cater for the varied ways in which information is presented by individual companies.

Summary Sheet 1 Summary of profit and loss accounts

Company:

Line		19... £...	19... %	19... £...	19... %	19... £...	19... %	Year ending 19... £...	19... %	19... £...	19... %	19... £...	19... %
1	**Turnover or sales**												
5	'Normalised' trading profit												
6	+ Associates												
7	+ Investment income												
9	− Interest paid												
4	± Adjustments (removed)												
	= Reported pre-tax profit		100		100		100		100		100		100
11	− Taxation reported												
	= Reported profit after tax												
	− Reported minorities												
	= Profits attrib. to company												
17	− Preference dividends												
	= Profits attrib. to ord.												
19	− Ordinary dividends												
20	± Extraordinary items												
	= Retentions												
23	Normalised e.p.s.												
24	Reported e.p.s.												
25	Reported fully diluted e.p.s.												
	Profitability ratios												
100	Trading profit/Sales												
101	Trading profit/Capital employed												
102	Sales/Capital employed												
103	ROCE												
104													
105	Interest cover												

Summary Sheet 2 Summary of assets employed

Company:

Line		19... £...	%	19... £...	%	19... £...	%	19... £...	%	19... £...	%
29	Land and buildings										
30	+ Surplus on revaluation										
31	+ Plant and equipment										
32	− Investment grants										
32A	+ Intangible fixed assets										
33	= **Total fixed assets**										
34	Associated and related companies										
35	Other investments										
36	Stocks and WIP										
37	+ Trade debtors										
38	+ Other debtors										
39	+ Cash and other liquid assets										
40	= **Total current assets**										
41	Trade creditors										
42	+ Taxation										
43	+ Dividends										
44	+ Other short-term creditors										
45	= **Subtotal**										
46	+ Loans (under 1 year) and overdraft										
47	+ Bills of exchange payable										
48	= **Total current liabilities**										
49	Trading capital employed										
50	**Overall capital employed**	100		100		100		100		100	

Year ending

Ratios

Line											
105	Current ratio										
106	Acid test ratio										
107	Stocks/Sales										
108	Trade debtors/Sales										
109	Trade creditors/Sales										
110	Working capital/Sales										

Summary Sheet 3 Summary of financing

Company:

Year ending

Line		19... £...	%	19... £...	%	19... £...	%	19... £...	%	19... £...	%
51	Ordinary capital										
52	+ Share premium a/c										
53	+ Other reserves										
32	− Investment grants										
54	+ Intangibles										
55	= Net assets attributable										
30	Surplus on revaluation										
56	Redeemable preference shares										
57	Other preference shares										
58	+ Minorities										
59	+ Deferred tax and other provisions										
60	+ Long-term creditors										
61	= **Subtotal**										
62											
63	+										
64	+										
65	+										
66	+										
67	+										
46	+ Loans (under 1 year) and overdraft										
47	+ Bills of exchange										
68	= **Total debt**		100		100		100		100		100
69	**Capital employed**		100		100		100		100		100
70	Net asset value (n.a.v.)										
71	n.a.v. + revaluation										
72	Contingent liabilities										

Ratios

| 113 | Debt/Capital employed |
| 114 | Contingent liabilities/net assets |

Summary Sheet 4 Summary of sources of funds

Company:		Year ending				
Line		19... £...	19... £...	19... £...	19... £...	19... £...
S1	Profits before tax (*less* minorities)					
S2	± Extraordinary items					
S3						
Non-monetary Adjustments						
S4	+ Depreciation					
S5	+ Other provisions					
S6	+ Minority retentions					
S7	− Retained in associates					
S8	± Exchange adjustments					
S9	− Profit } on disposal of					
S10	+ Loss } fixed assets					
S11						
S12						
S13						
S14	**= Generated from operations**					
Funds from other sources						
S15	+ Rights issue of shares					
S16	+ Other issues of shares					
S17	+ Increase in loans					
S18	− Decrease in loans					
S19	+ Sale of fixed assets					
S20	+ Sale of investments					
S21	+ Disposals					
S22						
S23	**= Sources total**					

Summary Sheet 5 Summary of application of funds

Company:							
Line		19....	19....	19....	19....	19....	19....
		£....	£....	£....	£....	£....	£....
A1	Tax paid						
A2	+ Dividends paid						
A3							
A4	+ Purchase of fixed assets						
A5	+ Acquisitions						
A6	+ Investment in associates						
A7	+ Purchase of investments						
A8							
A9							
A10							
A11	+ Increase } in working − Decrease } capital						
A12	+ Increase } in net − Decrease } liquid funds						
A13	= **Application total**						

Working capital

A14	± Increase (decrease) in stocks						
A15	± Increase (decrease) in debtors						
A16	± (Increase) decrease in creditors						
A11	= Net increase (decrease)						

Liquidity

A17	± Increase (decrease) in cash						
A18	± (Increase) decrease in overdraft						
A12	= Increase (decrease) in liquidity						

Chapter 26

REVELATION

Some years ago we met a young chartered accountant who had become a stockbroker's analyst in the days before the Extel league tables, when analysts' salaries were really quite modest. We asked him why he had changed careers: 'I got fed up with audits starting with an interview with the MD, who would tell us what he wanted the pre-tax figure to be.'

An exaggeration? He claimed not. However, since then refinements in company law plus the development of SSAPs have made creative accounting somewhat easier to detect, e.g. the *Financial Times*' comment on BUNZL's accounting policies: 'Bunzl seems to move the goalposts every year.'

But analysts must still expect some companies, particularly those headed by a 'strong personality' or fearful of a takeover, to try to show continuous growth year after year, and to 'pull out all the stops' to avoid reporting a downturn.

If companies stray too far from the fundamental accounting concept of *prudence*, the overriding concept, as you will remember from Chapter 1, the whole thing can come apart at the seams. Take the case of CRAY ELECTRONICS.

On 20 July 1989, Cray announced pre-tax profit of £17.03 million for the year ended 29 April 1989, up 29.8% with e.p.s. up 18.2%. Less than a month later it was announced that the Chairman/Chief Executive had decided to relinquish his position as chief executive, and that an independent firm of accountants, Price Waterhouse, had been called in to review the group's accounting policies. Their recommendations were adopted, reducing the pre-tax figure to £5.439 million; details were given in a circular to shareholders the following November:

CRAY ELECTRONICS *Extracts from circular to shareholders on revised results for the year ended 29 April 1989*

Review of accounting policies

Price Waterhouse were engaged to advise the Board as to the suitability of the accounting policies of the Group to the extent that they had a material effect on the results for the year ended 29 April 1989, having regard to best accounting practice in the electronics sector. Price Waterhouse did not conduct an audit. The key recommendations of the review, with which the Group's auditors, Ernst & Young, concur, were as follows:

Capitalisation of research and development expenditure
The capitalisation of development expenditure should cease . . . except to the extent that it is recoverable on contracts with third parties. Whilst the capitalisation of development expenditure is permitted under the relevant SSAP, the new policy accords with general practice in the sector.

Property profits
The 'sale-and-leaseback' property transactions carried out during 1988/89 should be reclassified as finance rather than operating leases . . .

Extraordinary items
The costs of closing the remaining . . . which are expected to be completed during 1989/90, should be provided for in the 1988/89 accounts. In future periods, Cray should restrict the use of extraordinary items relating to closures only to significant business segments such as these.

Recognition of income and costs
A generally more prudent approach should be adopted towards the point at which income and costs are

recognised, particularly in the area of long-term contracts.

Sales to joint venture companies

The profit on the sales of Cray Advance Materials machines to the Group's associated/subsidiary companies should be eliminated.

Use of merger accounting

The use of merger accounting should be restricted to acquisitions in which the commercial substance of the transaction justifies this approach.

Post balance sheet events review

The board has carried out a further review of the Group's main contracts and year-end stock provisions . . . The 1988/89 accounts have been adjusted to include additional provisions, principally those relating to losses on long-term contracts, which the Board considered appropriate.

Revised results

The effect on pre-tax profits of implementing the recommendations of the accounting policy review and the post-balance sheet events review is set out below:

	1989 £000	1988 £000
Profit before tax as previously published	17,030	13,120
Accounting policy changes		
– write off of development expenditure[1]	(4,196)	(2,298)
– reclassify sale and leasebacks of properties as finance leases	(2,473)	—
– other items[2]	(2,232)	—
Post balance sheet events review	(2,690)	—
Revised profit before tax	5,439	10,822

[1] The write off of development expenditure includes amounts included in work in progress relating to projects still in progress at the balance sheet date.
[2] Other items comprise adjustments relating to income recognition, long-term contract accounting and sales to joint venture companies.

CRAY ELECTRONICS was a particularly acute case of over-optimistic accounting: we hope the new Accounting Standards Board will tighten up the rules. Meanwhile here is a list of accounting practices that some companies use to enhance their profits, together with a few more examples.

Depreciation

- Stop depreciating freehold and long-leasehold buildings; e.g. KINGFISHER page 34. This is now fairly standard practice amongst retailers.
- Extend the estimated useful life of assets; e.g.

CITYVISION page 39 and CHRISTIAN SALVESEN page 73.

- Put an unrealistically high figure on the estimated residual value of assets, in particular computer-leasing companies not allowing sufficiently for the risk of obsolescence; e.g. ATLANTIC COMPUTERS, taken over by BRITISH & COMMONWEALTH for £410 million in July 1988 after the founder, who was also chief executive, had been killed in a motor racing accident, and put into receivership by B & C less than two years later.
- Do not amortise intangible assets, even if they become valueless at a known future date, unless the total value of *all* intangibles of that type, including those not capitalised, falls below the value shown in the balance sheet. For example, THORN EMI's acquisition of a portfolio of music publishing copyrights from SBK in June 1989 for $295 million:

THORN EMI *Extract of accounting policies*

Music publishing copyrights

Music Publishing Copyrights purchased up to and including 31 March 1989 have been written off to reserves on acquisition. Copyrights acquired on or after 1 April 1989 will be treated as an intangible asset in the Group balance sheet. The capitalised amount of such copyrights, being their purchase cost, will only be subject to amortisation to the extent that royalty income generated by the total music publishing copyright portfolio is insufficient to support its book value.

Capitalising expenses

- On start-up costs; e.g. SOCK SHOP, page 74, and HOGG ROBINSON:

HOGG ROBINSON *Accounting policy on intangible assets*

Deferred Revenue Expenditure

Net revenue losses incurred on the opening of new branches in Hogg Robinson Property Services up to the end of the first six months trading are capitalised and amortised over the five years commencing in the next financial year following opening of the office (if opened before November) or the beginning of the seventh month (if opened in November or later). These losses include revenue costs incurred in preparing the office for trading.

- Capitalise interest on costs incurred on patents. For example, LONDON INTER-

NATIONAL GROUP's accounts for the year to 31 March 1989 showed:

LONDON INTERNATIONAL GROUP *Note to the 1989 accounts*

Intangible assets

	1989 £m	1988 £m
Trademarks:		
Cost 1 April 1988 and 31 March 1989	32.0	32.0
Patents:		
Cost 1 April 1988	8.3	—
Interest capitalised	1.0	0.4
Other expenditure	0.3	7.9
Amortisation	—	—
Cost 31 March 1989	9.6	8.3
Intangible assets 31 March 1989	41.6	40.3

The previous year's accounts had only shown a single figure: 'Trademarks acquired during the year: £40,298,000.' Had the £1.0 million of interest capitalised in 1989 been charged to the profit and loss account, earnings per share, which were reported as increasing from 17.50p to 17.88p, would have been marginally *down*.

- Capitalise interest on borrowings to finance developments; *e.g.* SAINSBURY page 74. This is commonplace practice, but should be viewed with suspicion if interest is rolled up on sites before development starts, e.g. REGENTCREST page 75, or if capitalisation of interest continues after completion until a property is fully let, e.g. LADBROKE page 74. A variation on this theme is to issue a zero coupon bond and capitalise the discount on issue; e.g. GREYCOAT page 25.
- Be 'generous' in the amount of R & D capitalised, as CRAY ELECTRONICS was before the independent review of accounting policies.
- Capitalise the costs of obtaining new lessees; e.g. SOUTHERN BUSINESS GROUP (SBG), whose business is copier leasing:

SOUTHERN BUSINESS GROUP *Notes to the 1989 accounts*

Intangible and tangible fixed assets

	Expenditure to secure forward contracted income £000	Other assets £000	Total £000	1988 £000
Intangible	23,832	—	23,832	17,252
Tangible	16,780	14,196	30,976	24,239
	40,612	14,196	54,808	41,491

Expenditure to secure forward contracted income:

	Contract equipment £000	Settlement costs £000	Selling costs £000	Total £000
Cost:				
At 1 October 1988	18,352	6,560	19,479	44,391
Additions:				
In respect of companies acquired	279	109	520	908
Deferred consideration	—	629	—	629
Other	7,396	1,509	7,675	16,580
Disposals	(1,121)	(18)	—	(1,139)
At 30 September 1989	24,906	8,789	27,674	61,369

Accounting policy on amortisation and depreciation

Expenditure to secure forward contracted income is amortised on a straight-line basis over the periods of the contracts which range from between five and nine years. This expenditure represents the cost of the equipment, the selling and settlement costs incurred in placing the equipment. Depreciation on other fixed assets is charged at the following rates:

SBG maintains that capitalising 'Settlement costs', the costs of winding up the existing copier contracts of a new customer, and 'Selling costs', which cover the salesmen's commission, gives a true and fair view, as these costs are fully recoverable from the future income stream their contracts secure, and their auditors agree. The effect of this policy in 1989 was to produce a pre-tax profit of £10.251 million, with a tax charge of only £1.025 million!

Writing off direct to reserves

- In translating overseas earnings, change your policy from closing to average if the preponderance of those earnings comes from countries with softer currencies than Sterling; the difference between average and closing rate translation is then charged direct to reserves; e.g. BUNZL page 132. If the earnings come predominantly from harder-currency countries, translate at closing rate.

- Reduce interest charges by borrowing in a hard currency, where interest rates are low, to finance activities in soft-currency countries, where borrowing in local currencies would incur higher interest charges. Any currency losses can then be written off direct to reserves. For example, the analyst should ask questions about the figures that POLLY PECK reported for the 16 months to 31 December 1988:

POLLY PECK *Extracts from 1988 accounts*

Profit and loss account

	£m
Trading profit	146.7
Other operating income	10.2
	156.9
Finance costs (Note 7)	12.8
	144.1

Note 7 Finance costs

Interest payable:
On bank loans, overdrafts and other borrowings:

– repayable within five years	34.8
– repayable after five years	5.4
Finance lease interest	0.4
	40.6
Less interest receivable	27.8
	12.8

Note 22 Retained profit

. . .

Exchange variances	
On net investment overseas	(170.3)
On use of average exchange rates on overseas results	(12.1)

Acquisitions and disposals

- Write the assets of an acquisition down with 'the greatest possible prudence'. Doing so will increase purchased goodwill which can, at present, be written off direct to reserves. It will also give more scope for selling off some of the assets at a profit which can be taken above the line to boost future reported profits. But see the proposals of ED 44 on page 110.

- If you find that acquisitions prove more expensive to sort out than initially expected, write off further goodwill retrospectively; e.g. TI GROUP:

TI GROUP *Extract from note on reserves*

Goodwill written off

	£m.
At 31 December 1988	(268.8)
Goodwill written off	
– current year acquisitions	(32.4)
– prior year acquisitions	(59.3)
At 31 December 1989	(360.5)

TI gave details of the acquisitions concerned, with the amounts involved in each, and the Financial Review noted that 'Goodwill relating to acquisitions made prior to 1989 is now finally determined', but we would have preferred the previous year's accounts to have warned shareholders that the figure for goodwill written off was *provisional*.

- Merger account acquisitions made late in the accounting period to bring a whole year of their profits into the P & L account, see page 112. This is particularly useful for hiding a downturn in the profits of the original group.

- Make generous provisions for closure and reorganisation costs in acquired companies to avoid future charges to the P & L account and to increase the likelihood of being able to release some of these provisions back into the P & L account to boost profits in future years.

- Take trading losses of subsidiaries scheduled for disposal below the line, even when they have not been disposed of at the balance sheet date; e.g. BUNZL:

BUNZL *Extract from note to 1988 accounts*

Change in accounting policy

The Directors have adopted an accounting policy under which provision is made for the anticipated costs of withdrawing from business segments, including the trading results from the date of commencement of implementation of the decision to the anticipated disposal date. The adoption of this accounting policy has resulted in an extraordinary charge of £15.2 million, of which £4.4 million has been utilised during the period in respect of net losses from the commencement of implementation.

Consolidation

- Deconsolidate lossmaking subsidiaries, as METAL BOX (now the MB GROUP) did with its Nigerian subsidiaries in 1985 'in the light of the severe import restrictions in Nigeria', making a £9.4 million provision as an extra-ordinary item.
- Make marginal adjustments to holdings in partially owned subsidiaries to turn them into associates when they are not trading profitably, and vice versa. Similarly turn associates into investments in poor years, see page 125.

Extraordinary and exceptional items

- Take the profit on the sale and leaseback of properties above the line; e.g. KINGFISHER page 95.
- Take profits on equity investments above the line, but losses below the line; e.g. FARNELL ELECTRONICS page 154.

Income recognition

- Long-term contracts. As Cray Electronics demonstrated, there is plenty of scope for imprudence in the recognition of profits on long-term contracts.
- Leasing. SSAP 21 has tightened up the rules to prevent 'front-ending', see page 71, but there is still plenty of scope for adjusting provisions for bad and doubtful rentals.
- Take profits on sales to subsidiaries/ associates, as Cray Electronics did. A blatant example of this practice was FEEDEX AGRICULTURAL INDUSTRIES (now USBORNE) which in 1988 sold a development site from one joint venture to another and took the profit into the P & L account. When the auditors disagreed and qualified the ac-counts, they were replaced, see page 155.

Deferred taxation

- Take advantage of the discretion given by SSAP 15 in the provision of deferred tax; see page 86. (We recommend analysts to apply a full tax charge, see page 194.)

Fraud

Of course, fraud is another matter. It is particular-ly hard to detect if the company's auditors don't ring any warning bells. But even then a good analyst may have his or her suspicions aroused. For example, when INTERNATIONAL SIGNAL & CONTROL (ISC) created bogus clients in their international arms supply business and managed to pull the wool over FERRANTI's eyes in an alleged £215 million fraud, one analyst wrote over a year beforehand:

'ISC's disappointing results . . . inevitably rekindled the major investor concerns about the company: name-ly, the lack of knowledge about the products and customers of the International division.'

APPENDICES

APPENDIX 1 – CURRENT SSAPs AND EDs

The following Statements of Standard Accounting Practice and Exposure Drafts were current in June 1990:

		Date of issue
SSAP	Explanatory foreword (Revised Aug 1986)	Jan 1971
SSAP 1	Accounting for associated companies (Revised Apr 1982)	Jan 1971
SSAP 2	Disclosure of accounting policies	Nov 1971
SSAP 3	Earnings per share (Revised Aug 1974)	Feb 1972
SSAP 4	The accounting treatment of government grants	Apr 1974
SSAP 5	Accounting for value added tax	Apr 1974
SSAP 6	Extraordinary items and prior year adjustments (Revised Aug 1986)	Apr 1974
SSAP 8	The treatment of taxation under the imputation system in the accounts of companies (Revised Dec 1977)	Aug 1974
Addendum to SSAP 8		Mar 1988
SSAP 9	Stocks and long-term contracts (Revised Sept 1988)	May 1975
SSAP 10	Statements of source and application of funds (Revised Jun 1978)	Jul 1975
SSAP 12	Accounting for depreciation (Revised Jan 1987)	Dec 1977
SSAP 13	Accounting for research and development (Revised Jan 1989)	Dec 1977
SSAP 14	Group accounts	Sept 1978
SSAP 15	Accounting for deferred taxation (Revised May 1985)	Oct 1978
SSAP 17	Accounting for post balance sheet events	Aug 1980
SSAP 18	Accounting for contingencies	Aug 1980
SSAP 19	Accounting for investment properties	Nov 1981
SSAP 20	Foreign currency translation	Apr 1983
SSAP 21	Accounting for leases and hire purchase contracts	Aug 1984
SSAP 22	Accounting for goodwill (Revised Jul 1989)	Dec 1984
SSAP 23	Accounting for acquisitions and mergers	Apr 1985
SSAP 24	Accounting for pension costs	May 1988
ED 42	Accounting for special purpose transactions	Mar 1988
ED 43	The accounting treatment of government grants	Jun 1988
ED 45	Segmental reporting	Nov 1988
ED 46	Disclosure of related party transactions	Apr 1989
ED 47	Accounting for goodwill	Feb 1990
ED 48	Accounting for acquisitions and mergers	Feb 1990
ED 49	Reflecting the substance of transactions in assets and liabilities	May 1990

In addition to SSAPs and EDs, the Accounting Standards Committee (ASC) in 1984 introduced a new form of consultative document, the *Statement of Intent (SOI)*, designed to give early indication of how the ASC proposes to deal with a particular accounting matter. It also introduced the *Statement of Recommended Practice (SORP)*, to give guidance on topics where an SSAP would not be justified. Companies are encouraged to comply with SORPs, but they will not be mandatory.

APPENDIX 2 – PRESENT VALUE

£1 received in a year's time is worth less than £1 received today, because £1 available today could be invested to earn interest for the next 12 months. If £1 now could be invested at a rate of interest i (expressed as a decimal), it would be worth £$(1 + i)$ in a year's time. If the £$(1 + i)$ at the end of the year was left invested, it would be worth £$(1 + i)$ $\times (1 + i) =$ £$(1 + i)^2$ at the end of the second year, and £$(1 + i)^3$ at the end of the third year, and so on; in other words, it would earn compound interest at the rate of i per annum.

Present value is like compound interest in reverse: the value of £1 received in a year's time is worth £$1 \div (1 + i)$ now, and £1 in two years' time is worth £$1 \div (1 + i)^2$ now, and so on. For example, if i (known as the discount rate) is 10% p.a., then the present value of £1 received in a year's time is £$1 \div (1 + 0.10) =$ £0.9091. Similarly the present value of receiving £1 in two years' time is £$1 \div (1.10)^2 =$ £0.8264, and £1 in three years' time is £$1 \div (1.10)^3 =$ £0.7513, and £1 in n years' time is £$1 \div (1.10)^n$.

Tables of *present values* are available for various rates of interest and periods of years. The table below is a very simplified and abbreviated version of one:

Present value of 1 in n years' time

n	Rate of interest (the discount rate)						
	1%	2%	3%	4%	5%	10%	15%
1	.990	.980	.971	.962	.952	.909	.870
2	.980	.961	.943	.925	.907	.826	.756
3	.971	.942	.915	.889	.864	.751	.658
4	.961	.924	.889	.855	.822	.683	.572
5	.951	.906	.863	.822	.784	.621	.497
10	.905	.820	.744	.676	.614	.386	.247
20	.820	.673	.554	.456	.377	.149	.061

Present value tables refer to the value of 1, rather than the value of £1, because they can be used for any currency: the 1 may be $1, DM1, 1 peseta or 1 of any other currency you care to name.

The present value concept (which is also the basis of discounted cash flow, DCF) can be applied to any streams of future income and to repayments of capital. For example, £20 nominal of 5% loan stock redeemable in three years would be worth the interest payments of £1 at the end of each year plus the £20 in three years' time, all discounted at 10% per annum, to give a present value of:

$$\frac{£1}{(1.10)} + \frac{£1}{(1.10)^2} + \frac{£1}{(1.10)^3} + \frac{£20}{(1.10)^3}$$

$$= £0.909 + 0.826 + 0.751 + 15.026 = £17.512$$

The calculation of the present value of a steady stream of income can be assisted by the use of annuity tables, an annuity of 1 for n years simply being an annual payment of 1 for n years; such a table is set out below.

In our previous example, the present value of £1 per annum for three years, discounted at 10%, could have been obtained from the annuity table: three years at 10% = 2.487.

In practice, interest on fixed-interest securities is usually paid half-yearly in arrears (i.e. at the end of each half-year), and so the half-yearly discount rate, which is the square root $(1 + i)$, is used to discount each half-yearly interest payment. For example, £100 of 5% Loan Stock with three years to redemption, discounted at 10% per annum, would have a present value of:

$$\frac{£2.50}{(\sqrt{1.10})} + \frac{£2.50}{(\sqrt{1.10})^2} + \ldots + \frac{£2.50}{(\sqrt{1.10})^6} + \frac{£100}{(1.10)^3} =$$

$$2.3837 + 2.2728 + \ldots + 1.8784 + 75.1315 = £87.8734$$

Annuity table: present value of an annuity of 1 for n years

n	Rate of interest (the discount rate)						
	1%	2%	3%	4%	5%	10%	15%
1	.990	.980	.971	.962	.952	.909	.870
2	1.970	1.942	1.913	1.886	1.860	1.736	1.626
3	2.941	2.884	2.829	2.775	2.723	2.487	2.283
4	3.902	3.808	3.717	3.630	3.546	3.170	2.855
5	4.853	4.713	4.580	4.452	4.329	3.791	3.352
10	9.471	8.983	8.530	8.111	7.722	6.145	5.019
15	13.865	12.849	11.938	11.118	10.380	7.606	5.847

213

APPENDIX 3 – RETAIL PRICE INDEXES SINCE 1950

From 1987 onwards the Retail Price Index (RPI), as published in the Government Statistical Service's *Monthly Digest of Statistics*, has been based on 100 at 13 January 1987. Before this, the series was based successively on 100 at 17 June 1947, 17 January 1956; 16 January 1962 and 15 January 1974; in the table below all these earlier figures have been adjusted to base 100 at 13 January 1987.

Space has been left for the reader to insert RPIs month by month in the future, as they are announced. Alternatively, *Accountancy* magazine (the journal of the Institute of Chartered Accountants in England and Wales) includes an updated table each month.

Year	Jan	Feb	Mar	Apr	May	Jun	Jul	Aug	Sept	Oct	Nov	Dec	Average for year
1950	8.3	8.3	8.3	8.4	8.4	8.4	8.4	8.3	8.4	8.5	8.5	8.5	8.4
1955	10.7	10.7	10.7	10.8	10.8	11.0	11.0	11.0	11.0	11.2	11.3	11.3	11.0
1960	12.4	12.4	12.3	12.4	12.4	12.5	12.5	12.4	12.4	12.5	12.6	12.6	12.5
1965	14.5	14.5	14.5	14.8	14.9	14.9	14.9	14.9	14.9	15.0	15.0	15.1	14.8
1966	15.1	15.1	15.2	15.3	15.5	15.5	15.4	15.5	15.5	15.5	15.6	15.6	15.4
1967	15.7	15.7	15.7	15.8	15.8	15.9	15.8	15.7	15.7	15.8	15.9	16.0	15.8
1968	16.1	16.2	16.2	16.5	16.5	16.6	16.6	16.6	16.6	16.7	16.8	17.0	16.5
1969	17.1	17.2	17.2	17.4	17.4	17.5	17.5	17.4	17.5	17.6	17.7	17.8	17.4
1970	17.9	18.0	18.1	18.4	18.5	18.5	18.6	18.6	18.7	18.9	19.0	19.2	18.5
1971	19.4	19.6	19.7	20.1	20.3	20.4	20.5	20.5	20.6	20.7	20.8	20.9	20.3
1972	21.0	21.1	21.2	21.4	21.5	21.7	21.7	21.9	22.0	22.3	22.4	22.5	21.7
1973	22.7	22.8	22.9	23.4	23.5	23.7	23.8	23.8	24.0	24.5	24.7	24.9	23.7
1974	25.4	25.8	26.0	26.9	27.3	27.6	27.8	27.8	28.1	28.7	29.2	29.6	27.5
1975	30.4	30.9	31.5	32.7	34.1	34.8	35.1	35.3	35.6	36.1	36.6	37.0	34.2
1976	37.5	38.0	38.2	38.9	39.3	39.5	39.6	40.2	40.7	41.4	42.0	42.6	39.8
1977	43.7	44.1	44.6	45.7	46.1	46.5	46.6	46.8	47.1	47.3	47.5	47.8	46.2
1978	48.0	48.3	48.6	49.3	49.6	50.0	50.2	50.5	50.7	51.0	51.3	51.8	49.9
1979	52.5	53.0	53.4	54.3	54.7	55.7	58.1	58.5	59.1	59.7	60.3	60.7	56.7
1980	62.2	63.1	63.9	66.1	66.7	67.4	67.9	68.1	68.5	68.9	69.5	69.9	66.9
1981	70.3	70.9	72.0	74.1	74.6	75.0	75.3	75.9	76.3	77.0	77.8	78.3	74.8
1982	78.7	78.8	79.4	81.0	81.6	81.9	81.9	81.9	81.9	82.3	82.7	82.5	81.2
1983	82.6	83.0	83.1	84.3	84.6	84.8	85.3	85.7	86.1	86.4	86.7	86.9	85.0
1984	86.8	87.2	87.5	88.6	89.0	89.2	89.1	89.9	90.1	90.7	91.0	90.9	89.2
1985	91.2	91.9	92.8	94.8	95.2	95.4	95.2	95.5	95.4	95.6	95.9	96.0	94.6
1986	96.2	96.6	96.7	97.7	97.8	97.8	97.5	97.8	98.3	98.5	99.3	99.6	97.8
1987	100.0	100.4	100.6	101.8	101.9	101.9	101.8	102.1	102.4	102.9	103.4	103.3	101.9
1988	103.3	103.7	104.1	105.8	106.2	106.6	106.7	107.9	108.4	109.5	110.0	110.3	106.9
1989	111.0	111.8	112.3	114.3	115.0	115.4	115.5	115.8	116.6	117.5	118.5	118.8	115.2
1990	119.5	120.2	121.4	125.1	126.2								
1991													
1992													
1993													
1994													
1995													

INDEX

'A' shares, 12
AARONSON BROS, 41, 47, 142
acceptance credits, 64
accounting
  acquisition, 108–10
  equity method of, 123
  fundamental concepts, 2
  merger, 110–12
  policies, 2, 73–5
  standards, 1, 212
  year, of subsidiaries, 120
Accounting Standards Board (ASB), 2
Accounting Standards Committee (ASC), 1
Accountline, 162
accruals, 67, 87
  concept, 2
  effect on taxation, 87
accrued income, 54
acid test, 185, 186
acquisition accounting, 108–10
  avoidance of share premium, 112
acquisitions
  circular to shareholders, 157
  effect on e.p.s., 101, 102–3
ACROW, 13
ACT, *see* Advance Corporation Tax
administrative expenses, 77
admission of securities to listing, 8–10
ADR, *see* American Depositary Receipts
Advance Corporation Tax (ACT), 84, 90
  limitations on use, 91
  timing of payment, 91
AGM, *see* annual general meeting
'all stocks index', 89
ALLIED LYONS, 63, 96, 130
American Depository Receipts (ADRs), 14
amortisation, 33
Analysis Corporation, 162
analysis: how to tackle, 170
analysis pro-formas, 192–206
annual general meeting, 158
annuity method of depreciation, 38
annuity tables, 213
apportionment, 7
arrangements, schemes of, 18
Articles of Association, 6
ASB, *see* Accounting Standards Board
ASC, *see* Accounting Standards Committee
ASDA, 34
asset cover, 28

assets
  current, 3
  fixed, 33–42
  revaluation, 39, 87
  sales, 87
associated undertakings, 43, 123–6
  in funds statements, 136
ATLANTIC COMPUTERS, 208
Auditing Standards and Guidelines, 153
auditors' remuneration, 78
auditors' report, 153–5
AUTOMATED SECURITY (HOLDINGS), 105

back-to-back loans, 62
bad debts, 54
  protection against, 59
BAILEY, C. H., 13, 90
balance sheet, introduction to, 3
balancing allowances, 87
balancing charges, 87
bank facilities, 60, 62
bank loans, 61
BARRATT, HENRY, 17
BASS, 19, 46, 55
BAT INDUSTRIES, 168
'below the line', 94
BET, 24, 122, 124
bills of exchange, 63
BLACKWOOD HODGE, 90, 129, 184
'Blue Book', the, 162
board of directors, 148
BOC, 39, 120
bonds, 27
bonus issues, 16
  adjustment to e.p.s., 103
book profit, 85
book value, 34
BOOTS, 150
borrowing, 21
borrowing powers, of directors, 6
BOVIS, 53
BOWATER, 132
BP *see* BRITISH PETROLEUM
break-even, 184
Brealey, R. A., 14
BRITISH AEROSPACE, 109, 157
BRITISH & COMMONWEALTH, 208
BRITISH GAS, 168
BRITISH LAND, 15

BRITISH PETROLEUM, 60, 63, 146, 168, 186, 189
BRYANT HOLDINGS, 44
BULMER, H. P., 195
BUNZL, 132, 207, 211
BURNETT & HALLAMSHIRE, 115
BURTON, 159
Business Monitor, 162

CADBURY SCHWEPPES, 28, 110, 142, 145, 146, 167, 171–4
Cadbury, Sir Adrian, 179
capital allowances, 85
capital-based grants, 41
capital commitments, 69
capital cover, 28
capital gains, 88
capital reconstruction, 18
capital redemption reserve, 19
capital reserves, 18
  on consolidation, 109
capitalisation issues, 16
capitalising expenditure
  effect on profitability, 73
capitalising interest, 74
  disclosure, 9
cash flow statements, 140, 186
CCA, *see* current cost accounting
CENTRAL & SHERWOOD, 154
Central Statistical Office (CSO), 162
chairman's emoluments, 77
chairman's statement, 148–50
charging group, 24
charitable contributions, 147
chartered company, 7
CHLORIDE, 125
CHRISTIAN SALVESEN, 73
CHURCH, 128
circular to shareholders, 157
CITYVISION, 39
classes of business, 75
CLAYFORM PROPERTIES, 17
close company, 7, 148
closing rate (foreign exchange), 127
closing stock, 3
COLOROLL, 69, 187
commercial paper, 27
COMMERCIAL UNION, 25
commitment commission, 62
common size statements, 174

215

Companies House, 159
company
  control of, 148
  filing accounts of, 159
  incorporation, 6
  longer-term prospects, 150
  newsletters, 157
  purchasing own shares, 17, 147
  types of, 6–7
  visits, 159
COMPASS GROUP, 31
complex capital issues, 32
confidential factoring, 59
consistency concept of accounting, 2
consolidated accounts, 115–20
  interpretation of, 121–2
consolidated balance sheet, 115–17
consolidated profit and loss account, 118–19
contested bid, 157
contingent liabilities, 68–9
contingent liabilities/ord. shareholders' funds
  ratio, 187
Continuing Obligations (Listed Companies), 9,
  75
control of company, 148
convertible loan capital, 29
  treatment in a rights issue, 16
convertible preference shares, 12
convertible unsecured loan stock (CULS),
  29–30
COOKSON GROUP, 168
Corporation Tax, 82–93
  imputation system of, 83
COSA, *see* cost of sales adjustment
cost of control, 115
cost of sales, 77
cost of sales adjustment (CCA), 167
coupon, 23
court actions, 68
CPP, *see* current purchasing power
  accounting
GRAY ELECTRONICS, 49, 107, 207
credit controls, 61
credit insurance, 59
credit sale transactions, 56
creditors, 66
CRODA, 13
CROWTHER, JOHN, 69
CSO, *see* Central Statistical Office
CULS, *see* convertible unsecured loan stock
cumulative dividends, arrears of, 68
cumulative preference shares, 11
currency swaps, 62
current assets, 3
current cost accounting (CCA), 167–8
current liabilities, 3, 66
current purchasing power accounting
  (CPP), 166
current ratio, 184, 185

Dataline, 162
Datastream, 131, 161, 188
Dearing, Sir Ron, 2
debentures, 23–5
debt collection costs, 57
debt collection period, 55
debt/equity ratio, 28, 182
debtors, 54–8
declining balance, depreciation, 35
deep discount issues, 24
deferral method of accounting (taxation), 87
deferred income, 67
deferred shares, 13
deferred taxation, 86–8
Department of Trade and Industry (DTI),
  44
deposits, 67

depreciation, 33–9
  adjustment (CCA), 167
  Companies Act requirements, 34, 78
  effect on profitability, 73
  methods of, 35–9
directors
  emoluments, 77
  interests, 147
  non-executive, biographies, 9
  report, 147–8
  share schemes, 14
  transactions, circular to shareholders, 157
discounting (bills of exchange), 64
disposal of fixed assets, 40
disposals, circulars on, 157
distribution costs, 77
dividend cover, 92, 189, 190
dividend declaration, 100
dividend distribution, 98
  policy, 189
  proposed, 67
  taxation on, 90–2, 190
  yield, 189
double taxation relief (DTR), 89–90
doubtful debtors, 54
drawing down of loans, 62
DRAYTON CONSOLIDATED TRUST, 30
DTI, *see* Department of Trade and Industry
DTR, *see* double taxation relief

earnings before interest and tax (EBIT), 183
earnings per share (e.p.s.), 100–5
  inflation adjustment, 144
EBIT, *see* earnings before interest and tax
ECC GROUP, 41, 44, 185
Economist Intelligence Unit (EIU), 162
EDs, *see* Exposure Drafts
EDBRO (HOLDINGS), 35
employee share schemes, 14
e.p.s., *see* earnings per share
equity method of accounting, 123
ERSKINE HOUSE, 117
EUROTHERM, 167
exceptional items, 96, 97
excess depreciation, 39
exchange controls, 62
exercise period (warrants), 13
expenses disallowed for tax, 88
Exposure Drafts (EDs), 1
  list of, 212
  ED 8: 166
  ED 18: 167
  ED 43: 41
  ED 44: 110
  ED 45: 75
  ED 47: 146, 178
  ED 48: 107
Extel Cards, 160
extraordinary items, 96–7

factoring, 59
FARNELL ELECTRONICS, 154
FEEDEX AGRICULTURAL INDUSTRIES, 121, 155
FERRANTI, 211
FIFO, *see* first-in first-out method of valuing
  stock
filing of accounts, statutory requirements,
  159
finance leases, 70
financial ratios, 182–91
Financial Reporting Council (FRC), 2
financial statements, 153
Financial Times
  comment on BUNZL, 207
  published e.p.s., 102, 188
financial year, 84
finished goods, as stock, 46

Finsbury Data Services, 162
first-in first-out (FIFO) method of valuing
  stock, 48
first year allowances (Corporation Tax), 85
fiscal year, 84
FISHER, ALBERT, 16
FISONS, 140
fixed assets, 33–42
  significant changes in, 147
fixed charge (loan capital), 23
floating charge (loan capital), 23
floating-rate loans, 62
foreign currency borrowings, unmatched,
  132
foreign currency equalisation reserve, 19
foreign exchange, 127–34
foreign tax, 89
  relief for, 91
forex, *see* foreign exchange
Form 20-F, 157
forming a company, 6–7
franked income, 80, 88
fraud, 211
FRC, *see* Financial Reporting Council
'full distribution' earnings, 92, 191
fully diluted earnings per share, 105
funds flow statement, 135
fungible assets, 49

gearing, 28, 182
gearing adjustment (CCA), 167
GEC, 18
general meetings
  annual, 158
  increasing share capital at, 11
  procedure for, 6
geographical analysis, 75
Gillett Brothers, 63
GLAXO, 68, 102, 133, 134, 150
'going concern'
  concept of accounting, 2
  qualification of report, example, 154
going public, 7, 157
goodwill, 33, 115
  on consolidation, 117
  writing off, 98
golden shares, 12
Government grants, 41, 178
Government statistical publications, 162
GRAND METROPOLITAN, 27, 97, 166
GREAT PORTLAND ESTATES, 29
GREAT UNIVERSAL STORES, 13, 58
'Green Book', the, 10
GREYCOAT, 25
gross cash flow, 186
gross redemption yield, 26
group, definition of, 114
group accounts, 115–21
growth rates, 173
guarantees, contingent liability, 68
GUINNESS, 118, 155

half-yearly comparisons, 172
half-yearly reports, 156
HALMA, 101
Hambro Company Guide, 161
HAMMERSON PROPERTY, 24
HANSON TRUST, 101
HARRISONS & CROSFIELD, 44, 45
'heavy' share price, 16
HIGHLAND DISTILLERIES, 43
hire of plant and machinery, 78
hire-purchase transactions, 56
historical cost accounting
  shortcomings of, 164–6
historical rate (foreign exchange), 127
historical summaries, 142–6

Hoare & Co. Govett, 162
HOGG ROBINSON, 208
holding company, 114
horizontal analysis, 171

ICC Datacards, 161
ICC (Inter Company Comparisons), 176
ICELAND FROZEN FOODS, 152
ICI, 14, 97, 119, 130
IMI, 117, 137, 140
important events, 147
imputation system of Corporation Tax, 83
income cover, 28
income statement, 95
incorporation of a company, 6
indexation allowance, 87
Industrial Performance Analysis, 176
inflation, staggering impact of, 166
inflation accounting, 164–9
initial allowances (Corporation Tax), 85
intangible assets, 33
interest, capitalisation of, 9, 74
interest paid (pre-tax item), 80
interest rate sensitivity, 183
interest rate swaps, 63
interim reports, 156
interlocking holdings, 45
INTERNATIONAL SIGNAL & CONTROL, 211
introduction (Stock Exchange), 9
investment grants, 41
investment income, 80
investment properties, 40
investment ratios, 188–91
investments, 43–5
invoice discounting, 59
irrecoverable ACT, 91
issuing house, 9

JAGUAR, 130
JOHNSON MATTHEY, 148
Jordan & Sons Ltd, 160

Key Business Ratios, 176
Key Notes, 162
KINGFISHER, 34, 95
KWIKSAVE, 191

LADBROKE, 33, 74, 82
LAING, JOHN, 53
LAND SECURITIES, 24
last-in first-out (LIFO) method of valuing
    stock, 48
LAW DEBENTURE CORPORATION, 24
LEADING LEISURE, 14, 15
leases
    finance, 70
    operating, 71
leverage, 28, 182
leverage effect, 182
liabilities
    contingent, 68–9
    current, 66
liability
    limited, 6
    members' (shareholders'), 6
    unlimited, 7
liability method of accounting (taxation), 87
LIBOR, *see* London Inter-Bank Offer Rate
LIFO *see* last-in first-out method of valuing
    stock
limited company, 6
liquidation
    debenture rights, 24
    ranking in, 23, 24
liquidity ratios, 184
listing (Stock Exchange), 8–9
listing particulars, 8, 156

loan capital, 21–32
loan facilities, 62
loan notes, 27
London Inter-Bank Offer Rate (LIBOR), 62
LONDON INTERNATIONAL GROUP, 64, 209
long term contracts, 51–3
LONRHO, 142
losses, tax treatment, 89
    previous years, 90
Lowson, Sir Denys, 45
LUCAS, 66, 78

Macmillan's Unquoted Companies, 161
mainstream corporation tax, 84
    minimum rate, 91
market capitalisation, 191
MARKS & SPENCER, 12, 34, 40, 47, 87, 138
MARLEY, 56, 176
matching principle, 46
MAXWELL COMMUNICATION CORPORATION,
    101, 152
MB GROUP *see* METAL BOX
MCCARTHY & STONE, 156
McCarthy Information Services, 161
medium-sized company, 7
Memorandum of Association, 6
merger accounting, 110–12
    criticisms of, 112
merger reserve, 112
METAL BOX, 211
mezzanine finance, 31–2
MICROGEN, 111
minority interests, 94, 114
    calculation of, 116
    points to look for, 122
Mintel International, 163
Mirac, 161
monetary working capital adjustment
    (CCA), 167
money market, 64
mortgage debenture, 23
movement in reserves, 20, 106
multi-option loan facilities, 62

National Economic Development Office
    (NEDO), 162
National Institute of Economic and Social
    Research (NIESR), 163
NEDO, *see* National Economic Development
    Office
negative pledge, 62
net asset value (n.a.v), 191
net book value, 34
net cash flow, 186
net current assets, 3
net earnings, 92
net realisable value, 49
net redemption yield, 26
net tangible assets (n.t.a.), 145
'netting off', 136
new issues, 10
Newsline, 162
NEXT, 30, 119
next-in first-out (NIFO) method of valuing
    stock, 48
NIESR, *see* National Institute of Economic
    and Social Research
NIFO, *see* next-in first-out method of
    valuing stock
nil earnings, 92
nil distribution earnings, taxation of, 84–90
nominal value of shares, 11
non-executive directors, 9
non-recourse factoring, 59
non-voting shares (N/V), 12
NORMANS GROUP, 191
n.t.a., *see* net tangible assets

OCEAN TRANSPORT & TRADING, 69
offer for sale (of shares), 9
on-line services, 162
opening stock, 3
operating income, other, 77
operating leases, 71
operating ratios, 176–82
operational gearing, 183
options (share schemes), 14
ordinary shares, 12
ordinary shareholders' funds (OSF), 5
ordinary stock, 12
OSF, *see* ordinary shareholders' funds
overdrafts, 60–1
overseas income, taxation of, 89
overseas investment, financing, 62
own shares, purchase of, 17, 147

P & O, 7
par, 3
parent company, 114
    balance sheet, 120
    profit and loss account, 120
pari passu, 24
partially owned subsidiary, 114
participating interests, 43, 123
participating preference shares, 12
partly paid shares, 13, 15
payments on account, 67
payout ratio, 191
PEARSON GROUP, 117
pension costs, 78–80
pensions, provisions for, 67
PER, *see* price earnings ratio
perpetual warrants, 13
PER relative, 189
PILKINGTON, 150
PINEAPPLE GROUP, 112
placing (share issue), 9
    restrictions on, 15
plant and machinery, depreciation, 34
political contributions, 147
POLLY PECK, 151, 210
'pooling of interests', accounting method,
    111
PORTALS HOLDINGS, 68
post balance sheet events, 152
pre-acquisition profits, 111
preference dividends, 95
preference shares, 11
prepayments, 54
present value (discounting to), 213
press cutting service, McCarthy, 161
pre-tax profit, 81
price earnings ratio (PER), 101, 188
    relative, 189
price indices (CCA), 167
prior year adjustments, 97
prior year items, 97
priority percentages, 28
private company, 7
profit after tax, 94
profit analysis
    by class of business, 75–6
    geographical, 75
profit and loss account
    introduction to, 3
    formats, 72
profit margin
    gross, 47
    trading, 176
profit-sharing schemes, 14
profit/volume chart, 184
profitability, effect of accounting policies on,
    73
promissory notes, 27
prospective PER, 188

prospectus, 156
provisions, 67
  for doubtful debtors, 54
  hire purchase, 58
  reserves not to include, 18
prudence, overriding concept in accounting,
  2
public company, 7
public issue by prospectus, 9
purchased goodwill, 33
purchasing own shares, 17, 147
'put' options, convertibles with, 30

qualified auditors' reports, 153
quick ratio, 185
quotation (Stock Exchange), 8

RANK ORGANISATION, 12, 144
RANKS HOVIS MCDOUGALL, 179
ranking, in a liquidation, 23, 24
ratios, 175–91
  financial, 182
  investment, 188
  liquidity, 184
  operating, 176
  typical values, 176
receivables, 54
receiver, appointment of, 23
reciprocating loans, 62
RECKITT & COLMAN, 130
reconstructions, 18
redeemable preference shares, 12
redemption of loan stock, 25–6
redemption yield, 26
REDLAND, 96, 106
reducing balance, depreciation, 35
reduction of share capital, 18
REED INTERNATIONAL, 76
REGENTCREST, 75
regional development grants, 41
Registrar of Companies, 6, 159
related company, 123
replacement cost accounting, 168
research and development, 74, 147
reserve funds, 19
reserves, 18–20
  movements to and from, 20, 106
residual value of fixed assets, 35
rest period (convertibles), 30
restatement of accounts, 97
restricted voting shares (R/V), 12
restrictive clauses in trust deeds, 24
Retail Price Index (RPI), 145, 214
retained profit, 94, 119
Return on Capital Employed (ROCE), 21,
  178
revaluation of assets, 39, 87
revaluation reserve, 19
revenue account, 72
revenue-based grants, 42
revenue reserves, 18
revolving loans, 62
rights issues, 15
  adjustments to e.p.s., 104
ring fence, 24
ROCE, *see* Return on Capital Employed
rolled-up cover, 28
rollover relief, 88
Rowland, Tiny, 142
ROYAL BANK OF SCOTLAND, 86
ROYAL DUTCH SHELL, 70, 141
RPI, *see* Retail Price Index
RTZ CORPORATION, 16, 17, 47, 80, 122, 133,
  148, 165
RUGBY GROUP, 179
rule of 78: 57
running yield, 26

SAATCHI & SAATCHI, 142, 151
SAINSBURY, 8, 25, 34, 55, 74, 178, 191
sale and leaseback, 95
sales, 75–7
Sales/Capital employed ratio, 179
Sandilands Report, 167
SAYE share option schemes, 14
scrip dividends, 16
scrip issues, 16
  adjustments to e.p.s., 103
SEARS, 12
secondary offers for sale, 157
segmental reporting, 75
selective marketing (placing), 9
senior debt, 31
share capital, 11–18
share options, 14
share premium account, 16, 19
share price, 'heavy', 16
share splits, 16
  adjustment to e.p.s., 103
shares, 11–13
  company purchasing own, 17
  partly paid, 13, 15
Shearer v. Bercain, 111
significant holdings, 44
sinking funds, 25–6
small companies rate of Corporation Tax,
  84
SMITH W. H., 150
SMITHS INDUSTRIES, 80
small company, 7
SOCK SHOP, 74, 78
SORP, *see* Statements of Recommended
  Practice
SOUND DIFFUSION, 71
source and application of funds statements
  135–41
sources of information on companies, 156–63
SOUTHERN BUSINESS GROUP, 209
SSAPs, *see* Statements of Standard
  Accounting Practice
staff, particulars of, 78
standard price (stock), 48
starting-up costs, 74
statement of change in financial position,
  135
Statements of Intent, 212
Statements of Recommended Practice
  (SORPs), 2
Statements of Standard Accounting Practice
  (SSAPs), 1
  list of, 212
SSAP 1: 123
  misuse of, 125
SSAP 2: 2
SSAP 3: 100, 103, 105
SSAP 4: 41
SSAP 6: 40, 89, 94, 96
SSAP 7 (provisional): 167
SSAP 8: 82, 88, 91
SSAP 9: 46, 47, 48, 51, 53
SSAP 10: 135
SSAP 11: 87
SSAP 12: 34, 39, 40
SSAP 13: 74
SSAP 14: 114, 120, 121, 153
SSAP 15: 86, 87
SSAP 16: 167
SSAP 17: 152
SSAP 18: 66
SSAP 19: 40
SSAP 20: 127
SSAP 21: 56, 70
SSAP 22: 33, 110
SSAP 23: 107, 111
SSAP 24: 78

staff, particulars of, 78
starting up costs, capitalisation of, 74
stepped conversion (CULS), 30
sterling/DM exchange rate, 131
sterling/$ exchange rate, 131
stock, 46–51
stock dividends, 16
Stock Exchange
  listing, 8–10
  'Green Book', the, 10
  'Yellow Book', the, 8, 157
stock, ordinary, 12
stock relief (tax), 49, 89
Stock/Sales (Turnover) ratio, 49, 180
STOREHOUSE, 12
straight line, depreciation, 35
striking price (tender offers), 9
stripping of warrants, 13
stub (CULS), 30
subsidiaries, 114
  disclosure of information on, 120
  losses of, tax treatment, 89
  overseas, tax liability, 89
  owning holding company's shares, 120
substitution, 24
sum of the digits, depreciation, 36
swaps, 62

takeover bids, 108
tangible assets, 33
T & N GROUP, 69
TARMAC, 136
tax credit (ACT), 84
tax rates, 84
tax years, 84
taxable profit, 85
taxation, 82–93
temporal method of translation, 130
tender, offer for sale by, 9
TESCO, 34, 79, 112, 142, 178
Textline, 162
THORN EMI, 208
TI GROUP, 117, 210
'Tickler' clause, 24
timing differences (tax), 85
topping up, 24
trade bills, 64
trade creditors, 67
Trade creditors/Sales ratio, 181
Trade creditors/Stocks ratio, 181
trade debtors, 54
Trade debtors/Sales ratio, 181
trade publications, 162
trading profit, 77
Trading Profit/Capital employed ratio, 178
Trading profit/Sales ratio, 176
Trading profit/Wages ratio, 181
TRAFALGAR HOUSE, 82
tranches, of a loan, 62
transactions, classes of, 158
transfer price, 122
translation of foreign currencies, 127
treasury department, 132
trend analysis, 171–5
trust deed, 24
Trustee Investment Act, 17
TRUSTHOUSE FORTE, 31, 102, 111
turnover, 75–7
  analysis by class of business, 75
  geographical analysis, 75
Tweedie, David, 2

ULS, *see* unsecured loan stock
ULTRAMAR, 17, 54
undertakings, 115
unfranked income, 80
uniform dollar concept, 143

UNILEVER, 73, 117
unlimited company, 7
Unlisted Securities Market, 10
unrealised profit on consolidation, 119
unsecured loan stock (ULS), 23–5
USBORNE, 121, 155
USM, *see* Unlisted Securities Market

valuation of stock, effect on profitability 73
value added statements, 73
Value Added Tax (VAT), 75

vendor consideration, 17, 108
vertical analysis, 174–5
visits to companies, 159

warrants, 13, 31
    treatment in a rights issue, 16
wasting assets, 33
WATERFORD GLASS, 89, 97
WATTS, BLAKE, BEARNE, 68, 167
WEARWELL, 151
WEDGWOOD, 89

WEIR GROUP, 132
WHITBREAD, 13, 55
WIMPEY, 121
window dressing, 152
work in progress (WIP), 46
Working capital/Sales ratio, 181, 186
Writing-down allowances, 85

'Yellow Book', the, 8, 157
yields
    fixed interest, 26
    shares, 189